SURVEY RESEARCH

A COMPUTER-ASSISTED INTRODUCTION

▶ ▶ ▶ ▶ ▶ *WILLIAM SIMS BAINBRIDGE*

Illinois State University

Wadsworth Publishing Company
Belmont, California
A Division of Wadsworth, Inc.

Sociology Editor: Sheryl Fullerton
Production Editor: Leland Moss
Managing Designer: Mary Ellen Podgorski
Print Buyer: Barbara Britton
Editorial Assistant: Cindy Haus
Designer: Vargas/Williams/Design
Copy Editor: Anne Montague
Compositor: G&S Typesetters, Inc.
Cover: Vargas/Williams/Design
Signing Representative: John Moroney

Printed in the United States of America   34

1 2 3 4 5 6 7 8 9 10—93 92 91 90 89

Library of Congress Cataloging-in-Publication Data

Bainbridge, William Sims.
    Survey research : a computer-assisted introduction / by William
Sims Bainbridge.
       p.   cm.
    Bibliography: p.

    Includes index.
    ISBN 0-534-09774-X
    1. Social surveys—Computer-assisted instruction.   2. Social
surveys—Data processing.   I. Title.
HN29.B35   1989
301'.0723—dc19   88-19125
                                                      CIP

▶ ▶ ▶ ▶ ▶ ▶ ▶ ▶ ▶ ▶ ▶ ▶ ▶ ▶ ▶ ▶

CONTENTS

▶ ▶ ▶ ▶ ▶ ▶

▶ ▶ ▶ ▶ ▶ ▶

▶ ▶ ▶ ▶ ▶ ▶

▶ ▶ ▶ ▶ ▶ ▶ ▶ ▶ ▶ ▶ ▶ ▶ ▶ ▶ ▶

PREFACE

I have long been bothered that my students seldom got to experience for themselves all the excitement and mental challenge of real research. Like most professors, I enjoy lecturing, and much of my time is spent writing books. But the social sciences are far more than a cloistered debate among academics. And education is more than a matter of listening and reading. In the natural sciences, students even as early as the high school years get the chance to explore their subject directly, dissecting frogs, running electricity, mixing chemicals, and charting the skies through telescopes. Recently I have taken up the hobby of fossil collecting, and I am as ignorant as a student just beginning introductory geology. But from the very beginning I've had the chance to scramble over coal mine dumps and limestone quarries, finding and identifying my very own fossils, learning principles of science by doing as well as reading.

This book and software combination answers a profound need of students in the social sciences and related practical fields to take a more active role in their own education. It also answers the instructor's need to provide an interesting, valuable course on research methods without the vast funding required to launch a real survey every semester.

Intended for courses on survey research or on general research methods in business, education, political science, psychology, social psychology, and sociology, this package will also be of value for courses in other social sciences and practical fields. My mentor, George C. Homans, asserts there is only one social science, and the divisions between academic disciplines are largely the arbitrary result of the history of universities. However, surveys done by psychologists and sociologists, for example, tend to use somewhat different question formats and methods of analysis. Therefore I have selected concepts, examples, and statistics that represent the different fields and will be meaningful to students in each of them.

The *Survey Research* book and software have been written so that they can be used profitably by the complete beginner. A few sections, like the last chapter and the last program, are reserved exclusively for advanced users; other chapters and programs have a few advanced features. But my aim was to create a computer-assisted introduction to the field of survey research for which prior experience is not necessary. Although it is useful to know something about statistics, this book introduces many of the basic concepts, and much of it is quite suitable for students who have only begun to explore the mysteries of social science. For many, this book will also provide an introduction to computers. Everything has been prepared to give students a successful adventure in the world of survey research, a semester of excitement and discovery.

A New Way of Teaching

Survey Research is a complete teaching laboratory, a close partnership between book and software that gives the instructor richer teaching resources than ever before. The textbook is far more than a guide to the software: It is a comprehensive introduction to survey research. A chapter on open-ended questions, for example, and several other sections cover aspects of survey research that are not quantitative or readily computerized. Each chapter uses examples of research projects carried out by professionals in many fields, some of them famous landmarks in the history of social science, others exemplary practical investigations that illustrate good methodology. And each chapter concludes with a set of projects that lets students apply what they have read and heard about in class; some projects use the software, but others can be done away from the computer. A glossary/index defines the major concepts of the field, all clearly illustrated with examples from research and projects the student can do.

The disk contains data from two fascinating surveys, one of 200 college students and the other of 200 corporation executives, and the programs make it easy for instructors to add survey datasets of their own. A question processor lets students create a 48-item survey, in many question formats, and print it out or administer it right on the computer. Other programs analyze the results, even creating indexes out of groups of items and giving practice in such vital procedures as recoding and estimating reliability. Other programs simulate public opinion polls of a single town and of 289 metropolitan areas, illustrating sampling procedures for surveying the general public.

Easy to Use, Easy to Learn

Some instructors already use standard statistical packages in teaching methods, but they usually find that, because so much of the term is spent by students mastering the particular software, little time or mental energy is left for learning principles of research. The nine programs on the *Survey Research* disk were carefully designed for teaching, and students will find them easy to understand and control. Wadsworth Publishing Company and I have considerable experience writing "user-friendly" educational software. This is the fourth software package I have done for Wadsworth; two others included survey modules, one already in its second edition, and the third was an entire laboratory of programs allowing students to explore the concepts of sociological theory. Using that software in my classes has taught me much that has helped me write the most educationally potent programs for *Survey Research.*

Instructional software must be easy to run, but it should also provide a rich educational experience with many options for student experimentation. This set takes the student from the very simplest steps right up to the threshold of professional statistical systems. Far from trapping the student in the limited realm of programmed instruction, as so much current educational software does, it introduces the vast world of real research. So much is offered in the book and on the disk that the instructor can choose which topics to cover and how far to lead the student on the road to professional competence.

The statistical tools built into the nine programs cover a range of techniques widely used in the social sciences, and they were selected to be both useful and easily learned. For example, it is a short step from correlations, which I included, to regressions, which I did not, and my block modeling analysis takes the student a first step toward factor analysis. Although *Survey Research* was not primarily designed to teach statistical methods, parts of it can profitably be used in a statistical methods course, and in conjunction with a standard statistics text it will work well as the basis for a combined course on methods and statistics.

The software will run on IBM-type personal computers with 256K of random-access memory (and on some machines with less). Only one disk drive is required, and the computer does not need a graphics capability. A printer can be used but is not required. The programs were carefully written to handle most user errors, and computer sophistication is absolutely unnecessary. Although I give advanced users much power to manage files and datasets, beginners are not required to know anything about operating systems, files, or other mysteries of the computer.

Perfect for Beginners, Good for Advanced Students

Survey Research can be the sole resource for relatively short or introductory courses, but in more ambitious courses the students can switch with great ease to a professional statistics package for the final weeks. The same datasets can be used throughout, because my datasets (or any the instructor wants to enter into this software) can easily be transported to the standard statistical packages. The step from this teaching tool to professional survey systems is tiny.

For students who have a personal interest or career goal that motivates them to learn, *Survey Research* will serve them well even after the semester is over. Fun and valuable experience can come from doing extra projects in the book and from inventing completely new projects that can be tried with the software. Advanced students and instructors can even do pilot studies and complete research projects with this package. I began writing these programs because I needed them in my own questionnaire work, and I use several of them now in my own professional projects. If you want to employ them in your own research, you will have to determine that they are suitable for your purposes. Wadsworth and I have published *Survey Research* as an educational textbook, and we make no promises about its suitability for professional research. But I am personally sure that the programs are good for several kinds of pilot study—and even for some major projects—because I use them myself.

For example, the question processor program can be used to administer professional surveys over the telephone. At any point, you can switch over to one of my statistical analysis programs and see how the data are piling up, for example, to check whether you have enough respondents of a certain type or need to get more. And you can use the last program in the set (the advanced utilities) to enter data from a large printed survey very efficiently. Either way you enter the data, the utilities program can translate them into a form ready for analysis by a full-featured statistics package.

Thus we can say with justice that this is a complete introduction to survey research. It gets the beginner started with simple examples, builds experience through realistic projects, and takes students to the threshold of real professional research.

Acknowledgments

My greatest debt is owed to Rodney Stark, my frequent collaborator in research, who not only taught me more practical details of surveys than I imagined one could learn but showed me that research can be a fine art, requiring good taste and imagination. Sheryl Fullerton, my editor at Wadsworth, encouraged and guided me for several years, shaping me into a writer of textbooks and educational software, sharing with me her vast experience in providing teachers with the best possible resources. Professors Sheila Cordray, Oregon State University; Thomas M. Guterbock, University of Virginia; and Sidney M. Stahl, Purdue University, provided constructive criticism at a critical stage. Leland Moss and Anne Montague deserve much credit for greatly strengthening the clarity and teaching effectiveness of my manuscript. Many thanks are due Maryn Jacobson Teece for help preparing the datasets and collecting examples from psychology. Without the encouragement and tremendous tolerance of my wife, Erika Ohara Bainbridge, this project might never have seen completion. And boundless thanks are also due to the thousands of students, over the past fifteen years, whose ideas, reactions, and challenges have taught me how to teach.

▶ ▶ ▶ ▶ ▶ ▶ ▶ ▶ ▶ ▶ ▶ ▶ ▶ ▶ ▶ ▶ ▶ ▶

*GUIDELINES FOR THE USE OF SOFTWARE**

Software enables us to accomplish many different tasks with computers. Unfortunately, in order to get their work done quickly and conveniently, some people justify making and using unauthorized copies of software. They may not understand the implications of their actions or the restrictions of the U.S. copyright law. Here are some relevant facts:

1. Unauthorized copying of software is illegal. Copyright law protects software authors and publishers, just as patent law protects inventors.

2. Unauthorized copying of software by individuals can harm the entire academic community. If unauthorized copying proliferates on a campus, the institution may incur a legal liability. Also, the institution may find it more difficult to negotiate agreements that would make software more widely and less expensively available to members of the academic community.

3. Unauthorized copying of software can deprive developers of a fair return for their work, increase prices, reduce the level of future support and enhancement, and inhibit the development of new software products.

Respect for the intellectual work and property of others has traditionally been essential to the mission of colleges and universities. As members of the academic community, we value the free exchange of ideas. Just as we do not tolerate plagiarism, we do not condone the unauthorized copying of software, including programs, applications, data bases, and code.

---

*This essay was originally published by EDUCOM, a nonprofit consortium of colleges and universities committed to the use and management of information technology in higher education, and ADAPSO, the computer software and services industry association. For additional copies of the original brochure, contact EDUCOM, Software Initiative, P. O. Box 364, Princeton, NJ 08540 or ADAPSO, 1300 North 17th Street, Suite 300, Arlington, VA 22209.

QUESTIONS YOU MAY HAVE ABOUT USING SOFTWARE

a. *What do I need to know about software and the U.S. Copyright Act?* Unless it has been placed in the public domain, software is protected by copyright law. The owner of a copyright holds exclusive right to the reproduction and distribution of his or her work. Therefore, it is illegal to duplicate or distribute software or its documentation without the permission of the copyright owner. If you have purchased your copy, however, you may make a backup for your own use in case the original is destroyed or fails to work.

b. *Can I loan software I have purchased myself?* If your software came with a clearly visible license agreement, or if you signed a registration card, *read the license carefully* before you use the software. Some licenses may restrict use to a specific computer. Copyright law does not permit you to run your software on two or more computers simultaneously unless the license agreement specifically allows it. It may, however, be legal to lend your software to a friend temporarily as long as you do not keep a copy.

c. *If software is not copy-protected, do I have the right to copy it?* Lack of copy-protection does *not* constitute permission to copy software in order to share or sell it. "Non-copy-protected" software enables you to protect your investment by making a backup copy. In offering non-copy-protected software to you, the developer or publisher has demonstrated significant trust in your integrity.

d. *May I copy software that is available through facilities on my campus, so that I can use it more conveniently in my own room?* Software acquired by colleges or universities is usually licensed. The licenses restrict how and where the software may be legally used by members of the community. This applies to software installed on hard disks in microcomputer clusters, software distributed on disks by a campus lending library, and software available on a campus mainframe or network. Some institutional licenses permit copying for certain purposes. Consult your campus authorities if you are unsure about the use of a particular software project.

e. *Isn't it legally "fair use" to copy software if the purpose in sharing it is purely educational?* No. It is illegal for a faculty member or student to copy software for distribution among the members of a class, without permission of the author or publisher.

▶ ▶ ▶ ▶ ▶ ▶ ▶ ▶ ▶ ▶ ▶ ▶ ▶ ▶ ▶ ▶

SURVEY RESEARCH
A COMPUTER-ASSISTED INTRODUCTION

The modern world is built on information, and the most practical way to gather large quantities of information about human beings is through questionnaire surveys. Although this method has limitations, professional survey researchers have developed a refined toolkit of techniques to collect valid, reliable information of great value both to scholars and decision makers. All the social sciences use surveys, and no area of business, industry, or public affairs can get along without them. This book and the accompanying disk will introduce you to a wide variety of survey techniques, stressing practicality as well as scientific ideals, giving you the chance to do real survey research while you learn.

KINDS OF SURVEYS

The oldest kind of survey, the **census,** is still very important. The original aim was to count every person in the nation, city, or group of interest; modern censuses also collect all kinds of factual information about every person and family counted. Because the tally must be thorough, great effort is often invested in finding every possible person and getting the last scrap of desired information. Although national censuses are vast undertakings, you may find yourself doing a modest census some day. For example, your club or church may need a roster of all its members with basic data concerning each one.

The survey most often spoken about in the mass media is the **opinion poll.** A good poll seeks to be representative—to accurately predict, for example, who is going to win an upcoming election—but it does not have to

The Science of Surveys

survey every single voter or resident to succeed. Instead, a random sample is drawn that reflects the population at large, and its opinions are projected on the group as a whole. Opinion polls are very common in the business world, especially in market research, which evaluates the potential popularity of products and services.

In my own work I have mainly been concerned with scientific surveys designed to test various theories in such areas as the sociology of religion or ideologies about technology. Although random samples of the population are used in many scientific studies, surveys are more often done with specific groups within the population. Once we have findings about, for example, the capacity of religion to deter juvenile delinquency in one group, we can repeat the study on another, very different group. Indeed, many scientific surveys consist of what we call **replication** research, checking whether some published results are valid by administering a similar survey to some other set of respondents. When our aim is purely exploratory, hunting for some new and fascinating phenomenon that we'll examine systematically later, we often use some rather uninhibited methods of surveying.

The crucially important field of **psychological assessment** and counseling demands its own set of specialized surveys. Over the decades psychologists and others have developed many standard questionnaires to measure a person's talents, troubles, and personality type. Although the point of these surveys is to help single individuals, they are based on a tremendous amount of development and testing on hundreds or even thousands of people. Because precise analysis of human beings is extremely difficult, these questionnaires are typically very long, consisting of many items that are later combined into scales that measure various traits. Furthermore, because people should not be analyzed in a vacuum but in their specific environmental, sociological, and emotional contexts, these questionnaires are almost always administered by trained professionals who can bring many other kinds of expertise and sensitivity to their analysis: clinical psychologists, educators, counselors, and social workers.

Although ideas and ideals will be important in this book, its primary focus is the actual creation and analysis of surveys, giving practical experience designed to teach the principles you will need for future projects. Because I want to share with you the real challenges of questionnaire research, I will often tell you about my own work, bringing you as close as possible to the realities of actual surveying.

▶ ▶ ▶ ▶ ▶ ▶ ▶ ▶ ▶ ▶ ▶

USING SURVEY RESEARCH

With the accompanying disk for IBM-type personal computers, you will be able to create your own questionnaire, administer it, analyze the data, and also explore two datasets I have already collected for you. The projects at the end of this chapter tell you how to get ready, by helping you prepare backups of the computer disk as well as some work disks you will use with later projects and with surveys you may invent on your own. Turn to page 16 now and follow the instructions for Project 1.

Once you have a disk ready to use, it is very easy to begin. Although you may want to check the instruction manual for your particular computer system, the way to start on a standard IBM-PC is simple to describe.

First, place the computer's DOS disk in the main disk drive (Drive A or Drive 1), making sure to close the door or the latch. Then turn the machine on. If it asks you for the date and the time, just press the [ENTER] key, because my timeless programs don't care when they are run. (*Note:* On some IBM-compatibles, the ENTER key is called the RETURN key.) In a moment, you should see A⟩_ on the screen, signifying that the computer is ready to load a program from Drive A. Remove the DOS disk and place the *Survey Research* disk in Drive A. Press [S]—here, S stands for Start or Survey—and then press [ENTER]. Watch what appears on the screen, and, if all goes well, in a few moments you will see the *program menu.**

The Nine Programs on Your Disk

At the beginning of each session with *Survey Research*, or whenever you want to switch from one program to another, you must call up the *program menu*, a list of the nine programs that you can use. The program menu ap-

---

*When a character or word appears within brackets in this text, you should read it as referring to the key on the computer keyboard. Thus [S] means "the S key."

pears automatically when you start up the disk from scratch (after the title and copyright messages have flashed by). When you are in the middle of a program and want to switch, you can usually get to the program menu quickly by pressing [ESC] (the escape key) one or more times.

The program menu is easy to recognize. At the bottom it says P r e s s the letter key for your choice. Above this message it lists the nine programs, as follows:

```
[A] Random numbers
[B] Town survey
[C] National poll
[D] Question processor - write a survey
[E] Basic statistics - analyze data
[F] Recoding - transform variables
[G] Correlation matrix - blocks of items
[H] Scaling - multi-item indexes
[I] Utilities for advanced work

[Q] Quit SURVEY RESEARCH
```

To get any of these choices, do as the computer instructs: Press the letter key indicated in front of the program you want. Don't worry about whether to type a capital letter or a small letter; the computer is happy with either. Also, you don't need to press [ENTER] after the command; indeed, it is always safest *not* to press [ENTER] after pressing other keys (unless the computer specifically instructs you to do so).

When you select a program, the computer will ask you to wait while it loads the program from your disk. The disk drive will whir and—if it has a light to indicate operation—the light will go on. Soon the screen will display the beginning of the selected program, and you should consult the appropriate chapter in this book about how to run it. If you get the wrong program by mistake, press [ESC] once; the program menu will appear instantly, and you can try again.

[A] Random numbers is a set of three simple modules that all relate to the numbers we use when drawing a random sample for a survey. The first module lets you take the numbers 1 through 199 and shuffle them into a random order, useful not only for drawing small samples but also for arranging items in random order in your questionnaire. The second module allows you to draw random samples, large or small, from a list of between 200 to 9999 people or things. The third module is a probability pinball game that illustrates how chance can produce complex patterns based on very simple rules, how the normal curve can be derived from simple probabilities, and how we can think of statistical significance in terms related to sampling.

[B] Town survey gives you a town with 1000 voters who are about to decide a referendum issue. You take a sample of 100, survey them on the issue, then compare your simulated poll results with the outcome of the final vote. In addition to a simple random sample, you can draw other kinds: convenience sample, proportional sample, and three different quota samples. To make the simulation more interesting, you can decide how many men versus women and old versus young the town will have in its electorate. Further, you can decide whether each of these groups will tend to be for the referendum issue, neutral on it, or against it. All these choices, plus the operations of chance, will determine how well your sample represents the town as a whole, and thus whether you can accurately predict the outcome of the vote.

[C] National poll administers an 11-item questionnaire to a sample drawn from the 160 million residents of 289 American metropolitan areas. You can do simple random samples of all 160 million, of a single region, or of any single metropolitan area. You can then compare your sample with the population from which it was drawn and with the responses of all 160 million people. You can also try several different kinds of multi-stage cluster samples, and you can compare the accuracy of samples of different sizes. The data come from the United States census and my own research on religion, so the simulation is extremely realistic.

[D] Question processor-write a survey allows you to create a questionnaire of as many as 48 items and administer it to as many as 200 people—directly on the computer. This program has eight different question formats built in. The first seven, each offering many choices, are standard question formats, including agree–disagree items, magnitude items, and preference scales. The eighth allows you to write many kinds of free-form, closed-ended questions. If you have a suitable printer, you can run off a copy of the survey on paper. Once several people have responded to your survey, you can analyze the data with other programs on the menu.

[E] Basic statistics-analyze data is a simple-to-operate, small statistics package that will analyze data from your survey or from the two datasets already on your *Survey Research* disk. It includes frequencies, means, standard deviations, cross-tabulations, correlations (r, gamma, and tau), chi-square, and significance tests.

[F] Recoding-transform variables allows you to change the data from any of the surveys, such as combining "strongly agree" with "agree" responses to an agree–disagree item. Putting the data in the best form for various kinds of analysis and handling cases when people did not respond appropriately to some questions is an essential part of survey analysis. The program saves recoded data separately on your disk, thus allowing you to go back to the original form of the data at any time. This program also creates correlation matrixes for use by the next program.

[G] Correlation matrix-blocks of items deals with wholesale correlations, allowing you to inspect the entire set of correlations from a particular dataset. Not only can you instantly see any correlations you want, but the computer will also search for the largest coefficients in the whole set or the strongest correlations with a particular variable. One module of this program provides a simple alternative to factor analysis, finding the blocks of correlations among any sets of items you choose, displaying its work and the results in a highly visual manner. Depending on the correlation matrixes you choose to create, this program works with either the original or recoded data and can handle r, gamma, or tau matrixes.

[H] Scaling-multi-item indexes creates as many as 4 indexes, each composed of up to 20 items, and saves them on your disk for future use. In combining items, the program will either add an item's score or subtract it from the total score of the index, depending on your preference. One module offers you several statistics about an index, such as mean, standard deviation, and Cronbach's alpha. The module also lists all the items in the index and gives their correlations with it. Other modules correlate indexes with each other and with any items in your dataset.

[I] Utilities for advanced work, as the name implies, is a set of useful modules for performing relatively advanced tasks with your datasets. The simplest part allows you to write labels identifying each questionnaire item, which will automatically appear in the statistical analysis programs. Other modules let you create a separate data-input system for surveys of as many as 192 items with an unlimited number of respondents. The input system is extremely easy to use; you can even program it to make little sounds to mark the ends of pages or sections in your questionnaire. A verification mode allows you to check data easily and change them if incorrect. Finally, the utility program has a module that makes a new set of files for any dataset, in a form suitable for transferring to major statistical analysis packages, either on the IBM-type personal computer or on big computers.

[Q] Quit SURVEY RESEARCH, the last choice on the program menu, gets you out of the programs and returns you to DOS. If your computer system doesn't mind, you can always quit simply by switching off the machine, but this is not a good procedure with any program that might save data on your disk. If you quit via the program menu, you will be less likely to forget to save some work you have done.

So that you can get right to work doing some statistical analysis, I have included two interesting questionnaire datasets on your disk, in addition to the one for the simulated national poll. XYZ is a 40-item survey that was administered by mail to 200 executives of companies—presidents, vice presidents, and managers of corporations large and small. The questions focus on current debates about effective management practices, and the data will allow you to test some current ideas about business and economics in vogue in both popular and scientific literature. This survey is described in detail in Chapter 10, where we consider how to create a practical questionnaire on topics such as these. The other dataset, STUDENTS, is described at the end of this chapter.

Your Survey Textbook

With so much on your disk, you might think you don't need a book, too. But my purpose is to teach you how to be a survey researcher, not just to master a few useful computer programs. Each feature of the programs derives from a long tradition in professional research; hence this textbook describes the larger picture into which each part fits, as well as simply telling you how to get on with the many projects you can do with the programs. It cites many real research projects that have been carried out, as long ago as the 1850s and as recently as yesterday.

Chapter 2 could have been titled "The Philosophy of Survey Research," except that's rather too pompous, so I call it "Questions and Answerers." Examples from medical, anthropological, and other kinds of surveys show that the essence of survey research is good communication between the surveyor and the respondent. I consider the different roles respondents may be asked to play and sketch some general rules about how best to enlist them as willing partners in your research.

Chapter 3 is devoted to the random-numbers program and the two poll simulations that illustrate sampling. Chapters 4 and 5 not only show how to use the question-processor program but explain the virtues of many different kinds of questionnaire items, using concrete examples from professional studies. Chapters 6 and 7 introduce general principles of data analysis by showing how to operate the four statistical analysis programs on the disk using the STUDENTS dataset.

Chapter 8 considers the reliability and validity of questionnaire items and indexes, demonstrating the problems we have making sure our data really mean what we hope they do and showing the best, most widely used solutions. Chapter 9 focuses on open-ended questions, those that ask respondents to write answers in words of their own, showing how they can be used effectively in printed surveys and integrated with the more rigid fixed-choice items.

Chapter 10 creates the XYZ Management Survey, drawing on recent popular literature in the business field, particularly some influential work on democratizing the workplace and meeting the Japanese challenge. Chapter 11 considers four complex survey research designs: panel studies, experiments, linked-respondent surveys, and sociograms. Finally, Chapter 12 explains how to use the advanced procedures available through the utility program. A brief appendix tells the really advanced user how my programs keep track of all the files on the disk, thus making it easier to modify the files or even use the data in programs of your own.

Each chapter ends with a set of projects you can do, either as part of classwork or on your own. They are designed to offer you the best possible practice doing survey research before you actually create and administer a complete survey of your own. Many parts of the software allow you to do work at a professional level, and I am sure a number of you will complete serious pilot projects, from conception through analysis, entirely using *Survey Research*. Whether your work aims to test scientific theories or to collect data for practical purposes, you will find this computer-assisted introduction relevant.

I have provided far more student projects than could be required for any one course; each could be the assignment for a week of the term. Depending on the nature of your course, your instructor may select any combination of assignments, and indeed may skip some of the chapters and move others around. Whatever the assignments in your course, I hope you will consider trying a few extra projects, purely for your own interest. *Survey Research* is designed to encourage exploration of ideas and data, the essence of social-scientific creativity, and you should feel free to take full advantage of the novel educational experience it offers.

▶ ▶ ▶ ▶ ▶ ▶ ▶ ▶ ▶ ▶ ▶

A WORD ABOUT COMPUTERS, DISKS, AND PRINTERS

You should not have any problem running my software on any standard IBM or IBM-compatible computer. Your computer does not need special graphics capability or an especially big memory; 256K of RAM is certainly enough, and you might get by with less. Just follow the directions given in this book and on your computer screen. If anything goes wrong, don't panic. I have written my programs so that they will minimize the harm of any problems. If this is your first encounter with a computer, consider it an adventure. And adventures have at least a tiny element of danger. Nothing in this software will break the computer or give you an electric shock. The worst that will happen is that you might lose a little work you did and have to do it over.

The *Survey Research* disk is not copy-protected. That means you can transfer the programs and data to a hard disk (or "fixed disk," as IBM likes to call it) or to one of the new 3.5-inch microdisks. Most important, it means you can make a personal backup copy in case an accident ruins the original disk.

Repeatedly throughout this book, I urge you to make backup copies of your disk, including making different versions of the disk for different projects, as explained at the end of this chapter. If by any chance you ruin one disk, you can switch to the backup. Disk disasters are not very common, but they do happen. I had just about finished writing Chapter 4 of this book and was saving all my work on a disk when a "bug" in the software I was using caused the computer to crash while it was spinning the disk. In fact, the disk just kept spinning endlessly. After several agonizing minutes of hard thinking, I had no choice but to switch the machine off and lose all my work. The software that bombed had not been written by me but was a standard commercial word processor that had sold a couple hundred thousand copies; all software has bugs of some kind. Fool that I was, I did not have a second disk with the same information on it. I had to type the whole chapter in from scratch, following some fragmentary printed versions and odd pieces on various disks. I learned my lesson; learn yours less painfully. Make backup copies.

Also, do follow my instructions in Projects 2–4 to make work disks.

One of the most vexing moments in computer work is when you tell the computer to save some vital material on your disk and it turns out that the disk is full. With some software, the program may crash and all your work will be lost. I have written these programs so that on most current machines, at least, they will recover after experiencing a disk problem. Usually the computer will be able to tell you approximately what is wrong, such as a full disk, for example, and you will get the chance to try again, without your work vanishing in the process.

When you save something on the disk, it is put in a *file*, part of the disk's memory. If the computer is having trouble with the disk, it will probably tell you the name of the file it is struggling with. If you are trying to call up data from our STUDENTS dataset and type STUNUTS by mistake, the computer may tell you it can't find a file named STUNUTS.KEY. Don't worry about the KEY part; that is information for advanced users, explained in the appendix. But you should check the STUNUTS part, which will show you that you misspelled STUDENTS. The computer will expect you to press the [ENTER] key, acknowledging its complaint, and try again. It needs the exact name of a file in order to find it.

Other messages might appear, identifying other errors. "Disk full" refers to the problem I already mentioned. The solution is to find a disk with room on it and put the file there. If you have properly created work disks, following the project instructions, you should not have this problem. "Bad disk" may signify that the particular disk has been ruined, or that the disk was never properly prepared for data in the first place. A fresh blank disk, straight from the box, needs to be formatted before it can be used, something that happens automatically when you copy the entire contents of one disk onto another.

"Disk write protected" means that somebody has fixed the disk so that nothing on it can be changed. With 5.25-inch floppy disks, this is done by covering a notch on one edge with a piece of tape. With the new 3.5-inch disks, a tiny block slides in a slot at one corner to "write protect" the disk. Obviously, such a disk cannot have anything new put on it. Try a different disk, or remove the write protection by peeling off the tape or sliding the tiny block. If you contemplate doing this, make sure you know how the disk got write protected and are confident you won't do harm.

"Disk drive not ready" may simply mean there is no disk in the drive, or you forgot to close the door or latch after putting a disk in. It is a simple matter to check that the disk is in place and close the door. Then everything should work smoothly on a second try. "Disk or disk drive problem" refers to a range of other difficulties that might arise. Check your computer's instruction manuals.

Some of you may have printers attached to your computers and wonder whether you can print out some of the results you get. The answer is a firm "probably." Printers and computer systems vary greatly, and I have not attempted to take into account all the many types currently in existence; if I had done so, I could not have squeezed all the programs and data onto the *Survey Research* disk. However, the question-processor program will print out a simple draft of a questionnaire you create, suitable for photo-copying and administering. Many of the tables of data that will appear on your computer screen can be printed, using the PrintScreen function built into your IBM-type computer. Near the right on the standard IBM keyboard is a key labeled "PrtSc" for PrintScreen. Make sure your printer is turned on. Hold down [SHIFT], the key you use to type capital letters, and simultaneously press [PrtSc].

Maybe your printer will successfully copy what is on the screen, or it may give only a close approximation. A few printers will seize up. One reason a printer might not print the screen properly is that it does not possess all of what is called "The IBM character set." This is the set of letters and other shapes I use to write and draw on the screen. The printing capability of the question-processor program works on a different principle, and it should work perfectly on most machines.

If your computer is part of a network sharing one or more printers, I cannot promise you will be able to print material from this software. The design of these networks is still in flux. At present, most academic micro-computer centers are filled with isolated machines, few attached to printers, and I have designed *Survey Research* so that you absolutely do not need a printer to get full benefit from it.

The relationship between printer and computer is an uneasy one, and I have found that different machines react in quite a variety of ways to problems like the printer running out of paper, the cable connecting the machines getting unplugged, or a failure to switch the printer on in the first place. When you want to print, I suggest you check the paper supply, check the cable, and make sure the printer is properly turned on. With most printers, this means more than simply pressing the "on" switch, because one or two other switches have to be in the right position, too. Become familiar with your equipment, at least superficially, to get the most out of it and these programs. Often, my programs are able to recover from printer problems, but not always. But be of good cheer. These programs make losing data from a printer problem difficult, so an occasional printer disaster may merely add an element of excitement to an otherwise serene educational experience.

▶ ▶ ▶ ▶ ▶ ▶ ▶ ▶ ▶ ▶ ▶

THE STUDENTS DATASET

On January 28, 1986, I was sitting in the press room at NASA's Jet Propulsion Laboratory near Pasadena, California, collecting data on how the scientists and scientific reporters interpreted the information that was streaming back to Earth from the *Voyager II* space probe. *Voyager II* was at that moment speeding beyond the planet Uranus, which it had encountered four days before, and the flood of pictures and other information beamed from the probe across nearly 2 billion miles of space stimulated exciting scientific debates.

The pictures of far Uranus that had filled the many TV monitors around the hall were suddenly replaced by scenes of nearby Florida—nearby in astronomical terms, although at the other end of the continent. We began to watch NASA's direct feed from its base at Cape Canaveral, showing the 25th orbital launch of a space shuttle. In a few moments, in silence and deep shock, we watched the *Challenger* explode into a cloud of smoke and twisted metal, taking its seven astronauts to their deaths.

The catastrophe hit the people at Jet Propulsion Laboratory hard. Many of them knew members of the *Challenger* crew, and the careers of everybody at JPL were placed in jeopardy. An American probe had not been launched into deep space for eight years, and the work of many lifetimes had been dedicated to preparing the *Galileo* robot spacecraft, ready to be sent in May to the planet Jupiter. But without *Challenger*, there could be no *Galileo*. Without space shuttles, Jet Propulsion Laboratory, the nation's main link to the planets, was hopelessly crippled.

For some time, whenever I could briefly set aside my main research work on religion and writing computer software, I had been doing modest surveys on attitudes toward spaceflight. Now it suddenly seemed time to do more space research. Without funding, I found it just possible to afford a pair of questionnaires focused on the values of spaceflight, each completed by a thousand Harvard students. The STUDENTS dataset is based on responses of 200 of these students to 40 of the questions in the first of these 2 spaceflight surveys, administered in March, April, and May 1986.

The purpose was not to evaluate how the general public felt about the space program, so a random national sample was unnecessary. Instead, I wanted to collect a variety of thoughts about the possible value of the space program, using open-ended questions as described at the end of Chapter 9, which might form the basis of later surveys with different sets of respondents. So I needed a substantial number of respondents who had given some thought to the space program and would have a range of considered opinions in the wake of the *Challenger* accident. In other research, I had polled aerospace engineers, and this time I wanted respondents with a wide range of interests and opinions about space. With the help of students in one of my classes, I visited all the dining halls, distributing questionnaires from centrally located points.

This survey is the kind you could do. Indeed, much published research in the social sciences is based on modest research projects of no greater scope than this. Although we might prefer a random sample of the nation, or a set of samples of different groups, the exploratory work of science is usually done with little funding and limited datasets. This book will draw on many major survey research studies far more impressive than this one. But for our purposes here, the survey provides an interesting and convenient dataset for exploring the basics of questionnaire analysis.

There were 1007 respondents altogether, and the 200 represented in the STUDENTS dataset are essentially a random sample of the whole group. One stipulation was that the 200 had to have given valid responses to 33 of the 40 questions I have selected from the much larger number in the original survey, so that we could practice basic statistical analysis without worrying about how to handle missing data. Also, I selected equal numbers of both sexes and of students in each of the four undergraduate years.

Thirty of the questions asked students to rate each of a list of academic subjects, and I think you will find this set personally quite interesting. For one thing, the list includes most of the university departments that might teach a course in survey methods, and thus you can examine statistics on the particular subject you are studying at this very moment. You can compare the popularity of different subjects that interest you. And when we get to correlations, the fascinating possibilities multiply.

The printed questionnaires introduced the academic preference questions like this:

> **Preferences for College Subjects.** Following is a list of various subjects taught at universities. Please tell us how much you like each one of them, whether you actually have taken a course in it or not.
>
> Please circle the number 1 if you do not like the subject at all. Please circle the number 7 if you like it very much—if it is one of your very favorite subjects. Otherwise, please circle the *one* number in between that best indicates how much you like it.

Then followed a list of 30 subjects, with a scale of 7 numbers after each one. Actually, I have made a slight change in adapting the STUDENT dataset for our present purposes. In the original version, the scale of responses went from 0 through 6, and here I have given it as 1 through 7. The statistical programs on the disk are designed for items with 1 as the smallest valid response; they use the number 0 for cases when a person failed to give a valid answer—what we call **missing data** or missing values. Adapting the dataset in this way will not affect any of our statistical results, because I have merely shifted all the responses up by a factor of 1 to fit the 1-through-7 scale of preferences.

Here are the 30 academic subjects:

1. Botany
2. Astronomy
3. A foreign language
4. Law
5. Political science
6. Music
7. History
8. Classics (ancient civilization)
9. Physics
10. Geology
11. Business
12. Biology
13. Chemistry

14. Art	20. Ocean-	25. Engineering
15. Mathematics	ography	26. Sociology
16. Economics	21. Social work	27. Literature
17. Education	22. Drama	28. Medicine
18. Anthro-	23. Psychology	29. Zoology
pology	24. Communi-	30. Architecture
19. Nursing	cations	

As you can see, this list is highly varied. I originally developed it for some research I was doing at the University of Washington in Seattle on the basis of the departments and professional schools in which the university had a substantial number of majors. Philosophy was the only subject mentioned by several Harvard students as one they would have added to the list. I must offer apologies to any of you who are philosophers or work in some other field I failed to include, but perhaps you will find something in the list close enough to your field to satisfy you.

If your field of interest happens to be business, you can think of these 30 items as part of a marketing survey. Through them we learn how popular each academic subject is with the customers (students), just as we might evaluate any commercial product or service. By analyzing the data statistically, we can see how some of the subjects fit together and thus gain insight into who is a likely customer for which of them. For example, if we find that psychology and sociology tend to correlate—that people who like one also tend to like the other—then we can conclude that sociology would be easy to sell to psychology majors, and psychology courses to sociology majors. To be sure, colleges are not department stores, and the departments in colleges don't have sales personnel. But some of the same logic goes into surveys of which products to carry in a store of a particular kind, or which departments should stock which items.

Seven other questions focus on the space program. All of them are in simple check-the-box formats, but with various responses:

31. Should the amount of money being spent on the U.S. space program be increased, kept at current levels, decreased, or ended altogether?

    [1] Increased   [2] Kept at current levels   [3] Decreased
    [4] Ended   {5} No data

32. Some people say the United States should concentrate on unmanned missions like the *Voyager* probe. Others say it is important to maintain a manned space program as well. Which comes closer to your view?

    [1] Unmanned program only   [2] Manned as well as unmanned program   [3] No opinion   {4} No data

33. Do you think the United States should build a permanently manned space station in orbit around the Earth over the next few years, or not?

[1] Yes [2] No [3] No opinion {4} No data

34. Recently, there has been much talk about building a system of space satellites to defend against nuclear attack. Do you think research on this idea should continue, or should research stop?

[1] Research should continue [2] Research should stop [3] No opinion {4} No data

35. There has been much discussion about attempting to land people on the planet Mars. How would you feel about such an attempt—would you favor or oppose the United States setting aside money for such a project?

[1] Favor [2] Oppose [3] No opinion {4} No data

36. If you were asked to go along on the first rocket trip to the planet Mars, would you want to go, or not?

[1] Yes [2] No [3] No opinion {4} No data

37. Do you think we should attempt to communicate with intelligent beings on other planets, perhaps using radio?

[1] Yes, definitely [2] Yes, perhaps [3] No [4] No opinion {5} No data

Notice the number in the box for each response to each question. These numbers are the **values** or the codes for the responses. In question 31, if a person checked the "increased" box, I typed a 1 into the computer. If the person checked the "kept at current levels" box, I typed a 2, and so on for the other responses.

You will also see a number in curly braces labeled "no data." I typed this number if the person failed to check any box for the particular question. This is the **missing-values code** or missing-data code for the particular question. For some of these, the number is 4, and for others, it is 5. When a person checked two boxes, or otherwise fouled up the question, I typed this same number. The **coding** numbers and the curly braces were not actually printed on the questionnaire; I show them here to help you understand the responses when we do our statistical analysis, beginning in Chapter 6.

Because I selected 200 students who answered all 30 academic preference questions correctly, I have no missing values on those 30 items. But I wanted us to have some missing values on some questions, so we could practice dealing with this problem, as we will later on.

One question, concerning political orientation, was taken from the General Social Survey (Davis and Smith, 1986):

38. We hear a lot of talk these days about liberals and conservatives. Below is a seven-point scale on which the political views that people might hold are arranged from extremely liberal (point 1) to extremely conservative (point 7). Where would you place yourself on this scale? Please circle the *one* number that best indicates your general political views.

1 Extremely liberal
2 Liberal
3 Slightly liberal
4 Moderate, middle of the road
5 Slightly conservative
6 Conservative
7 Extremely conservative

{8} No answer or multiple answer

The last two questions identified the respondent's sex and year at the university; all 200 selected respondents gave valid answers and were in the first four class categories:

39. Your sex is: [1] Female [2] Male

40. Which category of student do you belong to?

[1] Freshman [2] Sophomore [3] Junior [4] Senior
[-] Graduate [-] Other

▶ ▶ ▶ ▶ ▶ ▶ ▶ ▶ ▶ ▶ ▶

PROJECTS

Note: These projects are explained in terms of DOS 2.10, the IBM disk-operating system that had been standard for several years at the time of this writing. Several more recent systems use the same commands, but you should check to make sure about yours. You may need to consult your DOS operating manual or a knowledgeable person to learn the commands that will work best on your system.

 1. Make a Backup Copy of the Survey Research Disk. It is essential to have an extra copy of the original disk, in case the one that came with this book gets lost or damaged. With older operating systems, unfortunately, one of the most dangerous processes for a disk is copying it; it might get erased accidentally. Be careful and check each step. It is also a good idea to protect the disk from being written onto. The older 5.25-inch disks have a little notch on the side. Cover it with a piece of tape (usually silver-colored) that came in the box of blank disks. The newer 3.5-inch disks have a tiny sliding plastic square at one of the lower corners. Slide it so you can see through the hole it covers, and the disk is protected.

With a standard IBM-type computer that has two disk drives, do the following:

1. Place the DOS (disk-operating system) disk that came with the machine in Drive A, making sure to close the door or turn the latch, whichever your disk drive requires to get the disk ready to go.
2. Start up the machine, and if it asks you what the date and time are, press the [ENTER] key a couple of times, until you get A>_ on the screen.
3. Type DISKCOPY A: B:. Notice the spaces before A and B and the colons immediately after A and B. Press [ENTER]. The disk drive will go into action, and shortly the computer will say: Insert SOURCE diskette in drive A: Insert TARGET diskette in drive B: Press any key when ready . . .
4. Remove the DOS disk from Drive A and put the *Survey Research* disk in its place.
5. Put a fresh disk—a brand-new one or a disk you are completely sure you want to erase—in Drive B.
6. Press a key, such as [ENTER], and wait. In a minute or so, the computer will finish its work and the disk in Drive B is now your backup.

2. Make a Work Disk for the STUDENTS Dataset.   (*Note:* This may not be necessary if you have made a copy on a system using disks having more than 360K capacity.) Your *Survey Research* disk is too full to take any more data of any kind; you need to make room on the disk to use all the programs. To do this, you need to throw away the data from the XYZ Management Survey. Project 3 explains how to make a separate work disk for XYZ.

First, make a second extra copy of the original disk, as explained in Project 1. Make an adhesive label for the disk with your name and a phrase like "STUDENTS work disk," being sure not to damage the disk by writing directly on it.

Start up the computer so that A>_ appears on the screen and place the work disk in Drive A. Now type DIR and press [ENTER]. The screen will fill with the names of all the files on the disk—all the programs and sets of data. Notice that several of them have names beginning with XYZ. Next—and this is the key part, so be careful—type ERASE XYZ.* and press [ENTER]. Type this exactly as it appears in the preceding sentence: ERASE, followed by a space, the letters XYZ right next to each other with no spaces between, followed immediately by a period and an asterisk (hold down [SHIFT] and press [8]).

The disk drive will work for a moment. When A⟩_ appears again, type DIR and press [ENTER] to see the catalog of the disk. All the XYZ files should be gone. There is now lots of room on the disk for you to work with the STUDENTS dataset.

3. Make a Work Disk for the XYZ Dataset. The procedure is the same as the one for making a STUDENTS work disk, except for the command that tells the computer what to erase. Again, make another copy of the original disk. Put it in Drive A and check to see all the STUDENTS files on it. Then type ERASE STUDENTS.* and press [ENTER]. Check the disk again to make sure the STUDENTS files are all gone and there is lots of room to work with the XYZ dataset.

4. Make a Work Disk for a New Dataset. Following the instructions for both Project 2 and Project 3, erase both the STUDENTS and XYZ files from a disk. Then it will have enough room for you to add a new dataset of your own, using programs described in later chapters.

Human beings have asked each other questions, and gotten answers in return, since long before the dawn of recorded history. I wonder whether an anthropologist or student of animal behavior has ever investigated how the first question got to be invented, for indeed questions are a great invention. I can imagine two protohumans sitting around the messy remains of a meal, resting. One catches the other's eye, inclines his or her head in the direction of the home cave, and goes, "Hmmm?" The other leans forward slightly, the beginning of a nod, and emits a dull "Hmmm." In modern terms: "Shall we go home?" "Yes, let's." The first question and answer.

The next step, if we are imagining the ancient origins of survey research, was when herding people first began counting their animals to see that none had strayed, the beginnings of censuses and quantitative research in general. Another important development was the invention of letter writing. I wonder which king first wrote to the dukes administering territories all around his kingdom and asked them to report on how things were going. This would have been the first mailed survey.

These imagined moments from the past are mentioned to remind us that questionnaires are but the scientific form of kinds of human communication that date to the beginnings of civilization and before. The key difference between modern, scientific surveys and the rambling investigations of the distant past is that today we have learned to be systematic.

From one perspective, the term **survey research** should refer broadly to any systematic collection of data from people at large, analogous to land surveys that chart the landscape. Our focus, however, will be on **questionnaires, standardized lists of questions and questionlike items**, whether they are administered through face-to-face interviews, over the telephone, via computers, or using the tried-and-true medium of the postal service.

Questions and Answerers

Through all these means, researchers ask questions of respondents; this chapter will examine the ways questions are asked and the ways answerers respond.

▶ ▶ ▶ ▶ ▶ ▶ ▶ ▶ ▶ ▶ ▶

THE ART OF SURVEYING

In today's society we encounter questionnaires of one sort or another practically every week. Most people hate filling out application forms, so it is probably good for survey researchers that people don't think of these nasty forms as questionnaires, but they really are. I once knew a fellow whose full-time job was designing forms for an insurance company. He was a master at fitting the most questions on the page in the most visually and logically satisfactory way.

Businesses commonly do surveys to determine customer satisfaction and to evaluate the sales potential of various products and services. I can recall staggering off a plane in London after a transatlantic flight, only to be confronted by a poll-taker for the airline. I was so tired I could hardly pay attention to all her questions about the food service, the music program, the in-flight movie, the drinks, and the safety drill. Finally, she asked whether there was anything she hadn't mentioned about the flight that I didn't happen to like. "Yes! With all the things you were giving us passengers, we never got a chance to sleep!"

The Face-to-Face Interview

Whatever the condition of the respondent, probably the most effective way of administering a survey is through a person-to-person **interview.** When we mail a questionnaire to someone, there is a good chance it will find its way into the wastebasket. But people are generally polite to a poll-taker who has come directly to their door or who approaches them in a supermarket. Thus interviewers tend to get a good **response rate,** the proportion of the people we seek to survey who ultimately give us valid sets of replies. Administering a questionnaire verbally also gets around the problem of people who cannot read or who read with difficulty. If properly prepared before going out into the field, the interviewer can explain some of the words in the questions when respondents are not familiar with them.

On the other hand, a major problem with interviews is that the interviewer, with the best intentions, often helps the respondent with the answers. The respondent starts to say something, hesitates, rambles, and breaks off into silence. Only a heartless or well-trained interviewer can resist the temptation to finish the sentence for the respondent.

Another problem is that the respondent may orient the answers to the kind of person he or she perceives the interviewer to be. For example, the respondent may not want to admit deviant behavior to a very conventional-looking interviewer. When respondent and interviewer are of different sexes, relations between the sexes may be a taboo topic, or the responses may be very different from what an interviewer of the same sex might get. Finally, if interviewer and respondent are of different social classes or ethnic groups, all the tensions and misunderstandings between these groups may intrude on the research.

Questions with a complex set of prepared response choices may not work well in interview settings. "I am going to read you what six different people have said about the quality of American automobiles. When I am through, please tell me which one comes closest to your own opinion." By the time the interviewer gets to the last quotation, the respondent will have forgotten the first five, and responding will be an exercise in memorizing rather than a free expression of opinion. Researchers will often print a complex list of response choices on a card that the interviewer hands to the respondent while asking the question. (See Chapter 9 for further discussion.)

The Telephone Interview

The biggest disadvantage of face-to-face interview surveys is the high cost of sending interviewers to the stores or the respondents' homes. Using the phone saves much money and effort. Rapport is more difficult to develop over the phone, however, and telephone surveys are generally limited to relatively short lists of questions. Some in-person interview surveys take as long as three hours per respondent, and it is quite common to expect a respondent to spend an hour on a printed questionnaire. But it is hard to keep most people on the phone for more than ten minutes. And the method assumes the respondent has a telephone in the first place.

A great disadvantage of telephone surveys is that the typical household receives many telephone sales solicitations during the month, some of them masquerading as surveys. People become quite resistant to answering a series of questions when the last three times they did so they were hit with a sales pitch at the end. This same problem afflicts mailed questionnaires, because printed surveys can get lost in the reams of junk mail many families receive.

Mailed Questionnaires

Generally, I have found that around half the people to whom I have sent a single-mailing printed survey were willing to fill it out and return it. Don A. Dillman (1978) has written a book about techniques to get high response rates for telephone and mailed surveys, and before you invest a lot of money in one of these approaches you might want to consider the large number of points he believes improve responses.

I think it helps to be associated with a bona fide educational institution and to include a **cover letter** with your mailed questionnaire, written on the institution's stationery. People still respect education, and they are usually sympathetic both to hardworking students doing a survey as part of their education and to scientists seeking to increase human knowledge through a survey.

Today it is far too easy to have computers crank out "personalized" letters with the respondent's name at strategic points. I may be wrong, but I suspect people still appreciate a personal letter with what appears to be a personally written signature. Many's the time my colleagues and I have sat around signing the name of one of us on a pile of cover letters when the researcher's own fingers were paralyzed with fatigue. You can consult Dillman on such points as whether real postage stamps work best, because they show a personal touch, or whether postage metering works better, because it looks official.

Perhaps out of pride more than scientific zeal, I always try to have my cover letters and questionnaires look as professional as possible. Some surveys are professionally printed on glossy paper and bound into impressive covers. But, frankly, I've also had good results with simple mimeographing when I didn't have the money for something better. The fact is, there is no one ideal way of doing a printed survey, and you should not become discouraged if you don't have the resources to send out something really fancy.

Production Pointers

When you compose the questionnaire, you should think the research process all the way through to the ways you intend to analyze the data. And even when you are using trained interviewers, a questionnaire that is both visually clear in the layout of the items and conceptually clear in how they are phrased and arranged is essential.

If the data are going to be entered by hand into a computer, putting item guide numbers on a printed survey can be useful. Each question can be numbered, and each response can have its own tiny number printed right on the survey. These help the data-entry persons keep track of where they are in the survey and tell them which key to press to register a particular answer. But though these numbers speed data entry and may help reduce mistakes in typing the answers into the computer, they may sometimes confuse or irritate respondents.

Another approach, ideal for researchers but awkward for respondents, is the use of **mark-sense forms**, special forms that can be run through optical scanners to put their data directly into the computer without the necessity of typing. Chances are, you have taken many tests in school using these forms. Not long ago I received a survey from my university's maintenance department that used mark-sense forms. I was supposed to put my answers on a separate blue sheet that was covered with numbers, letters, and little circles. Here is an excerpt from the directions and some sample questions.

> Please mark all of your answers on the attached computer readable form, using the number corresponding to the question number on the survey. Do not write your answers directly on the survey. Please use a number two lead pencil to mark your responses. Answers marked with ink cannot be read by the computer. Erase any stray marks on the form when you have completed the questionnaire.

> **Grounds Services**
>
> Grounds services include the upkeep of campus grounds, flower beds, trees, shrubbery and other open areas, as well as snow and leaf removal and grass cutting and solid waste removal. Please mark the letter which best characterizes how you feel about various aspects of this service listed below (A=Strongly Agree; B=Agree; C=Disagree; D=Strongly Disagree; E=No Opinion).
>
> 1. Grounds maintenance is satisfactory.
> 2. Snow removal and ice control are satisfactory.
> 3. Road and walkway maintenance are satisfactory.
> 4. Waste removal is satisfactory.

This is not an exciting survey, but worse than the dullness of its content is the fact that it may require too much complicated effort from the respondent. You should avoid giving the respondent any extra, distracting, or tedious tasks that might interfere with good answer-giving. Ideally, if your budget is high, you can use specially printed mark-sense forms that have the questions and responses on the same page, as in ordinary questionnaires.

Computer Questionnaires

A new alternative, represented by this book and the accompanying disk, is to administer your questionnaire directly on the computer. Chapters 4 and 5 show you how to operate a question-processor program that lets you write a survey into the computer. Then respondents can sit, one at a time, at the computer keys, giving their answers to your questions that appear on the screen and incidentally doing your data entry for you.

A few years ago, when computers were strange, threatening devices, this method would not have worked. But now that interest in personal computers is high, I think this method of administering surveys will win enthusiastic cooperation. And now that computers are common, you can have several going at once, all administering the same survey, their data to be combined for analysis once in the computers.

This method is exceptionally efficient for telephone surveys. The interviewer sits at a personal computer. A question flashes on the screen. The interviewer asks it over the telephone. The respondent answers, and the interviewer presses the appropriate key on the computer. Immediately, the next question comes up, and the process goes on. (The programs on your *Survey Research* disk are well suited for this purpose.) Advanced systems for telephone surveys go so far as to dial the number for you.

The next time you are in a car rental office or at the airport, watch the reservation clerks working on their computers. Some stores use a similar system. On the computer screen is a little questionnaire, the equivalent of a printed order form. The clerk types in the data. Instantly, the company's central computer knows that the car or plane seat has been booked, or that a particular piece of merchandise has been sold and must be deleted from inventory.

▶ ▶ ▶ ▶ ▶ ▶ ▶ ▶ ▶ ▶ ▶

RAPPORT WITH RESPONDENTS

However we do our surveys, we rely on motives within the respondents to get the job done. The at-home interview probably maximizes the motive of pure politeness in getting the person to respond. But anything that makes the respondent feel we really care about his or her opinion and have invested much in asking for it will stimulate a sense of pride and a desire to return the favor, giving us the cooperation we want. Some surveys have included money, or coupons that could be exchanged for money when the questionnaire was returned. I think this practice is seldom justified and never necessary, except for research in laboratory settings, where it makes sense to pay the research subject for helping us with our work.

A standard professional technique that proves to the respondents we really care about their answers, and that also jogs procrastinators to complete the survey, is **multiple mailings.** On the first of the month, we mail out 1000 surveys. As surveys come back, we check off the respondents' names. In three weeks, we send reminder letters to all the people who have not yet responded, politely stressing how valuable their opinions are for our very important survey. Two or three weeks after that, the people who have still not responded are sent a fresh copy of the survey with a nice letter urging them to do the job this time. Finally, the last few holdouts get a personal telephone call urging them to respond. I know of one case in which the researchers got the respondents' ministers to call them!

Often we want the questionnaires to be anonymous. Although people enjoy expressing their opinions, they want to be protected from public embarrassment and thus prefer anonymity. You might include a paragraph like the following, taken from a classic survey on religion (Glock and Stark, 1966), in your cover letter or in the instructions at the beginning of the survey:

> We should like you to feel that you are expressing your true feelings as you answer the questionnaire. Please write your comments in the margin when you feel a question is unclear, or doesn't allow you to express exactly how you feel. We are not asking you to sign your name so you can be sure that your answers will be confidential.

If you promise that your survey is anonymous and confidential, then you should keep it that way. I have heard of survey researchers putting secret marks on questionnaires so they really could identify the respondents, but I think this is a bad idea. Once you start cheating your respondents, it is too easy to slip into more and more sleazy practices that ultimately will destroy the relationship of mutual trust essential in questionnaire research, not just for you but also for future researchers.

But how can you send follow-up mailings if you don't know your respondents' identities? The standard technique is to include a stamped postcard along with the questionnaire, with the respondent's name on it, addressed to you. Instruct the respondent to mail the survey back in a stamped return envelope you have provided and to mail the postcard back separately to let you know he or she has done the survey. This way, you know that the respondent has sent the survey back, but you can't tell which one it is.

In many cases, working through an organization the respondents belong to and trust can be useful. For example, a student of mine who recently surveyed physicians and surgeons in three hospitals first persuaded top hospital administrators to add a special cover letter of their own and to make announcements in staff meetings promoting the survey. This assured a high response rate.

In many situations, respondents may have good reason to distrust you and your research. Often the best solution is to take the time to become known to your respondents and to get the public support of people or institutions the respondents trust.

In Third World countries, respondents may have a number of concerns about a survey project, based on their prior experience with superficially similar enterprises or rumors about threats from their governments. Kurt Back and J. Mayone Stycos (1973) reported that some of their Jamaican respondents were worried that the researchers were actually part of a scheme to conscript local men into the army or impose involuntary birth control on the women. In other cases, the respondent may fear that behind the surveyor stands the tax collector or the policeman.

The key to good surveys is good communication between the researcher and the person being surveyed. To examine this relationship further, we must consider two different roles the person may be asked to play.

▶ ▶ ▶ ▶ ▶ ▶ ▶ ▶ ▶ ▶ ▶

INFORMANTS AND RESPONDENTS

A person who fills out a questionnaire or answers interview questions can be conceptualized in two fundamental roles: informant or respondent.

An **informant** gives you objective information. In this sense, the informant is your assistant, telling you about things you could have observed yourself if you had only been on the scene at the right time. Anthropologists traditionally had *native informants,* members of the tribe who told the anthropologist all kinds of facts about it. Given enough time, the anthropologist could have learned these same facts directly. For example, the anthropologist could learn about native wedding ceremonies by attending several of them. But weddings don't take place every day, so it is more efficient to get information from natives who have attended dozens of them.

A **respondent** supplies personal, rather than objective, data: personal opinions, feelings, and attitudes. A question frequently used by the Gallup Poll that obviously puts the person in the role of respondent is: "Are you satisfied with the future facing you and your family?" Questions about attitudes sometimes appear to be seeking objective facts, but they really tap the personal judgment of the individual.

The line between the two roles is blurry. People who are asked to give objective information will often have none to offer and give vague hunches instead. Some questions may elicit answers of both types. And, of course, there can be considerable controversy over matters of fact. "Did the student activism of the late 1960s bring the Vietnam War to a quicker end, or did it prolong the war?'' People disagree on this question, some passionately; sociologist David Riesman has told me he thinks the activism delayed the end, even though he himself was part of the antiwar movement. As a social scientist I would like to believe that the right historical research project could decide the issue in an objective way. Potentially a question about objective fact, this one undoubtedly puts the answerer in the role of a respondent, expressing opinions that other reasonable people would not necessarily share.

A standard survey for evaluating social conditions in work organizations (Taylor and Bowers, 1972:133) contains a set of questions that straddle the line between factual and personal responses. Workers are asked items like: "How much does your foreman encourage people to give their best effort?" The response choices are [1] To a very little extent, [2] To a little extent, [3] To some extent, [4] To a great extent, or [5] To a very great extent. They are to answer this question twice. First, they are supposed to report "This is how it is *now*." Then they are supposed to say "This is how I'd *like* it to be." How they'd like the foreman to behave is clearly a matter of opinion. But how the foreman does behave now is in principle a matter of fact, even though the individual's judgment of it will be shaped by his or her own personal characteristics.

A series of questions about drinking will illustrate the range from pure information to pure personal response. "What is the legal drinking age in your community?" This is a matter of pure fact. No matter how people feel about the drinking age, they would agree on what the law was. "In a typical week, how many bottles of beer do you drink?" This question seeks objective information that other people could observe and report but gives the individual some opportunity to inflate or deflate the number reported. "Do you think that you drink too much?" Although the answer depends in part on how much the individual actually does drink, the question mainly taps his or her feelings about the proper amount to drink. "Which do you like better, wine or beer?" Now the person is a pure respondent, expressing nothing more than a personal preference.

When I taught a class in field research methods, one of the assignments was to find a pair of native informants and interview them about the culture they had come from. Among the best student projects was a pair of interviews with Russian emigrés about the Soviet school system. One informant had been a teacher and the other had been a student, so they did have different perspectives on the school system. But the questions were all factual, determining the rules and structure of the system, thus putting the two Russians in the role of pure informants.

Unfortunately, many of my students couldn't seem to make the distinction between informants and respondents, and their interviews elicited feelings and opinions, turning their interviewees into respondents, when the assignment had demanded informants. Perhaps we tend to consider our own personal opinions to be objective observations of the world, and some of us may naively extend the same courtesy to the opinions of people we are communicating with.

The Informant Tradition

In the history of social research, informant surveys came much earlier than respondent surveys. Indeed, the prime example of informant surveys is the census, a Latin word reminding us that systematic counting and assessment of the population dates to the days of Caesar Augustus. Modern census-takers never really counted heads or noses. Instead, they would ride from house to house getting information verbally from each head of household or from the first adult who answered their knock at the door.

I don't know who answered the door at the White House when census-taker H. H. Young knocked on July 30, 1860. Perhaps it was the Belgian butler, Pierre, or Richard the English steward. I can imagine a dramatic scene in which President James Buchanan himself gave Young the data on the household, although one might guess this job was delegated to James Buchanan Henry, his nephew and private secretary. In any case, like any ordinary household, the president's house was visited by the census-taker, and some person played the role of informant, giving Young the names, ages, genders, occupations, and birthplaces of all the residents.

Original copies of the old census forms still exist, and microfilm duplicates are available to the general public in several archives around the country. These records show that in addition to the president and his nephew, the White House in 1860 was home to his niece, Harriet Lane (who was then the First Lady for the bachelor Buchanan), and 11 live-in staff, including 3 maids, 2 laundresses, a footman, a coachman, a groom, and Thomas Stackpole, a 35-year-old native of New Hampshire who acted as watchman. Census-taker Young may have been nervous as he did his survey of the White House, because he got James Buchanan Henry's name wrong (he left off "Henry") and neglected to determine Miss Lane's age (perhaps a discreet omission).

It is a shame that Young and his colleagues could not have expanded the scope of their duties and administered a respondent survey on the issues of the day. Buchanan was struggling to hold together a nation that would split apart under his successor, Abraham Lincoln. Although Buchanan left many speeches and letters from which we could glean his opinions, a sampling of opinions of ordinary people in 1860 would be a gold mine for historians. But the respondent survey had not been invented yet. The 1860 census had a special questionnaire about slaves, including a question on those who had run away from their owners within the past year. But nobody was going door to door asking people how they felt about slavery or how they intended to vote in the 1860 presidential election.

Informant surveys of the day were being put to serious scientific use. Lewis Henry Morgan (1870) had already sent comprehensive questionnaires to informants around the world, giving him the data for a massive anthropological study on kinship and family structure. Edward Jarvis (1855) had published his study on mental illness and mental retardation, based on information provided by the doctors of Massachusetts, which tested the theory that mental illness and retardation are connected to poverty, as well as merely enumerating cases. Scientific informant surveys not only have a long tradition, but some of them are linked to each other across the decades, as the following set of examples on communes illustrates.

In 1851 A. J. MacDonald mailed a questionnaire to many leading American Socialists, seeking information about communal experiments they had been involved in. His aim was to write a book, "in which I propose giving a brief account of all the social and co-operative experiments that have been made in this country—their origin, principles, and progress; and, particularly, the causes of their success or failure" (quoted in Noyes, 1870:3–4). Among the questions were several that modern sociologists studying communes would have asked, including: "Was all the property put into common stock?" "What religious belief, and if any, how preached and practiced?" "Was there a written or printed constitution or laws?" "How were members admitted?" "When and where did the Association commence its experiment?" "What was the number of persons in the Association?"

Sadly, MacDonald died before he could complete his survey and take an honored place in the history of social science. But the trunkful of data he collected was eventually turned over to one of his informants, John Humphrey Noyes, founder of the Oneida commune, famous for its radical group-marriage experiment. Noyes incorporated some of this valuable material in his 1870 book *History of American Socialisms,* a landmark study in American sociology.

MacDonald visited many 19th-century communes, and Noyes had created one, but when Rosabeth Moss Kanter decided to investigate them in the 1960s, they were long gone, of course. Although she could not visit them or mail them a survey, she nonetheless used a questionnaire. Calling her questionnaire a "data summary form," she and her research assistants went through the historical record, writing down the answers to a couple of hundred questions like those MacDonald had framed. For example, the following question asked about the financial commitment that might be required of a recruit to the commune (Kanter, 1972:252):

> Was a financial contribution, a donation to community of money or property, required for admission?
>
> [1] Yes, it was required
> [2] Yes, it was preferred, though not required
> [3] No, it was not required or preferred

Kanter got the answer from historical accounts of Oneida, including Noyes's book. At the beginning of the 1970s, Hugh Gardner drove around Colorado, New Mexico, California, and Oregon visiting contemporary communes, with a data form based on Kanter's in the trunk of his car. He could answer some of his own questions simply by looking at the particular commune and observing the behavior of its members. In other cases, he could verbally ask members such questions as whether a fee or contribution was required for admission as a member (Gardner, 1978:261).

A Respondent Example

We can contrast these informant questionnaires with a respondent survey written by Benjamin Zablocki (1980:392–400) and completed by 398 members of urban communes in the 1970s. Some of the questions look as if they are simply seeking information, but an element of personal opinion is really involved. Among Zablocki's agree–disagree items was: "Most people in this commune are more inclined to look out for themselves than to consider the needs of others." Presumably, this question may have an objective answer that might be derived by observing the members interact with each other or by polling them individually in depth. But the respondents to Zablocki's survey in any given commune disagreed about their group and were expressing their personal opinions rather than reporting indisputable facts.

Some of Zablocki's other items were more obviously seeking personal opinions, feelings, and experiences: "I feel left out of things around me." "I prefer a dinner of brown rice and organically grown vegetables to a steak dinner." "Grading college papers according to the truth of what has been expressed in them is unfair because all truth is relative." "I prefer alcohol to marijuana." "There are odd moments now and then when I suspect I might go to pieces." These items put the person answering fully in the role of a respondent.

Zablocki did not have to invent all his questions, because many of them were taken from standard batteries of items. For example, he included a set of items that the Harris Poll and the General Social Survey have used to measure a person's feeling of alienation from the society. Indeed, when we want people to be respondents, revealing their personal thoughts and feelings to us, we generally have to use a large number of questions, each getting at just a part of the subtle opinions that people have. Over the years, survey researchers in many fields have constructed tests, scales, or indexes to measure a wide variety of attitudes and personality characteristics of respondents, and these sets of questionnaire items have become standard **instruments** used in many different studies.

Today whole encyclopedias are devoted to descriptions of the hundreds and hundreds of survey instruments available. There are encyclopedias of measures of political attitudes, social psychological attitudes, and occupational attitudes (Robinson, Rusk, and Head, 1968; Robinson and Shaver, 1969; Robinson, Athansiou, and Head, 1969). And you can consult volumes that cover tests and survey instruments in a wide range of areas (Sweetland and O'Connor, 1983; Keyser and Sweetland, 1984). We will consider some of these survey measures later in this book, but it should already be clear that lifetimes of effort have been invested in developing effective techniques for determining people's feelings, beliefs, and attitudes.

Competence of Informants

Much of this book is devoted to developing competence in the researcher to ask questions. But are respondents and informants always competent to give answers? One of the shortcomings of informant surveys of earlier years was that informants were often asked to make judgments that went beyond their knowledge and capacity. For example, the 1860 United States census attempted to count all the insane people in the country and to determine much about their condition and its origin. The local census-taker was usually the assistant marshal of the county and given very little training. The instruction book for the 1860 census-takers tried to give them criteria for identifying insanity and determining its origins:

> The various degrees of *insanity* often create a doubt as to the propriety of thus classifying individuals, and demands the exercise of discretion. A person may be reputed erratic on some subject, but if competent to manage his or her business affairs without manifesting any symptoms of insanity to an ordinary observer, such person should not be recorded as insane. Where persons are in institutions for safety or restoration, there can exist no doubt as to how you should classify them. As a general rule, the term insanity applies to individuals who have once possessed mental faculties which have become impaired; whereas *idiocy* applies to persons who have never possessed vigorous mental faculties, but from their birth have manifested aberration. The cases wherein it may be difficult to distinguish between insanity and idiocy are not numerous; should such occur, however, you may rely on the opinion of any physician to whom the case is known. It is to be hoped you will not fail to make record respecting all these classes of persons who may be in your subdivision.
>
> In all cases of insane persons, you will write in the space where you enter the word "Insane," the *cause* of such insanity, and you will in every case inquire into the cause or origin thereof, and write the word—as intemperance, spiritualism, grief, affliction, hereditary, misfortune, &c. As nearly every case of insanity may be traced to some known cause, it is earnestly desired that you will not fail to make your return in this respect as perfect as possible. (Kennedy, 1860:16)

Notice that these instructions suggest how the enumerator can identify "insanity" (mental illness), distinguish it from "idiocy" (mental retardation), and find the cause of the ailment. At the time, doctors believed they could generally determine the cause of a case of mental illness, whereas psy-

▶ ▶ ▶ ▶ ▶ ▶ ▶ ▶ ▶ ▶ ▶

TABLE 2.1   SUPPOSED CAUSES OF INSANITY FROM THE 1860 CENSUS

	Percent Attributed:	
Cause	Males	Females
Religious excitement	5.7	4.8
Spiritualism	0.9	0.8
Money trouble	5.4	2.3
Disappointment	3.3	4.9
Domestic trouble	3.7	10.7
Loss and grief	1.6	4.7
Love	1.2	0.7
Fear	1.3	1.5
Other intense emotions	2.2	2.1
Alcoholism	15.0	4.4
Drugs	1.1	0.9
Masturbation	17.7	2.1
Sin and bad habits	2.0	0.6
Overexertion	3.8	2.2
Hardship	1.0	1.4
Ill health	11.8	21.9
Childbirth	0.0	8.2
Feminine problems	0.0	7.7
Epilepsy	9.5	5.1
Paralysis	0.4	0.1
Injury	4.1	1.1
Exposure	1.3	0.5
Hereditary	5.7	7.1
All other causes	1.3	4.5
Total	100.0	100.0

▶

chiatrists of later generations were convinced their predecessors had been quite wrong in their judgments. Thus the doctors and ordinary citizens the 1860 census-takers interviewed were treated as competent informants about the cause of mental illness, but today professionals maintain that even the best specialist of the day was totally incompetent to answer the question.

I found it fascinating to look through the original manuscript census schedules, the data forms the 1860 census-takers wrote on, containing records for the largest insane asylums. I was able to find supposed causes of insanity for 2258 inmates of 17 asylums. In Chapter 9 I will explain how I distilled the data I found, but here in Table 2.1 we can examine the major kinds of cause the doctors running these asylums cited for 1230 men and 1028 women (Bainbridge, 1984b). Look through the list and ask yourself where the doctors could have gotten their ideas. In particular, you might look at differences between the patterns for men and women and consider whether these might reflect traditional stereotypes of the sexes in the minds of the doctors.

A main theme running through most of these supposed causes was the idea that great emotional stress or excitement could wear out the nerves, leading to a mental breakdown. This insight gives us a clue to the way 19th-century doctors conceptualized the human mind and the problems that might befall it. So although these data may be useless for an objective study of mental illness, they are quite valuable for a study in the social history of psychiatry. The census treated the doctors as informants, reporting objective information, but we can view them as respondents, expressing their personal opinions.

When one of the census-takers, a Mr. Ingraham, reached the vast New York City asylum on Blackwell's Island, he had tremendous difficulty getting answers to all the questions his instructions told him to ask. Moses Ramey, the resident physician, was able to give him the supposed cause of insanity for many of the inmates, but when it came to data about occupation and amount of personal property owned, the situation was quite hopeless. Ingraham wrote this apology on a page in his report:

> For the lunatic asylum many of the inmates had been there for years, and no history of their occupation previous to their admittance was on record; and in other cases those who brought them to the institution could give no information on the subject, and but little is known by the Resident Physician on this subject though the information is important in a medical point of view.
>
> All inquiries made of Paupers, Convicts or Lunatics as to the value of their real or personal estate would lead to no important result. One of the lunatics informed me his estate was worth $11,000,000, and another that he owned both sides of Broadway from the Battery to Union Square, including the City Hall, though it was but a few years since he first landed in this country.

Clearly, poor Mr. Ingraham had a rough time trying to get information about the inmates of the institutions in the census district it had been his bad luck to be assigned. But the general lessons are also clear. Sometimes there is no one competent to give us the information we want. At other times, we will be given wild opinions, even from experts, that must be considered respondents' views rather than informants' facts. Finally, the example that follows shows how important it is to get data from the right people.

In 1911, Australia sent interviewers to every household in the country to do its national census. One member of each household was supposed to give information about all the other members, including not only such standard data as age, sex, and birthplace, but also each person's religious preference. Besides the major denominations, such as Anglicans, Baptists, Catholics, Lutherans, and Methodists, the published volumes also enumerate all the tiny sects, cults, and splinter groups. Among the reported categories is "Other (Non-Christian)." The largest group in this category is Spiritualists, with 2362 members. The second most populous in this odd collection was Socialists, representing only 294 persons, and there were also 186 Realists.

Other subcategories with more than 50 members are bewildering: Deists, Undecideds, Cosmopolitans, Reasonists, Any Religionists or Anythings, Humanitarians, Metaphysicians, Pantheists, Universalists, and Calathumpians. There were also a few Monists, New Thought people, Spiritists, Freemasons, Communists, and Single Taxers. And there were 32 Wowsers, a category I originally found especially mysterious.

Wowser is the Australian word for an obtrusively puritanical person. I don't think anyone would describe himself or herself as a wowser. "Good morning. I'm the census-taker. Could you tell me your religion?" "Yes, happy to. I'm a confirmed bigot and snob, with tendencies toward obnoxious and obtrusive puritanicalism."

I am sure the 32 Wowsers were given that tag by other members of their households who were acting as census informant. "Yes, I'm an Anglican, myself, as are both my parents. My sister Sarah is a Methodist, however, and our brother George is a bloomin' wowser!" Obviously, it might be good to get George's own statement of his religious preference, because it might differ significantly from that attributed to him by his sister.

Exotic Respondents

Anthropologists and others interested in societies that Americans would consider quite exotic have found that it is quite feasible to do surveys in most parts of the world. Of course, people who cannot read must be asked the questions by an interviewer in their language. People who are not used to numbers cannot be asked to rate things on a seven-point preference scale.

A good example of what can be accomplished is a study by Robert B. Edgerton (1966) in the Culture and Ecology in East Africa Project. Edgerton was interested in the conceptions of severe mental illness held by members of cultures very different from the European–American culture that modern psychiatry is based on. He included questions about the nature and cause of psychosis in a survey administered to members of four widely separated tribes of East Africa: the Hehe, Kamba, Pokot, and the Sebei.

Respondents were selected for their lack of contact with Western culture; individuals who showed signs of such influence were excluded from the study. The survey went smoothly; only 5% of those contacted failed to answer the questions.

▶ ▶ ▶ ▶ ▶   ▶ ▶ ▶ ▶ ▶   ▶

TABLE 2.2   OPINIONS ABOUT THE CAUSE OF PSYCHOSIS IN FOUR "PRIMITIVE TRIBES"

Cause	Number Mentioning the Cause Among the:			
	Hehe	Kamba	Pokot	Sebei
Disease or illness	0	10	52	78
Witchcraft	50	70	1	18
God	28	1	0	2
Stress of life	1	35	0	2
Heredity	18	3	0	3
Other	0	5	0	1
Don't know	26	2	75	24
Total	123	126	128	128

▶

When Edgerton's interviewers asked the respondents what the symptoms of severe mental illness were, their answers were similar from tribe to tribe, and these answers were also similar to what Westerners would have replied. When Edgerton asked "What causes severe mental illness?", significant differences emerged.

Sadly, few "civilized" people are free of the false impression that members of "primitive tribes" are backward savages lacking intelligent opinions about the world. Even professional anthropologists, who should have known better, used to claim that members of "savage tribes" were uniformly gripped by the particular magical beliefs of their tribe. Now anthropologists know that members of many preliterate, nonindustrial societies differ as much from each other as do members of industrial societies. Both from tribe to tribe, and from individual to individual within a tribe, opinions may vary widely.

Table 2.2 shows, in simplified form, the ranges of opinions about the cause of psychosis held by members of the four tribes. Before you look at it, you might want to guess what these "primitive" respondents would believe. Perhaps they all hold foolish superstitions that madness is caused by witchcraft and evil spirits.

Indeed, 78 of the 123 Hehe (63%) responded that the cause was witchcraft or God, and so did 71 of the 126 Kamba (56%). But some members of these two tribes mentioned the stress of life or heredity, and 10 among the Kamba mentioned physiological disease. These are very "modern" ideas about madness—asserting that madness should be conceived of as "mental illness"—yet Edgerton's respondents got the ideas from their traditional cultures, rather than from the West.

Many among the Pokot and the majority of the Sebei conceived of madness as mental illness, the result of some kind of disease, yet they are no more influenced by Western psychiatry than are members of the two tribes that emphasize supernatural causes. Note that some members of all four groups responded that they did not know the answer to the question, and a majority of the Pokot expressed this ignorance.

Sometimes an admission of ignorance is the sign of real wisdom. Do you know the cause of psychosis? Thirty years ago many psychiatrists were telling us confidently that serious mental illness was caused by conflicts in relationships between patients and their parents. Today doctors confidently tell us that hereditary disorders affecting the chemicals in the brain are responsible. In another 30 years, some other cause may be confidently named by the experts. But right up to this very day, citizens of even the most modern society have not had a solid scientific basis for their opinions of the causes of psychosis.

You might not want to buy the witchcraft theory held by so many Hehe and Kamba, but it is possible that their opinions are closer to some held by modern people than we might want to admit. The difference might partly be one of language, of the metaphors a culture uses to express itself about human relationships. At least one personality theorist has suggested that modern people use the language of psychiatry to express concepts quite similar to those expressed by premodern people through supernatural metaphors (Rabkin, 1967, 1970). In any case, most modern people have only the vaguest understanding of what psychological or psychiatric terms mean, holding ideas about madness that are not greatly advanced over those of Edgerton's four primitive tribes.

To me, the great lesson of Edgerton's study is that people in all societies have active minds and develop opinions about key issues in life. If we can communicate with people in an exotic society, then we can survey them just as we survey people who live in our own neighborhood.

Questions in Translation

American researchers often write a survey in English, then translate it into another language. For example, a student of mine once took a standard American questionnaire about juvenile delinquency and translated it into Japanese, administering it to high school students in Japan, just as had been done earlier in the United States. Some surveys are designed from the start to permit international comparisons, and editions of the survey in several languages are developed simultaneously.

A standard technique for testing the quality of a translation is **back translation.** Say you have written a questionnaire in English. Then you hire a native Japanese to translate the survey into Japanese. Back translation involves getting a second translator to translate the Japanese version back into English. It is important to use a second translator, so that the person doing the back translation will not know what the original English version looked like. If the back-translated English version is very different from the original, you can suspect that the Japanese version needs more work.

A translation that takes every English word and replaces it with the best equivalent word in Japanese is not necessarily a good translation. Sometimes whole phrases have to be translated, using the metaphor that gets the idea across best in the new language. "Do you often feel down in the dumps?" might get back-translated as "Are you a frequent visitor of your community's garbage disposal facility?"

Even outside of metaphors and clichés, words may not have exact equivalents in different languages. What is Russian for "income tax"? Does the Russian word for "democracy" mean anything like the English word? Irwin Deutscher has noted that societies differ in the meaning they give to words describing family and friendship relationships, even when the words are *cognates*, words historically related across the two languages.

> The word "friend," for example, translates easily back and forth with the German cognate *"Freund."* But is *ein Freund* in fact a friend? Hardly! For the German, the term is reserved for a very few intimate associates of long standing. For the American, the English cognate has a much broader reference to a much wider assortment of acquaintances. Incidentally, the Spanish word which would provide a reliable back translation for the English "friend" is *amigo.* Yet among Mexicans that term is employed both as a form of direct address and as indirect reference to strangers with whom the speaker may have had only the most casual and superficial encounter. (Deutscher, 1973:168–69)

Another example, from my own household, concerns the word *yes.* When my wife says yes in response to something I said, I am never quite sure what she means. You see, my wife is Japanese, and the English word *yes* is usually translated into Japanese as *hai.* But the Japanese use *hai* simply as a polite response to almost anything another person says. Although it can sometimes really mean yes, often it is just an acknowledgment that the other person has spoken.

One should not despair of doing surveys in other languages merely because such problems of translation exist. Indeed, people speaking the same language can differ in their understanding of words. Parents and children in the same American household often seem to be talking different languages. It is said that a joint British–American command committee in World War II once got into serious trouble when the British moved to "table" an issue the Americans wanted to talk about. For the Americans, "to table a motion" meant to set it aside for possible later consideration. For the British, "to table a motion" meant to bring it up for consideration right now!

Despite these problems, it is possible to test general social-scientific theories through cross-cultural surveys. A good example has been provided by Adam Przeworski and Henry Teune, researchers who wanted to study political activity in the United States and Poland.

There are many theories about which kinds of people are most apt to be politically active. For example, you might want to test the theory that people who get involved in politics tend to be better educated than people who don't. Even though the educational systems of Poland and America are very different, you could measure education roughly in terms of how many years of education people have received. However, you might have to take into account the fact that more Americans complete college. Perhaps you would identify the highly educated as the top 20% in schooling in each country, even if this meant the Americans had to go to school longer to count as educated.

But your research project does not have to find the "right decision" on all matters like this. You could try your analysis both ways. One time, you could look at the political activity of citizens of the two countries, contrasting those who attended college with those who did not. And the other time, you could compare the top 20% in years of schooling in both countries. If you get the same general result, then you really don't have to decide which is the best way of translating "highly educated" from one country to the other.

Przeworski and Teune were more concerned with the issue of how to measure political activity in the two countries. Poland and the United States have very different political systems. Therefore, quite different actions might count as political in the two nations. Przeworski and Teune (1973:126) suggested the following two lists as valid questions measuring political activity in the United States and Poland:

United States	*Poland*
1. Contribute money to parties or candidates	1. Fight for execution of economic plans
2. Place sticker on car	2. Attempt to influence economic decisions
3. Volunteer help in campaigns	3. Join the party
4. Testify at hearings	4. Participate in voluntary social work
5. Write letters to members of Congress in support of or against policies or programs	5. Develop ideological consciousness

Much of the time, translation is not a serious problem for survey researchers. But one must always be aware of the potential problems and guard against them. Even when the questionnaire itself has been written correctly, communication with respondents may run into difficulty. The researcher must develop the right relationship with the respondent in order to get good results, and must phrase questions in terms meaningful to the respondent (Gordon, 1969).

▶　▶　▶　▶　▶　▶　▶　▶　▶　▶　▶

THE UNIT OF ANALYSIS

Whenever we count things, we must have a clear idea of what constitutes a unit—what we have to see before we can add 1 to our total. If you are doing an inventory of a fruit warehouse, you have to decide whether you are going to count grapes or bunches of grapes, bananas or bunches of bananas. Because the number of bananas in a bunch varies greatly, from lone bananas and pairs up to a mass of two dozen or more, counting single bananas might be more accurate. But you'd have to be crazy to count all the individual grapes, because they are so numerous, so for practical reasons you might select "a bunch of grapes" as your unit of analysis.

Another hypothetical example can help us see that there may be many ways to count and many different phenomena that could be your unit of analysis. Imagine you have just purchased the Bear Mountain Bridge and want to charge tolls on the cars and trucks that pass over. You have to decide how the toll should be figured. You could set the toll at $1 per vehicle. Then the unit of analysis is "a vehicle." But many toll roads and bridges charge big trucks more than they do smaller vehicles. For example, you could charge 50¢ per axle. In vehicle jargon, an axle is a rotating transverse shaft with a wheel at each end. Old-fashioned wagons and toy cars really have a little rod running across under the vehicle, with a wheel fixed to each end, though in real, modern vehicles the situation is more complicated. But it is easy enough to count each set of wheels, and a car would still pay $1 (50¢ for the front wheels and 50¢ for the back ones), while a multi-axle truck might pay $1.50, $2, or more.

Along comes a motorcycle. "One dollar, please," you say. "But wait," says the motorcyclist. "Cars pay that much, and I'm just riding a little motorcycle." You explain that the cycle, like a car, has two axles, so it has to pay two times 50¢, or $1. The cyclist replies that cars have four wheels, and you seem to be charging 25¢ a wheel. Therefore, a cyclist should pay only 50¢ for the two wheels a motorcycle has. Some motorcycles have a third wheel, usually on a sidecar, and they could pay 75¢. Perhaps this logic convinces you, and you change your unit of analysis from "an axle at 50¢" to "a wheel at 25¢." This does not alter the toll for cars and trucks, but it straightens out tolls for motorcycles.

Then you notice that the thousands of commuters crossing your bridge each day have started car pooling to save tolls. Originally, each worker drove a car, and you collected $1 each time one of them crossed the bridge. Now they are sharing rides, three and four to a car, and you are losing money. You could change the unit of analysis to "a passenger" and charge $1 for each person who crossed the bridge. You would not make so much money on trucks with this system, but you would really clean up on buses.

Still another possibility is to install scales and charge 1¢ for every 25 pounds that crosses. This system might be good if much of your traffic consists of trucks, because then you would be charging primarily for the cargo they transported across your bridge. Here the unit of analysis would be "25 pounds of weight." Every time 25 pounds goes over the bridge, you make 1¢. If you want to raise your rates a little bit, you could charge 1¢ for every 20 pounds, and then the unit of analysis would be "20 pounds of weight." Or you could charge ¼₅ cent for every pound, in which case "a pound" is the unit of analysis.

The **unit of analysis** is the basic unit counted in research. With surveys, the typical unit of analysis is the individual person who fills out the questionnaire—the respondent. Another common term for the unit of analysis in survey research is the **case**. Certainly, we often use the word *case* for units that might be counted, such as in "a case of whiskey" or "a case of the flu."

Although the individual respondent is typically the unit of analysis in survey research, sometimes we count families instead. A questionnaire could be filled out by a family as a unit, asking them about their dwelling and other facts of life that they share as a unit. Chapter 11's discussion of complex survey research designs describes a study in which the unit of analysis was a pair of respondents, rather than a single individual.

Here's a real example from survey research. The federal government frequently does surveys to see how much money people are making. It asks respondents how much money they made last year, as individuals, and it also asks what the total income of their family was. The government has been conducting these surveys for years, so these data show whether the American economy has been improving, holding steady, or even declining over the past few years. Clearly, this is an important question, and some political leaders have drawn dire conclusions from the "fact" that income did not go up at all from 1972 to 1987.

But this "fact" is partly a matter of interpretation. Median *family* income, the amount earned by the typical family, did not rise over this period. But the income of the typical *individual* did rise. The reason is that divorce and other social changes were affecting the average size of families, so the balance between the number of individuals and the number of families was changing (Flint, 1987). So one could say income was rising or just as validly say that income was not rising. The difference is the unit of analysis.

A survey carried out by my anthropologist colleague James Ito-Adler (1980) showed a similar paradox. He was studying Portuguese immigrants in the adjacent Massachusetts cities of Cambridge and Somerville. Even compared to other disadvantaged groups, the Portuguese immigrants appeared to have very low incomes, if the unit of analysis was the individual. But if the unit of analysis was the family, the Portuguese immigrants appeared to be doing much better. The fact is, many members of these families worked, and they pooled their incomes to invest in family businesses and real estate. By combining their small incomes, they were able to advance rapidly in economic status. The Portuguese immigrants of Cambridge and Somerville are a real success story—a story that might have been missed by a survey researcher who used only the individual as the unit of analysis.

A classic example of the necessity of choosing the right unit of analysis is the debate over the curability of insanity that raged in American medicine around the middle of the 19th century. In the 1840s and 1850s, several mental hospitals published reports showing very high rates of cure, sometimes over 80%, for patients suffering from serious mental illness (Rothman, 1971). But by the end of the century, doctors were quite pessimistic about cure, and the hospitals were reporting very low cure rates. What was going on?

One of the factors was that the concept of *case* or *unit of analysis* changed. Early in the century, doctors conceived of mental illness like many physical ailments. Consider the common cold. A person falls ill; he is sick for a week, and he gets better. Six months later, the same person catches another cold and again recovers quickly. We have just one person but two cases of the common cold. The unit of analysis is "an episode of illness" rather than "a person." One person can count as several cases of cure, which is quite reasonable for illnesses like the common cold.

Doctors thought of mental illness the same way. A person was struck ill, entered the hospital, got better, and left the hospital. The same person later re-entered the hospital (or went into another one) with a second episode of illness, got better, and left again. This person was counted as two instances of cure, even though he or she might have been hospitalized a third time and died years later still in the asylum.

Partly because of careful statistical studies by social scientist Pliny Earle (1887), doctors came to see that their mental patients were often leaving the hospital only slightly better than they had entered it. Their condition was not cured but only temporarily improved. Doctors no longer conceived of each time a person went into the hospital as a separate case but considered each patient to be a single case, no matter how many times the person suffered especially bad symptoms. The unit of analysis became the person, not the episode of hospitalization, and the apparent cure rate dropped far below the levels of the early days of optimism.

In your own surveys, you will want to think carefully about the unit of analysis. Usually, each questionnaire respondent will be a single case. But often you will want to collect data in which the respondent's family is the unit of analysis. At times you will want to collect data about limited portions of the person's life. For example, a study of juvenile delinquency might collect data about each time the respondent was picked up by the police—such as the reason for the arrest and the actions the courts took in each episode. Then the researcher could perform two separate analyses, one in which the individual respondent was the unit of analysis, and another in which each episode of arrest was a separate case.

A wrong decision about the unit of analysis might invalidate your research conclusions. But an awareness that alternate ways of defining a case exist can help you achieve much in even a modest survey.

▶ ▶ ▶ ▶ ▶ ▶ ▶ ▶ ▶ ▶ ▶

SAMPLING

We are seldom able to do a survey of all the people whose experiences and opinions are of interest to us. Instead, we administer the questionnaire to a **sample** of respondents, selected to represent the target group. The next chapter will explain many of the techniques of sampling, using three computer programs to demonstrate them.

The classic example of the virtues of scientific sampling comes from the 1936 presidential election. A popular magazine of the day, the *Literary Digest*, had done polls in 1920, 1924, 1928, and 1932 that accurately predicted weeks before the actual election who would become president. So a headline in its August 22 issue proclaimed: "THE DIGEST PRESIDENTIAL POLL IS ON! Famous Forecasting Machine Is Thrown into Gear for 1936."

The article went on to explain how the magazine selected its respondents:

> The Poll represents thirty years' constant evolution and perfection. Based on the "commercial sampling" methods used for more than a century by publishing houses to push book sales, the present mailing list is drawn from every telephone book in the United States, from the rosters of clubs and associations, from city directories, lists of registered voters, classified mail-order and occupational data.

Every week, the magazine announced progress, undoubtedly building circulation with all the ballyhoo. On September 5, it reported poll returns from Maine, New Jersey, New York, and Pennsylvania that showed the Republican candidate, Alf Landon, leading the incumbent Democratic president, Franklin Roosevelt. A headline in the September 19 issue read, "POLL RETURNS EXTEND TO 13 STATES—Landon Gains an Early Lead in Eight and Roosevelt in Five."

The final poll results, in the October 31 issue, showed Landon far ahead. Ten million questionnaires had been sent out, and a total of 2,376,523 were returned. Of these, 1,293,669 said they would vote for Landon, compared with only 972,897 for Roosevelt. The magazine was proud to quote James A. Farley, chairman of the Democratic National Committee, who had commented four years before:

> Any sane person can not escape the implication of such a gigantic sampling of popular opinion as is embraced in The Literary Digest straw vote. I consider this conclusive evidence as to the desire of the people of this country for a change in the National Government. The Literary Digest poll is an achievement of no little magnitude. It is a Poll fairly and correctly conducted.

Of course, when he spoke Farley's party was out of power, and one doubts he would have been so enthusiastic with the 1936 poll, which showed his man about to be kicked out.

Have your grandparents told you about President Landon? Do you recall hearing about how he got the United States out of the Great Depression and handled the rising storm clouds of war around the world? Of course not. Roosevelt was re-elected by an overwhelming majority. Pleading lack of time to change the printing plans, the *Literary Digest* refused to follow a reader's suggestion that it color its cover bright red, except for the message "Is our face red!" And its feature article for November 14 said that all the polls had been wrong, not its own alone. Nowhere in the article is there any hint that the polling method was anything less than completely scientific. It would have been interesting to see whether the magazine would have tried a different method of polling for the 1940 election, but it had disappeared by then.

The fact is that the magazine was not using up-to-date scientific methods, and a new type of scientific sampling was used successfully in the election by George Gallup, Elmo Roper, and Archibald Crossley (Gallup, 1976:64–67). In a newspaper article published July 12, 1936, George Gallup said that the *Literary Digest* poll would be wrong, and he went so far as to predict the poll would show Landon winning with 56% of the popular vote to 44% for Roosevelt. He had arrived at this prediction by sending just 3000 postcard ballots to a random sample of people on the lists used by the *Literary Digest*. It irritated the magazine greatly to see Gallup claiming to duplicate its 2,376,523-ballot poll on the basis of only 3000 respondents, but he was off by only 1% in predicting what the vastly larger poll would find.

Furthermore, Gallup was able to predict correctly that Roosevelt would win on the basis of another 3000-respondent poll he did of the electorate. Today, the *Literary Digest* is long forgotten, while Gallup's polling organization flourishes using the sampling methods pioneered by its founder.

It might seem that the huge set of respondents collected by the magazine would yield the better results. But the lists it had drawn up were best suited for finding prosperous people likely to make good customers for publishers and other businesses. In 1936 many of Roosevelt's voters had no telephones, charge accounts, or even jobs. According to Gallup, only 18% of the people on relief rolls favored Landon.

National Random Samples

The value of a set of respondents is not determined by how big it is but by how representative it is. Today most major national polls survey only 1500 people. But these people accurately represent the entire nation. Paradoxically, one of the very best ways of selecting a sample is to do it randomly. Every other method might introduce a bias of some kind that would reduce the representativeness of the sample. In the next chapter we will find that certain modifications of a simple random sample are often advisable for practical reasons, but we will also see clearly that a random sample tends to give the most representative data possible.

A random sample of 1500 gives as good results in predicting the vote for president of a large nation as it does in predicting the vote for mayor of a small city. Indeed, one of the ironies of survey research is that you need as big a sample for the small city as for the whole nation. When Gallup's organization does a poll in Belgium, it needs a sample of 1500, just as it does when it polls the United States. And for most purposes, it does not profit the researcher to increase the size of the sample much above 1500. A random sample of 3000 is only slightly more accurate than a sample of 1500, not twice as accurate, as you might guess.

The main reason for going beyond 1500 respondents is to be able to focus on subgroups of the population with as much accuracy as is achieved with large groups. Indeed, presidential polls often have to go to many thousands, because of the complex electoral college system in the United States. The poll must be able to predict the majority in each state separately, then add up the electoral votes of the states projected for each candidate. Otherwise, 1500 might be quite sufficient.

A random national sample has two chief advantages. First, your results will let you describe the whole public, rather than just a segment of it. This can be of journalistic importance, when you want to predict a national election or to ensure big headlines across the country publicizing your findings.

The second advantage of a national sample is that it guards against the possibility that the uniqueness of your population produced results quite different from those you would have achieved elsewhere. For example, Charles Y. Glock and Rodney Stark (1966) polled church members in northern California in a famous study that generated results of many kinds, testing all sorts of scientific theories. But, critics could complain, "Everybody knows Californians are weird. Variables that correlate for Californians probably don't for reasonable people." To guard against these possibilities, Glock and Stark also did a survey of the whole nation (which because of the high cost of a national poll included far fewer questions than the original questionnaire) that tested just the main findings of their more extensive local survey.

If I were given a large sum of money to test a scientific theory via survey research, I would probably spend it on several local surveys rather than on a national poll. By concentrating in a few local areas, I could afford a far larger number of respondents. Perhaps I would select a few varied geographic regions for random samples of the general public and add a few specialized populations that I guessed might have distinctive orientations toward the topic under study. A random national sample of 1500 people might simply be too small to reveal some of the differences that might exist in subgroups of the general public. You need a national sample to predict a national election, but good science can be done locally.

Choosing Your Population

The set of people from which you draw your sample is known as the **population.** This does not necessarily mean the general population, what the census bureau counts every ten years. It could be a much smaller group, such as the students in a particular school or the customers of a particular business. The population is the set of people you want to be able to describe through your sample, and it is the pool of potential respondents you hope are willing to help you by filling out your survey.

You should invest serious thought and research in identifying the precise population you will study. Who are the people you want to know about? What crucial variations in the general public must be taken into account? Which set of respondents will best help you achieve the aims of your research?

For example, if you have been hired to determine which new products a chain of stores should carry, you can consider several different populations. Most obviously, you can poll customers when they visit the stores. But perhaps the store chain wants to attract new customers. Then one possibility would be customers of all the businesses in the shopping centers in which the chain has stores. Another idea would be residents of the neighborhoods the stores serve. If the management of the chain has a clear image of its target group in the general public—for example, upper-middle-class married women with children—then you can narrow the population to just this segment.

It is said that psychologists understand the sophomore mind better than anything else, because the respondents to their surveys tend to be college sophomores. College folklore has it, however, that sophomores are a very strange bunch, prey to such unique disorders as "sophomore slump" and hardly representative of humanity as a whole. From one perspective, ideally your population should consist of Asian ghosts. Arthur C. Clarke contends that 95% of the human race are ghosts, because some estimates suggest that only about 5% of the humans who have ever lived are alive today. Only about 5% of the human race are Americans, so if you want to study basic human nature, a sample of living Americans will give you skewed results indeed. Better try Asian ghosts.

Of course, this is silly. No one study can pretend to plumb the depths of human nature, and survey researchers are always struggling to find the best compromise between ideal perfection and practical expediency. And the test of the right balance between these two is always what your ultimate purpose in doing the research happens to be.

Once you have decided in principle what your population should be, you have to get down to specifics and be precise in defining it. It is not good enough to say "residents of Anchorage" will be your population. You have to define "resident" in a way that is both unambiguous and relevant to your study. The city has a high rate of people moving in and out, so you may have trouble distinguishing people who live in Anchorage from those who are merely passing through. Do you include the people staying in hotels or don't you? Or do you approach hotel guests first with the question "Do you plan to stay in Anchorage?" and poll only those who say yes?

When Leo Srole (1962) and his associates were planning the famous Midtown Manhattan study, such issues were very important. A main purpose of the survey was to determine what proportion of the population could be considered psychologically impaired or mentally ill. Previous studies (Faris and Dunham, 1939; Hollingshead and Redlich, 1958) had counted the number of people receiving psychiatric treatment, but it was widely recognized that only a fraction of the mentally ill actually get into treatment.

Planning to do a lengthy at-home survey, Srole and his associates knew they could not afford a national sample; they relied on other researchers to try the same thing in different parts of the country, as indeed several subsequently did. Thus they were not ashamed to focus on a distinctive population that was readily at hand for investigation, residents of midtown Manhattan in New York City. But what definition of *resident* should they use?

The basic criterion "was that the individual be a resident for whom a Midtown dwelling is both his primary 'home base' and the place he now actually occupies." The researchers defined more precisely what they meant by "home base":

1. This included, of course, people in residential hotels and residence clubs but excluded those in transient hotels and clubs.

2. It included living-in staff members of Midtown institutions but excluded the patients and charges in those institutions.

3. It included non-kin members of households, like boarders and living-in servants, but excluded members of a family who, during the period of the survey's interviewing program, were away on extended or indefinite leave, e.g., occupied in military service, domiciled at college, engaged in foreign travel or distant assignment, or confined in institutions.

4. It also excluded people who had their home base elsewhere, usually out of New York City, but maintained a year-round Midtown dwelling for use on a sporadic or part-time basis. These were designated *secondary residents*. (Srole et al., 1962:33).

These criteria were a mixture of practicality and scientific judgment. If your town contains a state mental hospital, to include its inmates among the town residents when calculating rates of mental illness for towns in your state would seem unfair and theoretically indefensible. The inmates should be counted as residents of the towns from which they came. But the staff of the hospital are like employees of any other major business or institution that has a branch in your town. They should be counted. The criteria of the Midtown Manhattan study cannot be automatically applied to research projects that have other aims and experience other practical limitations, but they suggest the kind of thinking that must be done in defining a population.

But thinking is not enough. You also have to do a little research. Suppose you are studying school-age children in a particular county. You go to the superintendent of schools and get a list of children enrolled in the public schools. First, you must check how current the list is. Like the phone book, it may include several people who have moved away and exclude newcomers. You will have to ask whether the superintendent has a set of "new listings."

The public system may not be the county's only schools. There may be private day schools, some run by religious denominations, that must be included. Kids living in a far corner of the county may go to a school in the next county, and the local school may include a few who live outside. Some children attend boarding schools in other states, and a few may even be instructed at home by parents who have teaching certificates. Depending on state law, disabled kids may receive educations in exceptional institutions. A few children—many, if you are studying teenagers—may have quit school altogether.

In the early 1970s, an eminent sociologist (may he rest in peace anonymously) made a terrible mistake in defining his population. As part of an important international study, he had funding to survey adults who had graduated from Harvard. Now, Harvard is more completely described as Harvard–Radcliffe, because Harvard College was originally just for men, and women students attended Radcliffe, a separate but related institution. The sociologist was very busy, and he hired people to draw a random sample from a computerized list of Harvard alumni. Out went the questionnaires; back they came.

The responses were punched into the computer, and the first results astounded the sociologist. One hundred percent of the respondents were male! The people doing the sampling hadn't been told to include Radcliffe. All the alumni (male alums) were listed as Harvard graduates, and all the alumnae (female alums) were on a separate list of Radcliffe graduates. The sociologist had to beg for extra funding to send out surveys to the Harvard–Radcliffe women.

Drawing the Sample

Many towns annually publish a list of residents. For example, in 1986 one could go to the town hall of Watertown, Massachusetts, and get a book-size resident list arranged by streets and voting districts, plus an alphabetical list, all for just $10. Like telephone books and lists of registered voters, such lists quickly get out of date. Therefore, any sample drawn from them will leave out newcomers, which may bias the results against people who move often.

An alternative is to sample residences rather than residents: You can go through the Watertown residents book, marking people at random; when you arrive at a person's home, you may find that somebody else is living there instead. And this new person, not listed in the Watertown residents book, will take the place of the originally designated respondent.

The plan you adopt to draw your sample from the population is called the **sampling frame.** There are many different ways of drawing samples. At the practical level, it may be too much work to number all the thousands of people in the Watertown book, then have random numbers determine who gets into the sample. One solution is to pick the people in a certain position on each page. It generally is not good to take the first person on each page, because there may be a pattern that determines where people fall in the list. For example, each new page may begin with a new household, and the first name in the household may be the head of household, generally an older person. Each page of the Watertown book has 3 columns of names, with a maximum of 112 names in a column. So you might pick 1 name at random in each column by using a computer program described in the next chapter to pick a number at random from 1 through 112. Still, this method does not give exactly the same results as selecting individuals entirely at random, because it cannot select two respondents from the same column.

▶ ▶ ▶ ▶ ▶ ▶ ▶ ▶ ▶ ▶ ▶

PROJECTS

1. Examine Everyday Surveys. As I've noted, the typical person is asked to fill out many questionnaires and to respond to many other kinds of survey, such as application forms, subscription forms, school tests, and the like. Even some purchase orders ask for extra information, not needed to complete the sale, that the business uses to understand more about its customers. First, make a list of all the kinds of survey that you are likely to receive in the course of a year, including any telephone surveys as well as printed questionnaires of all types. You don't have to remember all the particular ones; just list the types you might encounter. Be imaginative, and try to recognize all the types of surveys that might come your way even when they don't at first look like surveys.

Next, actually obtain copies of five very different questionnaires, representative of different types on your list. Some, of course, can be quite short. Complete this project by writing brief descriptions of the five, explaining where each one came from and what information it sought to collect.

2. A Telephone Survey. Select a simple opinion poll, taken from a press report or from standard poll reports, such as the *Gallup Opinion Index* if you can find a copy in your library. The poll should be limited to about 6 questions, of a simple sort that could easily be asked over the telephone. Write out the questions, with spaces for answers, on a single sheet of paper, then make about 30 photocopies of it.

Then prepare what we sometimes call a *spiel,* a little introduction to the survey that you could read to a stranger over the telephone. "Good morning, I am Sam Pollster, a student at Central State Tech, and I am doing a very short survey as a class project. I have six simple questions, most of them about the recent troubles in the airline industry, and your thoughts about them would be very valuable. Could you help me for a moment while I ask them?"

Finally, choose 25 numbers from the telephone book, all belonging to strangers, and try giving the survey to each of them. Call each number twice, if necessary, but don't bother trying after the second time. Use a separate survey sheet for each number. If the person you get actually gives you answers, write them down. If the person refuses to answer, write down the reason for refusing or any other information you get about him or her during your attempt. In other cases, you will have to write down that nobody answered after 2 tries. Note, the purpose of this project is to give you some experience, not actually to succeed at getting data from all 25 people. Therefore, if you have a difficult time with 1 or 2 people, chalk it up to experience—all part of the adventure of research with real human beings. Although you should give your name, to protect yourself you probably should not give your phone number or address, merely the address of your college department, if a respondent asks.

3. *Designing a Multiple-Mailing Survey.* Think of a topic and a target population of respondents for a questionnaire. Do not actually write the questions or select respondents, but figure out the steps in a multi-mailing design for administering the survey.

One part of this assignment is a list of all the different things you might send a respondent who ignored your first couple of requests to fill out the questionnaire. How many times are you prepared to send the questionnaire itself? What else might you send? Return envelopes, a reminder letter, a reply postcard? Then draw up a schedule, with realistic dates, for each of the things you would send.

The list and schedule should be clear enough for someone you hired to do this work to follow without making mistakes. You may want to get estimates from your local post office of how long it would take for each mailing to get to its destination and for a completed survey to return.

Purely for the sake of thinking the practical issues through, and without pretending that your estimates are really accurate, suggest how many days the typical respondent takes to get around to the survey and guess what percentage might respond at each step in your multiple mailings.

4. *Informant/Respondent Interview.* Find a stranger willing to be the subject of a half-hour interview. You can prepare a few questions if you want to, and take a notebook, so that you can write down the questions you think of while doing the interview.

The point of the interview is simple: Get to know this stranger, developing a picture of the person he or she is. To be sure, different interviewers will concentrate on different aspects of the stranger's life and character, because people have varying perspectives on what is important to know about a person. Whenever you think of a question in the interview, write it down. Don't worry about the answers, for purposes of this assignment.

When this interview is over, prepare a report in which you consider each of your questions, writing it out clearly and commenting on it as follows. Decide whether each question places the person in the role of respondent or the role of informant. Some questions will be mixtures, undoubtedly, but then you can briefly describe this double aspect of the question.

If you are doing this project in a class, you and a classmate can do it on each other, combining two half-hour interviews, one with your partner asking the questions and one in which you are the interviewer. Then, as you write up your reports, you can discuss the role each question places the answerer in, perhaps finding some disagreements between you on exactly where the line between informant and respondent runs.

5. Census Schedule.   Design a simple census schedule, a brief questionnaire getting the basic facts about people such as a national census might use. You might imitate the form the 19th-century U.S. censuses employed. The census taker would go door to door with huge pages. Each line on the page was for information about an individual person, starting with his or her name. Across the top of the page were various headings for data, such as: Name, Sex, Age, Birthplace, Occupation. You can add other columns for other kinds of information that interest you.

Now the work begins. Read a novel, perhaps an old favorite of yours or a best seller you want to try, and do a census of all the characters in it who have definite names. Fill in the data on your census schedule for each one. Information about a particular character may be spread across several chapters, so you will have to be alert as you read. You are free to estimate data, if the novel gives you only approximate information, but then mark it as "estimated" or "approximate." For example, someone described as "elderly but spry" might get an Age notation of "75 est." But if you have no idea of a character's age or occupation, write "unknown."

Other data you choose to collect should be appropriate for the type of novel. For some murder mysteries, a column of data for the way in which the character died may be necessary. Or you may want to list the various crimes the characters commit in the course of the story. Be inventive in deciding what data to collect, but make sure all data are correct.

6. Competence-of-Informant Interview.   Select a friend for this interview, because you need someone with a lot of tolerance of the questions you are going to ask. Sit down with the person for half an hour to an hour and ask him or her questions about aspects of life that you really don't understand well—perhaps grand questions concerning the philosophy of life in general. Some questions should seek simple facts; others may probe for more general principles that would help you understand something you really care about personally. Obviously, there is some possibility that an interview of this sort could get too personal, so be alert to this danger. But ask questions you really would like answered.

As the interview progresses, write down your questions. When it is over, write a brief report, listing your questions and stating for each one whether you think your friend was really competent to answer it or not. In many cases you will decide that the person was not competent to give a valid answer, or only partly competent. Then you should also note why he or she was not completely competent. I think you may then discover several different ways in which questions may go beyond the territory of definite knowledge that informants have to give us.

7. Foreign-Language Survey.   This project is for students who are currently studying a foreign language or who have studied one previously. Select a short questionnaire, or a section of a longer one, that has already been used in your particular field of interest. For example, someone interested in medicine would look for a medical survey, and someone interested in education would find a school questionnaire. Next, carefully translate it into the foreign language.

Be careful to translate the ideas in each question rather than just the single words. You may find yourself torn between using special idioms in the foreign language and using words that are the closest equivalent to the English. In each case, you will have to decide how to get across the question most clearly, with as little change in meaning from the English as possible.

Next, get someone who knows the language well to translate your version back into English. Perhaps this person could be a classmate, exchanging mutual help with this assignment. But chances are, you could interest a language teacher or advanced language student in this project, because it is so revealing of the differences between languages. Finally, compare the back-translation (of your translation) with the original, and note any substantial differences between these two English versions.

8. Sampling Populations.   Conceive of three very different surveys, each designed to get very different data from very different respondents. Just sketch them, and don't worry about actually writing any of the items for them. Next, write a brief report for each, explaining exactly what the target population would be and how you could define the population precisely in a real research project.

For example, suppose you have decided one of the surveys should be of alumni of the local medical school. What do you mean by "alumni"?

Should your population include people who dropped out of school before graduating? What about people who transferred to another medical school but who did go on to be doctors? What about visiting students who did some work in the school while remaining registered in some other school? And should you include people who subsequently left the medical profession? Will you count doctors who left the country to practice elsewhere? Each question you raise must be answered in terms of the purposes of the study.

▶ ▶ ▶ ▶ ▶ Now we are ready to start working with the set of computer programs that came with this book, beginning with the program on random numbers.

 Start the computer and load the disk-operating system (DOS) as explained in Chapter 1. Then insert your *Survey Research* program disk in Drive A (or

 Drive 1), making sure to close the drive's door or turn its latch. Then press [S] for Start (or Survey, if you prefer), and press [ENTER]. If you are using an IBM-compatible computer made by some other manufacturer, [ENTER] might be called [RETURN]. The disk drive will whir, and you will briefly see the title page for the software and a copyright notice.

The screen will now fill with the program menu. A **menu** is a list of choices, and this one lists the nine programs on your disk, each identified by a letter from A through I. If you press a letter key, [A] through [I], you will get one of these programs. If you press [Q], the computer will "Quit SURVEY RESEARCH." It doesn't matter whether you type a capital letter or a small one.

▶ ▶ ▶ ▶ ▶ ▶ ▶ ▶ ▶ ▶ ▶

[A] RANDOM NUMBERS

The first choice on the program menu is: [A] Random numbers. Press the A key, and you will get the program we shall use for the next three sections of this chapter. A new menu will appear on the screen. It is the *main menu*, the primary set of choices, in the random-numbers program. Here are the options:

Sampling and Random Numbers

```
[1]     Arrange items in random order
[2]     Draw a random sample
[3]     Play Probability Pinball game
[ESC]   QUIT or switch Programs
```

The first three choices are the working parts of the random-numbers program; a section on each will follow. The last choice, which you get by pressing the ESC or ESCAPE key, returns you to the program menu, where you can select another program or QUIT altogether.

Until recently, producing sets of random numbers was very difficult, and most researchers relied on published lists that had been created in special projects (Rand Corporation, 1955). But now any microcomputer can generate strings of digits quite adequate for use in sampling. We will begin by showing how the random-numbers program can put a set of numbers (representing people, questions, or things) in a random order. To get that part of the program, press [1].

[1] Arrange Items in Random Order

Have you ever shuffled a deck of cards? Except for some card sharks, the purpose is to put the cards in random order. The definition of **random** order is that each card in the deck has an equal chance of being first, after the shuffle. And each has an equal chance of being second, third, fourth, and so on.

Suppose you want a random sample consisting of 10 cards taken from a deck of 52. One perfectly valid way of accomplishing this is to shuffle the deck thoroughly and then count off the first 10 cards from the top. The first choice on the main menu of the random-numbers program can shuffle imaginary cards or rearrange any list of as many as 199 items.

When you choose to arrange items in random order, the computer will begin by asking you How many items are in the list you want randomized? Type in a number no bigger than 199 and press [ENTER]. To see how the program works, try 20. That is, type [2][0][ENTER]. Instantly, the numbers 1 through 20 will run down the left of the screen in order, with equal signs after them. Then the numbers 1 through 20 will appear after the equal signs in random order.

Write down the numbers on the screen. I just put the numbers 1 through 20 in random order, and my list starts out: 1= 16, 2= 10, 3= 13, 4= 3. Your list will probably be different. It is as if I had written the numbers 1 through 20 on 20 cards, shuffled them, then written down the order they are in. You will notice the message Press [ENTER] in the lower right corner of the screen, telling you this is what you should do when you are through looking at the numbers. You can also "escape" the list of numbers by pressing [ESC] briefly. The result is the same: The main menu will reappear. Don't hold the [ESC] down, because the computer will think you are pressing it several times and it will send you to the program menu. This is no disaster, because you can easily press [A] to get back to the random-numbers program. But it's best to give [ESC] one quick press when you use it, so the computer won't misinterpret you.

Then ask the computer to put 20 numbers in random order again. You will get a different order the second time, and yet another order on a third try. One way of defining a random order is to note that you can't predict what order the computer will place the numbers in.

Now ask the computer to put the numbers 1 through 199 in a random order. This is the biggest list the program can handle, because it will fill the screen. The numbers 1 through 199 will appear in numerical order, followed by equal signs. Shortly, the 199 numbers will appear in random order after the equal signs.

Now, what use could the numbers 1 through 199 arranged in random order be? Suppose you have been asked to evaluate the athletic program at a school that has 199 students. For part of your study, you want to survey the students, asking them what improvements they would like to see in the athletic program. But the students may be too young for a written questionnaire, and you believe you need in-depth interviews so that you can get the kids to really express themselves and you can probe each of their answers. You estimate that each interview will take an hour, and you can't devote more than one week's work, 40 hours, to this part of the project.

Clearly, you should interview a random sample of the kids, 40 out of the 199 in the school. Our random-numbers program will help you. Get a list of all 199 kids. Write the numbers 1 through 199 in front of their names. Then run the program, asking the computer to put the numbers 1 through

199 in random order. The final step is to mark the names whose numbers are the first 40 listed by the computer.

For a different project you might need a random sample of 25 taken from a population of 150. Tell the computer to put the numbers 1 through 150 in random order, and take the first 25. It is easy enough to see how to work with other numbers, so long as the total is less than 200. The next part of the program and the next section of this book will explain how to work with populations bigger than 199.

There is another use to which you can put a randomized list of numbers. Sometimes you may want to randomize the order of items in a questionnaire. Let me give you a couple of examples from my own research.

In 1978 I took a carload of questionnaires to the World Science Fiction Convention in Phoenix, Arizona. The main part of the survey asked the fans who attended this annual gathering how much they liked each of 140 science-fiction authors. Eight pages in the middle of the questionnaire listed all the authors and gave the respondents a scale of numbers, asking them to circle one number for each author, expressing how much they liked that one. This was a big job, but the science-fiction fans seemed interested, and 595 of them dutifully filled out my questionnaire.

I suspect their enthusiasm slowly faded as they worked their way through the long list. This fatigue could ruin the results, because it might make the respondents rate the last author much lower than the first one. With this problem in mind, I had printed up five different editions of the survey, with the authors' names in five different random orders.

The first step was to put the numbers 1 through 140 in random order, and to do this 5 times. I did not have a computer program at my disposal, and so actual card shuffling was required. For part of the randomizing I employed my young son to run an electric pop-up bingo game that stirred a set of numbered balls and selected one at random every time he pressed the button!

Typing out 5 different versions of the survey was time consuming, and I had to write a special computer program to put the data from all 5 editions into the same order before I could analyze them. But good results do require effort. More recently, I did the same thing with a questionnaire I administered to 894 Harvard students, which focused on 125 somewhat different justifications for the space program. They too had to be put in 5 different random orders. I wrote this random-numbers program to do the job for me; it was much quicker and more thorough than shuffling cards would have been.

If you are really serious, at a professional level, in randomizing the order of items in a survey, you can far surpass my accomplishments in this area. A talented computer programmer can write a set of programs that produces a thousand editions of the survey, each with the items in a different random order. These could be printed out swiftly on a modern laser printer. Each one would need an ID number on it to identify which of the random orders it was based on. The program would save the thousand randomized lists of item numbers on a disk. When the questionnaires came back from the respondents and the data were typed into the computer, the program would automatically put responses to the items in a set order, so that analysis could proceed. But this is a big project, beyond the scope of the software I have written for *Survey Research*.

You shouldn't get carried away with the idea of randomizing the order of items in a survey. Much of the time, it isn't necessary. Indeed, there is often some logical order the questions should follow. Or you might use sets of items from other researchers' questionnaires that must be kept in their original order to give comparable results. But awareness of the possibility of randomizing items can help you think deeply about the issue of item ordering, and occasionally you may want to use this program in designing a questionnaire.

[2] Draw a Random Sample

The second option in the main menu of the random-numbers program, "Draw a random sample," is designed for serious sampling. To get it, press [2].

This option is designed for situations where the population is from 200 to 9999 in size. The sample can be as small as 1 or as large as half the population. That means that with a population of 200 you can have a sample as large as 100. With a population of 9999, the sample can be as large as 4999. If you want to sample a population smaller than 200, use the first option in the main menu, "Arrange items in random order," as explained in the preceding section.

As soon as you have chosen to draw a random sample from a large population, the computer will ask How large is the population? At the bottom it will tell you Type a number (200-9999) and press [ENTER].

Suppose we want to do a survey in a town of 5000 people, giving questionnaires to a random sample of 1000. We would get the town list, perhaps from City Hall, and write the numbers 1 through 5000 in front of the people's names. Then we would start up the random-numbers program and prepare to draw a random sample from a population of 5000: Type in 5000 for the population, and press [ENTER]. Do *not* type a comma, like this: 5,000.

The next step is to tell the computer how large the sample should be. It will ask How large a sample do you want? And at the bottom of the screen it will say Type a number (1-2500) and press [ENTER]. Notice that it sets a limit of 2500, half the population of 5000. We want 1000, so type 1000 and press [ENTER].

A hundred sets of numbers will flash onto the screen, and at the top will be the message Cases 1 through 100 in a sample of 1000 from a population of 5000. As with the first part of the random-numbers program, where we put a set of numbers in random order, you see a sequence of numbers (1 through 100) followed by an equal sign. After the equal sign is a number taken at random from the population you selected.

I have just done this, and the first four I happened to get were: 1=3321, 2=4696, 3=2555, 4=3966. To start drawing our sample from the town of 5000, we would look up persons numbered 3321, 4696, 2555, and 3966. Then we would mark each of these, perhaps with a simple check mark, to show that they have been selected to be in our random sample. Later, we would mail questionnaires out to these people, and only to these people.

When you have marked the first 100 people whose numbers appear on the screen, you can press [ENTER] to get the next 100 in the sample. When the whole sample has been listed, pressing [ENTER] will return you to the main menu. If you change your mind in midstream and decide not to see the whole sample, just press [ESC] to escape immediately back to the main menu, any time Press [ENTER] appears in the corner.

This part of the program can be used to take a random sample of telephone numbers, at least in the United States or where a similar system of numbers is used. Select the telephone exchange you want, the three numbers before the hyphen. Perhaps you decide this on the basis of the part of town you want to survey. Or you could select one at random from those in your area. Let's say you choose 637. All the numbers in the particular sample will begin with this prefix.

Now set the population at 9999 and indicate how big a sample you want. (I suggest you start with a sample much bigger than you actually need, because many of the numbers will not be working ones.) You will get a long list of four-digit numbers. To get phone numbers, stick the exchange number in front. When the number in the sample is less than four digits, such as 41, add zeros to complete it: 637-0041.

Start telephoning numbers from the beginning of your list, and stop when you have the right number of respondents. As explained in Chapter 2, this may not be a completely random sample of the individual people who are living within the boundaries of the exchange, but it will be a random sample of the phone numbers.

Occasionally, you might want a sample larger than half the population, say 200 students from a school that has 250. The way to get one, with this program, is to draw a sample of the people who will be left out of the study, rather than of those who will be included. In this example, draw a sample of 50 from the 250 at the school. Cross their names off the list, and do your survey on the 200 who remain.

[3] Play Probability Pinball Game

This game is not a terrific lot of fun, and it may not help you when you are designing an actual survey project, but it is a great demonstration of how simple probabilities can produce complex results. Furthermore, you can use this game to discover the intimate connection between random sampling and another important element of survey research: *statistical significance.* Later chapters, especially Chapter 6, will provide their own introductions to significance, but the pinball game gives a vivid picture of the key idea that fits well here, in the context of random sampling.

Get to the main menu of the random-numbers program and press [3] to play the probability pinball game. A set of 78 arrowheads will show up, all pointing to the left. In the lower left corner are two messages: [S]peed: Fast and Press [ENTER] to begin. Before I explain what the game means, let's see how to play it.

First, press [S] a few times, watching [S]peed:Fast to see what happens. It switches to [S]peed:Medium and [S]peed:Slow before returning to [S]peed:Fast. This is a command that tells the computer how fast to hurl the balls into the set of 78 arrowheads, the action part of the game. When you are actually playing, [S]peed:Fast is best. But to see how the ball flies, you should set it at [S]peed:Slow to start with. Press the [S] key enough times to set the speed command at Slow.

Now press [ENTER]. A starry ball will roll down from the top left corner of the screen, then shoot across at the first of the arrowheads. When it gets to the arrowhead, it will bounce either up or down, entirely at random. There are two arrowheads in the second column, and the ball will knock into one or the other of them. At this point, it will again bounce either up or down, entirely at random. Watch it go.

Now watch the next few balls as they shoot through the thicket of arrows. If you count, you will find that each ball experiences 12 bounces. Each time (I swear) it has a 50–50 chance of bouncing up or down. In essence, for each bounce the computer draws a random sample of 1 number from a population of 2. Imagine, if you will, that the computer has 2 numbers written on cards that it keeps in its hat. For each bounce, it pulls out a card. If it says 1, the computer makes the ball bounce up. But if the card says 2, it bounces down. After each bounce, the computer puts the card back into the hat, shuffles the 2 cards, and waits to draw another random sample of 1 card from a population of 2 cards.

It is hard to think of a simpler sampling procedure, but as you can see, the result is rather complex. Of course, the computer does the procedure 12 times for each ball. And 2 balls are very likely to experience different series of bounces. They may wind up at different levels in the 13 invisible horizontal rows on the right side of the screen. As the balls collect in the rows, can you guess which rows are likely to grow quickest?

If you guessed the rows near the middle, you are right. Of course, the game is run by chance, so any of the rows of balls could be the longest one. But the probabilities favor the middle rows. Why is that?

How could a ball get to the very top, and wind up over at the right edge, higher than any of the arrows? It would have to bounce up each time it hit an arrow. If it bounced down even once, it could not make it all the way to the top. Thus only one route takes a ball to the top. Similarly, only one route would take a ball all the way to the bottom. It would have to bounce down each time it hit an arrow.

In contrast, many, many different routes lead to one of the middle rows. Thus a ball has several chances to get to a middle row, each one reached by a different route. Watch the balls running through the set of arrows, each bouncing 12 times, and see how they collect near the middle of the screen. Chances are, no balls at all will make it to the very top or very bottom in a particular run of the game.

We will think more about these matters shortly. But first, let's learn the rest of the commands in the game. I assume you have run several balls through, and now there are several lined up in different rows. Stop the pinball machine by pressing [ENTER] once.

The last ball comes to rest, and a new set of messages appears in the lower left corner of the screen: [D]isplay:Balls, [R]estart, and Press [ENTER] to quit. If you were to press [R], the game would start over. Pressing [ENTER] would take you back to the main menu. But we don't want to restart or quit just yet. We should use the Display command to get some interesting information about the game and the balls that have run through it. So press [D] once.

The command will change to [D]isplay:Totals and the balls will vanish from the right side of the screen, to be replaced by numbers. Each row of balls becomes a number, telling you how many balls had been in that row. To the left of these numbers you will see the total number of balls that had run through, labeled Total.

Press [D] a second time, and you get [D]isplay:%Totals. The % means the numbers will be replaced with the respective percentages. If you had run 20 balls and 5 of them had gone into one row, that row would now say 25%. The grand total is always 100%. Percentages are useful when you want to compare one run with another that involved a different number of balls.

Press [D] a third time, and the command becomes [D]isplay: Routes. These routes are the different ways a ball might pass through the maze of arrows. The total number of different routes a ball might take happens to be 4096. Remember that only 1 of these will take a ball to the very top. Over at the right, in the column of numbers, the first number is 1, indicating that there is just this 1 route to the top. The bottom number also is 1. Table 3.1 shows the full set of numbers.

The second number in the list of routes is 12. This means that 12 different routes can take a ball to the second row. Figuring out how these 12 routes go is easy enough. To get to the very top, a ball must always bounce up. But if it bounces up 11 times and down 1 time, it will wind up in the second row, 1 step down from the top. Where this 1 downward bounce occurs doesn't matter, so long as the other 11 bounces are upward. And

▶ ▶ ▶ ▶ ▶ ▶ ▶ ▶ ▶ ▶ ▶

TABLE 3.1 ROUTES IN THE PROBABILITY PINBALL GAME

Bounces Up	Routes	Percent
12(top row)	1	0.02
11	12	0.29
10	66	1.61
9	220	5.37
8	495	12.08
7	792	19.34
6(middle row)	924	22.56
5	792	19.34
4	495	12.08
3	220	5.37
2	66	1.61
1	12	0.29
0(bottom row)	1	0.02
Total	4096	100.00

▶

there are 12 arrowheads where a downward bounce could happen, in a route with 11 upward bounces. Thus there are 12 different routes, depending on where the 1 downward bounce occurs.

To be completely clear, let's trace 2 of the 12 routes. First, imagine that a ball bounces up 11 times and gets to the last, highest arrowhead, at the right. When it hits that one, it bounces down to its place in the second row. Second, imagine a ball that bounces down at the very first arrowhead, and then bounces up the next 11 times to get to the same destination as the first ball. Ten other routes also involve 1 bounce down and 11 up, for a total of 12 routes to the destination.

If you press [D] one more time, you will get a set of percentages for the routes, the same ones shown in Table 3.1. (More presses of [D] after that will give you the other statistics over again, in case you want to look back at them.) The largest number of routes, 924, go to the middle row. And 924 is about 22.56% of 4096, the total number of routes to all 13 destination rows. The 1 route that goes to the top row is about 0.02% of 4096.

Another way to state this is to say 1 out of every 4096 balls will reach the top. Of course, that is just a prediction about what will happen on average, and it does not mean that every 4096th ball will zoom to the top. But if we run many thousands of balls, the average will be 1 out of 4096. This is the same as saying that on average, 0.02% of the balls will reach the top, or that the chance of a given ball reaching the top is 0.02%, or 0.0002 if you leave the % out.

But a ball has 924 different routes to the middle row. Thus it has 924 chances in 4096 of reaching that destination, or a 22.56% chance of doing so. And the probabilities of reaching any of the other rows are given in Table 3.1 or on your computer screen if you press [D] the right number of times.

Some of you who have taken statistics courses will recognize something familiar about the distribution of probabilities. In fact, you may have seen it as soon as a dozen balls had run through the game. The distribution of balls is close to what statisticians call the normal distribution or **normal curve.** To be precise, the distribution is called the **binomial distribution,** and as the number of rows increases, the binomial distribution comes closer and closer to the normal curve (Christensen and Stoup, 1986:215). And you may think of several important uses to which the normal distribution was put in your statistics course.

This textbook on survey research is not the place for a lengthy discussion of the normal distribution, but a simple survey example will show the connection between sampling and statistical significance. Those of you who already know about statistical significance may find the following very easy to understand. Those who have not yet encountered statistical significance can learn something, and subsequent sections of this book will give you further insights and examples to complete an introduction we can only begin here.

Once upon a time, I invented a little astronomy quiz for one of my questionnaires. I wanted to see whether students who knew a lot about astronomy had similar opinions about astrology and other popular myths concerning the heavens, so I needed a simple test of astronomical knowledge. I wrote a set of eight true–false questions like these: "Pluto is the largest planet in the solar system." "Venus is the planet closest to the sun." "An eclipse of the sun is actually caused by the shadow of the moon." "The pull of gravity on the surface of Mars is less than the pull of gravity on the surface of the Earth." The first two of these statements are false, and the second two are true. Well, sad to say, my astronomy quiz bombed. The average score was about half right, and it appeared that the overwhelming majority of the students responding hadn't the faintest idea what the correct answers were and just checked the true or false boxes at random.

Let's imagine I didn't give up on this project (as in fact I did) and that I created a new and improved astronomy quiz, consisting of 12 true–false items. And now I give this test to you. You read each of the 12 items and check either the true or the false box after it. We add up your score and find that you got 9 right. Does this prove you know something about astronomy?

We can use Table 3.1 to get an insight into the depth of your astronomy knowledge, as revealed in this score of 9 right out of 12 true–false questions, because the table tells us how likely each possible score on the test is purely as a result of random guessing. If you decided which box to check by flipping a coin, you would have a 50–50 chance of checking the right answer for a given question. This is exactly the same thing the ball experiences when it bangs into an arrowhead. It has a 50–50 chance of going either way. Indeed, you could have let a ball answer my quiz. Run it through slowly and note whether it bounces up or down at each of the 12 columns of arrows. If it bounces up, check the true box for the question. If it bounces down, check the false box.

But let's let an upward bounce represent getting the question right, and a downward bounce getting it wrong. Entirely by chance, you have a 5.37% chance of getting 9 right, because 220 out of the 4096 routes involve 9 bounces up and 3 down. Another way of looking at it is to figure out what the chances are of getting a score this good or better. You do that by adding together the chances of getting 9, 10, 11, and 12 right. The total number of routes to these scores of 9 or better is: 220 + 66 + 12 + 1 = 299, and 299 is 7.30% of 4096. Thus we would expect 7.30% of students to do as well as you (or better) on this test entirely by chance.

Frankly, that is not very convincing evidence that you know any astronomy. You are part of a minority who would score well on the test, but about 1 out of every 15 people would do as well as you even if none of them knew anything about astronomy. Generally, no social scientist would be impressed by a finding that could come about purely by accident 1 out of every 15 times.

What we have just calculated is the **statistical significance** of your score. You have a 7.30% chance of having gotten a score this good (or better) by pure chance, without possessing a glimmer of astronomical knowledge. If the figure were 5%, representing 1 chance in 20, social scientists might begin to take notice. We often speak of a survey finding as "achieving the 0.05 level of statistical significance." This means we got 5% or less when we figured the probability that the results could have come about by pure accident.

More commonly, we like to see the 0.01 level of significance, representing only a 1% chance of pure luck. If you analyze the top of Table 3.1, you can see that a score of 11 right does better than the 0.01 level. There are 12 routes to a score of 11 right, and 1 route to 12 right, so the probability of getting a score as good as 11 by pure chance is 0.32%. I got that figure by adding the routes together (12 + 1 = 13), dividing the result by the total number of routes (13/4096 = 0.0032), and multiplying by 100 to get percent (0.0032 × 100 = 0.32%). That is less than 1%, indicating a pretty good level of statistical significance, and a low probability that a score of 11 was a pure accident.

A score of 12 certainly looks great, but there is always a small chance that any score was an accident. Only 1 time out of every 4096 can you get a perfect 12 score on a 12-item true–false test by pure accident. That is a mere 0.02%, or about 2 chances in every 10,000 students (a 0.0002 chance). That surpasses the 0.001 level of statistical significance, a particularly impressive achievement among survey researchers.

To do better than that, you would have to take a test with more than 12 items. It is a general rule in statistics that the more things you have measured (whether items on a test or respondents filling out a questionnaire), the more solid your results are. And it is not uncommon to achieve even the 0.0001 level of statistical significance with results from a survey, 1 chance in 10,000 that the results were an accident.

Those of you who have already taken a statistics course might have several related issues to think about. You could use the probability pinball game to contemplate the differences between one-tailed and two-tailed tests of significance. And you might think about the many aspects of statistical reasoning that draw on concepts like those behind the game.

Whether you have taken "stat" or not, perhaps you can see a connection between the probability game and sampling. Whenever you run the game and let several balls run through, you get an approximate random sample of routes through the rows of arrows (though a route could conceivably be represented twice). Thus the percentage distribution of the balls' destinations will be a reflection of the full percentage distribution of all 4096 routes. The concept of "chance" or "probability" enters into both sampling and evaluations of statistical significance, and often you may gain insights by contemplating one of these issues in the light of the other.

▶ ▶ ▶ ▶ ▶ ▶ ▶ ▶ ▶ ▶ ▶

[B] TOWN SURVEY SIMULATION

It is time to get some practice working with various methods of sampling a population. Go to the program menu and press [B] to get the town survey simulation, the second of our nine programs. A **simulation** is a computer program that lets us pretend to study something out in the real world but actually keeps us within the safe confines of a gamelike fantasy. Good simulations should be realistic, and I have carefully designed this one to let us explore important issues of real social science.

A thousand M's, m's, W's, and w's will fill the left side of the screen. These letters represent the voters of the town of Bethel, Connecticut, all 1000 of them. Men voters are represented by the letter M or m and women voters by the letter W or w. The capital letters represent older people, the small letters younger people. To make these divisions perfectly clear, the bottom and right side of the square are marked with labels. The rows containing older men and women are labeled Old. The columns containing women of both ages are labeled Women. Similar labels identify Men and Young.

The numbers in each group are listed in the upper right corner; starting out there are 500 of each sex and 500 of each age group. Above this list is the command, Decide Population. This means you are not stuck with the population divisions we begin with. You can make the computer change the proportions of each sex and age.

To increase the number of old people, press [O] (the letter O, not zero). Similarly, to increase the number of young people, press [Y]. You can decide to add more men by pressing [M], or women by pressing [W].

When you press a key, the selected group will grow by one row or column of voters and the numbers in the list will change accordingly, so you can see how many are in each group at the moment. There is a limit to how far you can go, however. The computer will beep if you try to make it reduce a sex or age group below three rows or columns in size.

I suggest you play with the [O], [Y], [M], and [W] commands for a while, then set the commands as follows: 800 old people, 200 young people, 700 women, and 300 men. This age and sex distribution is very unlikely for a town, although a retirement community could conceivably have one like it, but it will help us see what some of the program's options do. When the population distribution is set exactly like this, press [ENTER].

Now we have to think of one question, for the world's shortest questionnaire. Let's try this one: "Should skateboards be banned from the town of Bethel?" Obviously, this is not an earth-shaking issue, but some of the voters may have been run over by these demon vehicles and may be strongly in favor of a town ordinance to ban them.

The computer is now asking us to decide the opinions of the age and sex groups in Bethel. As when we decided the population distribution, we press [O], [Y], [M], and [W] to set the simulation the way we want it. Try pressing [O] and notice what happens now. The message near the top right changes from [O]ld:Neutral to [O]ld:Pro. This means that old people have changed from being neutral on average toward the skateboard ban to being in favor of it. It makes sense for old people to favor a ban, because few of them ride boards yet many fear being victims of them.

Now press [Y] twice, watching what happens to the [Y]oung: Neutral message. It changes first to [Y]oung:Pro, then to [Y]oung:Con. Leave the young command at Con, meaning that young people generally oppose a ban on skateboards. Make sense?

At the risk of arousing charges of sexism, I suggest we thicken the Bethel political plot further by pressing [M] and [W] enough times to make men oppose the ban ([M]en:Con) and women favor it ([W]omen:Pro). At least in the towns I've inhabited, skateboarding was a predominantly male pursuit. Another time you run this program, if you wish, you can make the women oppose the ban and the men favor it.

When the commands are set as I suggest, press [ENTER] to move on to the next stage. Now the town residents will make up their minds about the skateboard issue. You will see the M's, m's, W's, and w's on the screen replaced by Y's and n's. Y stands for "Yes, ban the boards!" And n means "No, don't ban them." I used capital Y's and small n's so you could tell them apart as easily as possible, and the size of a letter no longer says anything about the age of the person.

In this simulation, chance plays a big role in how each voter decides to vote. But the commands about pro and con tendencies are also important. When we told the computer that older people should *tend* to be in favor of the skateboard ban, we made it significantly more likely that an old person would vote yes. And when we decided young people should *tend* to be against the ban, we made young people more likely to vote no.

Our commands also made men more likely to vote against the ban, and women for it. But you may have noticed that the town can be considered to be divided into four separate subgroups: old men, old women, young men, and young women. Consider what our pro and con decisions do for each of these subgroups. Young men have two reasons for opposing the ban: They are young, and they are men. Old women have two reasons to support the ban: They are old, and they are women. Look at the screen and see whether there are many Y's among the old women and a high proportion of n's among young men. The young men are rare enough that you can easily count their votes by eye. I have just run the program to this point, and only 10 of the 60 young men favor the ban, as indicated by the 10 Y's I see for this group. You may have a different number of skateboard-ban supporters among your 60 young men, because chance gives the simulation somewhat different results each time we run it.

Two of the four groups have mixed reasons for deciding which way to vote. Consider young women. They are young, which gives them a tendency to vote against the ban. But they are women, which gives them a tendency to vote for it. These two tendencies may cancel out, leaving them in the middle on the issue. Similarly, old men should be ambivalent about the skateboard ban.

At the right of the screen is a new set of commands, which can be achieved by pressing a number key, [1] through [6]. These will let you select six different kinds of sample of respondents for our short questionnaire. They are:

```
[1] Convenience
[2] Random
[3] Proportional
[4] Quota:Age
[5] Quota:Sex
[6] Quota:Age+Sex
```

We will go through them one at a time, beginning with the one that generally gives the worst results.

[1] A Convenience Sample

Hardly a day goes by when I don't see a "person-in-the-street interview" on television news. The network I usually watch is addicted to these journalistic shortcuts. If a government scandal breaks, a camera and microphone will poke into the face of someone caught walking by the TV studio, with the offscreen words, "And what do you think about the new revelations concerning Senator Bigbank's expense accounts?" If war is threatened in Latin America, a citizen trapped by the TV crew at a nearby shopping center will have to render an opinion on "the president's policy toward Latin America."

There is something to be said for collecting a range of opinions on the issues of the day, even if they are selected because of their human interest rather than representativeness. But enlisting certain citizens in a street poll simply because they are easily available is far from scientific and can give false impressions about the opinions of the citizenry.

A collection of respondents selected simply because they are readily available for polling is a **convenience sample.** They serve the convenience of the researcher rather than the scientific accuracy of the results. Perhaps the most common convenience sample in the social sciences is college undergraduates, often students in the particular classes the researcher happens to be teaching at the time.

Now, the disadvantages of convenience samples will become abundantly clear, but there are some things to be said for them. They are usually far cheaper to poll than a random sample of the population would be, which means that studies unable to find substantial funding must be done with them, particularly pilot studies and research in new areas where the methods and theories are not fully worked out. There is always time to replicate the research on a true random sample later on.

Psychologists are on pretty firm ground when they recruit convenience samples as subjects for experiments, because the experimental method gives the researcher nearly complete control over key variables. And a questionnaire can be designed to reduce inaccuracies that result from a convenience sample by including a number of items taken from other polls already administered to random samples, thus permitting examination of the ways the convenience sample differs from a random sample.

Let's try a convenience sample of the town of Bethel and see how it comes out. Press [1] to get a convenience sample; 100 of the Y's and n's will be highlighted in a block, 10 by 10 in size. The place the block appears is selected entirely at random by the computer, but the respondents will be neighbors of each other. As I imagine it, a month before the skateboard referendum you drove into the residential area of town and parked as soon as you could find a space. Then you went door to door, in the vicinity of your car, asking the first 100 people you could find whether they were going to vote for the skateboard ban or not.

Now it's time for the results. Press [ENTER]. A table will fill the screen, labeled Comparison of Sample with Population-Convenience Sample. Exactly what you get will be the result of chance; Table 3.2 shows what I just got on my screen. Let's look at my results first—you can use the principles illustrated by them to help understand your own results.

The first column of figures in Table 3.2 tells us how many voters are in each age and sex group, repeating information we saw before, when we were setting the population distribution. But now we also see the sizes of

▶ ▶ ▶ ▶ ▶ ▶ ▶ ▶ ▶ ▶ ▶

TABLE 3.2 COMPARISON OF SAMPLE WITH POPULATION— CONVENIENCE SAMPLE

Group	Number of People		Percent Who Agree	
	Town	Sample	Town	Sample
Old	800	90	73.5%	37.8%
Young	200	10	25.0%	20.0%
Men	300	100	29.3%	36.0%
Women	700	0	78.6%	?
Old men	240	90	32.5%	37.8%
Old women	560	0	91.1%	?
Young men	60	10	16.7%	20.0%
Young women	140	0	28.6%	?
Total	1000	100	63.8%	36.0%

▶

the 4 groups that make up the total. The largest subgroup consists of 560 old women, an absolute majority of the electorate, and the smallest group is the 60 young men.

The second column gives the corresponding numbers in my sample. I hope your convenience sample turned out better than mine! Mine had no women at all, even though women constitute 70% of Bethel's voters. Instead, it had 100 men, 90 of them old. The numbers in the second column should be exactly one-tenth the numbers in the first column if the sample is perfectly representative.

The third column shows the actual vote totals for each group. Look down the list and think about each percentage in terms of the Pro and Con commands we gave the computer. The difference between old women and young men is huge! Whereas 91.1% of the old women voted for the ban, only 16.7% of the young men did so. Notice the figures for the 4 subgroups. A majority in each of the 3 subgroups besides old women voted against it, but it passed for the total 1000 voters by achieving support of 63.8%! Of course, this happened because old women are the majority.

Now look at the fourth column in Table 3.2, the sorry results of my poll using a convenience sample. If the Bethel newspaper published my results, its editor must be gunning for me now. I predicted that only 36% would vote for the skateboard ban. Notice the question marks for the subgroups of women, reflecting the fact that I had no female respondents on whom to base a prediction about the women's vote. Let's hope that Mullaney's store, the toy center of Bethel for half a century, didn't stock up on skateboards in anticipation of the ban's defeat.

If you press [ENTER] again, you will see a small table showing the correlations (gamma or Yule's Q, for those of you who know about statistics) linking agreement with the ban to old age and to male sex, both among the town population of 1000 and among the 100 respondents to the poll. Those of you not yet familiar with correlations should not panic or let yourselves be mystified. We will introduce correlations step by step later on, especially in Chapter 6. But I could not resist calculating the correlations for those of you who might like to look at them.

A final press of [ENTER], and the simulation starts over from the beginning, with your population groups the way you set them, and you're ready to try the next kind of sample. If you don't want to repeat the program, press [ESC] to get the program menu, where you can select something different, or press [Q] to quit.

To be sure, I have written the simulation so that the convenience samples usually come out very far from the mark. As I have noted, serious researchers often have to find a way of balancing convenience (which may mean affordability rather than mere ease) with representativeness. Let's compare these results (and yours) with a true random sample of Bethel's electorate.

[2] Simple Random Sample

Start the town survey simulation again. If you pressed [ENTER] after finishing the preceding task, the population groups will start out the same way you last set them. You can change them, if you wish. But to keep the same populations, just press [ENTER] when asked to decide population. Similarly, when the computer asks you to decide the pro and con opinions of the groups, you can either change them or stick with the decisions you made earlier by simply pressing [ENTER]. But when it comes time to draw the sample for our survey, press [2] to get a **simple random sample.** This means that each voter will have an exactly equal chance of being selected for the sample, and the sampling will be done with random numbers.

Watch the 1000 voters carefully as the computer does its work. Individuals scattered at random all over the square will quickly acquire bright boxes around their Y's and n's, indicating they have been polled. It is as if you had taken an official list of Bethel's 1000 voters, numbered them, drawn 100 of them at random, and then driven around town like mad to find each and every one of those 100. When you are finished looking at the random pattern of bright boxes, press [ENTER] to get the results.

Now you will see the table, this time labeled Comparison of Sample with Population-Random Sample. The results I just got, when I did this a moment ago, are shown in Table 3.3. Yours will be somewhat different. In fact, this particular run of the simulation has given us a surprisingly good poll that reflects the whole population rather closely. Purely by chance, random polls will vary in their accuracy, and the smaller the sample the greater the variation of quality in polls. With a sample of only 100, we would expect many polls to be rather far from the mark.

But the random sample will hardly ever give you results as bad as

▶ ▶ ▶ ▶ ▶ ▶ ▶ ▶ ▶ ▶ ▶

TABLE 3.3   COMPARISON OF SAMPLE WITH POPULATION—
SIMPLE RANDOM SAMPLE

Group	Number of People		Percent Who Agree	
	Town	Sample	Town	Sample
Old	800	79	70.5%	70.9%
Young	200	21	18.5%	23.8%
Men	300	29	23.7%	27.6%
Women	700	71	75.7%	74.6%
Old men	240	23	27.1%	30.4%
Old women	560	56	89.1%	87.5%
Young men	60	6	10.0%	16.7%
Young women	140	15	22.1%	26.7%
Total	1000	100	60.1%	61.0%

those from a convenience sample. Nowhere near! In vast contrast to the convenience sample poll, this time we got an almost perfect overall estimate of the total vote. Look across the bottom line of the table and you will see that 60.1% of the 1000 citizens actually voted to ban skateboards, and a very close 61% of the sample felt the same way.

I have tried several simple random samples, running the program with exactly the same commands over and over, and I have not yet gotten a random sample poll that was so far off it didn't predict that the ban would pass. Usually the difference between the random poll and the vote was less than 5 percentage points.

Notice that our sample included almost exactly the right proportions of the age and sex groups. Whereas 80% of the voters are old, 79% of the sample are. The 71% of the sample who are women nearly matches the 70% in the population. The sample is exactly right in the numbers of old women and young men that should be in it, and off by only one each for the old men and young women. An exceptionally good sample! You should run a random sample and see how close you get.

Our simulation lets us compare our samples with the population to illustrate important methodological principles. But with real polls, we often have no way of knowing how many people in the population fall into each group, and until the election we cannot tell how they are going to vote. We will often have little information beyond the data provided by our samples to help us guess how well the sampling or the data collection went. So it is important to learn the right principles, and stick with them.

The smaller subgroups show the greatest disagreement in the percentages voting pro or con. This is a general tendency in research based on sampling, although it may not happen every time. Here, whereas 22.1% of the young women voters supported the ban, 26.7% of the sample from this group did, a difference of 4.6 percentage points. And the difference is greater still, 6.7 percentage points, for the young men. I should emphasize that this difference results from the small samples drawn from these subgroups, not from the small sizes of the subgroups themselves.

If you have to drive door to door to find your respondents, for example, a simple random sample can be costly. Therefore, researchers have looked for ways to reduce the cost without excessively reducing the accuracy. A standard technique that often accomplishes this, and under some circumstances may even be counted on to give more accurate results than a simple random sample, is described next.

[3] Proportional Sample

A **proportional sample** is one designed to include the same proportions of certain groups as are found in the population being polled. In our example, there are 800 old people in Bethel, so we would want exactly 80 old people in a proportional sample of 100. And there are 140 young women, so exactly 14 of them should find their way into our sample. Unlike with the simple random sample, you have to know a good deal about the population's characteristics before you can draw a proportional sample.

The best kind of proportional sample, often better even than a simple random sample, is the **proportional random sample.** You would proceed exactly as with the simple random sample, except that when you had polled enough of some subgroup you would stop looking for members of that subgroup, and you would keep on until you had polled enough of each group.

For example, suppose you had polled all 30 of the men and all 56 old women your sample demanded, but not yet all 14 young women. You knock on the door of the house of the next person identified in your random sample and find that it is an old woman. You cannot use this potential respondent, because you already have enough in her category. If you wanted to be polite, you could administer the survey to her, but you would have to tear it up privately later. Because you have polled all the men you need, you would bypass them as well, just polling young women until this category, too, was full. You have to prepare a somewhat larger random sample than you need, and the last few respondents can be hard to find.

Here, in our program, a proportional sample is automatically done in terms of both sex and age, to get you as close as possible to the right proportions of each subgroup in your sample. In real research, you have to decide which variables to use. Two questions must be considered. First, can you get good information on a particular variable in the population? You might like to sample in terms of people's religious affiliations, but if you don't know how many belong to each denomination in town, you just can't do it. Second, which variables do you have good reason to believe will make a difference? If religious denomination is unlikely to influence attitudes toward skateboards, it is unnecessary to use it.

But the proportional sample in our program is not a random one. Instead, it resembles the convenience sample. As I imagine it, you pick a place in town by accident and begin walking down the street, polling everybody you meet until you have exactly the right number in each subgroup. Once you have enough of a particular subgroup, you start skipping people of this kind. And you move on until you have all the respondents of each type that you need. I chose this kind of proportional sample for the program because it gives a graphic picture of the way the method requires you to hunt for respondents of particular kinds.

Try running the program, with the same settings of the age and sex group commands as before, then draw a proportional sample, and you will see what I mean. Our proportional samples of Bethel will give very good results, even though they are not random, but that is only because we can sample in terms of the variables that matter: age and sex. If some third variable, such as athletic interests, predicted attitudes toward a skateboard ban but could not be sampled for, our results might be much further off. This would especially be the case if athletic interests varied in some systematic way from one part of town to another. Thus proportional samples are not magic, and it is best to stick to the random proportional variety if at all possible.

Proportional sampling is used in many national polls, for the reason that complete lists of residents are not generally available from which to draw a simple random sample. Many areas have no lists of residents at all, and the lists in other areas are old and incomplete. A common tactic is to send interviewers out to randomly chosen locations to find respondents who fit the proportion plan.

In sampling a city, for example, the researchers would first look at the latest census statistics to estimate how many people of various types are in each district of the city. Then they figure how many people with each set of characteristics they need from each district to represent the city as a whole. Next, interviewers are sent into each district, to randomly chosen addresses. Then they are supposed to travel through the neighborhood, in a predetermined route, until they find enough respondents of each specified type. As you can imagine, this can be a big job that requires careful training and high motivation to carry out well.

If the target numbers are proportional to the sizes of the groups in the population itself, then we have a proportional sample. But in some cases it is better to set target numbers of respondents from the groups that are not proportional to their size in the population.

[4] Quota Sample

A quota sample is like a proportional sample, because both involve getting predetermined numbers of respondents from groups in the population. But in a **quota sample,** the researchers seek disproportionate numbers of respondents from certain groups. The purpose is to make sure that enough respondents are drawn from groups of interest to the researcher, so that the characteristics of those groups in the population can be accurately estimated. Earlier we noted that the predicted votes from such minority groups in Bethel as young men can be way off, just because our sample of the group was itself so small. An obvious choice is to increase the number of respondents we draw from the minority group.

A good example is a study of juvenile delinquency done by Travis Hirschi which I shall mention often in this book. Hirschi gave a questionnaire to a representative sample of high school boys in western Contra Costa County, California. The main minority group in the schools was black students, and he wanted to make sure he had data that expressed their attitudes and experiences as accurately as data he would get from the majority whites. So he intentionally oversampled blacks. As the term suggests, **oversampling** means drawing more respondents from a group than its proportion in the population would require. Hirschi included 85% of the black high school boys in his sample and only 30% of the other boys (Hirschi, 1969:35).

Our town survey simulation program has three options for quota sampling: Quota:Age, Quota:Sex, and Quota:Age+Sex. Start the program the same way as for the previous examples and select a Quota:Age sample.

Quota:Age will give you exactly equal numbers of old and young respondents, 50 old and 50 young. Otherwise, they will be selected at random. The program proceeds as for a simple random sample, but it counts how many people in each age group it has gotten. Once it has its quota of 50 for an age group, it stops accepting potential respondents from the group. It continues to locate people at random, but it selects only those in the group for which the quota of 50 has not yet been met.

When the computer has finished selecting the Quota:Age sample, you should look closely at the picture of the 1000 voters. You don't have to count to make sure there are really 50 from each age group. But it should be quite obvious to your eye that a higher proportion of the young voters has been polled, as indicated by the greater density of little boxes around Y's and n's in their part of the picture. When you have exhausted your interest in this, press [ENTER] to get the table of data.

Table 3.4 shows the results I got in a typical run with a Quota:Age sample. A proportional sample would give us 80 old people and 20 young ones, but here we have 50 of each. The purpose is to get a more accurate picture of attitudes among the young, and this time we may not have succeeded too well. In our simple random sample, shown in Table 3.3, the difference between the actual vote of 200 young people and our poll was just 5.3 percentage points. But here, the difference is 7.5 percentage points— the difference between 23.5% and 16%.

Remember that the simple random sample run I report was an especially good one. Furthermore, 50 respondents is a very small quota for a group, and we cannot count on it to give us very accurate results. I have selected a run to tell you about this time that was not particularly good, even though the method was right, so you will not get discouraged with your own samples. The point is to learn the principles involved, and if you really

▶ ▶ ▶ ▶ ▶   ▶ ▶ ▶ ▶ ▶ ▶

TABLE 3.4 COMPARISON OF SAMPLE WITH POPULATION—
QUOTA : AGE SAMPLE

Group	Number of People		Percent Who Agree		Estimated Percents
	Town	Sample	Town	Sample	
Old	800	50	74.0%	78.0%	←
Young	200	50	23.5%	16.0%	←
Men	300	32	28.7%	15.6%	25.0%
Women	700	68	79.0%	61.8%	84.7%
Old men	240	16	32.9%	31.3%	←
Old women	560	34	91.6%	100.0%	←
Young men	60	16	11.7%	0.0%	←
Young women	140	34	28.6%	23.5%	←
Total	1000	100	63.9%	47.0%	66.8%

▶

want to prove that quota sampling is the best way of describing subgroups in the population, you will have to do several quota runs, adding or averaging the results together.

Although quota samples may be good for describing small groups, they will typically do less well with big groups that get undersampled. Therefore, in studies like Hirschi's, enough effort is put into polling the majority groups that they do not suffer from undersampling. Our program does not do this but sticks with a total sample of 100, thus surveying fewer old people to increase the number of young. In a real study you should spend the extra time and money to keep the number of respondents from the big groups high, while investing extra attention in the smaller groups.

Furthermore, quota sampling gives you a set of data that does not automatically represent the general population, although it can easily be made to do so. Look at the total number of respondents who are for the skateboard ban, 47%. This is not only far below the 63.9% in the population, but below 50%, so that it gives a false prediction about how the referendum will come out.

The reason this prediction is so low is that we intentionally oversampled young people, and young people tend to be against the ban. But it is not hard to correct for this, and you will find an extra column in the table of results for quota samples, labeled Estimated Percents. Here is how the computer makes its estimate of the total vote. The computer works with responses from the 4 subgroups. Among the old men in the sample, 31.1% would support the ban. Because there are 240 old men in the population, the computer estimates that 31.1% of them, or 74.64 voters, would also support the ban. Although there is no such thing as 0.64 voters, the computer hangs onto such fractions until it has finished with all 4 subgroups and has an estimate for the total vote.

Because 100% of the old women in the sample supported the ban, the computer is forced to guess that all 560 old women in the population also support the ban. Similarly, because 0% of the young men in the sample support the ban, the computer has to guess that none of the 60 young men in the population will support it either. Finally, the computer sees that 23.5% of the young women in the sample support the ban, so it estimates that 23.5% of the population's 140 young women, or 32.90 voters in the category, will support it.

Having estimated the vote for each subgroup, the computer now combines them. It predicts that the skateboard ban will get the vote of 74.64 old men, 560 old women, 0 young men, and 32.90 young women. The total is 667.54, which represents 66.8% of the 1000 voters. This is the computer's estimate of the vote, and it is not very far from the 63.9% who actually voted for the ban. It is a much better estimate than the 47% of the quota survey.

Despite the many assumptions that went into this estimate, it is much better than a guess. True, to predict that every old woman and not a single young man would vote for the ban is unreasonable. But we are always dealing with approximations in research based on samples, especially when the sample is as small as 100. And the estimating procedure we just went through does a good job of compensating for our oversampling of young people and gives a decent estimate of the population's vote on the basis of a quota sample.

You will notice, while using the quota sample options in our program, that the computer also calculates estimates for the larger age and sex groups, when appropriate. Here, we oversampled young people among the men and among the women, so we have to correct for our age quota in estimating the votes from each sex. When we use Quota:Sex, we will provide estimates by age group. And when you try Quota:Age+Sex, you will get estimates for both age and sex groups.

▶ ▶ ▶ ▶ ▶ ▶ ▶ ▶ ▶ ▶ ▶

[C] NATIONAL POLL SIMULATION

However difficult it may be to poll a good sample of Bethel's 1000 voters, a poll of the entire nation is a project of a vastly greater difficulty. The third program on the *Survey Research* disk simulates such a poll, using the final technique we must consider in this chapter, **multi-stage sampling.**

Though it might be ideal to draw a random sample of the entire population of the United States, then travel to their homes to collect the data, the cost in time and money is prohibitive. An alternative that gives similar results is to draw random samples at 2 stages. For example, the first stage might be to draw a sample of all the counties in the United States. As of 1980, there were 3137 counties and similar geographic divisions in the nation. You could draw a sample of 100 of these. Then, in the second stage, you would sample individuals within each county, perhaps getting 10 respondents per county, for a total of 1000 respondents. Traveling to each of the 100 counties will cost something, but not as much as if you had to visit nearly 1000 different locations to find your respondents.

We can explore these possibilities further with the national sample simulation, which you get by pressing [C] in the program menu. When the program starts, the computer will say NATIONAL POLL and instruct you Press [ENTER] to load national poll data. The reason I put this step into the program was so that you could escape this program easily if you selected it by mistake. If you press [ESC], you will get immediately back to the program menu. But now, press [ENTER].

The computer will begin work that may take a full minute on some computers. It has to load a tremendous amount of information, highly realistic data from 159,969,104 people living in 289 metropolitan areas.

Where did the data come from? A chief source was the publications of the 1980 U.S. census concerning counties and SMSAs, or Standard Metropolitan Statistical Areas, geographic units defined by the census bureau for use in statistical analysis. They were invented because data on cities often turned out to be messy to deal with.

As I look out my window, I can see the houses of Cambridge, Massachusetts, and directly behind them the skyline of Boston. The subway takes us in eight minutes across the narrow Charles River to the very heart of Boston, yet in formal governmental terms, Cambridge and Boston are wholly separate entities. Data on Boston completely ignore Cambridge and the other parts of the Boston metropolitan area that don't happen to have the same mayor or police force. Yet Boston and Cambridge are indisputably parts of a single economic and social unit.

The SMSA was invented as a way of getting around the accidents of local government, to allow metropolitan areas to be described as units. Outside New England, SMSAs are created by combining major cities with the suburban counties that really belong to them. For example, in 1980 the New York City SMSA included not only the boroughs represented in Bronx County, Kings County, New York County, Queens County, and Richmond County, but also Putnam County, Rockland County, Westchester County, and even Bergen County in New Jersey. Minneapolis and St. Paul, the twin cities, are part of an SMSA that includes several Minnesota counties.

Unfortunately, the counties in New England are large compared to the metropolitan areas, so various systems have been tried to divide New England into its components, and the result is that some important data are not available at the SMSA level. The crucial omission in my research was data on membership in the different religious denominations, which exist only for counties. Over the past couple of years I have labored to construct a religion-oriented SMSA dataset for a variety of research purposes, but I had to limit myself to the 289 SMSAs outside New England. So that's what you've got on the *Survey Research* disk, data concerning all the metropolitan areas outside New England for the year 1980.

To make the simulation clear, imagine we have constructed a short questionnaire to determine various facts about the metropolitan population of the United States outside New England. The questions are too simple to use in a real poll, but they will suffice for present purposes. Indeed, a couple of them are pretty crude, and they might get sarcastic replies from real respondents! The survey looks like this:

1. What is your sex?

   [1] Male   [2] Female

2. Are you a member of the black race?

   [1] Yes   [2] No

3. Have you moved to a new home in the past five years?

   [1] Yes   [2] No

4. Are you living below the federally defined poverty level?

   [1] Yes   [2] No

5. Where were you born?

   [1] In the state I live in today   [2] In a different state   [3] In a foreign country

6. How much formal education have you received?

   [1] Little (I did not graduate from high school)   [2] High school graduate   [3] College graduate

7. How old are you?

   [1] Age 0–17   [2] Age 18–64   [3] Age 65+

8. What is your marital status?

   [1] Single or widowed   [2] Married   [3] Divorced

9. Are you the formal member of a church or other religious organization?

   [1] Yes   [2] No

10. If you answered "Yes" to question 9, above, which religious tradition do you belong to? (If you answered "No" to question 9, please skip this question.)

    [1] Protestant   [2] Catholic   [3] Jewish

11. Have you ever practiced Transcendental Meditation?

    [1] Yes   [2] No

Well, I said it was a crude survey! But the 11 questions cover quite a lot of territory, and I think you will have fun giving this survey to many different samples of the metropolitan population. We won't be able to look at correlations between these variables or do other advanced statistical analysis, but we will be able to inspect answers from samples drawn from particular cities, regions, or from the whole nation west of New England.

When the data have been loaded into the computer, the sampling menu will appear, with the following choices:

```
[0] individuals
[1] 10 clusters
[2] 20 clusters
[3] 30 clusters
[4] 40 clusters
[5] 50 clusters
[6] 60 clusters
[7] regionally balanced 60 clusters
[8] a single city
[9] a single region
```

The first choice, individuals, will give you a simple random sample of the metropolitan population of 160 million. We should try this option first, to get familiar with the results our poll can give us. So press [0] (zero, not the letter O).

Next, the computer asks How many respondents do you want? The choices run from 10 to 2000. Let's be ambitious and poll 1000 respondents, by pressing [7]. When you do, the computer will announce that it is polling the nation, and you will see the number of respondents it has tallied building rapidly in the center of the screen. When the full sample has been polled, the computer will ask Which would you like? The following menu will appear:

```
[1]    General information
[2]    Birthplace
[3]    Education
[4]    Age
```

```
[5]    Marital status
[6]    Church membership


[7]    DRAW A NEW SAMPLE
[ESC]  QUIT
```

I set option 7 apart from the others because it erases the data you are working with and prepares you to draw a new sample. Before you select this option, make sure you have finished analyzing the sample you have just drawn. Perhaps you will recognize the first 6 options in the menu as the topics of the survey. Try the first one, general information, by pressing [1]. You will get a table that shows data about the population, 159,969,104 people, compared with your simple random sample of 1000. You will see what percent are males, what percent are blacks, what percent have moved in the past 5 years, and what percent are below the poverty line.

The reason I selected some of these questions for our survey was that they vary considerably from one region to another. For example, a quarter of the residents of Alabama are black, compared with 12.9% of those in Michigan, and only 0.4% in North Dakota. Thus we can watch the percentage black as an indication of how well our sample represents the population. As it happens, a poll done just in Michigan would give us about the same proportion black as in the total population. Polls done only in Alabama or North Dakota would give us very inaccurate estimates of the proportion black throughout the nation.

I believe the other tables of results will be quite clear, with the possible exception of the one about church membership. So let us look at the religion table I got when I just did a simple random sample of 1000 respondents, shown here as Table 3.5.

Now, I can't tell you exactly how my program accomplishes its realistic simulation of a huge national poll. That's a trade secret. But I promise you that the results are completely honest. The program really does go through a process equivalent to finding individuals at random and asking them the questions. So when the results of the poll come out very close to the percentages in the population, the reason is simply that *random sampling works*. A random sample of adequate size really does reflect very closely the population from which it was drawn.

Table 3.5 reveals that 53.9% of the population are formal members of religious organizations, and my sample is very close to this at 56.2%. The percentages for Protestants, Catholics, and Jews add up approximately to 56.2%, rather than to 100%. If you ask people what denomination they consider themselves, most Americans will mention one. But only a bit over half the population actually belong to churches or other religious organizations, and that is what our poll measures.

Transcendental Meditation is an international movement founded by an Indian guru that was very popular in the mid-1970s. As you can see

▶ ▶ ▶ ▶ ▶ ▶ ▶ ▶ ▶ ▶ ▶

TABLE 3.5   PERCENT IN EACH CATEGORY OF RELIGIOUS MEMBERSHIP

| | Formal Members of Congregations | | | | TM |
	Total	Protestant	Catholic	Jewish	Meditator
Actual nation	53.9%	31.0%	21.9%	1.1%	0.5%
Your sample	56.2%	33.4%	21.7%	1.1%	0.6%

from Table 3.5, about half a percent of the population, something like a million people, have practiced TM. The extent to which TM is a religion is a matter of hot debate. I have included this variable in our survey so we would have one question to which the overwhelming majority of our respondents would give the same answer, in this case no. The tiny proportion who meditate means that some samples will estimate two or even three times as much participation in TM as other samples will, illustrating the problems we can have studying minority phenomena through survey research.

I think you can see that simple random samples of the nation can give very accurate results. But they are so expensive that few researchers can afford to do them. We will now explore the procedures and virtues of multi-stage sampling.

Multi-Stage Sample

Start the national poll program and get to the point where the computer asks Which kind of sample would you like? Notice that options 1 through 7 refer to "clusters." This means **clusters** of respondents; all respondents in a cluster come from a given neighborhood or other small area. The sampling works as follows.

In the first stage, the computer will draw a random sample of polling locations in the 289 cities. If you press [6] to get 60 clusters, it will draw a sample of 60 places. The chance that a selected location is in a particular city is proportional to the population of the city. This means that every person residing in the 289 metropolitan areas has an equal chance of being selected, just as he or she would in a simple random sample. One consequence is that you often get several polling locations from the same city, particularly the biggest ones: New York, Los Angeles, and Chicago.

In the second stage, the computer goes to each location on its list and draws a simple random sample of the people living there. These become a cluster of respondents. Actually, I don't have data on the parts of all the cities, so the computer is really sampling from the city as a whole. But in real projects like this, you would probably arrange the first stage of the sampling so that each cluster came from a different neighborhood, even if several came from a given city.

Let's try a big poll, starting with 60 clusters. Press [6] to get 60 clusters, then press [2] when the computer asks How many respondents do you want per cluster? This will give you 60 clusters with 20 respondents in each, for a total of 1200 respondents.

Next, the screen will fill with a list of the locations of the 60 clusters. Look through your list, and you will probably see the same city listed more than once. I just did this, and I got 6 clusters each in Los Angeles and New York and 4 clusters in Chicago. I also got 1 each in Beaumont, Galveston, and Laredo, Texas.

If you wish, you can write down the cities that the particular sample includes. When you are through with the list of cluster locations, press [ENTER] and the actual polling will take place. One by one the clusters will be highlighted in a bright box, until the survey is complete. Then the computer will give you the menu of analysis choices and ask Which would you like?

At this point you can inspect your survey data, compare with the percentages for the whole 160 million potential respondents, and decide whether you think a multi-stage sampling approach gives results comparable to a true, simple random sample. Technically, the simple random sample is better. But if you have a reasonably large and well-selected set of clusters, the lower cost of administering a multi-stage sample makes it an attractive alternative.

The method we have just used selected the cluster locations at random, proportional to the populations of the individual cities. However, you might want to draw a multi-stage sample that properly reflected the eight regions of the United States covered by our data as well. Option 7 on the sample selection menu gives you a regionally balanced set of 60 clusters. They are chosen at random, but each region will be represented by the proper number of clusters to reflect the size of its metropolitan population.

Sometimes multi-stage cluster samples can have a special research advantage over simple random samples. You wind up with data that allow you to describe each cluster as a whole, thus learning something about the social environment of respondents. An excellent example is a research study done by Rodney Stark, Lori Kent, and Daniel Doyle (1982), focusing on regional differences in the influence of religion.

Recent survey research has shown that religion has a very different impact on people's behavior in different parts of the country. This is extremely interesting, because it shows that religion operates in a complex alliance with other aspects of a community, rather than having a constant, direct influence. In most regions, religious teenagers are far less likely to commit delinquent acts than are nonreligious teenagers. But Stark and his associates found that in the Far West—in California and Washington State, for example—religious teenagers and nonreligious teenagers are equally likely to be delinquent. Their most persuasive evidence came from a re-analysis of a multi-stage cluster survey done by Jerald Bachman (1970).

In the first stage, Bachman had drawn a sample of 87 high schools across the country. Then within each high school, a sample of about 25 boys was randomly drawn. The reason for the 2-stage sampling was simply to save money, but Stark made excellent scientific use of the fact that the respondents came in clusters. The questionnaire contained 4 questions about religion, which were used to identify religious boys. Then the 87 high schools could be described as relatively religious or not, based on the responses the 25 boys from each school had given.

Next, Stark divided the sample into 2 groups, one consisting of 1518 boys who were in relatively religious clusters and 281 who were in clusters very low in religion. Of course, some boys in the religious clusters were not themselves religious, and these boys were especially likely to be delinquent. Some boys in nonreligious clusters were themselves religious—but they were *not* significantly better behaved than the nonreligious boys around them. This is a complex analysis, and you might have to think it through several times. But Stark's study exploits a cluster sample to show that the social context of religion greatly determines the influence it will have on individuals.

Sampling a Region or City

The two final sampling options in the multi-stage program allow you to administer a survey to residents of a single city or region (other than New England) in the United States. If you choose to sample residents of a particular city, pressing [8] from the sample selection menu to get this option, the computer will first ask you what region the city is in. As I explain more fully in Chapter 9, these are the census bureau's eight "divisions" of the country other than New England.

```
[1] Middle Atlantic
[2] E.N.Central
[3] W.N.Central
[4] South Atlantic
[5] E.S.Central
[6] W.S.Central
[7] Mountain
[8] Pacific
```

It won't cost you much to guess which region your city is in, so press the key you think describes its region. All the metropolitan areas I have data on in the region will be listed in alphabetical order. Look for your city in the list. In case you forget, the name of the region you selected is shown at the top. You might want to look on a map or consult a government publication about the 1980 census to see exactly which towns might be included in a given metropolitan area. For some reason, the census bureau called Scranton "Northeast Pennsylvania," and Long Island is called "Nassau." If you have the wrong region, it is easy enough to press [ESC] and start over.

To select a city, type its identification number and press [ENTER]. Next you get to decide how many respondents should be in your sample. In a moment, the computer will have your survey results for you.

As an added bonus, the tables of results will give you percentages not only for your sample and the 160 million people in my dataset but also for the whole city you selected. Thus you can compare your sample with the city from which it was drawn, just as we can compare a simple random sample of the 160 million with their actual statistics.

When you decide to sample a region, you will select it just as you selected the region a city was in. Then the computer will show you the metropolitan areas in that region, just for your information. When you've finished looking at the list, press [ENTER] and the polling will begin. This will be a simple random sample of the region's metropolitan population. The tables of results will give you statistics on the whole region, as well as on your sample and on the 160 million total population in the dataset.

The results you get in any particular simulated poll will depend on luck in drawing your sample, and thus you often may want to do a particular study twice, to see how consistent your findings are. The projects that follow will give you extensive practice in thinking through the issues of sampling and comparing results achieved by different methods.

▶ ▶ ▶ ▶ ▶ ▶ ▶ ▶ ▶ ▶ ▶

PROJECTS

1. Arrange Items in Random Order. Take a piece of lined paper (with at least 25 lines) to make a data sheet and number lines 1 through 25 at the far left. Above the first line, starting to the right of this column of numbers, write the letters A, B, C, D, and E, separated across the page, to serve as the headings of 5 columns of figures. Start the random-numbers program and select the option for arranging items in random order. When the computer asks how many items are in the list you want randomized, tell it 25.

Write the randomized numbers from the second column on the screen in column A of your data sheet, in the same order as shown on the screen, one number to a line. At this point, the numbers on your sheet will look the same as the ones on the screen.

Now press [ENTER] to get back to the main menu and select Arrange items in random order a second time. Again, tell the computer you want 25 items, and press [ENTER]. This will give you a second, different random order for the numbers 1 through 25. Write them down in column B of your sheet. Do the same 3 more times, until you have all 5 columns filled with 5 different random orders.

Does any line have the same number on it twice, in 2 of the 5 random orders? Can you find numbers that wound up in consecutive order in a column, despite being randomized? (I just did this, and in one column I see the number 1 in 6th place and the number 2 in 7th place. Also, 5 is in 14th place followed by 6 in 15th.) Are there any pairs of numbers that are together in two lists? For example, 17 could be followed immediately by 23 in 2 of the 5 columns, although at different places, such as 6th–7th in one and 19th–20th in the other.

What seem to be patterns often emerge in lists of random numbers, but they happen entirely by chance. And the human mind is very good at seeing patterns, even when they aren't really there. Thus honest, randomized lists don't always look completely random even when they are.

2. Draw Random Samples.   To illustrate the drawing of random samples, we will do this project three times, with very different lists of things. If you wish, you could limit your project to only one or two.

First, obtain an up-to-date list of the members of a legislature, like the U.S. House of Representatives, with at least 200 members. Number the members—in the case of the House, write the numbers 1 through 435 in front of their names. Then use the D r a w   a   r a n d o m   s a m p l e part of the random-numbers program to select 50 whom you might interview. On the full list, mark the 50 drawn in the random sample.

Second, obtain a list of at least 200 cities, and similarly draw a random sample of 50. Finally, do the same thing for a list of at least 200 novels or motion pictures. Although you cannot interview cities, novels, or movies, samples of them would allow you to select representative cases to study. For example, you could write a thesis on the role of women in 50 novels randomly selected from (and thus representative of) a list of all best-selling novels of the past decade. As illustrated in our simulation of a national poll, drawing a random sample of cities might be the first step in finding questionnaire respondents, the next step being drawing a random sample of residents of each of the 50 cities selected.

3. Probability Pinball Game.   Play the game 10 times, letting it run each time until it stops by itself. Make a big but clear table with 10 columns of data, showing how many balls wound up in each of the 13 rows on each run.

Add the numbers up for each of the 10 runs. This should give you the number winding up in each row for all 10 runs, out of a total of 1000 or more. Does the middle row have the largest total number? Are the rows arranged symmetrically—in pairs of about equal size on either side of the middle row?

If this project is done for a class, the next step is to add data together from all the students. Examine the new distribution of balls from all the students' runs combined. Does the middle row have the largest number? Is the distribution more symmetrical than with just 10 runs? Each student could calculate the percentage of balls in each row, for his or her 10 runs combined, and compare with the percentages for the whole class. With luck, the more balls in the sample, the closer the distribution will be to the binomial distribution in Table 3.1 or to the normal distribution.

4. Town Survey Simulation. Select *Survey Research* program B, which simulates a survey of a small town. Let's imagine an election for mayor is coming up, and there are two candidates. Thomas Jones is the present mayor, an elderly man whose main interest is duck hunting. Molly Flanders, the challenger, is a young woman concerned with establishing a day-care center for children of working parents. The vote is essentially whether to throw Tom out and replace him with Moll—that's what "Pro" means for this simulation.

Set the town population so there are 600 old people and 400 young people. Then set it so that 600 are women and 400 are men. When the commands to decide opinions come on the screen, set them like this: Old: Con; Young:Pro; Men:Con; Women:Pro.

Now try two polls, using any two different types of sample you wish. But intentionally select types of sample that you think will give different results. Write a short report, giving both election results and your poll results from both runs, commenting on the differences between your polls and suggesting which was a better choice for predicting the election.

Note: To make the simulation more interesting, I have written the program so that "agree" and "disagree" (or "pro" and "con") do not have equal strength to start with in the community. If you don't like the results of the election, try a couple more runs, with the same opinion settings but changing the sizes of age and sex groups in the population to give your candidate a large enough constituency to win.

5. National Religion Poll. Select program C, the simulated national poll. Do four polls, each time writing down all the results on religion (including Transcendental Meditation). You should wind up with a table like this:

Formal Members of Congregations

Respondents	Total	Protestant	Catholic	Jewish	TM Meditators
Actual nation	53.9%	31.0%	21.9%	1.1%	0.5%
Random sample (Individuals)	53.6%	30.4%	21.1%	2.1%	0.7%
Middle Atlantic region	55.2%	45.4%	9.7%	0.1%	0.5%
South Atlantic region	50.2%	32.1%	17.3%	0.8%	0.7%
Pacific region	50.4%	35.5%	14.5%	0.4%	0.2%

For the first sample, select Individuals and tell the computer you want 1000 respondents. This gives you a simple random sample of the 160 million people in the dataset. The 3 other samples should be single regions: Middle Atlantic, South Atlantic, and Pacific, with 1000 in each sample. Each regional sample will give you 2 more rows of percentages to add to your table, "Your sample" and "Cities sampled." Label each row of your table clearly, so we know what data it represents.

Write a brief report, describing the results you see in your table. In particular, discuss the differences you see across regions and the advisability of using each of the four samples in an actual research project designed to study American religion.

6. Economy in National Polling. Your task is to get data from 1000 respondents through a national poll, tabulating the percentages male, black, moved, and in poverty ([1] General information on the menu). You will do this 4 times, using the national poll program, comparing samples that would cost very different amounts to obtain in reality.

Sample 1, the cheapest, is 1000 persons living in your own city (or some city you select to be your own for purposes of this project).

Sample 2, second cheapest, is a cluster sample consisting of 10 clusters, taking 100 respondents from each cluster (likely to be in 10 different cities).

Sample 3, a bit more expensive because of travel costs, will be a cluster sample with 50 clusters, 20 respondents from each.

Sample 4, the most expensive, is a simple random sample of the nation, consisting of 1000 individuals.

Prepare a table of results, similar to the one for Project 5, but tabulating percentages male, black, moved, and in poverty. Write a brief report comparing the merits of the four samples. If you were going to do a real poll of this kind, how would you decide which sample to use?

4

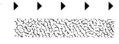

▶ ▶ ▶ ▶ ▶ In this chapter we will create a questionnaire of as many as 48 items, using the question-processor program on your disk. We will discuss 7 different question formats, each with its own set of response alternatives, that are built into the program. Then we will discuss revising existing surveys, ending with instructions on how to administer the survey to as many as 200 people, right on the computer, and how to print out the survey on paper.

Before you can create a new survey, you will need a work disk. A good principle to follow is to make a separate work disk for every questionnaire you create. Project 4 in Chapter 1 explains how to make one. Write a clear description of the disk and its purpose on a label and stick it on the disk. Do not write on the disk itself, especially if you are using one of the traditional, vulnerable floppy disks in a weak jacket.

The main menu of the questionnaire-writing program gives you the following choices:

```
[1]   Create a NEW questionnaire
[2]   Revise an EXISTING questionnaire
[3]   Administer an existing questionnaire
[4]   Print an existing questionnaire
[ESC] QUIT or change programs
```

The words NEW and EXISTING in the first two choices are important. When you start this program, you should be very clear whether you will be working with an existing questionnaire or creating one from scratch. Obviously, you cannot revise a questionnaire unless it exists and you have a copy of it on your work disk. But if a questionnaire exists on the work disk and you set out to create a new one with the same name, the existing ques-

Writing a Questionnaire

tionnaire will be obliterated in the process, perhaps wasting much previous labor.

▶ ▶ ▶ ▶ ▶ ▶ ▶ ▶ ▶ ▶ ▶

[1] CREATE A NEW QUESTIONNAIRE

As soon as you press [1] to select the first choice from the main menu, the computer will ask What is the name of the survey? A bright rectangle flashes in the middle of the screen, showing you where the name will appear as you type it. Near the bottom are the instructions Type a name, from 2 to 8 letters long, and press [ENTER]. Below that, you will see a warning: Press [ESC] if you do not want to CREATE a survey after all. Check this warning carefully, because it will remind you which key you pressed, and thus tell you if you pressed the wrong one. For example, if you pressed key 2, the warning will have the word REVISE in it instead of CREATE. To return to the menu, press [ESC].

You should invent a name that clearly reminds you what your project is. If you name it something ordinary, like DATA or SURVEY, you may not be able to distinguish your disk from that of someone else who happened to choose the same, all-too-obvious name. On the other hand, you want a name you can remember easily, so you don't have to bother looking it up every time you start work.

IBM has set various limits on the names we can use. Most important, they cannot be any longer than eight letters or numbers long. WILLIAM is an okay name for a questionnaire, but BAINBRIDGE won't work—too long. At the other extreme, the name has to be at least two letters or numbers long. The reason is that I have used up several of the single letters (A, B, C . . .) in naming my programs. Remember that your original disk contains two datasets, named STUDENTS and XYZ, which I have provided for you to analyze. Thus you should avoid the names STUDENTS and XYZ as well.

Punctuation marks and strange characters aren't allowed, just letters and numbers. Capitalization of letters doesn't matter; the computer interprets all the letters as capitals. Finally, you cannot use a few particular names because IBM already has technical functions for them: CON, AUX, COM1, COM2, LPT1, LPT2, LPT3, PRN, and NUL. It is possible that your computer will reject some other name, and you might consult its instruction manual to make sure.

Once you have entered the name of your survey, the screen will fill with a new menu: SELECT ITEM TYPE. Across the screen runs a horizontal line, with ITEM 1 in the middle of it. This means you are set to create the first item of your questionnaire. As you do so, completed parts of the item will appear below the horizontal line. Various decision menus and the parts of the item you are working on at the moment will appear above the line.

The computer asks you to select the item type from eight alternatives:

```
[1] Yes-No or True-False
[2] Agree-Disagree
[3] Magnitudes
[4] Self-reported behavior
[5] Preference scale
[6] Satisfaction scale
[7] Paired opposites
[8] Free-form item
```

To select one of these eight, simply press the appropriate number key. Now I will explain how to create items of the first seven kinds; instructions for the eighth are in Chapter 5.

[1] Yes–No or True–False

When you select item type 1, the top half of the screen will reveal a large box with a flashing cursor in it. You will also see an instruction: Type item's stimulus above. Press [ENTER] when it's right. This box is where you will write the main part of your questionnaire item, known as the **stimulus**. If I ask you a question, my question is a stimulus. Your answer is a **response**. But not all questionnaire items are phrased as questions. I call the box at the top of the screen a *stimulus box*, not a ques-

tion box, because often the item will be in statement form rather than question form. Here are two examples, both designed to fit the yes–no or true–
false format.

1. In your opinion, are foreign cars generally better built than
   American cars?

   [1] Yes   [2] No

2. German cars are generally better built than Italian cars.

   [1] True   [2] False

These items are very similar, although the first is phrased as a question,
complete with question mark, and the second presents the respondent
with a statement to be evaluated.

To see how the box works, type in the following traditional typing exercise, which includes all the letters of the alphabet: "The quick brown fox
jumps over the lazy dog." Do not press [ENTER] at the end, just type these
nine short words. If you make a mistake, you can back up by pressing
[BACKSPACE] (or ←, often in the upper right corner of the keyboard).
Let's say you want to modify the sentence, while still using all the letters of
the alphabet, by replacing *lazy* with *sleazy*. Just press [BACKSPACE] nine
times, or until *lazy* disappears, and type in *sleazy dog*.

Now, backspace nearly to the beginning and change the sentence to:
"The quick, bright psychologist jumps over the lazy sociologist." Before
you finish, you will reach the edge of the stimulus box and find there is not
quite enough room on the first line for everything. On old-fashioned me-
chanical typewriters, you would hit the carriage return key, the equivalent
of our [ENTER] key, but don't do anything like this now. Just type the sentence itself. As if by magic, the sociologist hops down to the second line,
where there is room for him or her.

Now backspace several times to erase the sociologist. Notice that the
cursor leaps back up to the end of the first line, where you can begin typing
again. This time, type in *social-psychologist* to finish the sentence. It will automatically break at the hyphen. The question-processor program has been
written to handle simple line ends like this for you. Do not hit the [ENTER]
key until you are finished with the stimulus and want to enter it into the
computer's memory.

The stimulus box can hold as much as 4 lines of 60 letters, spaces, and
other characters. If you want the items to be numbered, simply type each
item's number as I have done with the 2 items about foreign cars. If you
want to indent the first line of the stimulus, just type a few spaces to begin it.

You can type a brief instruction into the stimulus box, if you want.
For example, you could start a set of true–false questions with a brief instruction by typing it into the box for the first item in that set: "In your

view, is the following statement TRUE or FALSE?" Or you could include a brief reminder or other comment inside parentheses. To put a blank line between lines of text in the stimulus box, hold down the space bar to get a line full of spaces.

Once you have the stimulus just the way you want it, press [ENTER]. The stimulus will appear just below the middle of the screen, for your reference, and a menu of eight response choices will appear in the top half. Press [1] through [8] to select one. So you can design your questionnaire away from the computer, I have listed these response choices below.

```
[1]  Yes, No
[2]  Yes, Not sure, No
[3]  Yes, Don't Know, No
[4]  Yes completely, Yes mostly
     No mostly, No completely
[5]  True, False
[6]  True, Not sure, False
[7]  True, Don't Know, False
[8]  True completely, True mostly,
     False mostly, False completely
```

When you have selected one, it will appear at the bottom of the screen, under the stimulus, giving you an idea of how the question will look to the respondent. The top of the screen will become a new menu of choices:

```
[1]    Change response categories
[2]    Rewrite the stimulus
[3]    Junk the item and start over
[4]    Go to the next item
[ESC]  Return to the main menu
```

The first two alternatives let you rewrite part of the item, while keeping the current version of it on the bottom of the screen for your reference. If you want to change the whole format of the item, press [3]. This wipes the screen clean and asks you again to select the type of question you want for the item. The fourth alternative moves you on to the next item, which you should do when you have a good draft of the one you have been working on. You can always come back and revise selected items after you have created them and saved the set on your disk.

If you decide to return to the main menu, and press [ESC], the computer will politely ask Do you want to save your work? If so, press [Y] for yes. If you were just practicing, press [N] for no.

Remember that our question-processor program can create a survey with no more than 48 items. But, it can contain any mixture of types of items that you want.

[2] Agree–Disagree

Among the most common survey items are statements with which the respondent is supposed to agree or disagree. These are often called Likert items, and an index composed of them is often called a Likert scale, after Rensis Likert, who developed systematic methods for using them. If you press [2] when the computer asks you to select a question type, you will be able to create an agree–disagree item.

You will get exactly the same stimulus box and instructions as you would for a yes–no question, except now you are supposed to type a statement rather than a question into the box. Chapter 10 describes how to create a complete survey based on agree–disagree items, and thus extensive examples are not needed here. But here are three from a survey of Harvard and Stanford graduates (Skelly, 1986): "To improve the economy, we will have to buy only American-made products." "Computers have improved our lives tremendously." "Staying in good physical shape is very important." Do you tend to agree or disagree with each of these?

You might want to put a brief instruction in the box for the first agree–disagree item in your survey. Here's an example that fits on one line: "To what extent do you agree or disagree with the following?" If there is room, you can type a line of spaces between this instruction and the first agree–disagree stimulus. When you've finished typing the statement, you can press [ENTER] to register it with the computer and get the six response-type options, which are listed below:

```
[1] Agree, Disagree
[2] Agree, Neutral, Disagree
[3] Strongly Agree, Agree, Disagree, Strongly
    Disagree
[4] Strongly Agree, Agree, Neutral, Disagree,
    Strongly Disagree
[5] Strongly Agree, Agree, Slightly Agree,
    Slightly Disagree, Disagree, Strongly
    Disagree
[6] Strongly Agree, Agree, Slightly Agree,
    Neutral, Slightly Disagree, Disagree,
    Strongly Disagree
```

Notice that half the sets of responses have a neutral category. Some survey researchers believe a middle or neutral category is a bad idea, because it gets used as a cop-out by respondents who otherwise would express a definite opinion. Others maintain that a neutral response can be completely valid, and thus it should be included.

Another issue is how finely respondents can make distinctions. I have usually used option 4 for my own agree–disagree items, and I personally suspect that six or seven choices are too many for most respondents. But you have to make up your own mind about the responses for your items. Perhaps you want to force people to choose between agreement and disagreement, and thus you will avoid a neutral category. Perhaps your topic is one, such as hot political issues, on which people will have a wide range of intensities of opinion, and thus you will use the maximum number of responses. It's up to you.

When you select the set of responses you want, your agree–disagree item will appear below the horizontal line, and you will be asked whether you want to make any changes. You can work over the item, revising it repeatedly on the computer, with the material below the line as a guide. But remember, you can always come back later and revise the question again, after you have saved your new survey on the disk.

[3] Magnitudes

When we want respondents to express opinions about how complete or big something is, we use questions about magnitudes, choice 3 on the question-type menu. As with the two previous types, you must first write a stimulus in the stimulus box, this time in the form of a question. The response type menu has four choices:

```
[1] To a very great extent, To a great extent, To
    some extent, To a little extent, To a very
    little extent
[2] Very large, Large, Medium, Small, Very small
[3] A very great deal, A great deal, Quite a bit,
    Some, Little or none
[4] Extremely, Very, Moderately, Slightly, Not at
    all
```

We can illustrate these four sets of responses with four questions from a hypothetical survey of factory employees:

1. In your opinion, to what extent do your factory's managers care about the welfare of their workers?
2. How large is the building in which you work?
3. How much confidence do you have in the management of your company?
4. In general, how careful are you while working with machines?

The first of these would use the first set of responses, the second would use the second set, and so on. In fact, questions like these are very often used in real surveys of workers. The following **magnitude items,** taken from a standard survey administered to thousands of employees of many companies (Taylor and Bowers, 1972), all use the first set of responses:

1. To what extent do you enjoy performing the actual day-to-day activities that make up your job?

2. How much do you look forward to coming to work each day?

3. To what extent are there things about working here (people, policies, or conditions) that encourage you to work hard?

4. When you talk with your supervisor, to what extent does he [or she] pay attention to what you're saying?

5. How much does your supervisor encourage people to give their best efforts?

6. How much do persons in your work group encourage each other to work as a team?

7. To what extent do you find it difficult to sleep at night because you keep thinking of what happened at work during the day?

Another example comes from the field of marketing research (Lusch and Lusch, 1987:216). In a survey administered to potential customers of a travel agency, we could include a series beginning like this:

1. How helpful do you believe a travel agent would be in answering your questions on the following topics for a trip you are considering to a foreign country? Questions about . . . currency conversions?

2. How helpful would a travel agent be answering questions about . . . climate?

3. How helpful would a travel agent be answering questions about . . . shopping?

4. How helpful would a travel agent be answering questions about . . . restaurants?

As phrased, these questions might go best with response set 4: Extremely, Very, Moderately, Slightly, Not at all. But you could rephrase the questions with the word *help* instead: "How much help would a travel agent be answering questions about restaurants?" Then response set 3 would be appropriate: A very great deal, A great deal, Quite a bit, Some, Little or none. Or you might prefer this: "How much could you rely on a travel agent to answer questions about restaurants?" Then set number 1 would work: To a very great extent, To a great extent, To some extent, To a little extent, To a very little extent. Just make sure that the responses harmonize with the stimulus. If you have a list of similar items you want to include, you would do best to stick with one set of responses for all of them, and put items with different responses in sections separated by items of other types, so that respondents will not be confused. Often, one or two hard-to-phrase items will decide which responses you use for all.

[4] Self-Reported Behavior

Many survey items inquire about the respondent's attitudes and opinions, and others seek factual information about the respondent's background and current circumstances, but some of the most powerful questions concern the respondent's behavior. You can couch these questions in any of the three previously discussed formats, but here I describe a special format that might serve your purposes better.

Let's say you're doing market research for one of the chains of computer stores that have sprung up in recent years. One of the things you need to know about is the respondent's purchase of computer software. You could ask "Have you ever purchased computer software?"

Yes or no might be all the answer you need. In that case, you could use the yes–no question type. But perhaps you would like to know how recently the respondent has bought software. The recent computer owner might have done it within the past week, but not earlier. Someone who acquired a computer and then put it in the closet when it turned out far less useful than expected may have bought software long ago, but not recently. A steady computer user and potential steady customer of your stores may have bought software long ago as well as recently. The computer will fit a particular span of time into these alternatives, depending on which of the following four choices you select.

You begin, as in the previous formats, by writing the stimulus. When you've got it right, and press [ENTER] to register it, the computer will want you to select a period of time, from a day to a year, that will be incorporated in some of the responses, indicating when the person may have engaged in the behavior:

```
Performed the behavior in the past . . .    [1] day
                                            [2] week
                                            [3] month
                                            [4] year
```

You have to pick the right time interval for your particular question. Perhaps you decide a month is a reasonable span of time for software. People who buy much are apt to do so every couple of months or so, and real addicts will purchase software monthly. Press [3] and the respondent will get a question that looks like this:

```
Have you ever purchased computer software?
[1] No, never
[2] Yes - More than a month ago
```

```
[3] Yes - During the past month
[4] Yes - During the past month AND more than a
    month ago
```

You don't have to think in terms of these four groups while doing your analysis, however. Once the data have been entered into the computer, you can do what is called **recoding**, a very useful procedure described in Chapter 6 that lets you combine two or more responses. For example, you could recode responses to our software purchasing item so that respondents were put into two categories: those who had not purchased software in the past month, a combination of responses 1 and 2 to our question, and those who had, a combination of responses 3 and 4. So a question format such as this gives you flexibility in how you analyze your data.

When Travis Hirschi (1969:256) included questions of this form in his landmark study of the causes of juvenile delinquency, he used the time interval of a year. This time interval allowed Hirschi to divide his respondents into four substantial groups. First, of course, would be those who never violated the law. Second would be a group that used to be delinquent but had stopped performing delinquent acts. Third were the boys who had only recently started acting delinquently, after a prior life of virtue. And the fourth group were the long-term, habitual delinquents who do the deeds now and have done them for a long time.

Hirschi's delinquency items also provide a good illustration of a point that cannot be stressed too often: Questions must be phrased in language the particular set of respondents will understand. Hirschi wanted to know about the crimes the boys had committed. Crime is defined by criminal laws and courts, which give illegal acts technical names. But Hirschi didn't ask the boys "Have you ever committed petty larceny?" "Have you ever committed vandalism?" "Have you ever committed battery?"

Such terms would have mystified many of the high school students. Thus any correlations in the statistical results might merely have reflected which students understood the questionnaire and which did not, rather than which had done the delinquent deeds.

Instead of asking about petty larceny, Hirschi inquired "Have you ever taken little things (worth less than $2) that did not belong to you?" Instead of referring to vandalism, he asked, "Have you ever banged up on something that did not belong to you on purpose?" And instead of mentioning battery, he asked, "Not counting fights you may have had with a brother or sister, have you ever beaten up on anyone or hurt anyone on purpose?"

[5] Preference Scale

A **scale** is a measurement device, like a thermometer or a ruler. A thermometer measures how hot something is. A ruler measures how long it is. A **preference scale** measures the amount of liking a person has for the stimulus.

When you select the preference scale question type, you get a small stimulus box. Previously, you could type as many as 4 lines, 60 letters or spaces long. Now you get only 1 line that length. When the computer administers the questionnaire, it will automatically ask "On a scale from 1 (do not like) to 9 (like very much), how much do you like . . ." All you have to type in the stimulus box is the phrase to follow this, the thing the respondent is to judge on the preference scale. For example, if you want a preference rating of Italian cars, you should type *Italian cars?* into the stimulus box. If you want a question mark at the end of the stimulus, you have to type it in.

When you press [ENTER] to register the stimulus, the following will appear below the horizontal line:

```
On a scale from 1 (do not like) to 0 (like very
   much),
how much do you like . . .
Italian cars?
```

Do not worry about the zero in the first line. When the respondent gets the item, it will have another number in this place. If you want *Italian cars* to be indented, for visual appeal, simply type some spaces into the stimulus box before typing the phrase.

Above the horizontal line, an instruction now reads: Type a number from [2] to [9] to set the number of responses. This is how you can determine the number of different degrees there will be in the preference scale. If you press [2], there will be two degrees: 1, 2. If you press [9], there will be nine: 1, 2, 3, 4, 5, 6, 7, 8, 9.

If you pressed 7 in the Italian car example, you would get:

```
On a scale from 1 (do not like) to 0 (like very
   much),
how much do you like . . .
Italian cars?
            7    Like very much
            6
            5
            4
            3
            2
            1    Do not like
```

Notice that the low-numbered response, 1, is at the bottom here. I felt that people will instinctively expect the lowest response to be at the bottom in this kind of question.

A major use of such items is in market research. Say you have a grocery store and need to decide what new products to stock. On the simplest level, you could list a number of brands of breakfast cereal and use the overall ratings to decide which ones you should stock. But on a more subtle level, you could discover which products correlated with the products that already sell well in your store, because they should sell well, too.

The greatest use I have made of this type of item was in my book on science-fiction literature (Bainbridge, 1986a), based on a questionnaire filled out by several hundred participants in the 1978 World Science Fiction Convention. The point of the study was to chart science-fiction authors' competing images of the future and ideologies about science. In the process of doing some preliminary research, I decided that it was essential to map the different groups of authors, charting which were most similar to which. Then I would need to find objective ways to describe each of the groups.

I first considered a question format known as **pair comparisons.** If you have a list of things you want respondents to evaluate, you write a questionnaire pairing these things with each other. In a study of how people conceive of the animal kingdom, for just three animals the items might be:

1. On a scale from 1 (not similar) to 7 (very similar), how similar are bears and rabbits?

2. On a scale from 1 (not similar) to 7 (very similar), how similar are bears and foxes?

3. On a scale from 1 (not similar) to 7 (very similar), how similar are rabbits and foxes?

For 3 animals, there must be 3 items, to get all possible pairs. But see what happens if we add pigs. We must compare pigs and bears, pigs and rabbits, and pigs and foxes. Thus we have to add an item for every one of the animals already in our list. If we already had 20 animals in our list, and added one more, we would have to add 20 new items in the pair-comparison format. This means that even a relatively short list of animals requires rather a long questionnaire. And my final list of science-fiction authors included 140, which would have produced a questionnaire with at least 9730 items!

After experimenting with other approaches, I found that preference questions were a very efficient way of getting information about similarities. You ask people how much they like each of a list of things and then correlate these preferences with each other. If you are not familiar with the concept of mathematical correlations, you will get a proper introduction to them in Chapter 6. But for now, we can say that a positive mathematical correlation between questions about two animals implies that people feel similarly about the two creatures.

Positive correlations will reflect similarities that people respond to in the liking ratings. Foxes and rabbits are small. Foxes and bears are carnivorous. Bears and rabbits are lovable. If people who like bears tend to like rabbits but not especially to like foxes, then you know that people consider bears and rabbits to be similar. If rabbit-lovers are not fond of foxes, then you can conclude that rabbits and foxes are not similar, in the estimation of your respondents.

In my science-fiction study, I found four main groups of authors, each group including both well-liked and poorly liked writers. One group consisted of classic authors from the early days of science fiction, such as H. G. Wells, Jules Verne, and Edgar Rice Burroughs. The characteristic they all shared was antiquity, and this objective characteristic came out perfectly well in the apparently subjective preference ratings of my respondents.

A second group wrote various kinds of fantasy fiction, including J. R. R. Tolkien, the creator of cute Hobbits, and Robert E. Howard, who gave us the brutal character Conan, featured in several recent muscle movies. Such wild fantasy has little to do with science, but types of fantasy based on ancient myths have always had a place in the subculture of science fiction. The heart of the science-fiction field is a third group consisting of hard-science writers, whose stories concerned discoveries in the physical sciences and technological inventions. Isaac Asimov and Arthur C. Clarke are perhaps the best known. A fourth group, often called the new wave, included such writers as Harlan Ellison, Joanna Russ, Barry Malzberg, and Norman Spinrad.

New wave can be our example, showing how preference questions can reveal much about the nature of the things they ask about. My questionnaire contained not only 140 preference items about authors but 62 items asking respondents how much they liked various kinds of literature. Table 4.1 lists 9 literature types that correlated significantly with new-wave science fiction in preference responses from 409 conventioneers who proved to be especially knowledgeable about the authors.

Read through the nine kinds of literature in the table and you will have a good picture of the new wave. Most important, new wave experiments with new styles of writing, and thus could be called avant-garde. Whereas respondents who liked the competing hard-science style also tended to prefer fiction based on the *physical* sciences, new-wave fans prefer fiction based on the *social* sciences. Indeed, many of the new-wave stories are based on speculations in psychology, sociology, anthropology, political science, or economics.

New wave is critical of our society and worried about the possible harmful effects of scientific progress. It deeply probes personal relationships and feelings, and thus it emphasizes characters who are sensitive and introspective. Several writers have used new wave as a vehicle for feminism. The first conscious movement of new-wave writers appeared in Britain. The correlations do not tell the whole story, by any means, but I think you can see that preference questions have a potential far beyond merely determining which things are people's favorites.

Notice that people who like new wave tend to like science fiction of the 1960s and 1970s. In contrast, those who like hard science tend to like

TABLE 4.1   CORRELATION BETWEEN PREFERENCE FOR NEW-WAVE SCIENCE
FICTION AND FOR RELATED TYPES

Correlation (r) with New Wave	Literature Type
0.65	Avant-garde fiction that experiments with new styles
0.40	Fiction based on the social sciences
0.39	Science fiction of the 1960s and 1970s
0.38	Fiction that is critical of our society
0.37	Fiction that deeply probes personal relationships and feelings
0.34	British science fiction
0.31	Feminist literature
0.29	Stories in which the main character is sensitive and introspective
0.27	Fiction concerned with harmful effects of scientific progress

science fiction written in the 1940s and 1950s. Again, apparently subjective questions about preferences can give results about objective facts, such as when different literature types predominated.

[6] Satisfaction Scale

Satisfaction scales are very much like preferences scales. Are you satisfied with your job? Do you like your job? These questions are similar, if not precisely identical. Sometimes it is more natural to phrase personal evaluation in terms of satisfaction rather than in terms of liking or preference. For example, asking people whether they like their incomes may be slightly confusing; they may have a quicker, surer answer if we ask whether they are satisfied with their incomes.

The satisfaction stimulus box is identical to the one for preference items. You can type in the part of the stimulus that is specific to the item you are working on. For example, if you typed in "the job the president of the U.S. is doing right now?" the full stimulus would be: "On a scale from 1 (not at all satisfied) to 9 (perfectly satisfied), how satisfied are you with the job the president of the U.S. is doing right now?"

After you type in the specific part of the stimulus, you are asked to decide how many responses there should be, from 2 to 9. Then, as with the preference items, the full item will appear in the bottom half of the screen, and you will get the chance to revise it. Again, don't worry about the fact that the stimulus on your screen says that the scale runs from 1 to 0, because the zero will be replaced with the right number when the item is shown to respondents.

The Gallup Poll, which has asked satisfaction questions for years, compares the national level of satisfaction from one year to another. You have to be a bit careful when you compare the satisfaction level of one kind of person with the satisfaction level of another kind, however. As George Homans (1974:252) and many other social scientists have pointed out, people do not possess objective standards for judging their personal success or well-being. Thus when we ask whether they are satisfied with their incomes, they may not compare themselves with the population as a whole but with some **reference group** or comparison group. Poor people may report being satisfied despite having less than the average if they have as much as they expect a person in their situation to have. Rich people may report being dissatisfied if they compare themselves with the super-rich. Be aware of this possible problem with satisfaction items, and be prepared to look up some literature on it in your field if you contemplate using them. Often they work quite well.

I used modified forms of Gallup's questions in a couple of small surveys I did related to the space program. In 1974 I sent questionnaires to editors of amateur science-fiction newsletters and magazines, and 130 surveys came back from this very unusual group of respondents. Science-fiction fans are utopians, dreaming of societies vastly different from the one they live in, so I hypothesized that they might be especially dissatisfied (Bainbridge, 1986a:165–67). Following are the 5 items taken from Gallup; the questionnaire offered only 3 responses: satisfied, dissatisfied, and no opinion.

1. On the whole, would you say you are satisfied or dissatisfied with the future facing you and your family?
2. On the whole, would you say you are satisfied or dissatisfied with the education children are getting today?
3. On the whole, would you say you are satisfied or dissatisfied with your standard of living?
4. On the whole, would you say you are satisfied or dissatisfied with your family income?
5. On the whole, would you say you are satisfied or dissatisfied with the work you do?

In the survey Gallup carried out just a few months before mine, 53% of American adults said they were "satisfied with the future facing you and your family" (Gallup Opinion Index, 1973). Only 41% of the science-fiction fans were satisfied with their families' futures, but this difference of 12 percentage points is not very solid evidence of fan dissatisfaction, because with only 130 respondents the 41% figure is just a rough estimate of how typical fans feel.

Whereas 71% of the general public were satisfied with their standard of living, 65% of fans were happy. On a related matter, 61% of citizens, but

50% of fans, were satisfied with their family income. When the stimulus was "the work you do," 79% of Gallup's sample and 70% of the fans were satisfied. The fans do appear less satisfied, but the differences are quite small.

A huge difference appeared when the stimulus was "the education children are getting today": 61% of Gallup's respondents were satisfied; only 17% of the fans were. Just 29% of the general population expressed actual dissatisfaction with children's education, compared with 70% of the fans. This is a vast difference, expressing the disdain of this group for an educational system in which most of them excelled.

I included the item about satisfaction with "the future facing you and your family" in a survey about the space program completed by 225 Seattle-area voters (Bainbridge, 1986a:167). These respondents were quite different from Gallup's random sample of the population, not only because of their location in one particular Western city but also because many citizens are not registered to vote and those who responded to my survey had more considered perspectives on the space program than do ordinary voters.

This spaceflight voters survey included items about reading science fiction and watching science-fiction movies and television shows. Of those who never read science fiction, only 24% were dissatisfied about the future, but of those who read it often, 48% were dissatisfied. Of those who never watched science fiction, only 22% were dissatisfied, compared with 49% of those who often watched it. These responses indicate that science fiction is connected with dissatisfaction. Perhaps dissatisfaction drives people to read escapist literature, like science fiction, but it is also possible that images of radically different futures stimulate dissatisfaction with the present conditions.

These two surveys were quite modest, of course, but they illustrate how satisfaction items can produce significant results even with a small number of respondents. Furthermore, their satisfaction items offered only three responses, whereas the satisfaction scale built into our question processor can offer as many as nine responses, measuring attitudes more sensitively. Also, you can increase the sensitivity of your survey by combining several satisfaction items into a satisfaction index, as explained in Chapter 7.

[7] Paired Opposites

The paired-opposites format is used to get respondents' judgments of a particular thing or concept on a series of scales. Each of these scales can be identified by a pair of concepts that describe each end of it. For example, let's design some items to describe the IBM corporation. And let's give respondents a set of seven-point scales like the following: Small 1 2 3 4 5 6 7 Big. Thus a person will rate IBM in terms of how small or big it is by typing one of the numbers 1 through 7, typing [1] if the person thinks IBM is very small, [4] if IBM seems in between, or [7] if IBM seems very big.

The first step is to write the stimulus for the item. As with preference scales and satisfaction scales, a one-line stimulus box will appear at the top of the screen. In it, you should type your stimulus, which in our example will be *the IBM Corporation?* You should invest some care in getting the stimulus just right, and you might consider stating this one at greater length, like this: *IBM—The International Business Machines Corporation?* If you want a question mark at the end, type it.

When you press [ENTER] to register the stimulus, the following question will appear just below the middle of the screen: On the following scale, how would you describe... the IBM Corporation?

The top of the screen now looks just like the stimulus box, but the computer is asking for something different: Type LOW scale label above. This means you type a word or phrase that will describe the low end of the scale, the end starting with the number 1. In our example, you should type *Small* and press [ENTER]. At the very bottom of the screen, you will now see LOW: Small, to remind you what the low end of the scale is while you are deciding the high end.

The one-line box remains at the top of the screen, but now the instruction is Type HIGH scale label above. In our example, you should type *Big* and press [ENTER]. Near the bottom, just above LOW: Small you will see HIGH: Big.

The computer says Type a number from [2] to [9] to set the number of responses. Our example called for a scale of seven steps, so you should press [7]. Now the full item can be seen:

```
On the following scale, how would you describe...
the IBM - Corporation?
7    Big
6
5
4
3
2
1    Small
```

You can go on to produce many more IBM items. For each one, you have to type in the second half of the stimulus. A questionnaire of 48 items could be composed of 4 groups of 12, each consisting of the same set of paired opposites but with a different stimulus, such as 4 popular computer companies: IBM, Apple, Tandy Radio Shack, and Compaq. Let me imagine 12 pairs of opposites that might be used to describe personal computers. Here they are with a 5-point scale:

Small	1 2 3 4 5	Big
Expensive	1 2 3 4 5	Inexpensive
Blue	1 2 3 4 5	Red
Friendly	1 2 3 4 5	Unfriendly

Uncreative	1	2	3	4	5	Creative
Pictures	1	2	3	4	5	Words
Unconventional	1	2	3	4	5	Conventional
Modern	1	2	3	4	5	Old-Fashioned
Work	1	2	3	4	5	Fun
Simple	1	2	3	4	5	Complex
Sour	1	2	3	4	5	Sweet
Incompatible	1	2	3	4	5	Compatible

You could arrange the items in your survey following either of two basic plans. Following one plan, the first 12 questions would ask the respondent to rate IBM on these scales, the second 12 would present the same scales but with Apple as the stimulus, and the third and fourth sections would cover Tandy and Compaq. This is the standard way of arranging such items, and it has the advantage of asking people to focus clearly on one stimulus for several items in a row, before switching completely to another stimulus and contemplating it for the next several items. But a second plan is possible, having the first item judge IBM on *small–large*, the second item judge Apple on *small–large*, the third item judge Tandy on *small–large*, and the fourth item judge Compaq on *small–large*. Then you would continue in this fashion, rotating the stimuli while keeping the scale for every block of four items.

Notice that the list of 12 scales varies the end of the scale with what we might call the positive label. For example, we have *friendly–unfriendly* but *uncreative–creative*. With *small–big*, *big* is at the high end of the number scale, but with *expensive–inexpensive*, the conceptually bigger one in the pair is at the low end of the scale. You probably want to vary which end the conceptually higher or lower half of the pair of opposites is on, so that the number scale itself doesn't come to dominate people's responses, and they will really pay attention to the labels at both ends of the scales.

Some of the pairs really seem appropriate dimensions on which to describe personal computers—for example, *expensive–inexpensive, compatible–incompatible,* and even *friendly–unfriendly.* But others are not so obvious—for example, *sour–sweet* and *blue–red.* You may have heard that IBM is familiarly called "Big Blue," and many of its big computers formerly had blue-colored panels on them. Some people associate the color red with Apple computers, although the company's official apple-with-a-bite-out symbol is rainbow-colored. But psychologists have found that often very strange pairs of opposites turn out to reveal something very meaningful about people's judgments of stimuli. If you were a computer manufacturer, wouldn't you worry somewhat if people judged your machines to be sour while calling your competitor's machines sweet?

The example of *blue–red* might cause you to question whether all the pairs really represent perfect opposites or merely relatively different qualities referring to a given characteristic. In terms of human visual experience of colors, the opposite of red is a bluish-green, and the opposite of blue is orange. Of course, the way the items are presented to the respondent encourages him or her to think of each pair as a set of opposites. Thus when presented with the pair *work–fun*, the respondent will react to these two concepts in a way that considers them to be opposites. You may run into trouble, with grumpy respondents or uninterpretable results, if you use pairs that are very far from being opposites, such as *happy–cheerful*. When a scale measures distance between two equally meaningful opposite concepts, we say that the entire scale expresses a **bipolar concept**, and if you want an easy way to remember this term, think of the way distances north and south run between the two poles of the Earth.

Thus each one of a pair gets some of its meaning from its opposite. Consider the meaning of *blue* in *blue–red* compared with *blue–cheerful*. In the latter, *blue* becomes the name of a mood, synonymous with *depressed*. When you are devising a series of these items, it is worth asking some friends or colleagues to say what the pairs meant to them. It is possible that you, personally, have an interpretation somewhat different from that of your typical respondent. I don't know how many people are aware of the associations of blue with IBM and red with Apple, for example.

The paired-opposites format was developed most successfully by Charles Osgood and his associates, who developed a psychological instrument based on them, called the **semantic differential**. Several somewhat different sets of paired-opposites scales were used, in a tremendously varied set of studies. What follows are 12 representative pairs from a standard list of 50 that Osgood used in some early research, with a 7-point response scale (Osgood et al., 1957:37).

Good	7	6	5	4	3	2	1	Bad
Beautiful	7	6	5	4	3	2	1	Ugly
Nice	7	6	5	4	3	2	1	Awful
Honest	7	6	5	4	3	2	1	Dishonest
Large	7	6	5	4	3	2	1	Small
Strong	7	6	5	4	3	2	1	Weak
Heavy	7	6	5	4	3	2	1	Light
Rugged	7	6	5	4	3	2	1	Delicate
Sharp	7	6	5	4	3	2	1	Dull
Hot	7	6	5	4	3	2	1	Cold
Active	7	6	5	4	3	2	1	Passive
Fast	7	6	5	4	3	2	1	Slow

After trying such items on a number of respondent populations, and using statistical techniques like factor analysis, Osgood and his associates concluded that people judge stimuli primarily in terms of three dimensions: The items I selected for the preceding abbreviated Osgood list were those most representative of the three, and you might spend a moment looking through the list to see whether you could easily divide them into three groups of four pairs in each.

The first four items come from Osgood's *evaluation* dimension. It expresses people's judgments of how good or bad something is. The next four items represent the *potency* dimension, basically how strong respondents judge the thing to be. The third dimension is *activity*, how much movement the thing exhibits or perhaps how much of a contrast with the environment it offers. If we are to believe many of the studies done with the semantic differential, people commonly judge all kinds of stimuli according to these three dimensions, from sounds emitted by a Navy sonar machine to painted works of art.

To make the three dimensions most clear, I presented the pairs with what might be called the positive or high end of each scale on the left. If you were using these in a survey, you might want to reverse every other pair in the set. Instead of *good–bad* and *beautiful–ugly*, you would have *good–bad* and *ugly–beautiful*. Also, it might be wise to separate the four items in each dimension, perhaps presenting them in rotation: *good–bad, large–small, sharp–dull*.

But you certainly don't have to keep to the traditional list of pairs. Fred Fiedler (1958) adapted the semantic differential method to research on relations between leaders and groups, using a specially written set of 24 pairs that focused on the qualities that coworkers might have. Below I have listed 12 of these items, with the 6-point scale Fiedler employed. You can see how these scales might be effective tools for describing fellow members of a work group.

Friendly	1	2	3	4	5	6	Unfriendly
Cooperative	1	2	3	4	5	6	Uncooperative
Quitting	1	2	3	4	5	6	Persistent
Confident	1	2	3	4	5	6	Unsure
Shy	1	2	3	4	5	6	Sociable
Energetic	1	2	3	4	5	6	Tired
Careless	1	2	3	4	5	6	Careful
Practical	1	2	3	4	5	6	Impractical
Intelligent	1	2	3	4	5	6	Unintelligent
Responsible	1	2	3	4	5	6	Undependable
Unrealistic	1	2	3	4	5	6	Realistic
Efficient	1	2	3	4	5	6	Inefficient

In one of his studies, Fiedler (1958:65) had respondents judge 4 different people on his 24-item scale: "yourself," "the person with whom you can work best," "the person with whom you can work least well," and "the man who has been president of the board of directors of your company during the past year." Much can be learned simply by looking at the ratings for each of these 4 types of person. But Fiedler also analyzed how similar they were judged to be, in pairs and triads. How similar are you to a good worker in comparison with a bad worker? And what are the traits that most strongly distinguish a good worker from a bad worker?

You might want to create paired-opposites items with labels in the middle of the scale—for example, *small–medium–large* or *blue–green–yellow–orange–red*. Or you might want intermediate labels on preference scales or satisfaction scales. You can create items like these, and a wide variety of other fixed-choice items, with the eighth option on the item format menu, which is the subject of the next chapter.

▶ ▶ ▶ ▶ ▶ ▶ ▶ ▶ ▶ ▶ ▶

[2] REVISE AN EXISTING QUESTIONNAIRE

Once you have saved a few items on your work disk, you can quickly go back and revise them or add to them. Get to the main menu of the question-processor program and press [2] for Revise an EXISTING questionnaire. Next, the computer will ask What is the name of the survey? You must type the name in, spelled exactly right, and press [ENTER]. If you get even just one letter wrong, the computer won't be able to find the questionnaire on your disk.

The disk drive will go into action, and then the computer will ask you which item you want to start working with. Suppose the name of the survey were HOPE, and you had started with only four items. Then the computer would say Which of HOPE's 4 items to begin? Press [+] or [-] to change item number. Press [ENTER] when done. In the middle of the screen will be displayed Item: 1. This means the machine is prepared to start working with the first item. To get a different item, press [+] to increase the item's number or [-] to lower it. When you have the one you want, press [ENTER].

You start with a menu of choices:

```
[1]   Change response categories
[2]   Rewrite the stimulus
[3]   Junk the item and start over
[4]   Go to the next item
[ESC] Return to the main menu
```

If you merely want to add another item after the ones you have already written, select the last item in the existing survey, and when you get it, press [4] to go to the next item. Otherwise, pick an item that needs changing and start work on it.

When you decide to return to the main menu, the computer will ask whether you want to save your work. If you are seriously revising a questionnaire, rather than just experimenting, you should indeed save your work. The computer wants to update the disk every time it returns to the main menu. Therefore, if you revise item 4 and then decide to go back and revise item 2, you have to save your work after item 4 before you return to the main menu.

You may want to throw away the last item in the survey. To do this, start the question-processor program, tell the computer you want to revise an existing survey, and give the machine its name. Then go to the last item, the one you want to discard, and select option 3 to junk the item. Then press [ESC] instead of selecting a question-type format. Save your survey, and it will be one item shorter the next time you call it up.

If you are writing a complex questionnaire to be printed on paper, I suggest you design it using an ordinary word-processing program. You can always create a duplicate of it using this question processor if you want also to administer it via computer. The program on your *Survey Research* disk is based on principles very, very different from those of a word processor, and it is not very good at moving items around in the list—for example, switching the places of items 2 and 4. If you must change the order of items using the question-processor program, type each one in afresh where it should be.

It is a bad idea to revise a questionnaire after you have started administering it. Oh, I must admit I have occasionally caught a spelling mistake or typographical error in one of my questionnaires and corrected it in a second printing. But if you change the substance of items, later data will not be comparable with earlier data. And if you go so far as to change the number of items in the midst of administering the survey, everything will go crazy. Your data will be hopelessly fouled up, and the program is likely to crash.

These warnings are not meant to frighten you but merely to suggest you think through the survey you want to create and settle on a final version of it before you start collecting data. Of course, it is quite appropriate to start with a pilot version of the survey, administer it to a few people, look at the pilot results, and then revise the survey a bit before administering it to your final respondents. If you plan to do this, you should create the pilot survey on a work disk called something like "Pilot for——Survey." After creating the pilot version of the survey, but *before* administering it to any respondents, make a copy of it called, say, "Draft of——Survey." Then use this draft work disk to make the final version of the survey.

There are two reasons for using separate disks for pilot and final versions of a survey. First, you probably want to keep the pilot version, and any data collected with it, for future reference. Second, once the computer starts administering the survey, it keeps track of how many people have responded, and you want the final version to start from scratch, from a new case number 1. Once you are familiar with how these programs work, and are also familiar with the general principles of operating the computer, you can use the utilities program described in Chapter 12 to do such advanced jobs as telling the computer to forget the pilot respondents. But I don't advise this for a beginner.

▶ ▶ ▶ ▶ ▶ ▶ ▶ ▶ ▶ ▶ ▶

[3] ADMINISTER AN EXISTING QUESTIONNAIRE

We use the same program to administer surveys as to write them. Get to the main menu of the question-processor program and press [3] to administer a survey. As usual, the computer will ask you the name of the survey.

Then it asks you

```
              Which do you want?
   [1] Respondent must press ENTER after each answer
   [2] Respondent just presses answer keys
              Press 1 or 2
```

This governs a very important option.

If you select [1] Respondent must press ENTER after each answer, the following happens when the respondent deals with a question: First, the question and the response choices appear on the screen. Next to the choices is a set of bright-boxed numbers representing the keys the respondent must choose from in answering. The respondent presses a key. The question stays on the screen, but the bright boxes vanish from all answers except the one for the key the respondent just pressed. Thus the respondent can see whether he or she pressed the right key and can reconsider the answer. A message at the bottom of the screen will say Press [ENTER] if the correct number is bright. Or, type a number to change it. Typing a number changes the answer. Typing [ENTER] moves the respondent on to the next question.

The other option, [2] Respondent just presses answer keys, is much simpler. As soon as the respondent presses an answer key, the question vanishes from the screen, to be replaced by the next question.

The first option may be better for respondents who are unfamiliar with answering a computer's questions, and thus may want to go slowly and carefully. But if you or a trained assistant wants to use this program to conduct surveys over the telephone, you may want the quicker, second option.

After you make your choice, the computer will ask Is respondent number 1 ready for the survey? Press Y for Yes, or N for No. If you press [N], you will exit the administration part of the program, and you will get a chance to save the respondent's data. If you press [Y], the computer will prepare the first question for the respondent. Note that the computer tells you which number respondent you should be on, thus also reminding you how many have already responded.

Of course, you should practice taking the survey yourself, several times, before you inflict it on somebody else. Indeed, you may want to make two or three copies of your final survey-administration work disk: one to practice on, one actually to administer, and one as a backup. As you practice taking the survey yourself, you can do two things. First, give the items one last check to see that each is worded properly and that all of them make sense in the form and order you have them. Second, think about exactly what you want to tell the respondent when bringing him or her to the computer.

It is a good idea to prepare a brief introduction for the respondent. This could be a printed page or in the form of a paragraph or two that you will read aloud. It should explain how the respondent is to answer the questions that appear on the computer screen, and it should give whatever topical introduction you think your survey needs. Keep this brief—just the minimum necessary to prepare the respondent.

Look at some old questionnaires to see how other researchers have communicated instructions to the respondents. One purpose of instructions is simply to get the respondent to do the right things, checking one box instead of two in response to an agree–disagree question, for instance. But a more subtle purpose is to get the respondent into the right frame of mind for the questions, in particular to convince the respondent to get into the spirit of the questions and give answers honestly, unselfconsciously, and with the proper mixture of spontaneity and deliberation.

In the paired-opposites section, I mentioned Fiedler's study of work groups. Paraphrasing some of his instructions to adapt them to our computerized method of administering surveys, here is how you might prepare respondents for this type of item (see Fiedler, 1958:64–65).

People differ in the ways they think about themselves and about those with whom they work. [These qualities] may be important in working with others. Please give your immediate, first reaction to the following questions about different people.

You are asked to describe yourself and several of the people with whom you have worked, by pressing a number key on the computer. Each question on the computer screen gives you a pair of words that are opposite in meaning. A set of bright numbers runs from one of these words to the other. Look at this scale and decide where on it the particular person falls. Then press the number's key on the top row of the computer keyboard.

For example: If you were to describe yourself, and you ordinarily think of yourself as being *quite talkative,* you might press the 2 key in response to a scale like this:

Talkative   1   2   3   4   5   6   7   Quiet

If you ordinarily think of yourself as somewhat *more quiet than talkative,* you might press the 5 key because it is a little on the quiet side of the middle. If you think of yourself as extremely quiet, you might press the 7 key.

Look at the words at both ends of the scale before you make up your mind and press a key. Please remember, there are *no right or wrong answers.*

Tell respondents to take their time and read the questions and instructions on the computer screen. In my experience, most respondents have no difficulty figuring out how to answer via the computer.

If respondents will need to press [ENTER], you should show them where this key is. Because it looks very much like the BACKSPACE key right above it on many computers, respondents unfamiliar with personal computers may have trouble telling which one to press, even after you have shown them. One solution is to put a brightly colored piece of plastic tape on top of [ENTER], making sure the tape is a kind easily removed later on.

I have written the program so that respondents can go back to a previous question, if they want to, by pressing [B] for back. There is no need to encourage them to do this, and if they press [B] more than once they will have to reanswer any later questions they already answered. One advantage of computer administration is that respondents cannot skip questions. You may have to tell them, "If none of the answers to a particular question seem quite right to you, please select the one that seems best out of the choices you are given."

When the respondent is done, definitely thank him or her. It is both polite and good policy to chat briefly with the respondents. They are your valuable helpers in your research, and they deserve kind attention. You may have to refrain from discussing the full aims of your study with them, because they might communicate them to future respondents whom you want to keep naive or open-minded. If anything about the survey troubled your respondents, it is your duty to put their minds at rest. They should leave the computer feeling they have done a good job, happy to have contributed to your research and harboring no lingering embarrassment or nervousness.

It is important to avoid panicking yourself, or getting too ecstatic over the adventure of doing research. Administering a survey, like taking one, should be easy and pleasant. But it is hard not to get excited to the point of panic with your first survey. And then, you are prey to all kinds of error, even erasing your valuable data by mistake! Thus another purpose for a pilot survey, even with just a half dozen friends as respondents, is to get yourself accustomed to the process of administering.

When you have some valuable data on your work disk, copy it. I always have to point out to beginners that backing up your disks is essential; ironically, copying a disk is one of the riskiest procedures—the chances of ruining it are high. So check over the projects section of Chapter 1 about copying, and check the disk-copying instructions for your machine and operating system as well. In classes and computer labs, let an experienced consultant handle the copying if possible.

When everything is working perfectly, you can administer your survey to as many as 200 respondents, using your IBM-type microcomputer. This is the maximum number of respondents our statistical programs can handle. But if you plan to upload the data to a big computer or transfer it to other suitable software on the micro, you can collect far more than 200 by using several duplicate work disks, 200 respondents on each one. Then you can consult Chapter 12, which explains how to transform your data into a form usable by mainframe statistical packages and by some micro software.

▶ ▶ ▶ ▶ ▶ ▶ ▶ ▶ ▶ ▶ ▶

[4] PRINT AN EXISTING QUESTIONNAIRE

My question-processor program cannot possibly compete with full-featured word-processor programs that often fill an entire disk. Indeed, the word-processor program on which I wrote this book fills the equivalent of two traditional 360K disks. You might want to print out a simple version of a questionnaire you have created with the question processor, though, so I added a module that does this, without giving you any options for complex manners of printing or rewriting.

Before you can print out a questionnaire, you have to have created it and saved it on your disk. Printing can be hazardous, especially because my small program cannot possibly take account of all the different kinds of printer currently available. Therefore, I thought it best to do the printing from the disk, so that if anything went wrong, you would not lose any information. When you press [4] from the main menu to print an existing questionnaire, you will be asked the name of the survey and get the warning `Press [ESC] if you do not want to PRINT a survey after all`. After that, you have no further instructions to give until the job is done, and the computer will draw the survey up from the disk and put it directly on paper.

You need a printer attached to your computer, probably directly attached because my limited program could not take into account all the various networking systems that are proliferating for IBM-type systems. The printer must have fan-fold paper, the standard connected sheets, because it will print straight through until the end, without dividing questions into pages.

My experience with different computers and printers tells me that they will react very differently if any problems arise. I don't want to frighten you, but you might check out how to interpret my program on your computer in case the printer goes wild or the computer freezes up. A standard combination of keys, typically pressing [CONTROL], [ALT], and [DEL] simultaneously, will start an IBM-type computer over from scratch, thus stopping any program, but you should check what to do with your system. Also, your printer should have some simple way of switching off, at the very least an on/off switch.

Most likely, you will want a paper copy simply for your own reference, but I designed the format so that the printed-out questionnaire could actually be administered. The title of your survey will be at the top, such as PRODUCT SURVEY if your survey were named PRODUCT. Then comes a simple instruction telling respondents to circle numbers to indicate their answers. The questions will print in order, with each response introduced by a number that could be circled.

If you want to make copies of this printed survey in order to administer it, you should first decide whether to reduce the print size when you duplicate it on a photocopier. Many photocopy machines let you make copies smaller than the original, and this can be useful to get more questions on a page. You can even get two pages of questions on each side of a page (perhaps legal size) by arranging the print in two side-by-side columns on a piece of paper with its long dimension running left and right. Once you have decided this, you can cut the printed survey apart into what will be separate pages, making sure to keep the stimulus and responses of each item together. Paste them up the way you want them; add page numbers, and make your final copies.

Unless you typed question numbers in front of the items, they will not be numbered when you print them out. I purposely did not insert item numbers, because you might want your own numbering system. Perhaps items in different sections would be numbered afresh starting from 1. Or perhaps you would number consecutively throughout the questionnaire but put a page or two of other questions first.

Once your printed surveys have been completed, you can use this program to enter them into the computer, telling the machine you want to administer your survey but then typing the data in yourself from the pages. Or you might consider the advanced options for entering data, explained in Chapter 12 and made possible through the utilities program. That is a more complex option, and it is not right for beginners, but if you have the experience to use it effectively, it is more efficient.

▶ ▶ ▶ ▶ ▶ ▶ ▶ ▶ ▶ ▶

PROJECTS

1. Yes–No or True–False Items.   Select an academic subject that you know quite a lot about. Then write 2 versions of a 20-item test that could be given to students taking a course on that subject. Each item should be clear and unambiguous, with a definite, correct answer. One version should present the 20 items as yes–no questions. The other version should present the same 20 as true–false statements. Your report should include the answers to the questions!

2. Agree–Disagree Items.   Make a list of 20 proverbs that offer advice on several aspects of life. You should try to include proverbs that contradict each other, and the proverbs should show great variety both in the advice given and the form they are written in. For example, my list includes: "Look before you leap," "Slow and steady wins the race," "The early bird catches the worm," and "Seize the day!" Note that the first 2 urge you to be cautious in life, and the second 2 urge speedy, decisive action.

Next, rewrite the proverbs so that they are statements suitable as the stimulus in an agree–disagree item. "Look before you leap" is a command, not a statement. You could turn it into a statement like this: "You should look before you leap." But merely turning each proverb into a statement is not enough. You should translate them from the poetic form of a proverb into ordinary English. "Look before you leap" might become "You should examine the situation carefully before taking action." "Seize the day" might become "It is best to take advantage of opportunities immediately, before they are lost."

Finally, you should consider whether a slight change in wording would give the statement just the right scope. The scope of an item is the range of people and situations it applies to. For example, you might decide to avoid using *you* to make the items more general in scope, applying to people in general rather than just the particular respondent: "A person should examine the situation carefully before taking action." Proverbs can be dogmatic, asserting that their advice is true for everyone in every case. For some, you may want to include a phrase that tones the proverb down, so it will attract more respondents to agree with it: "Most of the time, it is best to take advantage of opportunities immediately, before they are lost."

3. Magnitude Items.   Construct a 40-item questionnaire evaluating the respondent's family relationships, using magnitude items. First, think about the ways people in a family relate to each other, listing any that can be expressed in magnitude questions. I won't offer any examples here, because that would give the assignment away. But think of any ways you could describe family relations through questions that ask "how much?" or "how great?" about some aspect of the family.

You could assume that your respondents have families consisting of a mother, father, one brother, and one sister. Thus you could think of ten aspects of family life and ask, in turn, about the respondent's relationship to each person with respect to each of these. You may also want to include questions about the respondent's relations with his or her family as a whole and include magnitude questions concerning how the other family members relate to each other.

Finally, write a brief essay explaining why you believe your questionnaire covers the most important aspects of family life.

4. Self-Reported Behavior Items. Create a questionnaire consisting of 30 items asking teenage respondents to report their deviant behavior. By "deviant" I mean any acts the typical teenager's parents would be likely to forbid or at least frown on. Although the list should include a few illegal activities, it can mainly consist of common actions teenagers are tempted to perform but that their parents would object to.

Try to achieve great variety in your list and also to group the items so that several of them cover each of a half-dozen areas of behavior, such as sexual activity, fighting, consuming various mood-altering substances, and the like. When your list is complete, select a reasonable time period for the computer to insert the responses, as explained in the section of this chapter that introduces self-reported behavior items. Finally, write a brief essay explaining why you believe your items cover the significant areas in which teenagers may violate the wishes of their parents.

5. Preference Scales. Visit a supermarket and collect information for a 40-item survey on customers' preferences for 8 different kinds of product they might buy there. First, identify 8 very different kinds of products that consumers commonly purchase and that are represented by at least 4 different brands each.

Here's an example, but don't use this one. One kind of product commonly purchased is soft drinks. Two of the most popular are Coke and Pepsi, so these could be the first 2 items out of 4 that will all be soft drinks. You could complete the list with 2 other brands of cola, such as RC (Royal Crown) and Shasta. Or you could broaden the scope by adding distinctly different soft drinks, such as Canada Dry Ginger Ale and Seven-Up.

This survey has 2 purposes. First, you can compare respondents' preferences within each of the 8 kinds of products. Second, you can compare respondents' average preferences for the 8 groups of items. You have room in the questionnaire for a few questions about the respondents—for example, asking how old they are. Young people might rate all the soft drinks relatively high, for example, while giving lower ratings to some other kind of product. This allows you to identify different types of consumer on the basis of their preferences for different categories of products.

6. Satisfaction Scales. Write a questionnaire of 40 satisfaction items designed to evaluate the working and living conditions of people in a particular occupation. First, select *one* of the following occupations to be the targeted respondents:

1. farmers with small, family-owned farms
2. enlisted personnel in the United States Navy
3. agents for an insurance company, selling directly to individuals
4. university professors

Second, write a list of 40 stimuli that together cover the full range of working and living conditions that are likely to be important for the particular type of respondent. Your report should include a brief justification of the items you have chosen.

7. Paired Opposites.   Interview a man and a woman, separately, asking them to list the qualities they would like their romantic partner to have and the qualities they would hate their romantic partner to have. The point of these interviews is to get a long list of nouns and adjectives, perhaps as many as 100, that describe both good and bad qualities one might find in a romantic partner.

Next, go through the list and cross out any words that might be unfamiliar to many potential respondents, difficult words such as *impecuniousness* or *indefatigability* and specialized slang words that some people would not know. When you find several words that say pretty much the same thing, cross out most of them, leaving a few that communicate the idea of all of them. If your original list includes *boring, tediousness, real blah, uninteresting, unexciting*, and several others of the ilk, you could reduce this part of the list to just two or three. In boiling your list down, you want to keep great variety, so that all the main qualities a good or bad romantic partner could have are included.

Write this shorter list on a pad of paper, one word per line. Then after each word write its opposite, making sure that a noun has a noun for its opposite, and an adjective has an adjective. If you cannot find a clear opposite for a given word, cross it out. You probably will find that many of the opposites are already in the original short list of words. Cross out all duplications; if you have *short–tall* and *tall–short*, cross out one of these pairs, leaving the other.

Finally, select 20 of these pairs for a survey of 40 paired-opposites items, trying to cover the full range of qualities important for romantic relationships. We get 40 items out of 20 pairs in the following way. The first 20 items will be your 20 pairs, asking the respondent to describe his or her ideal romantic partner. Items 21–40 would be the same list of 20 pairs, but this time presented as describing "the qualities you yourself actually possess." Do you know what you have created? A dating service questionnaire! Perhaps you could make money giving it to lovelorn individuals, then comparing their responses to match them up.

▶ ▶ ▶ ▶ ▶ Your question-processor program, introduced in Chapter 4, allows you to create free-form items with as many as six specially written responses. If you are working in the question processor, creating a questionnaire, this is question format number 8. When the computer says SELECT ITEM TYPE, press [8].

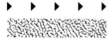

As with several other item formats, you will next get a large stimulus box. For our first example, type the following: "Should the amount of money being spent on the U.S. space program be increased, kept at current levels, or ended altogether?" Then press [ENTER]. The next step is to select the number of responses the item needs. The computer lets you choose from 2 to 6. Press [4] to get 4 responses.

A small box for the first response now appears at the top of the screen, with the instruction Type response number 1 above. When it's right, press [ENTER]. Type *Increased* and press [ENTER] to register this first response.

Now a box for the second response will appear; type in *Kept at current levels*. Type *Decreased* for the third response, and the fourth should be *Ended*. The full item is now written out under the horizontal line, and you get the menu for revising this item:

[1]   Change response categories
[2]   Rewrite the stimulus
[3]   Junk the item and start over
[4]   Go to the next item
[ESC] Return to main menu

If you decide to change the response categories, the computer will again ask you how many you want. Try this and tell it 5 responses. You will

Free-Form Items

not have to type each of the 4 existing responses in afresh but can simply press [ENTER] to keep a given response. For your fifth response, add *No opinion*. (If you wanted to put a new response first, such as *Greatly increased*, you would have to type them all in again. But the original set of responses will stay on the bottom of the screen as a reminder, until you change each one.) By now, the features of the question processor should be quite familiar to you. Create a new questionnaire, calling it SPACE, and type in the following 7 free-form items:

```
1. Should the amount of money being spent on the
U.S. space program be increased, kept at current
levels, decreased, or ended altogether?

1 Increased
2 Kept at current levels
3 Decreased
4 Ended
5 No opinion


2. Some people say the United States should con-
centrate on unmanned missions like the Voyager
probe. Others say it is important to maintain a
manned space program as well. Which comes closer to
your view?

1 Unmanned program only
2 Manned as well as unmanned program
3 No opinion
```

3. Do you think the United States should build a permanently manned space station in orbit around the Earth over the next few years, or not?

1 Yes
2 No
3 No opinion

4. Recently, there has been much talk about building a system of space satellites to defend against nuclear attack. Do you think research on this idea should continue, or should research stop?

1 Research should continue
2 Research should stop
3 No opinion

5. There has been much discussion about attempting to land people on the planet Mars. How would you feel about such an attempt--would you favor or oppose the United States setting aside money for such a project?

1 Favor
2 Oppose
3 No opinion

6. If you were asked to go along on the first rocket trip to the planet Mars, would you want to go, or not?

1 Yes
2 No
3 No opinion

7. Do you think we should attempt to communicate with intelligent beings on other planets, perhaps using radio?

1 Yes, definitely
2 Yes, perhaps
3 No
4 No opinion

As you type these into the computer, you can see how easy it is to create free-form items. Have you recognized these seven? They are the space questions from the STUDENTS survey quoted in Chapter 1. Although there is no one best way to write free-form questions, a few points about these seven are worth calling to your attention.

A few of them include phrases like "some people say" or "there has been much talk about." These phrases help respondents feel it is okay to hold various opinions on the topic of the item, and they encourage them to think about their own personal views. Such introductory phrases can be overdone, and when writing your own survey you might save them for a few items you think need such help either because they are so controversial or so noncontroversial that the respondent must be encouraged to express an opinion.

"Which comes closer to your view" helps the respondent select an opinion even if none seems ideal. The same can be accomplished in directions for the survey as a whole: "Please select the answer closest to the view that you, personally, hold." A message like this on an occasional item may help the respondent with the next few items as well.

Several of the items' stimuli incorporate the responses, or a short version of the responses: "Do you think research on this idea should continue, or should research stop?" The point of this duplication of the responses in the stimulus is to make the choices very vivid in the respondent's mind when he or she is about to select one. Poorly written closed-ended questions may give the respondent an impossible set of choices. The classic "When did you stop beating your wife?" assumed the respondent was no gentleman.

Shortly after the space shuttle *Challenger* exploded in 1986, a national news magazine did a quick survey to assess the nation's reaction. The inclusion of schoolteacher Christa McAuliffe in the crew had generated much publicity, and the disaster heightened debate over which people should be sent into space. Two members of Congress had already been sent aloft, and many other nonastronauts were waiting in line for a launch. Although the press ignored the fact, another of the *Challenger* crew was not an astronaut, Gregory B. Jarvis of the Hughes corporation. Thus the following question was newsworthy:

Do you think that putting civilians into space is important—or is it too dangerous?

[1] Important   [2] Too dangerous   [3] Don't know

This item struck me as presenting respondents with an incomplete set of choices, but needing items from national polls for the spaceflight survey I was then hurriedly writing, I decided to include it and see what happened. I provided a space after the boxes and asked respondents for any comments they might have on the issue.

Most of the 1007 Harvard students who filled out my spring 1986 survey dutifully checked one of the three boxes, but several wrote in comments and others invented new boxes to check. One added a "Neither" box, checked it, and commented, "I think it probably isn't too dangerous, but I don't think it's important." Many respondents added "Neither" or "Not important" boxes. Other added boxes were: "Neither good nor bad, but neutral," "OK," "OK, but not too important," "Not too important," "Unimportant," "Doesn't matter one way or the other," "Other," "None of above," and "Stupid." One changed the second box to indicate "Not pertinent"; another transformed the third box into "I know."

Others wrote: "Limited responses here. I do have an opinion, but it isn't polarized to the extremes as the given responses are." "This is not an either/or question. One cannot be, for example, either happy or thrilled. It should be either important or unimportant." "I checked no box because: (a) I don't think it's important, (b) I don't think it's too dangerous, and (c) I know how I feel about it." "Dangerous does not mean important." "It isn't too important, but I don't think it's too dangerous. They aren't mutually exclusive!" "The converse of 'important' is not 'dangerous.'" "The two terms are not on the same continuum."

The question also suffers from ambiguity over the meaning of the word *civilian*. As one student said, "This is a poor question—how do you define civilian? If you remember, Neil Armstrong [first man on the moon] was a civilian." I guess that *civilian* is supposed to mean "nonastronaut," but many respondents took it to mean "nonmilitary." One commented, "NASA *is* civilian," and another noted, "Many astronauts are civilians, not military." "What the hell's a civilian, anyway?" Others assumed a military definition; one said, for example, "The shuttle should *not* be limited to military uses."

Many respondents suggested that launching nonprofessionals might be too dangerous right now but important in a few years when the space shuttle had proved its safety. One specifically complained that the lack of a time frame made the question ambiguous: "Bad question. It is important, but, at least for the time being, appears to be too dangerous. I don't expect it to be too dangerous forever."

When a question gets as many complaints as this one, it is probably doing a poor job with the respondents who don't complain, too. Those who define *civilian* as "nonmilitary" are answering a markedly different question from those who define it as "nonastronaut."

▶ ▶ ▶ ▶ ▶ ▶ ▶ ▶ ▶ ▶ ▶

VARIED FORMATS

No one can count all the different question formats possible. I can offer you a range of examples, but you will have to scan research studies in your own field to find the ones most appropriate for your particular kind of work. Of course, you can use the free-form option to produce slight variants of the seven other question types the question processor offers. For example, here is a question taken from a recent textbook on marketing (Lusch and Lusch, 1987:101):

> Would you consider purchasing a new television in the next six months?
>
> [1] Definitely yes
> [2] Probably yes
> [3] Not sure
> [4] Probably not
> [5] Definitely not

Also, you can write the responses in any European language, putting Ja, Si, or Oui instead of Yes in the yes–no format, for instance. Although the directions that appear on the screen will be in English, they are few and simple enough that you can provide your own translation for non–English speakers, and use the free-form option to write the items and responses in the respondent's own language.

Many surveys contain a variety of questions seeking simple information that require a different set of responses for each item. A few years ago the researchers at the Institute of Community Studies in London did a survey of people who had lost their jobs, many of them middle-aged folk who would never find full-time work again. The point of their research was to understand the experiences these people were going through and get some hints about how they could be helped. One section, which provides us with several examples of varied response items, was focused on previous times in the respondents' lives when they were out of work:

> 49. Have you ever had a spell without work before?
>
> [1] Yes but under 1 month   [2] Yes   [3] No   [4] Maternity leave
> [5] Not sure
>
> 50. How many times did this happen?
>
> [1] 1–2 times   [2] 3–5 times   [3] 6–10 times   [4] Over 10
> [5] Not sure
>
> 51. When was the last time this happened?
>
> [1] Within the last year   [5] 10 to under 20
> [2] 1 to under 2 years ago   [6] 20 or more
> [3] 2 to under 5 years ago   [7] Not sure
> [4] 5 to under 10 years ago
>
> 52. What was the longest time you were out of work?

[1] 1 to under 3 months   [4] A year or more

[2] 3 to under 6 months   [5] Not sure

[3] 6 to under 13 months

53. What was the reason for it?

[1] Unemployment   [5] Child care

[2] Sick leave   [6] Just time off

[3] Domestic reasons   [7] Other

[4] Retirement   [8] Not sure

Just by looking at these items, can you guess how the survey was administered? Notice that the questions and the responses are very simple. Notice also that question 53 has response choices that are a little vague, and that "maternity leave" in question 49 is not mutually exclusive with the first two responses. These are not defects of the items, but clues about how the survey was given to respondents.

It was administered through interviews, face to face in the respondents' homes. The questions had to be simple so that the respondent could have them clearly in mind, without the chance to look them over a couple of times on a printed page. Question 53 expects the interviewer to classify the answer the respondent gives verbally, even if the response is long and complex; the interviewer will have been trained to do this reliably. Question 49 is not ruined by the nonexclusive maternity leave choice, because the interviewer is trained to handle the categories of response, marking "maternity leave" as a special kind of "yes" that was bound to mean being away from work for more than a month.

These items show how questions with highly varied response choices may be necessary to get information on a variety of cut-and-dried topics. Now we will go to the opposite extreme, seeing how responses can be written to get the highly subjective feelings of the respondent about subtle matters.

In 1925 E. S. Bogardus introduced a new kind of question he called the **social distance scale.** These are items written to determine how close the respondent feels to particular categories of people. In the original version, the respondent was presented with a list of different nationalities or races (Germans, Italians, Russians, Caucasians, Asians, American Indians, blacks, and so on) and was asked what his or her policy toward each would be:

According to my first feeling reactions, I would willingly admit Germans (as a class, and not the best I have known, nor the worst members) to one or more of the [following] classifications.

[1] To close kinship by marriage

[2] To my club as personal chums

[3] To my street as neighbors
[4] To employment in my occupation
[5] To citizenship in my country
[6] As visitors only in my country
[7] Would exclude from my country

The seven responses are arranged from the closest to the furthest in social distance. Somebody you would let live on your street certainly must be allowed to visit your country; somebody excluded from the country logically is rejected from doing any of the closer things in the list.

Apparently, people were quite willing to express rejection of national and racial groups when they were given social distance scales earlier in this century. Today we have been so thoroughly educated to the norms of tolerance and fairness that even the bigots among us may be unwilling to express much social distance in a scale like this. Milder versions, consequently, have been written to tap the more tentative prejudices people are willing to admit today.

A good example is a social distance scale used by Charles Glock and Rodney Stark (1966:278) in their landmark study of American religion. Notice how the wording prepares the respondent to express a personal feeling and how the language is very mild compared to the original Bogardus item. Purely to get the respondent started and in the right frame of mind, Glock and Stark begin with *a Baptist,* a standard and widely accepted religious denomination but with the potential of eliciting very mild disapproval. (My father was a Baptist, my mother an Episcopalian, and when Mom wanted to needle Dad she began talking about how irritating the Baptists were.)

It sometimes happens when we first meet a person that we know only *one* thing about him. We may know what he does for a living, or what his religion is, or where he comes from, and so on. We all tend to form a first impression of this person on the basis of this one thing we know about him. Now, . . . put yourself in the situation of just having met a person and the *only* thing you know about him is that he is a Baptist. Knowing only this *one* thing about him, what would your immediate reaction tend to be?

[1] I think I would feel friendly and at ease
[2] I think I would feel friendly, but somewhat uneasy
[3] I think I would feel uneasy and somewhat unfriendly
[4] I think I would feel quite unfriendly
[5] I guess I would feel nothing either way

Now we would like you to read each of the following characteristics and assume for each that it is the ONLY thing you know about a person, and do the same thing you just did above.

1. A Communist
   [1] Friendly and at ease
   [2] Friendly but somewhat uneasy
   [3] Uneasy and somewhat unfriendly
   [4] Quite unfriendly
   [5] Nothing either way

After the Communist came a Methodist, a German, an African, an alcoholic, a Roman Catholic, a left-winger, and a long list that included what were really the key stimuli for this section of the Glock and Stark survey: a Jew, a Zionist, and an Israeli. The goal of the study was to discover the possible causes of anti-Semitism, but Glock and Stark knew they could not simply ask the respondents whether they felt uneasy in the presence of Jews. Instead, they had to go to the extreme lengths you see in the preceding example to convince the respondents it was all right to express different feelings about a variety of groups, and then slip the target stimuli in with a great variety of others, hoping this way to get the respondent's true feelings despite modern norms that one is supposed to feel uniformly positive about members of other groups.

This example suggests that great care may be needed to write and introduce items that explore sensitive and personal topics. The questionnaire should communicate that it is all right for the respondent to hold any one of a number of views. One way to do this within the narrow context of a single item is to include a variety of views among the responses, all presented as opinions that are equally valid.

Menu Items

A survey question that offers several, complex choices, specially designed for that particular item, can be called a **menu item**. Many of this type ask the respondent to select just one of the choices. A good example is a question about belief in God written by Glock and Stark (1966:273):

Which of the following statements comes closest to expressing what you believe about God? (Please check only one answer)

[1] I know God really exists and I have no doubts about it

[2] While I have doubts, I feel that I do believe in God

[3] I find myself believing in God some of the time, but not at other times

[4] I don't believe in a personal God, but I do believe in a higher power of some kind

[5] I don't know whether there is a God and I don't believe there is any way to find out

[6] I don't believe in God

[7] None of the above represents what I believe. What I believe about God is _____

_____
_____ (please specify)

Note the key features of this kind of question. First, the choices are mutually exclusive, for all practical purposes, and thus a person would have little trouble choosing among them. People might vacillate between one response or another, but only the most quibbling respondent will fail to find one statement that is closest to his or her personal belief.

Second, the choices are arranged in a logical order, so that people will be able to scan quickly down the list, easily comparing each choice with the others. Here, all the responses but the last are arranged from the most religiously conservative at the top to the most irreligious near the bottom.

Third, the "none of the above" response comes last, so that people will be most likely to check an appropriate box before they come to this hard-to-analyze choice. Although having such a miscellaneous response in the list is often essential, we don't want people to use it as a cop-out when they could just as easily have expressed themselves by checking a more specific box.

Finally, the list of responses covers the full range of commonly held opinions about the topic. Do you find your own belief in this list? If you were a classical pagan, you might not, because there is no box to check if you believe in a pantheon of a dozen different, competing gods. You would have to check the last box and write something in. But this is not a defect of the question, because there were no classical pagans among the respondents. All of them were members of Christian churches. The purpose of this item was to identify different groups among these particular respondents, and thus there was no need to include every possible theological opinion that human beings have ever held.

Notice that the alternatives represent main orientations to God that numbers of people actually hold today. The first response is typical among religious conservatives; the second is common among religious liberals. The third probably represents the ambivalence felt by many rather secular people who are not deeply committed to religion. The fourth, fifth, and sixth choices are technically called deism, agnosticism, and atheism. But respondents may feel uncomfortable with these labels, or even be unfamiliar with them, so each item is phrased in ordinary language that anybody can understand.

Even though theological debates have raged since the early 1960s when Glock and Stark wrote their survey, this item is general enough that it probably serves well today as a measure of belief in God. But you might want to supplement it with other questions about the nature of the deity. One source of alternatives for a second menu item on God would be the theological debates that have been carried on in religion journals and in books. You could discover what they are by a trip or two to the library, but you'd have to phrase the alternatives carefully in ordinary language.

Another approach is to do a set of brief interviews, or circulate a brief open-ended survey, with people of the same sort who will be your respondents, a method that will be illustrated in detail in Project 7 of Chapter 9. This way, you can sketch the different beliefs that are actually common in the population under study. Here is an example I developed in a class on survey research, one that illustrates problems you must solve in developing your own questionnaire items.

I gave each class member two file cards and asked them to write on one card a brief statement of what they, personally, believed about God. On the other card they were to write some other opinion about God that they'd heard but that they themselves didn't happen to hold. I told them not to indicate which was which. This kept each person's beliefs private, yet included these beliefs in the set we would be examining.

As a class, we then attempted to sort the cards into piles, each consisting of cards that expressed roughly the same idea. It became immediately clear that many different images of God existed, and that they seemed to have several dimensions. Thus a full study of people's beliefs would have to include several different questions. Suppose we had not had this insight and unthinkingly had turned the most common responses into a single menu item. We would have gotten something like the following mess, assembled from the statements written by the class.

Which of the following statements comes closest to expressing what you believe about God? (Please check only one answer)

[1] One all-powerful God created the universe

[2] I believe in one God who heeds the prayers only of those who truly follow my church and its beliefs

[3] There are three persons in one God: God the Father, Jesus the Son, and the Holy Spirit

[4] God does not punish man; He governs out of love, and He loves unconditionally

[5] God governs by a reward and punishment system, rewarding obedience and punishing sin

[6] God is the creative life force that exists in every human being

[7] God does exist, but one cannot explain what God is except that he is something like air: It has no shape, distinct smell, or feeling, yet we all know that it is there though we cannot see it

[8] Whether God exists or not, I do not know

[9] God is a creation of man to explain many of the phenomena of the world that were not understandable when consciousness provoked a desire to understand

[10] God does not exist but in the minds of people who need a crutch in life

[11] God is a cultural belief system that provides order and structure for society

[12] God is only a belief, a socializing force used by the power elites as a pacifier for the masses

[13] None of the above represents what I believe. What I believe about God is _____

_____

_____ (please specify)

This question overflows with flaws. First, it is too long. The Glock and Stark item offers about the maximum number of complex alternatives we can safely use in a question aimed at the general public. Second, the alternatives are not mutually exclusive. You can believe in the first alternative, that one all-powerful God created the universe, and also hold any of the four opinions that follow it.

For both these reasons, we should break this question apart into several questions. An obvious dividing line is at alternative 8, which represents agnosticism. All the items above it express some kind of faith in God; those below it (except the last) are various irreligious analyses of why it is that other people might believe. One possibility would be to start with a question that made people say whether they tended to believe in God or not, and then have two conditional questionnaire sections, one to be answered by believers and the other by nonbelievers, an approach I explain in detail at the end of this chapter. On the other hand, so many people may be fence-sitters on the question of God's existence that perhaps you'd better phrase the questions so that all respondents can answer all questions. Here's one way of handling the irreligious analyses of religious faith:

Philosophers have long debated why it is that so many people believe in God. Below is a list of explanations that have been offered. Please check the box before the ONE explanation that comes closest to your own opinion of why people believe in God.

[1] God actually exists, and many people have a personal relationship with God

[2] The idea of God provides people with an explanation of many phenomena in this world that otherwise they would feel they could not understand

[3] Faith in God gives comfort and emotional support that many people need to get through life

[4] God is a cultural belief system that provides order and structure for society

[5] Belief in God is a tool of political repression, used by the power elites to pacify the masses

[6] None of the above represents what I think about belief in God. What I think is _____

_____

_____ (please specify)

Note that I have rewritten some of the responses, to sharpen them and focus them all on the question of why people believe in God. The original statement about God being merely a crutch seemed too judgmental in tone, so I substituted "comfort and emotional support" for "crutch." Also, I wrote an introduction to the question that would detoxify it somewhat. Probably, many respondents would feel offended by some of the responses in this list, or by the tenor of the whole set, so I framed it in terms of the blandness and abstractness of philosophical theories. A few provocative questions can liven up the experience of being a respondent, but too much irritation will drive respondents to rebel and either throw the survey away or start giving capricious answers.

The set of irreligious analyses begins with a general religious response, so that the many religious respondents will be able to answer the question. Of course, depending on the particular population you are studying, you might find the majority checking this box and only small numbers checking the others. Thus the question might be better without the first alternative, forcing more people to select among the irreligious theories, but it also might offend more people. One way to decide whether to include the first, religious alternative is to think carefully about the purposes of your survey and how best to achieve these purposes with your particular respondents. If you can, you should also include a couple of versions of the items in a pilot survey, and get the respondents to write comments next to any questions they thought needed improving.

So we have transformed four of the responses from our messy religion menu into a new question. What about the others, the first eight from that list? I suggest our survey should include the Glock and Stark item, which has an agnostic response and thus takes care of number 8. Starting a set of God questions with the Glock and Stark item would also let many people feel they had expressed their main belief, thus making them more tolerant of otherwise toxic items like our irreligious theories.

The seven remaining God opinions still represent several dimensions, mainly concerning what kind of a "person" God is, in relationship to human beings. Is God merely an impersonal life force, or is He an active being shaping the course of our lives according to His plan? Does God love people unconditionally, or is He a stern judge inflicting punishment on the sinful? Is God a single being, or is He somehow divided into different aspects, such as the Father, Son, and Holy Ghost? Is God the Lord of all humans, or does He pay special attention to the members of one, particular denomination? Is God's nature clearly known to us, or is God primarily a great mystery?

I leave it to your imagination to create a set of questions on these different points. You might find that menu questions on all these aspects of God would fill up your questionnaire, monopolizing the respondents' time and thus would be simply too costly to include. You might consider writing them as a short set of agree–disagree items.

Single-choice menu items, which require the respondent to check one and only one box, are best when a definite range of mutually exclusive opinions exists in the population. By having the main opinions listed together, you orient the respondents to this range, and encourage them to make clear, significant choices.

Perhaps the four irreligious theories about religious faith are not mutually exclusive, although they clearly are based on four different principles. One is intellectual, considering God to be an explanation, and another is emotional, considering God to be a source of good feelings. The other two are sociopolitical. Sociologist Émile Durkheim and his followers would have chosen the next alternative, about God providing order and structure for society, whereas Marxists would argue that God is a tool of the repressive elite. Depending on the purposes of your survey, you might want to ask people how much credence they give to each of these theories, rather than forcing them to choose just one as their favorite.

One more example will emphasize how important it is to find the right set of responses; at the same time, it illustrates the great utility of free-form items designed for a particular purpose. For a study on respondents' sense of their duties in handling problems concerning friends or strangers, Samuel A. Stouffer (1962) developed a series of items that asked college students to imagine they had caught someone cheating on an exam.

1. Imagine that you are proctoring an examination in a middle-group course. About halfway through the exam you see a fellow student openly cheating. The student is copying his answers from previously prepared notes. When he sees that you have seen the notes as you walked down the aisle and stopped near his seat, he whispers quietly to you, "Okay. I'm caught. That's all there is to it." *You do not know the student.* What would you as proctor do?

   [1] Take away his notes and exam book, dismiss him, and report him for cheating

   [2] Take away his notes, let him finish the exam, but report him for cheating

   [3] If he can be led to withdraw from the exam on some excuse, do *not* report him for cheating; otherwise report him

   [4] Take away his notes, but let him finish the exam, and *not* report him for cheating

   [5] Act as if nothing had happened and *not* report him for cheating

2. Suppose now that a proctor's action would be: *Take away his notes and exam book, dismiss him, and report him for cheating.* How would the university authorities feel if they knew you as a proctor did this?

[1] Would expect one to do something like this

[2] Would not necessarily expect one to do this, but would not disapprove

[3] Would disapprove

[4] Would not tolerate it

3. How would your friends in the student body feel if they knew you did this?

[1] Would expect one to do something like this

[2] Would not necessarily expect one to do this, but would not disapprove

[3] Would disapprove

[4] Would not tolerate it

Stouffer's survey went on to ask how the university authorities and student friends would react to each of the other action alternatives given in item 1. Note that the story about the exam cheater was written to make the particular set of five responses seem complete. There is absolutely no doubt that the cheater cheated; he admitted it. Thus actions a proctor might take to investigate the case did not have to be included in the list of responses. Notice also the way that Stouffer uses free-form items to build a whole section of his survey that fits tightly together, items linking with each other and sustaining a unified image in the respondent's mind.

Multi-Response Menu Items

Menu questions can be written to permit more than one choice, but you should be wary of such multi-response items. Some respondents will feel they have done their duty after checking one box; others will overdo box checking. **Multi-response menu items** are probably most appropriate when the issues are cut and dried, such as the following question about "fanzines" (amateur fan magazines) I once included in a survey mailed to members of the New England Science Fiction Association:

To what fanzines do you currently subscribe? Please check as many boxes as apply, and write the names of any other fanzines you subscribe to at the end.

[1] *Locus*   [4] *Energumen*

[2] *Granfalloon*   [5] *Science Fiction Commentary*

[3] *Speculation*   [6] *Outworlds*

Others _____

_____

The purpose of the question was to determine how deeply the respondent was involved in the communication channels of the science-fiction subculture. To extract analyzable data from this item, I simply counted how many boxes were checked and how many other titles were written in. This item was much more efficient, in use of physical space on the survey and of the respondent's time, than asking seven different questions of the form: "Do you subscribe to the fanzine *Locus*? [1] Yes   [2] No."

Ranking Items

A form of multi-response menu item that one sees quite often asks respondents to rank a short list of items. Here is one I administered to Harvard students, an item adapted from research that Raymond A. Bauer (1960; Furash 1963) published in the *Harvard Business Review*:

> This question was originally asked in a Harvard questionnaire administered in 1960. Below are five possible objectives for the space program. Please rank these in terms of your own personal priorities. Place the number 1 in front of the objective that is most important to you, personally. Then place the number 2 in front of the one that you feel is second most important, and so on, until you have placed a 5 in front of the one that is least important to you.
>
> _____ Pure science research and gaining of knowledge
> _____ Control of outer space for military and political reasons
> _____ Tangible economic payoff and research results for everyday life on Earth
> _____ Meeting the challenge and adventure of new horizons
> _____ Winning the prestige race with the Soviet Union

In my experience, respondents don't like this kind of question. Some of them skip it. Others violate the instructions, for example putting 5 in front of two responses to register extreme disapproval of both, and skipping the number 4 in their ranking. Still others pretend to fulfill the instructions, writing the numbers 1 through 5 in order. This is a troublesome trick, because it is quite possible a person actually ranks the five choices in this order. One person answered with a rocket countdown: "5 . . . 4 . . . 3 . . . 2 . . . 1 . . . BOOM!"

Ranking questions generally should be kept short, because people have to compare all the responses carefully, and too many difficult choices will overwhelm them. As with single-choice menu items, you have to make sure the alternatives are distinct and yet all relate to the same issue. From the computer's standpoint, each of the alternatives is a separate question. "What's the rank of pure science and gaining of knowledge?" "What's the rank of control of outer space for military and political reasons?" And each alternative's rank is a separate variable.

One feature of this question format that I hate is the fact that these different variables are only partly separate. To rank one alternative high is to rank all the others somewhat low. This means that a built-in negative correlation will appear between all the variables derived from a ranking question. A problem arises when you want to know whether any of them are intrinsically correlated with each other, not just as a result of how the question was written. For example, "Control of outer space" and "Winning the prestige race" are both about international competition, and we would expect people who rank one high to rank the other high as well. But the question format forced a negative correlation between the two, and it may be very hard to overcome this in your statistical analysis to see whether the two have an intrinsic positive correlation.

The main advantage of ranking questions is that they elicit comparative judgments from the respondents. They can't just say all five reasons are "good," giving you no variation to analyze. Furthermore, and this may be an advantage or a disadvantage depending on the nature of your research, ranking items automatically compensate for the fact that some respondents may habitually give very positive reactions to stimuli, and others habitually negative ones, regardless of what the stimuli are. Here, each respondent rates something in terms of other stimuli, producing exactly the same average rank as each other respondent.

You might want to use a ranking format to get a high-quality response on just one of the alternatives, which you would then examine in the light of other data in your survey. For example, you could focus just on the first of our five space alternatives, "Pure science," as a measure of attitudes toward *science,* and then look at correlations with other items in your survey, such as the sex of respondent. Unfortunately, the built-in negative correlations created inside a ranking item can contaminate correlations with other items as well. Let's imagine men like science better than women do. But surveys often show a greater acceptance of military items among men, too. Women might rank space science very high, simply as a way of avoiding the military and international competition alternatives, and men might rank science lower because some of them are attracted to the military alternative. Thus you might not find a correlation between being male and ranking science high, even if men were much more likely to prefer science.

Perhaps the best use of ranking items is sheer description. A good example is found in a survey of popular attitudes toward technology, administered to Boston-area residents in 1970 by Irene Taviss.

> In order to determine the relative priorities among technological and social problems, we asked our sample to rank order the following programs: space program, pollution prevention, national defense, urban housing, mental health, welfare

and poverty programs, and crime prevention. The highest priority went to welfare; the lowest, to the space program. National defense was ranked next to last, and pollution prevention in the middle, after crime prevention and mental health. The social programs were clearly ranked ahead of the technical programs. (Taviss, 1972:617)

The ranking format can be used with long lists of alternatives, if the respondents are highly motivated and research justifications are compelling. Perhaps the most famous example is the approach to measuring values invented by Milton Rokeach (1973). The heart of this technique is a pair of ranking questions, each with fully 18 alternatives. Rokeach's value questions have been used by many other researchers, and they can be adapted to somewhat different kinds of questionnaires. We will focus on the 18 items that identify the main things the respondent wants to find in life:

1. A comfortable life (a prosperous life)
2. An exciting life (a stimulating, active life)
3. A sense of accomplishment (lasting contribution)
4. A world at peace (free of war and conflict)
5. A world of beauty (beauty of nature and the arts)
6. Equality (brotherhood, equal opportunity for all)
7. Family security (taking care of loved ones)
8. Freedom (independence, free choice)
9. Happiness (contentedness)
10. Inner harmony (freedom from inner conflict)
11. Mature love (sexual and spiritual intimacy)
12. National security (protection from attack)
13. Pleasure (an enjoyable, leisurely life)
14. Salvation (saved, eternal life)
15. Self-respect (self-esteem)
16. Social recognition (respect, admiration)
17. True friendship (close companionship)
18. Wisdom (a mature understanding of life)

Rokeach's questionnaire was specially printed so that each of these 18 values was on an adhesive label that could be easily removed from the page. A set of boxes was also printed on the page, each large enough to hold one of the stickers, numbered 1 through 18. Instructions on the previous page said the following:

On the next page are 18 values listed in alphabetical order. Your task is to arrange them in order of their importance to YOU, as guiding principles in YOUR life. Each value is printed on a gummed label which can be easily peeled off and pasted in the boxes on the left-hand side of the page.

Study the list carefully and pick out the one value which is the most important to you. Peel it off and paste it in Box 1 on the left.

Then pick out the value which is second most important for you. Peel it off and paste it in Box 2. Then do the same for each of the remaining values. The value which is least important goes in Box 18.

Work slowly and think carefully. If you change your mind, feel free to change your answers. The labels peel off easily and can be moved from place to place. The end result should truly show how you really feel. (Rokeach, 1973:358)

The adhesive labels seem a good idea, not only because they make it easy for respondents to indicate their choices, but also because they let the respondents feel the researcher is very serious about these items and needs careful answers. Indeed, I think respondents would enjoy answering via these adhesive labels and invest more care than they would if merely asked to write in numbers. Printing labels may be expensive but probably impresses the respondent favorably.

The one time I used these questions myself, however, I had neither money nor time to use Rokeach's excellent labels. In 1985, a British sociologist, Michael Young, suddenly gave me the opportunity to survey people who had volunteered to live for a year in an experimental environment designed to simulate a base on the planet Mars. Young is highly respected for the research he did on urban family patterns (Young and Willmott, 1957; 1973), and he has played important roles in British education and politics. Young had noted two interesting facts about space exploration: (1) Many nations have begun developing their own space technology. (2) Cooperative joint projects in space have some power to bring nations together. Young concluded that it was time to start vigorous international ventures in space as a means of promoting international understanding and world peace. Realizing that a focus was needed for such efforts, he decided that international exploration and eventual settlement of the planet Mars could be a popular rallying point.

With some associates, he founded a small organization, called Argo Venture, to promote Mars and to lobby the European Space Agency to begin research on this neighboring planet. To galvanize public interest, he decided that a simulated Martian community, established here on Earth, would be a practical and exciting near-term project. For a year, people would live and work as if they were on Mars, reporting their experiences to the world through a series of television programs.

My questionnaire was the application form for the first wave of volunteers, mainly Britons but including citizens of several nations, who learned about Argo Venture through a couple of news reports. This is the only time one of my questionnaires ever enjoyed a 100% response rate. By definition, a volunteer was somebody who filled out my questionnaire, so all the prospective Mars dwellers did so!

Creating the survey on a tight deadline, I needed useful items in a hurry. It seemed to me that volunteers for the first settlement on another planet were a little like the utopians who found communes and other radical societies here on Earth. Benjamin Zablocki (1980) had published a large book on utopians and commune members, based partly on some surveys he had administered, so I went immediately to his work for inspiration.

Zablocki's questionnaire had included Rokeach's value items, and 174 of his communal respondents had given valid answers. I also included Rokeach's items. I drew a line in front of each value on the list, and instructed as follows:

> QUESTIONS ABOUT VALUES. Below are 18 values listed in alphabetical order. Your task is to arrange them in order of their importance to YOU, as guiding principles in YOUR life. .
>
> Study the list carefully and pick out the one value which is the most important for you. Write the number 1 on the line in front of that value.
>
> Then pick out the value which is second most important for you. Write the number 2 on the line in front of that value. Then do the same for each of the remaining values. You should finish by writing the number 18 in front of the value which is least important for you.
>
> Work slowly and think carefully. If you change your mind, feel free to change your answers. Make sure that when you are done, each of the values has a different number (1 to 18) in front of it. The end result should truly show how you really feel.

Notice that I have based my instructions closely on Rokeach's, merely altering those parts about adhesive labels to refer to written numbers. I did this not merely because his instructions are good, nor to save myself some work, but in order to make my data as comparable as possible to his and Zablocki's. You can't easily compare different groups' responses unless the questions were the same. Some respondents took me at my word about changing answers and scratched out one set of numbers to write in another. The result was far messier than adhesive labels would have been, and I suspect a few respondents were discouraged from changing answers because they wanted to be neat. Several respondents wrote in pen, and so they couldn't erase their answers. One respondent even used a typewriter!

Of the 131 Martian volunteers, 122 correctly answered this battery of questions. Each person ranked the 18 values from 1 to 18, and one way of summarizing their responses is simply to calculate the mean rank for each value. Suppose you have 3 respondents, A, B, and C. A ranks wisdom

▶ ▶ ▶ ▶ ▶ ▶ ▶ ▶ ▶ ▶ ▶

TABLE 5.1   AVERAGE RANKING OF VALUES BY MARTIAN VOLUNTEERS AND
COMMUNE MEMBERS

Value	Martians' Mean Rank	Group Ranking	
		Martians	Communards
Wisdom	6.18	1	2
Freedom	6.42	2	7
Self-respect	7.07	3	5
Inner harmony	7.14	4	1
A world at peace	7.16	5	9
True friendship	7.26	6	4
Happiness	7.51	7	6
An exciting life	8.01	8	10
A sense of accomplishment	8.37	9	11
Equality	8.62	10	8
Family security	9.19	11	13
Mature love	9.25	12	3
A world of beauty	9.76	13	12
Pleasure	13.00	14	15
Social recognition	13.21	15	16
A comfortable life	13.62	16	14
National security	14.26	17	18
Salvation	14.84	18	17

▶

first, giving it a 1. B gives wisdom a rank of 7, and C gives it a rank of 10. To
get the average you add 1 + 7 +10 = 18, and divide by 3 to get an average
rank of 6.

Table 5.1 shows my results, the average ranks the 122 Martian volunteers gave to the 18 values. The average for wisdom was 6.18, the lowest
average of any of the values. Ranking is like the game of golf: Low numbers
are better than high numbers. So wisdom is the value the Martian volunteers favor most.

I have put the 18 values in order of their average ranking, so the ones
most favored by the Martian volunteers are at the top. You can get an image
of this unusual group of respondents simply by considering which values
are on top of the list, and which on the bottom. The first 4 values listed in
Table 5.1 are all about personal, individual qualities, mainly qualities of
mind. Some other group might have put social values at the top: true
friendship, equality, family security, social recognition, and national secu-

rity. It seems that the volunteers are individualists who place the most emphasis on their personal freedom and inner tranquility.

Notice the big gap in the mean rankings from a world of beauty at 9.76 to pleasure at 13, more than 3 points lower. Clearly, the group has a strong consensus that the five values from pleasure on down are not attractive qualities of a good life. The lowest one, salvation, probably suggests a particular religious orientation that few of the respondents have. Social recognition, fourth from the bottom, is almost the opposite of the individualistic qualities the Martian volunteers value most. A comfortable life might seem very dull to people prepared to leave this planet and create a new society on a distant world. Pleasure is defined in parentheses by Rokeach not as active ecstasy but as "an enjoyable, leisurely life," thus sounding rather staid. Finally, national security is conventional and collective rather than individualistic.

Because Rokeach's items have been given to many different groups of respondents, it is possible to compare the values one group expresses with those expressed by many different kinds of person. One way is to compare the *group rankings* from two different groups. Table 5.1 shows the 18 values in order of their *mean individual rankings*. The group ranking is simply this order. The right side of the table has a column labeled Group Ranking—Martians. It is just the numbers 1–18, counting off the values from top to bottom in the table. Zablocki's book has a similar table, listing the values in the order of average individual rankings by his 174 commune members. These numbers are given in the last column of my table.

The rankings by Martians and communards are very similar. Both put wisdom near the top and salvation and national security near the bottom, with most other values having similar positions for the two groups. You could compare such a set of rankings many ways. For example, you could simply correlate the two sets of numbers. Rokeach and Zablocki used a different approach that gives points for how similar the first three and last three values are across groups. But simply looking down the final columns of Table 5.1 gives a clear impression that Zablocki's commune members and my Martian volunteers hold very similar values.

The fact that Rokeach's value items are standard questionnaire batteries that have been administered to many different groups is a major point in their favor. Of course, the list is long and getting a high proportion of your respondents to answer validly may be difficult. The fact that mine had to do the questionnaire to become official volunteers for a project in which they were willing to invest a year of their lives probably helped. It is rarely advisable to invent new ranking items of this size for inclusion in ordinary questionnaires. But I think you can see that under conditions when respondents' motivations are very high and your research purpose is very clear, even these complex, difficult items have their place.

Because of its disadvantages, I have not included the ranking format among the ready-made question formats available on the *Survey Research* disk, but it is easy enough to get a similar effect out of a series of separate items. One question could introduce the set of alternatives: "Below is a list of government programs. Which one would you give the highest priority?" A second question could present the same list, with a different instruction: "Below is the same list of government programs. Ignoring the one you just gave highest priority, which of the following would you say should have the second highest priority?"

If you give them many items in this format, respondents might lose track of which answers they had given, and there probably is no point in going through the entire ranking of priorities. But a set of three such items might be useful, ending with: "Now look through the same list of government programs and find the one you would rank lowest. Which of the following should have the lowest priority?" Of course, this approach does not give the respondent's ranking for each of the things in the list, but the highest and lowest priorities should still be of research interest.

Contingent Questions

Some questions are not relevant for all respondents. Single people cannot answer some questions designed for married people, for instance. If you know which respondents are in which category even before you start administering the survey, you might have different versions of the questionnaire, such as one version for single people and one for married people. Alternately, you can write your questionnaire so that there is a special section of questions for married people, marked off clearly so that single people can skip it. Items that only a subgroup of respondents are supposed to answer are called **contingent questions.** Questions that are used to separate people into subgroups are called **screening questions.**

One of my students, Daniel Dohan, recently surveyed Boston-area physicians and surgeons concerning their views about the malpractice insurance crisis in the state. One set of simple questions sought to determine the personal experiences respondents might have had with malpractice cases, data to be compared with the doctors' opinions about the cause of the crisis and what should be done.

3. Has a patient of yours ever brought a malpractice action of any kind (notification of action, preliminary hearing, out-of-court settlement, etc.) against you?

   [1] Yes   [2] No

   If Yes, please answer question 4 below; if No, please skip to question 5.

4. a. How many actions have been brought against you?

   [1] 1   [2] 2   [3] 3-4   [4] 5-6   [5] 7+

b. Have you ever appeared in any court (preliminary or trial) as a defendant in a malpractice suit?

[1] Yes   [2] No

c. Have you ever been a defendant in a malpractice suit in which an award was granted to the plaintiff in court?

[1] Yes   [2] No

d. Have you ever been the defendant in a malpractice suit in which an award was granted to the plaintiff in an out-of-court settlement?

[1] Yes   [2] No

5. How many times have you served as a witness in a malpractice suit in which you were not the defendant or plaintiff (i.e., as an expert witness)?

[1] 0   [2] 1   [3] 2–5   [4] 6–10   [5] 10+

All respondents answer items 3 and 5, but those who answer no to the screening question, number 3, are told to skip down to 5. Notice that questions 4b, 4c, and 4d could logically be asked of every respondent, and that 4a also could be if a box for zero actions were added to the set of responses. Item 3 is included to get a clear, quick answer to the most general question possible about malpractice actions. The parts of item 4 then get specific. And doctors with no actions brought against them are allowed to skip 4 in order to save them time, an important consideration with busy respondents who might quit in mid-survey if it took too long.

Another good example of a contingent question is a three-part political item used by the Stanford Research Institute (SRI International) in a number of market research surveys (Mitchell, 1983:276):

9. Generally speaking, do you usually think of yourself as a Republican, a Democrat, or an Independent? (Please Check *One* Box)

[1] Republican (Please Answer Question 9a)
[2] Democrat (Please Answer Question 9a)
[3] Independent (Please Answer Question 9b)

9a. IF YOU ARE A REPUBLI-CAN OR A DEMOCRAT, would you call yourself a strong or not very strong Republican or Democrat? (Please Check *One* Box)

9b. IF YOU ARE INDEPEN-DENT, do you think of yourself as closer to the Republican or Democratic Party? (Please Check *One* Box)

[1] Strong Republican
[2] Not very strong Republican
[3] Not very strong Democrat
[4] Strong Democrat

[1] Closer to the Republican Party
[2] Not close to either party
[3] Closer to the Democratic Party

In a printed questionnaire, you can increase the clarity of the directions by drawing arrows on the page, showing different subgroups of respondents where they are supposed to go next. Although SRI's political party question may be clear enough as it stands, you could draw an arrow from the Independent response to question 9 down to question 9b, and other arrows from the Republican and Democratic responses down to 9a.

It may help clarify questions that only married people are supposed to answer by putting a big box around them labeled "If you are married, please answer these questions." Another way, as in Daniel Dohan's survey, is to set the instruction for a subgroup to skip down in boldface type. Suppose question 20 asks for the respondent's marital status, and questions 21 through 25 are just for married people. After question 20, you could write, "Questions 21–25 are for married people only. If you are single, divorced, or widowed, please SKIP down to question number 26."

In fully computerized surveys, where the data are entered directly into the computer and there is no printed questionnaire, the program can be written to do the skipping automatically. If a respondent answered "married" to question 20, the computer would then ask question 21. If the person answered "single," the computer would immediately go to question 26.

Although contingent questions are standard tools of the survey researcher, I have not included them in the questionnaire modules of the *Survey Research* disk. They would greatly complicate your statistical analysis of the data, educationally a bad idea. But they also are best employed with large numbers of respondents that include substantial numbers in each subgroup, rather than with the more limited number we work with here.

The special data input program, the utilities described in Chapter 12, does permit contingent questions, so long as you give a different question number to each item in the survey that anybody might answer. In the preceding SRI political examples, you would only have to renumber questions 9, 9a, and 9b as 9, 10, and 11.

The possibilities for free-form items are limited only by your imagination. Chapter 11 introduces some other examples while discussing complex survey designs that go far beyond the modest complexity of contingent questions. Now it is time to see what happens when all the respondents have completed our survey and the data are ready to analyze.

▶ ▶ ▶ ▶ ▶ ▶ ▶ ▶ ▶ ▶ ▶ ▶

PROJECTS

1. A Current Public Issue.   Write ten free-form items on a current public issue—some government policy, social problem, or important event that is being widely discussed. Our seven questions about the space program provide examples. Three aspects of the space program were highly controversial at the time I did my study. First, of course, the *Challenger* had just been destroyed, raising many questions about the manned space program. Second, President Reagan had recently committed the nation to building a space station, a project that many scientists opposed, as did some who believed it would become a tool of the military. Third, for several years Reagan's Strategic Defense Initiative (the Star Wars missile defense plan) had drawn fire from his political opponents and from many groups with different views both of international relations and of the technical feasibility of the project. The general public was not debating an expedition to Mars or radio contact with extraterrestrials, but these were issues discussed among certain aerospace groups, so I included them in my survey.

In creating your own set of ten questions, you should first define the issue or controversy they will be about. Then try to identify the main aspects of this issue, subtopics that should be the material of separate questions. Identify also the major alternative opinions that many respondents might hold. Because rival political groups typically use different language to talk about the same issues, you may need two or three questions for each part of your issue, framed in the terminology of different political groups.

2. Poor Professional Polling.   Look through professional poll reports, such as are often featured in certain newspapers and magazines or can be obtained from polling organizations directly, looking for free-form questions that strike you as badly worded. In some, the stimulus may be ambiguous. In others, the responses may not be mutually exclusive. And often some important possible responses may simply be absent. Write a brief report on two to five such poll items, pointing out the defects you find in them.

If you want an example, look at what we said about the bad space question in this chapter: "Do you think that putting civilians into space is important—or is it too dangerous?" You may not find examples as bad as this one, and you don't have to be absolutely right in criticizing the wording of professional poll items. The point is to develop and demonstrate a critical eye when it comes to questions. Professional pollsters often waste thousands of dollars and the time of hundreds of respondents on lousy questions.

3. A Survey on Employment History.   Look at the part of this chapter that introduced items from a London survey on unemployment. Notice how short, free-form questions were used to get a picture of the person's previous episodes of being jobless. (Remember, however, that the London survey was administered through interviews, and a couple of the questions are worded poorly for a printed questionnaire.) Think about the main information you would need if you wanted to describe the history of a person's employment, the various jobs of various kinds he or she has held in the past, for various periods of time with various salaries or wages.

Now write a set of 20 or 30 short, free-form questions that could be used to get the main facts about a person's employment history. In doing so, keep in mind the different aspects of employment that you would want to know about. It is not enough to have 20 identical questions about 20 different times a person might have been employed. Instead, write items that will give a detailed picture of the work a person has done.

4. A Social Distance Scale.   Create a set of 25 social distance questions, in the free-form format, 5 each about 5 different groups in your population. First, consider the most highly visible and different groups in your community or on your college campus. Then find a way of naming each in a few words so that respondents will definitely recognize each group. This will give you the names of 5 different groups.

Second, write 5 different social distance questions that could be applied to any of the groups. Be inspired by the examples we gave, but use your imagination, too. Your final survey would consist of 5 sections. For example, the first section could be the same question asked 5 times, once for each group. Or the first section could be the 5 different questions asked about a single group. The other sections would complete the set so that each of the 5 questions got asked about each of the 5 groups.

5. Menu Items on Government Policies.   Write eight free-form items, with five to eight appropriate responses, about four major areas of government policy, two items about each. I will use the military as my example, so you should not use it in your project. I am sure you will be able to find far more than four different areas in which the government makes policy and where political controversies rage, but four is enough.

If you were writing about military policy, there are many issues that could become one of the pairs of free-form items. For example, you could focus on nuclear strategy and on the issue of the draft:

> 1. There has been much debate about when we should be prepared to use nuclear weapons in war. As you know, there are many different opinions about this, some based on moral considerations and some on how the enemy might respond. Although you may feel these issues are extremely complex, please check the

ONE box below that best describes the circumstances under which you think nuclear weapons might properly be used.

[1] Never, not under any circumstances
[2] Only when the other side has already used nuclear weapons against us
[3] To defend against a massive non-nuclear attack, as well as in response to the enemy's nuclear weapons
[4] Whenever it is clear that our side would benefit from using them
[5] I do not know, because this decision should be left up to national leaders
[6] None of the above. What I think is: _____

2. In our nation's history, we have sometimes drafted young men against their will to serve in the military, and at other times we have relied entirely on volunteers. Under what circumstances do you feel it would be appropriate to draft people (whether just men or both men and women) into the military? Please check the ONE box that comes closest to saying when you feel a draft would be justified.

[1] Never, not under any circumstances
[2] Only when it is absolutely necessary to preserve our freedoms from a foreign aggressor
[3] When a draft is needed to defeat foreign tyranny like the Nazis, as well as to defend our freedoms at home
[4] Whenever it would help achieve desirable national goals
[5] At all times; we should never be without the draft
[6] I do not know, because this decision should be left up to national leaders
[7] None of the above. What I think is: _____

These two items are not perfect, but perhaps they communicate what you should achieve in this project. You should write four pairs of items, on questions of government policy other than the military, using this general format.

6. Group-Generated Menu Item.   Check over the section of this chapter on questions about the existence and nature of God. Then use 12 respondents to help you write a menu item about another religious question, life after death. These 12 respondents can be fellow students, friends, family members, or even strangers you poll on the street.

Give each respondent three file cards. Tell them you are collecting opinions about what happens after a person dies, for a class project. Use a standard question you have written, perhaps three or four sentences long, that focuses them on the question of whether there is an afterlife and what it might be like if there is one. Then ask them to write their own opinion on one file card, in a single sentence describing what happens to a person after death. And ask them to write a different opinion they had heard, but not their personal opinion, on each of the other cards.

When you have obtained 3 cards from each of 12 respondents, for a total of 36, create a menu item for a questionnaire, based on their ideas. You will want to sort the cards on a large table, combining any that seem to express the same viewpoint. Your final questionnaire item should have 5 to 8 mutually exclusive responses. Therefore, you may have to discard sentences that seem unrelated to the others, combine similar cards into a single response, and look for distinctions in opinion that will give you several response categories. If you encounter any special difficulties in doing this assignment, you should note them in a 1-page report attached to your questionnaire item.

7. A Value-Ranking Item.   With the Rokeach values item as a model, create a completely fresh value-ranking item for a survey in an area of your interest. The item should begin with your own introduction, telling the respondent to rank the values. Then should come a list of values relevant to the subject of the item. I will give you two examples, but you will do better to think of your own.

Such an item could be about the value of sports. You could list 15 or 20 different values that various people find in sports, such as: physical exercise, fresh air, developing a sense of balance, and losing weight. Some might be fairly contradictory—for example: building the spirit to compete, learning to cooperate with others.

Or the item might be about art. You could list a number of criteria for a good painting and ask the respondent to rank them from the one he or she thinks is most important down to the least important one. Examples might be: accurate illustration of the subject of the painting, excitement from a novel image, sensitive treatment of color, purity of visual abstraction. In making such a list, you should include values favored by different schools of thought in art today, because one of the main uses of such an item is to place the respondent on the map of contemporary artistic debates.

8. Contingent Questions on a Family's Investments.   Pretend you are a financial adviser, with prosperous families as your clients, creating a questionnaire of about 30 items to get some basic information about the investments of new clients. The point of this project is to gain experience with contingent questions. Therefore, you should have some screening questions about major kinds of investments of all kinds that a prosperous family might have. Once a screening question has determined that the family has the particular investment, you should ask a few questions to zero in on the specifics of the investments of that type which they have.

I can't tell you too much about this assignment, or I would be doing your work for you. But think about the general kinds of investment that a family might have, check some references in the library if you wish, or even contact real investment advisers of some kind. You should have several screening items that determine whether the respondent has a given type of investment. Then, ask follow-up questions written on the page in a clearly contingent format, to learn precise details of that investment.

▶ ▶ ▶ ▶ ▶ The *Survey Research* disk includes four programs for analyzing data. Two are designed for the basic work of analyzing and recoding your data, and they are the subject of this chapter. Two more advanced programs that let you work with many variables simultaneously are covered in the next chapter. When you actually work with your own data, the first step will usually be recoding data to put them in the best form for analysis. But it is hard to do that unless you first have some idea what analysis you will do. Therefore, this chapter will start with the basics of statistical analysis, and then it will explain how you can recode data for maximum effect.

As I explained in Chapter 1, a dataset called STUDENTS can be used to practice statistical analysis. It is based on responses by 200 Harvard students to a 40-item survey. You may want to go back at Chapter 1 to look at the questions.

▶ ▶ ▶ ▶ ▶ ▶ ▶ ▶ ▶ ▶ ▶

[E] BASIC STATISTICS

 Using the STUDENTS work disk you made in Project 2 of Chapter 1, select [E] from the program menu.

The computer will ask `What is the name of the survey?` To work with our student data, simply type STUDENTS and press [ENTER]. Just STUDENT will not work; you have to type in the exact name of the survey that we have given to the computer. If you have a new survey of your own on a disk, use that disk and type its name to get that dataset.

Let's work with STUDENTS to start with. Type STUDENTS and press [ENTER]. A message will appear on the screen saying what the computer

Basic Statistics and Recoding

is doing. First it says Loading information about STUDENTS. The computer is taking a pair of files from the disk, one with general information about the survey, the other with labels I have written that name the 40 items. Then the computer will say Now loading data from file STUDENTS.D1. This is the first batch of responses from the first 25 students. In a moment, the computer will be loading data from file STUDENTS.D2, the second batch. It will continue loading data until they are all in the machine, which for this survey means going through file STUDENTS.D8.

Next, the main menu will appear, with the following choices:

    [1]   Data from one case
    [2]   Frequencies on one variable
    [3]   Crosstab of two variables
    [4]   Partial correlations of three variables
    [ESC] QUIT or change programs

Notice that there is no option to save anything onto the disk. This basic statistics program merely analyzes data; it does not create or transform any. Thus it is a rather safe program to run, and any mistakes you make will be purely temporary. Start by pressing [1] to get data from one case.

[1] Data from One Case

The computer will now say You have data on 200 cases. Select one. Of course, if your own dataset has fewer than 200 cases, the maximum handled by our programs, the correct number would be displayed instead of 200.

149

This option lets you look at the responses from a single individual. When you are working with your own data, you might use this option to check a suspicious case in which you think the person gave wild answers or where some mistake was made entering the data into the computer. Here, we can use it to get acquainted with the variables.

To select a particular case, you have to type in the respondent's ID number, a number from 1 through 200 (or whatever the total number of your surveys happens to be) assigned in the order the data were entered into the computer. Then press [ENTER].

Try respondent number 41, an interesting case who refused to answer 3 of our space questions. Type 41 and press [ENTER]. The upper right corner of the screen will say Responses from case 41, and the screen will fill with numbers and brief names of the 40 items. Notice 4 #1 Botany at the upper left. The first of the preference questions is about Botany, and this explains the "#1 Botany" part. The "4" part is explained by the fact that respondent 41 gave a 4 preference rating to Botany. This is smack in the middle of the 1–7 preference scale, so it indicates that she likes this college subject a bit but not a whole lot.

Under the Botany entry you will see 4 #2 Astronomy, indicating that respondent 41 feels the same way about astronomy courses. A little below that, you will see that she has given a top rating of 7 to both Law and Political Science. Think about that for a moment. Do you think that law and political science tend to go together in people's minds? Do people who like law tend also to like political science? Answers will have to wait until we are ready to correlate two items, later in this chapter.

Down a little lower in the list, you will see 1 #9 Physics. Apparently, respondent 41 absolutely loathes Physics, giving it the worst possible rating of 1. Check through the list of 30 academic fields and look for other 1 ratings. This respondent loathes 3 other fields: Education, Nursing, and Social Work. While none of these strike me as having much in common with Physics, they do seem similar to each other. All 3 involve helping people, although in 3 different ways.

Perhaps you are getting a picture of what respondent 41 is like. You can look through the full set of questions and see how vivid an image of respondent 41's personality you can get. Question number 40 gives her year in school, which is 2. So we know she is a sophomore. But how do we know she is a she? Question 39 tells us her sex. Our survey codes the sexes as 1 and 2. But which is which? Look at question 39 in the section describing the survey in Chapter 1. You will see a 1 inside the box for females, so a person with sex number 1 is a female.

Now look through the space questions, numbers 31 through 37. As you will see them on your screen, here are the responses person 41 gave:

```
5 #31 Space funding
2 #32 Unmanned missions
2 #33 Space station
```

```
2 #34 Satellite defense
4 #35 Mars expedition
4 #36 You go to Mars
2 #37 Communicate with ETs
```

If you look back in Chapter 1 at the questions and how I coded them, you will see that response 5 to item 31 about space funding means she failed to answer the question in a valid way. In fact, I just checked the original survey and found that she wrote in a comment saying she didn't know how much was being spent on the space program and thus couldn't check a box. Of course, few people really know how much is being spent, but most have no difficulty expressing their opinions by checking a box.

Respondent 41 had firm negative opinions about the space station project and the system of space satellites, both of which were being promoted heavily by the Reagan administration at the time of our survey. She responded "2" to both, indicating negative sentiments. But note that 2 means something different for the two questions. For Item 33, asking whether a space station should be built, 2 means simply no. For Item 34 on satellite defense, it means "research should stop." When analyzing data, you must always pay close attention to what the coding numbers mean.

The two questions about Mars, Items 35 and 36, both got 4 as a response, which for these particular items indicates a failure to give a valid answer. The survey encouraged students to write comments after the space questions, and this respondent did so. After failing to check a box expressing an opinion about funding an expedition to Mars, she wrote: "I'm not sure, depends on risks and costs. We might learn something—new frontiers are always exciting." And after failing to check a box about going to Mars herself, she wrote: "I don't have the time to soul search this question. I like adventure, but . . ."

These written comments suggest she should have checked the "no opinion" box. But perhaps she felt that "no opinion" did not quite capture the sense of ambivalence or uncertainty she felt. Furthermore, some people might be reluctant to admit they lacked an opinion, and others might have well-articulated opinions that they could not fit into the particular boxes offered them. Our program that administers questionnaires right on the computer prevents people from skipping an item, something we cannot achieve with printed surveys. Thus with printed questionnaires you must anticipate occasional refusals to answer a question.

Finally, respondent 41 gave a valid "yes, perhaps" answer to the question about communicating with intelligent beings on other planets. She did so by checking the 2 box. Of course, this 2 means something very different from the 2s she gave to the items about travel to Mars. When you are finished inspecting case 41, press [ENTER] to return to the main menu.

[2] Frequencies on One Variable

Press [2] and you will get the second menu choice, statistics on a particular item in the survey. A list of the 40 items in the STUDENTS survey will appear, with the numbers 1–40 in front of them. In the top right corner of the screen is the instruction Select the item that is to be Variable X. And at the very bottom, you see Type a number from 1 to 40 and press [ENTER].

For practice, let's begin with Item 38. This is the question about political liberalism and conservatism, taken from the General Social Survey. Type 38 and press [ENTER]. In a moment, the screen will be full of statistics. Some of these are easy to understand; others require a little statistical background. We will start with the easiest ones.

The left half of the screen is a table showing how many people gave each possible response to the political question. The first column of figures is labeled *Value*. Each numeral representing a different response to the question is a **value.** For example, everybody who marked the "extremely liberal" response to the question got a 1 score for the political item. Thus the value 1 represents extreme liberalism. The extreme conservatives got scores of 7, and thus extreme conservatism has a value of 7.

We don't mean that conservatism is more valuable than liberalism. We are using the word *value* in a technical sense to identify whatever score some students got for their response to the question. We could have assigned very different numbers to the different responses. For example, extreme conservatism could have been given the value of 1, and extreme liberalism could have been counted as 7. But once we have adopted a particular system of values, we generally have to stick with it, or we will get hopelessly confused.

The liberal–conservative item is a measure of the respondent's politics. And once we have the responses inside our computer, it becomes a variable we can analyze. The term **variable** is often defined in mathematics as "a quantity that can assume any of a set of values." This is a little abstract. But I think you can get the idea through the example of our political question.

People give various answers to the question. Another way of putting this is to say that individuals' responses vary. One person circles the number 1, indicating that he or she is extremely liberal; another circles the number 7, indicating extreme conservatism. As we go from one person to another, the response varies. The response can be any one of the values set for the question, any of the numbers from 1 through 7. To know what each value means, you have to check the original questionnaire. That is how you can be sure that 1 represents liberalism rather than conservatism.

The political variable is an example of variables known as scales. The word *scale* is familiar, although in statistics we give it a particular meaning. Good analogies are musical scales and weight scales for finding out how heavy things are. The notes in a musical scale go from low to high. Similarly, weight ranges from light to heavy. In survey research we use the term **scale** for a questionnaire item or combination of items that measures a person's responses from low to high in a series of steps, and often we imply that the steps are equal in size. Here, politics can be measured in seven steps from liberal to conservative.

I am sorry this section has to present so many definitions, but most of them draw on some terms that are already quite familiar to you. An example is *frequencies*, the name of this part of the program. The **frequencies** are the number of respondents with each particular value. How many students circled the "extremely liberal" response, number 1? Look at the bottom of the second column in the table on the screen, under *Cases* across from value 1. You will see the number 16. This means that 16 of the 200 students gave the "extremely liberal" response. That is the frequency for extreme liberalism.

As you look up the column labeled *Cases*, you will see the frequencies for all the other values, until you get to value 7, representing extreme conservatism. Wow! Only one person gave that response. If you are interested, that respondent was a male senior. I hope he was not too lonely in his four years surrounded by liberals at Harvard.

The table of frequencies has room for the values 8 and 9, but we did not assign these numbers to any possible responses to the political question. Therefore, you will see zeros in the rows after values 8 and 9.

The two remaining columns of the table report percentages. If you look at them carefully, you can quickly see how they differ. The third column, labeled simply *Percent*, tells us what percent of the 200 respondents gave each of the 7 possible responses. For example, the 16 extreme liberals represent 8% of the total 200. The lone extreme conservative represents only 0.5%.

The last column shows the *Cumulative Percent*. To figure this out, start at the bottom. The cumulative percent for extreme liberals is 8%, just as it is for the simple percent column. But the cumulative percent for the second group, "liberal," is 38%. We get this cumulative percent figure for value 2 by adding together the people in the first two groups—the 8% who are extreme liberals plus the 30% who are just liberals. As you go up the cumulative percent column, you keep adding people and percents, until you reach 100%. For politics, that happens at value 7.

You can think of it this way. The 38 cumulative percent for value 2, liberals, means that 38% of the students are at least this liberal. The 65 cumulative percent for value 3, those "slightly liberal," means that 65% of the students are at least slightly liberal. Notice that cumulative percent offers some small conveniences in reading the frequencies table quickly. You can immediately see that 65% of the respondents are on the liberal side of the scale.

Cumulative percent can be helpful in looking for the middle of the distribution of values. If 38% are at least "liberal," and 65% are at least "slightly liberal," then you can imagine a line between values 2 and 3 that divides the 200 students in half. This would be the 50% line, although there is no value that has a cumulative percent of 50% on this political item. Using the cumulative percents, you could say that the typical student was somewhere between "liberal" and "slightly liberal."

Now, at this point some readers will be congratulating themselves for sharing the liberalism of the students surveyed, while others will be disgusted that so few of the respondents are conservative. Survey research can get emotional at times. You will find yourself reacting in various ways to the opinions of your respondents, and sometimes you will be surprised and shocked to see that most of them disagree with you.

In my philosophy of survey research, it is quite all right for the researcher to get emotional. But you must not let your feelings distort your judgment. Instead, let your emotions energize you. Then they will fire up your imagination and drive you to seek explanations for your research findings.

All research involves comparisons, and frequently you will find yourself comparing your respondents' answers with those you would have given yourself. The next step in systematic research is to compare your respondents with some other group, or to compare two subgroups among your respondents. Our politics question was taken from a standard national poll, the General Social Survey, so a logical step is to compare the distribution of responses given by Harvard students with those of the American public. Indeed, one of the main reasons for incorporating items in your survey that came from earlier questionnaires is the opportunity of comparing your respondents with other people. And a national sample is an especially valuable comparison group.

Table 6.1 shows the distribution of responses from the 200 space-survey students and from 1401 respondents to the 1986 GSS who gave valid answers (Davis and Smith, 1986:90). Conveniently, the GSS was administered at exactly the same time as our STUDENTS survey, so we can compare the two groups without having to worry about political shifts that might be changing the public's responses. If the data came from different years, differences might have merely reflected such general trends, rather than demonstrating essential differences between the groups.

The first two columns of figures in Table 6.1 show the numbers giving each response. For example, 16 of the Harvard students said they were extremely liberal, compared with 25 in the GSS national sample. These two numbers, 16 and 25, are quite similar. But, of course, you must not leap to the conclusion that the two groups are about equally liberal. The GSS group is seven times as large as the Harvard group, 1401 respondents compared with 200. A valid comparison requires us to look at the percentages rather than the **raw numbers.**

In percentage terms, far more of the students than GSS respondents are extremely liberal, 8% compared with a mere 1.8%. The plain liberal category is much larger, too, 30% compared with 9.4%. If you combine the three liberal categories, you get 65% for the students versus only 23.8% for

▶ ▶ ▶ ▶ ▶   ▶ ▶ ▶ ▶ ▶ ▶

TABLE 6.1   POLITICS OF HARVARD STUDENTS COMPARED
WITH A NATIONAL SAMPLE

Response	Number		Percent	
	Students	National	Students	National
7 Extremely conservative	1	38	0.5%	2.7%
6 Conservative	9	209	4.5%	14.9%
5 Slightly conservative	38	242	19.0%	17.3%
4 Moderate	22	579	11.0%	41.3%
3 Slightly liberal	54	176	27.0%	12.6%
2 Liberal	60	132	30.0%	9.4%
1 Extremely liberal	16	25	8.0%	1.8%
Total	200	1401	100.0%	100.0%

the national sample. The students also seem much more willing to express political partisanship. Only 11% of them are moderates, compared with fully 41.3% of the GSS respondents.

As you can see, much can be learned by inspecting a frequency distribution, and even more by comparing one with another. But the raw numbers and percents may provide almost too much information, so we often use statistics, such as various kinds of average, that can summarize the frequencies for us.

Averages and Measures of Dispersion

Everybody knows what a simple average is, and the frequency table displays one on the right side of the screen, near the top, after the word *mean*. **Mean** is just the technical term for the arithmetic average. The mean score on the political scale is 3.18. To get this, the computer added up the responses of all 200 respondents, for a total of 637. Then it divided by 200 to get the average response, which is 3.18. Notice that this is very close to 3, the "slightly liberal" answer to the question. The average score for the 1401 GSS respondents is 4.18, slightly on the conservative side of moderate.

But there are other kinds of average. Two that our program calculates for us are the mode and the median. The mode for the political question is 2. Look at the frequencies and you will see that more students (60 of them) gave the "2" response ("liberal") than any other; "3" came in second with 54 cases. The **mode** is the most common value among the respondents. For the GSS national sample, the mode is 4; the largest number chose "4 (moderate)."

Sometimes there can be more than one mode. If you want to see an example, press [ENTER] to get the political question off the screen. Then press [2] to get other frequencies, and type 40 [ENTER] to get the frequency distribution for year in college. Remember that I selected exactly equal numbers of freshmen, sophomores, juniors, and seniors for our 200 respondents. Lo and behold, you will see that 50, exactly 25%, have the value of 1 (freshmen) for their year in college. And precisely equal numbers have values of 2 (sophomores), 3 (juniors), and 4 (seniors). The mean year is 2.50, which is halfway between sophomore and junior year. But instead of just one mode, we have four: 1, 2, 3, and 4. All four different values are tied for most common response, or mode. Now you should get back to frequencies on the political question, so we can consider the remaining statistics.

The third kind of average is the median. The median for the students on the political scale is 2.94, which is close to the mode, 2, and the mean, 3.19. In principle, the **median** is the score that exactly divides the group of respondents in half. Precisely half the respondents should have scores above the median, and precisely half, below.

Unfortunately, in survey research our distributions seldom permit us to find a median that really achieves this division. Look at the cumulative percentages again. Thirty-eight percent of the students have scores of 2 or less. But this isn't quite half. Sixty-five percent have scores of 3 or less. But this is more than half. There is no way we can really cut the 200 into equal halves, on the basis of the political variable.

But this is easy to do with year in college. For that variable, the median is 2.50. Exactly 100 students have scores less than this, and 100 have scores that are higher.

Two other statistics tell us something about the shape of the frequency distribution: variance and standard deviation. I have put these just under the mean on the right side of the screen because they are closely related to it. Those of you who have taken a statistics course will know all about these two, but perhaps I should attempt a very brief introduction for those who have not.

Both **variance** and standard deviation are measures of how spread out the respondents are around the mean. These are often called measures of variability or measures of **dispersion.** Like many statistics we use in survey research, they are a bit of a pain to figure by hand, because they require lots of calculations, but the computer spits them out almost instantly. The most logical but tedious way to calculate the variance is as follows.

Calculate the mean, the average score for all your respondents on the particular variable. We have already seen that the mean for the political variable is 3.19. Now go through the 200 scores and figure out the difference between each one and the mean. For example, suppose the first respondent was slightly liberal and gave the 3 response. The difference between 3 and 3.19 is 0.19 (3.19 − 3 = 0.19). And let's say the second person was slightly conservative and gave the 5 response. The difference between 5 and the mean is 5 − 3.19 = 1.81. You would continue on, doing 200 subtractions, finding how far from the mean each respondent's political score is.

Then you have to square each of these 200 difference numbers; that is, multiply each one by itself. The square of 0.19 is 0.04, and the square of 1.81 is 3.28. This gives you another set of 200 numbers. Each one is the square of the person's difference from the mean. Add all these together and divide by 200.

You will have to consult a statistics book for good explanations of why we want to go to all this trouble (Loether and McTavish, 1976:143–59; Christensen and Stoup, 1986:83–110). But I think you can see that the variance measures how spread out the scores are around the mean. If everybody gave the average response, the variance would be zero. Imagine everybody was a moderate, for example. The mean would be 4. Every difference from the mean would be zero. Every square of the difference would also be zero. And the average of these 200 zeros would be zero, too.

If we had 100 extreme liberals and 100 extreme conservatives, the mean would still be 4, the middle of the scale. But with everybody at the ends of the distribution, the variance would be big. Indeed, under these extreme circumstances, it would be 9.00. The actual variance in our data is more modest, 1.94.

Like percentages, variances can be used to compare different distributions. Recall that 41.3% of the GSS respondents were moderates, and the national sample seems very bunched together in the middle of the political scale. In addition to being more liberal, on average, the students seem more spread out along the scale. But mere impressions can be false. How can we compare just the amounts of spread in the two distributions, when the averages are so different?

One answer, of course, is through the variances. The variance for the GSS respondents is 1.64, somewhat smaller than the 1.94 variance for the students. Sometimes, researchers like to take one more step and divide the variance by the mean, getting what is called the **variation ratio.** For the 200 students, the variation ratio is 0.61 (1.94/3.19 = 0.61), much larger than the 0.39 for the GSS national sample (1.64/4.18 = 0.39). If you want, you can easily figure the variation ratios by hand or with a calculator, from the mean and variance that the computer displays.

I didn't want to fill your computer screen with statistics, and there are many more we could calculate if we were greedy for numbers. But the standard deviation is used so frequently that I could not possibly avoid it, even though it's a cinch to calculate. The **standard deviation** is simply the square root of the variance. The standard deviation in politics for the students is 1.39. If you square this number—multiply it by itself—you get about 1.94, which is the variance. The standard deviation for the GSS respondents is 1.28.

The final number shown on your screen is **missing cases,** the number of respondents who failed to answer the question. All 200 answered this one, so the missing cases are 0. If 5 of them had failed to answer, the missing cases would be 5, and the total in the table would be 195.

It is important to check missing cases, or the total number of good cases, so that you don't misinterpret the other statistics. When the number of missing cases is quite large, we really don't know the real distribution of opinions. All we have is the distribution among people who responded to the item. But when few cases are missing, we can have greater confidence in the other statistics.

[3] Crosstab of Two Variables

Crosstab is short for **crosstabulation,** a fancy way of describing a table that tabulates two variables against each other. It is the next step up from frequencies, and in statistical software it is one of the most common approaches to correlation. We often want to know whether two variables go together. For example, do students who like Economics also like Business?

It certainly makes sense to guess that they would. The two subjects seem related. Both are about money. People in business usually know something about economics, and economists are forever analyzing data about businesses. Even in everyday language we might say, "Business correlates with Economics." For our questionnaire data, a better way of putting it is: "Preferences for Business correlate with preferences for Economics."

But this is only an educated guess, a hypothesis. We think it is true, but we haven't proved it yet. How could we find out whether this hypothesis is true or false in our data? We would have to look at people's preferences for both subjects. A correlation means that people who like Business tend to like Economics. But more than that, it also means that people who hate Business tend to hate Economics. And people who give Business a middling rating would tend to do the same for Economics.

These would only be tendencies, however. There might be somebody who loved Business but hated Economics. To say that two things correlate does not mean they must *always* go together, just that they go together more often than not. To check this hypothesis in detail, we would have to look at all the possible combinations of attitudes toward Business and Economics and see how many students held each of them. This is what crosstabs accomplish.

From the main menu, press [3] to get crosstabs. You will get the list of 40 items, with the instructions Select the item that is to be Variable X. Type a number from 1 to 40 and press [ENTER]. Business is Item 11, so type 11 and press [ENTER]. Now, the 11 in front of Business in the left column of items will begin flashing, to remind you that you have chosen it to be Variable X, while you select Y. This time, Variable Y should be Economics. Press 16 and press [ENTER] to select economics.

The computer goes furiously to work; it has a lot to do to give you a crosstab and all the statistics that go with it. A message appears in the upper left corner of the screen: Crosstab of Item 11 (Variable X) and Item 16 (Variable Y). Much of the screen is filled with a big square composed of 49 small squares. This is the crosstab itself. The small squares are called **cells,** just like prison cells. Indeed, if you are unfamiliar with this kind of analysis, it might help you understand the crosstab to imagine that it is a prison with 49 cells into which we can put the 200 students. Just as prisoners might be assigned to different cellblocks in terms of the crimes they have committed, all the robbers in one place and all the arsonists in a different (fireproof) cellblock, we will assign students to cells in terms of their attitudes toward Business and Economics.

Across the top of the big square are Item 11 Business and the numbers 1 through 7. These numbers represent the seven different values—the seven scores people might give Business—taken from the frequencies, with 1 meaning "do not like at all" and 7 meaning "like very much." At the bottom left corner of the square you see Item 16 Economics, with arrows pointing up. The numbers 1 through 7 run up the left side of the big square. These numbers represent the values for Economics.

Consider just the first column of the big square, the seven cells under Business 1. These are the prison cells where we put all the students who gave Business the lowest possible rating of 1 on the 1-to-7 scale. The cell at the very bottom, under Business 1 and just to the right of Economics 1, has the number 19 in it. These are the 19 students who thoroughly hate both Business and Economics. They gave each a 1 rating.

Right above them is a cell with the number 6 in it. These six people also gave Business a 1 rating, as did everyone in the left-hand column of cells. But they gave Economics a 2 rating, not quite so bad. And above them are four people who rated Business 1 and Economics 3. Another four rated Business 1 but gave a middling 4 score to Economics. And one person rated Business 1 but Economics 5.

Nobody hated Business but loved Economics. The top two cells in the column have zeros in them: No students rated Business 1 but Economics 6, and none rated Business 1 and Economics 7.

So far, we have a hint of a correlation. People who hate Business also tend to hate Economics. But correlation is a two-way street. Have we shown that people who hate Economics also tend to hate Business? Not yet. To do that, we have to scan across the bottom row of cells in the crosstab.

Again, 19 people hated both subjects, the 19 in the cell in the lower left corner. Look at the cell at the bottom with 5 in it. The bottom row represents people who rated Economics at 1, so we know these 5 hate Economics. How do they feel about Business? Their cell is under Business 2, so they rated it 2 on the preference scale, quite low but not the absolute worst.

To the right of that cell is one with 1 in it, representing a person who rated Economics at 1 and Business at 3. Then comes an empty cell with 0 in it. Then a cell with one person who rated Economics 1 but gave Business a 5. Then another empty cell. And finally, in the lower right corner cell, a strange person who hates Economics but loves Business. Frankly, I worry for the future of this person if he or she ever tries a career in business. How can you succeed in business without some appreciation for economics?

Clearly, people who hate Economics tend to hate Business as well. But what about the other end of the distributions? Do people who love Business tend to love Economics? The place to start looking for answers is the upper right corner cell of the crosstab. You will find that 11 people love both subjects.

And what about people who rate Business in the middle, giving it a 3, 4, or 5? Look at the cells in the middle of the table. You will see three in a row with 11, 15, and 13 students in them, and several cells with 6, 7, or 8 nearby. Indeed, people who rate one of these subjects in the middle tend to rate the other one in the middle, too.

If you gaze over the whole crosstab, all 49 cells, you will see that most of the students are in cells running from the lower left corner, up through the very middle, to the upper right corner. Hardly anybody is in cells near the upper left or lower right. People tend to feel the same way toward the two subjects, and very few love one subject while hating the other. This is the picture you will get with a strong positive correlation.

Notice the numbers running under the bottom row of cells: 34, 35, 37, 31, 32, 12, and 19. Each of these is the total of the numbers in the column of cells right above it. These are the same numbers of cases you would see if you asked the computer for the frequencies distribution for Business. Thirty-four people gave Business a 1 rating, for example.

At the far right of the cells, running up outside them, are the frequencies for the Economics ratings. For example, 27 people gave Economics a 1 rating. These frequencies on two sides of the crosstab are sometimes called the **marginals,** perhaps because they are on the physical margins of the crosstab.

The total number of cases, the number of students whose opinions are crosstabulated, is shown near the top left of the screen: Cases: 200. If there were missing cases (missing values), the number would be less than 200.

The bottom left corner of the screen has a useful option. You see the word Display, with the D in a box, followed by Counts. This means that at the moment, the cells in the crosstabs show the actual numbers of students—the counts of students—in the 49 cells. But maybe you'd like to see them in terms of percentages. Simply press [D] to change the display.

The counts will change to percents. It is important to see how they are figured. Take the right-hand column of cells, under Business 7. The percentages in the cells, from top to bottom, are: 58%, 32%, 0%, 0%, 5%, 0%, and 5%. These all add up to 100%, and so at the bottom of this column is 100%. The percentages are figured for each column separately. Thus you can see that 58% of those who rated Business most highly also rated Economics most highly.

The left-hand column, representing the students who hated Business, shows that 56% of these Business haters also hated Economics. The figures in the left-hand column of cells may not add up exactly to 100%—they seem to total 101%—because some small error was caused by rounding off the percentages to the nearest whole percent. But the percentages in each column should add to about 100%. Each column of cells reports on students who gave a particular response to Variable X, which is Business in the example. Each percent represents the students in that group who gave a particular response to the Y variable.

If you want to see the percentages figured the other way around, return to the main menu, select crosstabs, and then choose Economics to be Variable X, Business to be Variable Y. Professional statistical software usually prints two or even three sets of percentages at once on its crosstabs. I have found that this confuses even advanced students, so I have put only one set of percentages in a given crosstab. A second set is always available to you by simply selecting the same pair of items again in the opposite order.

To get rid of the percentages and see the counts again, just press [D] to change the display a second time. Now it is time to tackle the summary statistics printed to the left of the crosstab, starting with the correlation coefficient.

Correlation Coefficients

Scrutinizing all the cells of the crosstab can be illuminating, even for practiced researchers, but it is also time consuming and often bewildering. When two items are strongly correlated, like Business and Economics, the pattern can be quite clear. But a weak relationship between two variables is usually hard to see in a crosstab with many cells. And it is very useful to have a way of measuring the different strengths of various correlations in your data. This is where correlation coefficients come in.

Correlation coefficients are modest little numbers that express the strength of the association between two variables. In previous software publications, I have introduced correlations in several different ways (Bainbridge, 1986:52; 1987a:187, 1987b:3), and perhaps most of you have already gained some familiarity with correlations. The way I originally learned about them myself was simply through example. Long before I ever learned how to calculate correlations, I had been reading articles that used them to analyze data. We will look at some correlations from the STUDENTS dataset and through them get the general feeling of what correlations mean. If you seriously plan to do your own statistical research, you will have to take courses that cover the real mathematical basis of these useful numbers.

At the left side of the screen is the phrase Correlation (r): 0.69. The most commonly used correlation coefficient is called r (always written as a lowercase r, never a capital R). The highest r can possibly get is 1.00, and we almost never see one this big. Indeed, 0.69 is a very strong correlation as survey research goes. The computer calculates r by putting all the data from the crosstab into a somewhat complicated formula, boiling the relationship between Business and Economics down to this one, simple number.

If you want to see a "perfect correlation" of 1.00, you really have to correlate an item with itself. You could do a crosstab in which Business was Variable X, and Business was also Variable Y. Try it, if you like, and see how a 1.00 correlation looks in the cells of the crosstab. All it would mean is that people who like Business like Business.

When two items are not related at all, we say there is a *zero* correlation between them. Try a crosstab in which Business is Variable X, and Item 9, Physics, is Variable Y. Do you see any pattern in the cells of the crosstab of Business and Physics? Well, I don't. And the correlation between these two items is 0.01, about as close to zero as you will get.

A correlation coefficient doesn't have to be dead zero to indicate a lack of correlation between the two variables. It just has to be close. But how close is close? Certainly, a correlation of 0.01 is essentially the same as zero. But what about one of 0.10? The answer to these questions is a bit complicated, and we can touch only the surface here.

Researchers often speak of the statistical significance of their findings. This must not be confused with the importance of their findings, which is a value judgment. I suppose every researcher thinks his or her discoveries are important. Rather, statistical significance concerns our confidence that the correlation is not really zero, inflated accidentally by the workings of pure chance. We illustrated basic concepts of statistical significance in Chapter 3, when we played the probability pinball game and discussed a true–false astronomy quiz.

When people fill out a questionnaire, sometimes their fingers—or their minds—slip and they check a box that does not really express their true feelings. And our questions can show a lot of slippage, ambiguities we write in by mistake that confuse the respondents and produce some meaningless responses. Chance plays a role in all our statistics, although we can hope it is a small one.

One of the reasons survey researchers like to get a big heap of questionnaires from a large number of respondents is that a large number of cases reduces the impact of chance. Thus the statistical significance of a given correlation is greatly determined by the number of respondents.

Imagine we had a brief riot in our student prison, with all 200 students running madly from cell to cell in the crosstab. Then the guards regain the upper hand and lock all the cell doors. We can then calculate the statistics for the new distribution of students across the 49 cells of the crosstab. If students got into cells entirely by chance, there will be a correlation close to zero between the two variables. Let's imagine it came out 0.05.

If we had a second riot, and then figured the correlation, we'd probably get a new figure, let's say 0.02. And if we did it 100 times—exhausting for all concerned—we'd get a set of correlations, a couple of which would be pretty far from zero, such as 0.15.

The **statistical significance** of a correlation is the probability that we would get this correlation purely by chance. For 200 respondents, a correlation of 0.18 has a statistical significance of 0.01. Notice that 0.01 is the same as the fraction 1/100. This means we would get a correlation as far from 0.00

as 0.18 only 1 time out of 100, purely by chance. That is, on average, in every 100 riots in our prison we would get 1 crosstab that gave us a correlation this big.

The 0.69 correlation between Business and Economics is far more solid than this. Right below `Correlation (r): 0.69` you will see `Significance: 0.001`. This means that we would not expect to see such a big correlation purely by chance even once in 1000 tries. In fact, for 200 respondents, every correlation beyond about 0.23 will achieve the 0.001 level of significance.

There are four possible messages about statistical significance that a crosstab might give you: 0.001, 0.01, 0.05, and n.s. The third, 0.05, means there is 1 chance in 20 that the correlation could really be zero. This is not very solid, especially because our dataset can produce hundreds of correlations. One out of 20 of them would achieve the 0.05 level entirely by chance. The message "n.s." stands for "not significant." That is certainly what you get with a correlation of 0.02, and from others in the vicinity of zero.

If you want to see a moderate correlation, try the crosstab of Business with Item 25, Engineering. I think if you squint at the cells in that crosstab, you can see that people who like Business tend to like Engineering, but the pattern is a weak one. The correlation coefficient is 0.21, significant at the 0.01 level.

Correlations can be below zero, as well as above it. Just as they cannot surpass 1.00 on the positive side, they cannot go beyond -1.00 on the negative side. So all the correlations you will ever find run between -1.00 and $+1.00$. Try a crosstab with #4 Law for Variable X and #9 Physics for Variable Y. The correlation is -0.25, significant at the 0.001 level.

With negative correlations, we should expect to see the fullest cells of the crosstab running from the upper left corner down to the lower right corner. The crosstab of Law and Physics doesn't give a perfect picture like this, but it's close. The fullest cells do run down from left to right, but they don't exactly start in the upper left corner, just very near to it. Still, this example gives a pretty good picture of a negative correlation, and we don't have many very strong negative correlations in this particular dataset.

A negative correlation between Law and Physics means that people who like Law tend *not* to like Physics. People who like Physics tend not to like Law. As with positive correlations, people middling toward one tend to be middling toward the other. The correlation is not very strong as negative ones go, but the tendency is there.

To summarize: In a positive correlation, people who love subject X tend also to love subject Y, and people who hate one also hate the other. But in a negative correlation, people who love X hate Y, and people who hate X love Y. A correlation near zero, whether just below zero or just above it, indicates no relationship between X and Y.

Another way of thinking about correlations is in terms of prediction. How would you predict David Innes feels about Economics? No idea, right? You don't know anything about David's college preferences. But if we tell you he loves Business, then you have some information on which to base a prediction about Economics. Our research showed that preferences for Business have a strong positive correlation with preferences for Economics. Knowing he likes Business, you would predict he also likes Economics. Because the correlation between these two subjects is a very strong one, you will have confidence in this prediction, although it is possible you are wrong in the case of David.

How does David feel about Physics? We just told you he likes Business, but there is no correlation between Business and Physics. Therefore, it doesn't help your prediction about Physics to know he likes Business. So without further information, you can't really predict how he will feel about Physics.

How does Jane Porter feel about Physics? Again, you can't answer, because you don't yet know anything about her college preferences. Suppose we tell you she loves Law. Then you would have some basis for suggesting she will dislike Physics, because Law and Physics have a negative correlation. But the correlation is a fairly weak one, so you won't have great confidence in your prediction that she dislikes Physics.

Gamma, Tau, and Chi-Square

Right below the r correlation on your screen, you will see two very similar coefficients, gamma and tau. Their names are the Greek letters for G and T. When social scientists or statisticians say "correlation coefficient," without giving it a specific name, they usually mean r, the one we have been using. But gamma and tau are really correlation coefficients, too.

Look again at the crosstab for #11 Business and #16 Economics. The r is 0.69, the gamma is 0.66, and the tau is 0.48. Well, if they're all correlation coefficients, why don't they agree? At the simplest level, they disagree because they use three different mathematical formulas. Which one is correct, then? The answer depends on the kind of data you have and the purpose of your analysis.

Think for a moment about the different kinds of questions we ask in surveys. A question like age gets a definite number for its answer. I am 46, and one of my sons is 23. I am twice as old as my son. Over the next year, each of us will age exactly 1 year. All this seems pretty obvious, but I want to stress that age is the ordinary kind of number we are used to dealing with in arithmetic. But take our question about space funding:

Should the amount of money being spent on the U.S. space program be increased, kept at current levels, decreased, or ended altogether?

[1] Increased   [2] Kept at current levels   [3] Decreased   [4] Ended

Notice that we have put numbers inside the four boxes the respondent is supposed to choose from. And we type these numbers into the computer. The number 1 is for respondents who want funding for space increased, 4 for those who want spaceflight ended. Thus, because of the way we gave numbers to the four boxes, this questionnaire item measures a person's *opposition* to the space program. The higher the number, the greater the opposition. Just as each respondent has an age number, such as 23 or 46, inside the computer, each one has a space opposition number, such as 2 or 4.

But though a person aged 46 is twice as old as someone aged 23, we cannot say that a person with a space funding score of 4 is twice as much against the space program as someone with a score of 2. The numbers from the space funding item are not necessarily the same distance apart. They are much less precise numbers than those from an age question.

Age can be described as a *ratio* scale, and space funding is an *ordinal* scale. Statisticians distinguish four kinds of variable, and they have devised different statistical measures for dealing with each. In terms of survey questions, the four are as follows:

1. **Nominal variables.** These are questions that place people in categories, but the categories are not in any particular order. For example, we could ask which religious tradition a person had grown up in, giving four boxes to choose from:

   [1] Protestant   [2] Catholic   [3] Jewish   [4] Other

   These responses could have been offered in any order. It is common to see them in this order, simply because more Americans will check the first box, a sizable number will check the second, and few will check the last two. But there's nothing very logical about this order. We could have put Jewish first, because it's the historically most ancient of the first three. Or we could have put Catholic first because it comes first in alphabetical order.

   With nominal variables, we are using numbers instead of names, but we have no right to do anything with them we could not do with the names. We cannot do much arithmetic on numbers that are values of nominal variables. For example, we gave the number 4 to Other and 2 to Catholic. But it doesn't mean anything to divide this 4 by this 2. In what way are the Others twice the Catholics? In no way at all, so far as I know. The numbers in nominal variables should be considered names, and nothing more.

2. **Ordinal variables.** These are questions that place respondents in categories, and the categories are in a meaningful order. The space funding item is a good example. People who want funding ended checked the 4 box; those who wanted funding merely

decreased checked the 3 box. Those who checked 4 are more opposed to the space program than people who checked 3. Those who checked 2 ("kept at current levels") are still less opposed, and those who checked 1 ("increased") are the least opposed of all.

It doesn't make sense to do regular arithmetic with these numbers, for example dividing this 4 by this 2. But we can do some crude measuring with such a scale. It is as if our thermometers didn't have nicely ruled degrees on them, but instead said: [1] Cold, [2] Cool, [3] Warm, [4] Hot. If it's hot today, we know the thermometer has to go through warm and cool to get to cold. The numbers are in a particular order, but the distances between them might be irregular. For example, Cool might be 50 degrees; Warm might be 80, and Hot might be 90. Many types of questionnaire item are ordinal variables—for instance, agree–disagree items.

3. **Interval variables.** These questions have a set distance—interval—separating all the steps in the scale. Common thermometer scales are a good example. The difference between 79 degrees and 80 degrees is exactly the same as the difference between 80 and 81. And the difference between 10 and 20 is the same as between 90 and 100. You can validly add and subtract with these variables. If it is 80 degrees and it gets 10 degrees hotter, we know it is exactly 90.

However, multiplying and dividing cause problems. Perhaps by instinct, we avoid saying things like "Today is exactly twice as hot as yesterday." Oh yes, today could be 80 and yesterday was 40. But is 80 really twice as hot as 40? No, and the reason is that the zero point on most of our temperature scales is not where it should be. There is a temperature called absolute zero, which really is a point of no temperature. It's about 460 degrees below zero Fahrenheit and 273 degrees below zero Celsius (Centigrade). A lower temperature than this is physically impossible. And scientists often use a temperature scale called Kelvin or Absolute that has this for its zero. But ordinary temperature scales have faulty zero points, so it is wrong to multiply and divide in them.

4. **Ratio variables.** These are questions that have proper zero points, as well as meeting all the requirements of an interval variable. An example we have already mentioned is age. A person just born is zero years old. At 46, I am twice as old as my 23-year-old son. We give variables of this type the name *ratio*, because it is mathematically correct to make ratios out of these variables—that is, to divide them by each other.

You can consult any statistics textbook written for the social sciences to learn more about these four kinds of variables. But, as you can see, we encounter each of these types in questionnaires, and we have to use somewhat different statistical formulas for the different types.

The r correlation coefficient is designed for interval variables and ratio variables. It is not mathematically right for ordinal variables; it just wasn't designed for them. Often, researchers boldly use r and some related coefficients when their data are really of the ordinal kind. Technically, this is not correct, but it appears that the errors produced by using r with ordinal data are usually small, and a large proportion of professional social scientists go ahead and use r in this way, despite the complaints of purists (Boyle, 1970; Vigderhous, 1977).

Although you may get an argument from some professionals, it is widely considered okay to use r with nominal variables that have just two values, what are sometimes called **dichotomous variables.** For example, we have a question about gender in our STUDENTS survey, with half the respondents being female, and half, male. Now, the difference between males and females can't be quantified. We don't have a third sex to worry about, so we don't really have to decide how big that difference is. But when you have a nominal variable with more than two categories, such as Protestant, Catholic, and Jewish religious affiliation, you would get into serious trouble using r.

Today, I suspect that sociologists are more apt than practitioners of the other social sciences to complain when someone uses r with ordinal data. Psychologists seem especially ready to use r or related statistical procedures when their data are not technically the right kind. In the next chapter, we will follow the psychologists some distance in this, because r and related measures are especially convenient when you are combining several items to make a psychological index. But you should be warned that other coefficients are more appropriate than r when you have ordinal or nominal questions in your survey.

This is where gamma, tau, and chi-square come in. **Gamma** and **tau** are correlation coefficients designed for use with ordinal data. It is mathematically quite correct to use them with interval and ratio variables as well, but unlike r, they work for the cruder ordinal variables. **Chi-square** can handle nominal variables, as well as having some use with the three other kinds.

You can use gamma and tau with confidence for our space funding question or for the typical agree–disagree item. Their formulas make no assumptions about the distances between the responses, and all they require is that the responses be in a logical order. To add to the confusion of students and researchers alike, there are three commonly used versions of tau (tau-a, tau-b, and tau-c) with different formulas. I place gamma and tau on the screen next to each other because the particular version of tau the program computes, tau-a, is closely related to gamma.

Tau is a bit more conservative a coefficient than gamma, and with very uneven frequency distributions on one or both of your variables, gamma can become misleading. On the other hand, with the typical survey data, tau cannot reach very close to -1.00 or $+1.00$, and gamma can.

Chi-square is not a correlation coefficient, and it can be greater than 1.00. It reflects the extent that the numbers in the cells of the crosstab are in a pattern you would expect purely on the basis of the frequencies of the individual variables, and chi-square is typically a step on the way to determining the statistical significance of patterns in the data. Unlike correlation coefficients, chi-square is not very good for comparing different pairs of variables, especially because its size is strongly influenced by how many cells the crosstab has. But, although doing so is not strictly correct, it is sometimes used as a test of the statistical significance of gamma or tau.

If you look once again at the crosstab of Business and Economics, you will see that the chi-square is 213.92. That's certainly bigger than our correlation coefficients! Right below chi-square is some information necessary to interpret it: Degrees of freedom: 36. This number simply reflects the size of the crosstab, being the number of rows in the table minus 1 multiplied by the number of columns in the table minus 1. A table of numbers called the *chi-square distribution* appears in the back of every statistics textbook. Look up both the chi-square and the degrees of freedom and you will find the statistical significance.

In the case of the crosstab of Business and Economics, the chi-square is significant far beyond the 0.001 level, just as the r correlation is. I give you the r, gamma, tau, and chi-square, rather than just one coefficient, for several reasons. Of course, your computer does not know whether your variables are ordinal or interval, so you have to decide. Also, different fields of social science will give more or less emphasis to one coefficient or another. And all students should be aware that various different statistical methods exist, and that they have to choose intelligently among them.

The last program on your disk enables you to move data from my software into other statistical packages, especially those on large, "mainframe" computer systems. Those professional statistical packages will offer many different analytical techniques, and with them you can choose just the right one for your purposes. But our limited set of statistics, selected for its variety and educational value, does provide valid means for analyzing the kinds of data we typically get from surveys.

If you are using *Survey Research* in a course, the instructor will know the right way of approaching correlations for your particular field of study. I believe you already have a sense that much mathematical training may be necessary for really advanced work. But you have also just seen that practical survey researchers have traditionally bent the mathematical rules a bit. Personally, I think you should be very aware of the technical limitations of various analytical procedures, and you should always be ready to improve your grasp of them. But I have often seen students unnecessarily paralyzed by the realization that statistics is a wide, complex field.

For our purposes, it is much more important at this point to get on with the exciting job of analyzing survey results than it is to study the mathematical details. That is an important job, too, but one best tackled at another time. Keep in the back of your mind the realization that high-level, professional survey research requires a precise understanding of mathematical statistics. But a rudimentary sense of what correlations are is enough for us now.

As you work with correlations, and quickly make interesting discoveries of your own, you will gain practical experience that is valuable in its own right and should make learning statistics easier when you study it. Conversely, if you have already taken statistics courses, you can benefit from your knowledge in tackling the problems of survey research, and you will also give your knowledge greater practical scope by applying it to real data.

[4] Partial Correlations of Three Variables

The last option on the basic statistics main menu lets you analyze correlations linking three variables simultaneously. When you choose Partial correlations of three variables, the computer will ask you to select three, which it will call X, Y, and Z. Once you have done this, you will get a pair of tables, mostly giving you information you could have gotten from frequencies or crosstabs.

On the left of the screen, near the top, you will find a list of the three items you choose and a message about the number of valid cases. The computer will do the analysis only for respondents who gave valid responses to all three items you selected, and these people are the valid cases.

Below these messages stands Table 1, which gives you the means and the variances for the three variables. Note that these may or may not be exactly the numbers the frequencies option would have given you. For example, suppose that everybody in a sample of 200 gave valid answers for Items X and Y, but only 150 people gave a valid answer for Item Z. Here, the means and variances will be calculated only for the 150, thus giving you somewhat different statistics than you would have gotten from the frequencies on X and Y, which would have been based on all 200 cases.

On the right side of the screen is Table 2, which gives you the three r correlations that link the three variables in pairs, and you will see something called the **partial correlation**. I think the best way to explain this is with an example. To do that effectively, we have to invent a scientific hypothesis.

Start by looking at a crosstab in which Variable X is #39 Sex and Variable Y is #9 Physics. You will find that the r correlation between the respondent's sex and preference for Physics is 0.19, significant at the 0.01 level. At first thought, this coefficient may seem a bit mysterious. But remember that the Sex item gives each female a value of 1 and each male a value of 2. Again, this says nothing about the relative merits of the two sexes; these are just the numbers we arbitrarily used to input the data into the computer. Recall, also, that although sex is a nominal variable, it may be safe to use the r correlation because there are only two categories, even though it normally is used for interval or ratio variables.

The r of 0.19 between Sex and Physics means that males are more apt to like this particular academic field. If you look at the relatively simple crosstab itself, I think you will find the picture pretty clear. More men (column 2) give high ratings to Physics. In contrast, the women (column 1) rate it lower.

Let's think of an explanation for why men might like Physics more than women do. I am sure you can imagine many logical reasons. But one possible explanation can be tested further with the data at hand, so let me propose it: Men like Physics because more of them are apt to enter careers in Engineering, and people seeking a career in Engineering can use some background in Physics. I like this explanation, partly because it does not assume any innate differences between the intellectual predispositions of the sexes, and also because it suggests that students make rational decisions about college subjects based on their career plans. But do our data support this explanation? Or do the data weigh against it?

First, you could try looking at the crosstab between Sex and Engineering. You would indeed find that men prefer Engineering, and the correlation is 0.25, significant at the 0.001 level. But you can take the analysis even further if you do a partial correlations analysis, with the three items as follows: X is #39 Sex, Y is #9 Physics, and Z is #25 Engineering.

When the tables of the partial correlations analysis appear on the screen, look at Table 2. The top row should say this:

Pair of variables	Corre- lation	Control variable	Partial correlation
X-Y	0.19	Z	0.05

The first part is easy enough to understand. Sex of the respondent is Variable X. The respondent's feelings about Physics is Variable Y. The first row gives the correlations between X and Y; its pair of variables is X-Y. The ordinary, r correlation between these is 0.19, just what we found in their crosstab.

But we are interested in whether the real cause of the correlation is actually Variable Z, the respondent's interest in Engineering. The computer brings Engineering into the equation as a **control variable**. When we control for the influence of a third variable on a correlation, we calculate what the correlation would be if its influence did not exist.

The particular statistical method the computer is using is called **partial correlations**. And at the end of the first row of the table we see that the partial correlation between X and Y, controlling for Z, is 0.05. This is very close to zero, and is certainly not statistically significant.

One way of understanding this is to say that when we controlled for the influence of Engineering, the correlation between Sex and Physics collapsed. It dropped from 0.19 to 0.05, and this brings it essentially to zero. In other words, the analysis shows that the tendency for men to like Physics more than women do could indeed be entirely because more men anticipate a career related to Engineering.

If there were some very different reasons for the sex difference in attitudes toward Physics, the partial correlation between Sex and Physics, controlling for Engineering, would still have been sizable. But when we took out the influence of Engineering, using the partial correlations method, *no* significant correlation between Sex and Physics remained.

The two remaining rows in Table 2 on your screen try the same thing for the two other pairs of items, X-Z and Y-Z. For example, the correlation between Sex (X) and Engineering (Z) is 0.25. When we control for Physics (Y), this drops to 0.17, but does not collapse to near zero. Thus it is not so plausible to hypothesize that men like Engineering because of their love for Physics. No, apparently they like Physics because of their love for Engineering!

Now, I don't mean to say that we have proved that this is so. Rather, the data support my hypothesis about Physics, and we should take the hypothesis more seriously after seeing the results of this analysis. Many secrets can be hidden in a set of data, however, and statistical techniques don't have magic powers. In scientific research, we gather evidence that relates to theories and hypotheses we are interested in. We do an even-handed analysis, and usually some hypotheses will come out better than others. Our confidence will increase in the theories that receive statistical support, and our doubts about the others will increase. Ultimate truth is beyond the grasp of a single, modest research study. But even a small dataset like STUDENTS can inch us in the direction of truth.

The sort of partial correlations used in this analysis is based on r. You can do something similar with tau, and statisticians have invented a partial gamma calculated by very different means. In fact, there are many different methods for controlling for the influence of extra variables. Some of them require more advanced kinds of statistics, and others need large numbers of cases to work effectively.

I included a simple version of partial correlations in this basic statistics program for two reasons. First, they let you see that we can work with more than just two variables at once. Second, they show it is possible to evaluate whether we have the right interpretation of research results. We will follow up on these themes in the next two chapters. Chapter 7 and a pair of programs it introduces let us work with many variables at once. And Chapter 8 revives the issue of control variables in examining the reliability and validity of questionnaire items and our interpretations of correlations between them.

Before we can contemplate more elaborate analysis, and before we can fully utilize the four options of our basic statistics program, we need to get our set of data in the best possible shape. This is accomplished by a program on your disk that recodes data.

▶ ▶ ▶ ▶ ▶ ▶ ▶ ▶ ▶ ▶ ▶

[F] RECODING

Get to the menu of nine programs, the table of contents of the disk. Select the recoding program. This works only if you have a set of data to recode, and we will use our now-familiar STUDENTS dataset to show how to do recoding.

In a moment, the top row of the screen will say RECODING - What is the name of the survey? Type STUDENTS and press [ENTER].

Later on, when you have saved a recoded version of the dataset on your disk, the computer will next ask you Do you want to work with the ORIGINAL data or RECODED data? That choice allows you to make further changes to the recoded version of your dataset, or to start fresh with the data in their original form, before any recoding was done. But I did not recode any variables in the STUDENTS dataset, so you won't get this option until you have done some work yourself.

The STUDENTS dataset will load into the computer, and a menu will appear:

        [1]   Recode a Variable
        [2]   Create correlation matrix
        [3]   Create GAMMA matrix
        [4]   Create TAU matrix
        [ESC] QUIT or change programs

[1] Recode a Variable

Be careful! Don't press [2], [3], or [4]. We'll explain them in the next section, but they all give the computer a vast amount of work to do. Instead, press [1] to do some simple recoding.

The screen will fill with the familiar instructions for selecting a variable, this time to transform it rather than merely look at some statistics about it. For our first example, let's work with the space funding item. Type 31 and press [ENTER] to recode it.

Now the screen will show you something that looks very much like the frequencies options from the basic statistics program, with a set of instructions listed on the left. The first one says Move the recode arrow by pressing + for up or − for down. The recode arrow is the bright shape with the word *Recode* inside it, at the bottom center of the screen.

Find the + key on your keyboard. Actually, there should be two of them. Over at the lower right edge is a key with just a + on it, and in the upper right-hand corner is one with + and =. This latter key makes you hold down the shift key to get a +, so I suggest you use the key just for +. Press it a couple of times.

The recode arrow will jump up. Now press [−] and watch it move back down. Wherever the arrow points, the computer is ready to change the data. Move the arrow until it points at the number 5 in the *Value* column of the frequencies table. Look across that row and you will see that eight cases—eight students—gave the 5 response to the space funding question.

But wait, the item had only four legitimate responses: [1] increase funding, [2] keep funding at current levels, [3] decrease funding, or [4] end funding for the space program altogether. The value 5 was given to students who failed to give a valid response. Either they checked no box at all or they checked a couple of boxes.

Do we want these bad responders in our analysis? The way the table is set up, their 5 score on the space funding question implies that they were even more negative about it than the people who wanted funding ended. But some of them may simply have lacked any opinion. What we have to do is throw these eight respondents out of the data for this item.

The way we do that is to recode the 5 response to a 0. When we recode a value, we change it to a different number. The way I wrote these programs, the computer ignores any value of 0, so if we recode the 5s to 0, that is the same as throwing them out.

Make sure the recoding arrow points at the value 5, with its eight respondents. Notice the instruction at the left edge of the screen that says, `Recode the value by pressing a number key (0-9).` Press [0]. Make sure you press the zero key, rather than the letter O. In an instant, the eight bad respondents are thrown into the 0 category. From now on, the computer will ignore them whenever it is working with the space funding item.

Now look over the two right-hand columns of the table, labeled *Percent* and *Valid Percent*. I didn't mention them at the beginning, because they started out identical, and only now can we tell them apart. The *Percent* column tells you what percent of your total sample of respondents have a particular value on the given item. It includes those recoded to 0. The *Valid Percent* column gives you the percentages after throwing out the respondents with a value of 0.

For example, 79 students checked the 1 box in response to the space funding question, indicating they want funding increased. They represent 39.5% of the total set of 200 students. But they are 41.1% of the 192 students who gave a valid answer. Divide 79 by 192, multiply by 100, and you get 41.1%.

We are not finished recoding the space funding item yet. Notice that only one person checked the 4 box, indicating that he or she wanted funding for the space program stopped altogether. That person sticks out like a sore thumb. For some kinds of statistical analysis, having just one person giving an extreme response can distort results a bit. So perhaps we should recode this one person's response.

Logically, if he wants funding ended, he also wants it reduced. So it would be quite appropriate to recode him into the 3 category along with all the others who want funding reduced. You don't have to do this. Getting rid of the eight who failed to respond validly really was necessary, but recoding this extreme response is optional.

To recode this person, move the recoding arrow until it points at the 4 value. You want to recode this person to a 3, so press [3]. Don't press [0], because that would throw him out altogether. As you will see, the person gets recoded smoothly into a 3, and the number in the 3 category increases from 34 to 35.

It may occur to you that recoding data can be dangerous. What if you make a mistake? Will you ruin your dataset?

Don't panic. Whatever recoding you do, the original dataset will stay on your disk. It will merely be joined by a recoded version of the dataset, and you can select either version you want for one of the analysis programs.

Also, I have written the recoding part of the program so that the actual changes are not made right away. They look as if they were, because the table changes immediately. But really the computer is just showing you what would happen if you made the recodes. It remembers your set of commands (up to a limit of about 40 recodes for any variable) and will follow them when you press [ENTER]. But if you press [ESC] instead, the recodes will be forgotten, and you can consider a different way of recoding the variable.

Whichever way you finish working with a particular variable, by pressing [ENTER] or [ESC], the computer will ask you to select another variable for recoding. If you don't want to do any more recoding now, press [ESC]. Then the computer will ask you whether you want to save your work. If you were just practicing or experimenting with how recoding works, perhaps you want to answer no. But if you want the recoded version of the dataset to be saved on the disk, you must answer yes.

Let's try another example, to see some of the other ways a variable can be recoded. Select Item 33: "Do you think the United States should build a permanently manned space station in orbit around the Earth over the next few years, or not?" The three valid responses were [1] Yes, [2] No, and [3] No opinion.

When you get the frequencies table on the screen, you will see that 9 cases have a value of 4 on this item. These students failed to give a valid response, so you should probably recode them to 0, to throw them out of the analysis. But what should you do with the 43 people who said they had no opinion? At the moment, they have the value of 3, but shouldn't you recode this to 0 also?

You could. There are two other ways you could recode, however, and each one would be a reasonable decision. One possibility is to recode 3 into

2. You already have 101 respondents who said "Yes, build the space station." By recoding 3 into 2, you would get 90 respondents who were not willing to support the space station, 43 of whom had no strong opinion, and 47 who were definitely against the space station.

The advantage to this choice is that you would have two groups of comparable size to compare, and you could base conclusions on almost all of your 200 respondents. But in interpreting your results, you would have to make sure you remembered that the 2 value had a new meaning after your recoding. Originally, it meant "No, don't build the space station." After recoding, it would combine those who were against the space station with those who couldn't decide either way. Perhaps you should describe this group of 90 as "lacking positive support for the space station."

But you could recode this variable another way. The "No opinion" group could be put between the "Yes" and "No" groups. Those in favor of the space station are at one extreme, and those opposed to it are at the other. Logically, those with no opinion could be considered fence-sitters with a viewpoint between those of the more opinionated groups.

There are different ways to move group 3 between groups 1 and 2, but here's a simple one. You should probably keep notes on each step in the move, because it is slightly complicated. First recode 2 to 9. That's right, move the people who said no up out of the way, recoding them to value 9. Now the 2 value is free, and you can move the people in group 3 down to it. So the second step is to recode 3 to 2. Finally, recode 9 to 3. This last step takes the people who originally were at value 2, and who had been visiting up at 9, down to 3.

This gives you three groups of valid responders. Group 1 is the 101 students who said "Yes, build the space station." Group 2 is the 43 students who had no opinion. And Group 3 is the 47 students who said no. Again, you should write this recoding information down, stating it clearly so that you will understand it weeks later.

Once you have finished your recoding, you can save your work and shift to a different program. The other programs will automatically ask you whether you want to work with your original data or the recoded version.

You may want to try different recoding decisions, even to have two differently recoded versions of a dataset available for different kinds of analysis. The way to do this is to make an extra copy of your data disk and have one set of recodes on one disk, the second set on the other disk. For sake of simplicity, I have written the programs so that they expect to see only one original dataset and one recoded version. By using two or more disks, each with a different recoded version, you can work with any number.

[2] Create Correlation Matrix

A **correlation matrix** is simply a table containing many correlations. Our recoding program can create several kinds of correlation matrix, each containing more than 1000 correlation coefficients. So far, we have dealt with correlations one or two at a time. But now we can get into the wholesale correlation business.

Perhaps you think that is a bad idea. You might feel it was hard enough to understand just one correlation coefficient, let alone hundreds. But Chapter 7 will show that it is not so hard to extract new discoveries from a whole matrix of correlations, and the matrix program that the next chapter describes will let you accomplish things that would be very difficult without a correlation matrix.

We will conclude this chapter by explaining how to create one or more correlation matrixes. I have already created one matrix and put it on your disk, giving all the r correlations in the original STUDENTS dataset, so you do not actually need to create any before turning to the next chapter and learning how to use them. Therefore, you might want to read quickly through the following instructions, then start the next chapter, until you have gained some experience in the virtues of matrixes and want to create some of your own.

To create a correlation matrix, you must first select the data the correlations are calculated from. Just go back to the beginning of the recoding program and tell the computer the name of the survey you want to work with. If you happen to have recoded some of the variables in it, the computer will then ask whether you want to work with the original data or the recoded form of the data. After you have decided, you will get the main menu. Pay attention to options 2, 3, and 4:

```
[2] Create correlation matrix
[3] Create GAMMA matrix
[4] Create TAU matrix
```

Each of these choices will calculate a huge number of correlations and save them on your disk. Option [2] gives you a matrix of r correlations; [3] and [4] give you heaps of gammas or taus. Depending on the kind of questions in your survey, you might consider r correlations most appropriate, or perhaps one of the others. Make your choice, and press the appropriate key.

Now the computer will launch into furious but invisible calculating activity. It is correlating every item with every other item and placing the answers in the cells of a table. If you have the maximum number of items, 48, the computer will calculate a total of 1128 correlation coefficients. This can take 10 minutes or more, for r correlations, and as much as half an hour or more on a slow computer for gammas and taus. Take a break. Have a snack. When the computer is done, it will flash and beep at you.

The computer will ask Do you want to save your work? Almost certainly, you do. Press [Y] to answer yes, and the freshly created matrix will be saved on the disk.

If you are part of a group using *Survey Research,* such as a college class, you may want to save time by having one person create all the matrixes for the dataset you are collectively analyzing. Then you can make several copies of that person's data disk.

(For those of you familar with the disk-operating system who might want simply to copy the matrix files from one disk onto another, leaving all the other files as they are, rather than copying the entire disk: This won't work unless you also copy the file for the dataset with the extension ".KEY" after the dataset's name. As explained in the appendix, this is the file that keeps track of what other files are on the disk. If you don't copy the KEY file as well as the new matrix, the computer won't know the matrix is on the disk. Of course, the KEY file should not be moved to a disk that is in any other way different from the one KEY is on, because it will have false information about the contents of the disk.)

You can make as many as six correlation matrixes for any dataset. Three of them would be based on the original data, and three would be based on the recoded version of the data. In each set of three, one would consist of r correlations, one of gammas, and one of taus. Whenever you want to look at a matrix, using the program described in the following chapter, the computer will list the matrixes you have created from the particular dataset, so you won't have to remember how many you have.

▶ ▶ ▶ ▶ ▶ ▶ ▶ ▶ ▶ ▶ ▶

PROJECTS

1. Data from Individual Cases.   When I prepared the 200 questionnaires for the STUDENTS dataset, I selected 100 female respondents and 100 males, including 50 from each of the 4 undergraduate years: freshmen, sophomores, juniors, and seniors. These surveys were sorted into piles before entering the data into the computer, so all the students in each group were kept together.

Use the "Data from one case" option in the basic statistics program to figure out how these groups fit together. Which cases are male, and which, female? Which groups of case numbers identify freshmen? Sophomores? Juniors? Seniors?

I must admit that the answers to these questions are buried in a later chapter of this book, but you should figure them out on your own. Work out an efficient plan for checking the sex and year of a number of cases, to find where the groups are in the series of case numbers (1–200). Then check these cases out, adding other cases when you develop a hypothesis about where the groups are. Write a brief report communicating your results.

2. Your Best and Worst Subjects.   Go through the list of 30 college subjects in the STUDENTS dataset and select the subject you like best and the subject you hate most. You will find the list of subjects in Chapter

1, but you will be using the basic statistics program, and they are listed there also.

Next, decide your personal preference ratings of the two subjects on the scale from 1 ("do not like") to 7 ("like very much"). Note, you do not have to give the subjects the extreme ratings of 7 and 1, unless you really love and hate them this much. But if they really are the courses you like best and worst, you cannot give more extreme ratings to any other subjects.

Use the "Frequencies on one variable" option on the main menu of the basic statistics program to see how the 200 students rated your best and worst subjects. You should copy down the two sets of information, just as they appear on the screen. On each table, you should mark the value you personally gave the subject, using an asterisk, and at the bottom of the page put a footnote explaining what the asterisk means: "*My personal preference rating of this subject."

Finally, write a brief report comparing your ratings with those of the 200 students. What percentage of the students gave the same rating as you did to each subject? What percentage gave higher ratings? Lower ratings? On average, do the students rate your best subject higher than your worst one?

3. Correlates of Classics. Perhaps the most mysterious of the 30 academic subjects in the STUDENTS dataset is "Classics (ancient civilization)." Just two or three generations ago, the study of Roman and Greek civilization was the heart of a liberal education. But today, in America at least, it has nearly vanished.

What does Classics mean to students today? Answer this question with the "Crosstab of two variables" option of the basic statistics program. Try a number of crosstabs, with Classics as your Y variable and the six subjects listed in the table below as your X variables. On a big sheet of paper, construct a large table. Down the left side, list the seven statistics given to the left of each crosstab on the computer screen. Each column of the table should represent the results of crosstabbing Classics with another subject. It should look like this:

			Crosstab of Classics with:			
	A Foreign Language	History	Anthropology	Literature	Art	Architecture
Correlation (r)						
Significance						
Gamma						
Tau						
Chi-square						
Degrees of freedom						
Significance						

You can analyze other subjects as well, if you think they will help you understand the meaning Classics has for students today.

Of course, the serious student of Classics has to study foreign languages—Latin, Greek, perhaps Hebrew or others—but do students think of Classics in terms of foreign languages? If so, there should be a significant correlation between Classics and A Foreign Language. Classics may also be seen as a branch of History, and much early Anthropology drew on information about the Greeks and Romans. But many students may encounter ancient civilizations primarily through their Literature, Art, and Architecture classes. Find the subjects that correlate most highly with Classics, and from them deduce what Classics means to our respondents.

4. Politicized Subjects. Perhaps you were sitting peacefully in a college class one day, when suddenly you were struck by the feeling that what the professor was giving you was political propaganda, most likely of a kind you disagreed with. This project asks you to use the crosstabs part of the basic statistics program to see which subjects have significant political bias in the minds of our 200 student respondents.

You should first look through the list of 30 academic subjects and find 5 that you suspect are politically conservative, and 5 that look politically liberal. Then run a crosstab for each with Item 38 (Political conservatism) as Variable X, and the subject as Variable Y. If a significant positive correlation between political conservatism and the subject appears, then conservatives tend to like the subject, perhaps because it is biased in their direction. If the correlation is significantly negative, political liberals are the ones who like the subject, perhaps because it leans in their political direction.

To complete this project, write a brief essay reporting the correlation between conservatism and each of the ten subjects, trying to explain why it came out the way it did—positive, negative, or insignificant.

5. Recode the Space Items. Switch to the recoding program, being careful *not* to select the options for creating a matrix. Get the STUDENTS dataset, and when you see the main menu, press [1] to recode variables.

Now, keeping notes on what you are doing, recode Items 31 through 37, the outer space questions, to get rid of bad responses, to get responses in a logical order, and to combine some of the valid responses into reasonable, large categories.

Write a report showing the frequencies you wind up with for each of the seven space items and justifying briefly each of the recoding decisions you made.

7

▶ ▶ ▶ ▶ ▶ This chapter will show you how to analyze simultaneously correlations linking many variables and how to combine questionnaire items into composite scales or indexes. In so doing, we look deeper than the separate questions we ask in our surveys, to see general ideologies and personality traits our respondents reveal through the patterns of their responses. In the practical realm of business, these techniques can help us identify groups of potential customers.

The subject of this chapter is vast enough for many books, and you can easily find thousands of technical publications that focus on this or that aspect of it. Although we must consider a few technical matters here, we will avoid all but the most essential mathematics or theoretical abstractions. Rather, we will apply a pair of programs to the STUDENTS dataset to give a practical introduction. We will begin with a matrix program that lets us inspect all the correlations in our dataset efficiently, sifting it to find general patterns that might otherwise escape our notice.

▶ ▶ ▶ ▶ ▶ ▶ ▶ ▶ ▶ ▶

[G] CORRELATION MATRIX

Using the STUDENTS work disk you made in Project 2 of Chapter 1, start up the matrix program; your computer will ask a familiar question, What is the name of the survey? For our examples, type in STUDENTS and press [ENTER]. If you want to analyze another dataset, make sure you have used the recoding program to create a suitable correlation matrix. Then type the survey's name and press [ENTER].

Matrixes and Indexes

If more than one matrix exists on your disk the computer will ask you which you want. Your disk contains one matrix from the STUDENTS dataset, and you should select it by pressing [1].

The main menu will now appear. At the top it will say `Original data - correlation matrix - Which do you want?` Note that it identifies the kind of matrix you are working with, so you can be sure you have the right one. The menu reads:

```
[1]     Correlation matrix
[2]     Correlations with one variable
[3]     Rank all correlations
[4]     Find blocks of correlations
[ESC]   QUIT or change programs
```

Select the first choice, the correlation matrix. The item selector will appear on the screen, and you will be told `Select the item that is to be Variable X`. Just to see what happens, select Item 1 by pressing [1] and [ENTER]. Then you will be asked to select Variable Y. This is just as if you were selecting a crosstab in the basic statistics program. I suggest you select Item 21, so type 21 and press [ENTER].

In a flash, 100 correlation coefficients will appear. The instruction seemed to call for just one correlation, that between Items 1 and 21. And if you look in the upper left-hand corner of the table on your screen, you will see the number 0.29 under *Var1* and to the right of *Var21*. This means that the correlation between Items 1 and 21 is 0.29. Just to the right of 0.29 is −0.16. This is the correlation between *Var2* and *Var21*—between variables (or Items) 2 and 21. And just below 0.29 is −0.03, the correlation between variable 1 and variable 22.

181

I am sorry I didn't have room on the screen for the names of the items, just for these "Var" abbreviations. But if you want to remind yourself of what the items are called, you can zip back to the item selector part of the program, then return instantly to the section of the matrix you want to inspect.

The full correlation matrix of our STUDENTS dataset is an immense table of coefficients, 40 columns wide and 40 rows high, for a total of 40 times 40, or 1600 coefficients! The correlation matrix option lets you see a chunk of the full matrix. When you select Variable X and Variable Y, the computer displays a 100-coefficient table with the correlation between X and Y in the upper left corner.

Of course, if your dataset has fewer than 10 variables, you can't get a table as big as 100 coefficients. Also, if you select items near the end of your list to be Variable X and Variable Y, the computer won't put the correlation between X and Y in the upper left corner, but in some other convenient place. For example, if you selected Item 40, the last one in the STUDENTS dataset, to be both X and Y, the correlation between Item 40 and itself would be in the lower right corner. You can experiment to see what I mean.

Now get another part of the correlation matrix by selecting Item 1 to be Variable X, and Item 1 to be Variable Y as well. Of course, the correlation between a variable and itself is 1.00, and you will find 1.00 in the upper left corner, the correlation between Var1 and Var1. The correlation between Var2 and Var2 is also 1.00, and so is the correlation between Var3 and Var3. In fact, the table has a diagonal line of 1.00s running from upper left corner to lower right corner. (Strictly speaking, a variable will not have a tau of 1.00 with itself, but for simplicity's sake, 1.00 is shown in our tau matrix.)

Now look back at the upper left corner, where the correlation between Var1 and itself is given as 1.00. To the right of it is 0.27, the correlation between Var2 and Var1. And below it is also 0.27, the correlation between Var1 and Var2. Of course, I have just named the same two variables, 1 and 2, merely mentioning them in different orders. The correlation between Var1 and Var2 is the same as that between Var2 and Var1. The order doesn't matter.

These observations let us do a quick inventory of the coefficients in the full correlation matrix. As I've noted, it contains a total of 1600 coefficients. But 40 of them are 1.00s, the result of correlating each item with itself, and are thus not very interesting. Subtract these 40 from 1600 and you get 1560. But half the coefficients in the 1560 are just duplicates of the other half. So you can divide 1560 by 2 to get 780, the number of completely different, and therefore interesting, correlations in the set.

If you want to figure the number of unique correlations in a dataset of your own, there is a simple formula to do it. Let the number of your items be N. Then the formula is: $N(N-1)/2$. For our 40 items, N = 40. N − 1 is 39. Multiply 40 times 39 and you get 1560. Divide by 2, and the result is 780.

You can use the correlation matrix option to browse through your correlations, looking here and there at random to see what you can find. Or you can walk your way down the columns, or across the rows, to see all the correlations with a particular variable you might be interested in. The next option lets you see all the correlations with one item more efficiently.

[2] Correlations with One Variable

When you select this option from the main menu of the correlation matrix program, the item selector will appear. Select the item you want, press [ENTER], and watch a list of correlations grow on the screen.

If you select Item 38 from the STUDENTS dataset, Political Conservatism, the first correlation you will get is 0.28 #11 Business. This means a correlation of 0.28 exists between being politically conservative and liking Business as an academic field. Next comes a correlation of 0.24 between being conservative and liking Economics. This is not surprising, because Business and Economics are so closely linked.

The third largest positive correlation is 0.23, linking Political Conservatism with the sex of the respondent. Recall that the sex variable has the value 1 for every female and 2 for every male. Thus a positive correlation between Political Conservatism and Sex means that males tend to be more conservative.

Let's pause for a moment and think again about how these variables are coded. The preference questions about Business and Economics have a logical direction to their coding. That is, it makes sense for a person who likes Business to have a higher value for Business than someone who doesn't like Business. The question is how much the person likes Business, so we give a low number to someone who likes it little, and a high number to someone who likes it a lot. The lowest possible rating for Business, as with all our preference items, is 1, and the highest rating is 7.

But the two questions about politics and sex have *arbitrary* codings; we could just as well have coded them a different way. A political conservative gets a high number, and a political liberal gets a low number, so the politics item is coded to measure the degree of political conservatism. The more conservative a person is, the higher the value on the politics item.

But we could just as easily have given a high number to liberals and a low number to conservatives. If you wanted, you could use our recoding program to change the item around in this way. Then it would be logical to call the item "Political Liberalism."

We have already discussed this briefly. But it becomes a crucial issue when we are examining correlation coefficients. Before you can interpret one of these coefficients, you have to remember how its variables are coded. Calling the political item "Political conservatism" is a reminder that high scores on it indicate conservatism. Had I labeled it just "Politics," we might forget this.

I intentionally did not give the sex item such a clear label, so that you would see the issue of labels and direction of coding. In its present form, the sex item expresses how male the person is. A male has a value of 2, and a female has a value of 1. If we had reversed this, giving females 2 and males 1, the item would measure the femaleness of the respondent. The original decision was purely arbitrary. In fact, I put the female box first on the questionnaire for the trivial reason that the old etiquette rule "ladies first" popped into my mind.

If we had forgotten that the politics item was coded to give high scores to conservatives, and the sex question was coded to give the higher score to males, we would not know how to interpret the 0.23 correlation between sex and politics. We would be able to see that one sex was politically different from the other, but not in which way.

Now look at the other end of the list of correlations, the bottom of the second column of figures on the screen. Next to last comes −0.27 #21 Social Work. The correlation is negative. This means that someone high in Political Conservatism will tend to be low in preference for Social Work. The reverse is also implied by the −0.27. A person low in conservatism— that is, a political liberal—will tend to rate Social Work higher. I think you can recognize that this is a reasonable finding.

Finally, a rather big negative correlation, −0.41, exists between being politically conservative and attitude toward the satellite defense project. If the satellite defense item were recoded to get rid of people who failed to respond to it properly or had no opinion, an even stronger negative correlation might result.

Well, we all know that political conservatives are more likely to support the so-called Star Wars program (Strategic Defense Initiative), part of which is research on a system of space satellites to defend against nuclear attack. So wouldn't you expect a *positive* correlation between conservatism and satellite defense, rather than this negative correlation? Again, it depends on how the items were phrased in the original questionnaire and coded for entry into the computer.

The satellite defense item reads: "Recently, there has been much talk about building a system of space satellites to defend against nuclear attack. Do you think research on this idea should continue, or should research stop?" The first box respondents could check was "Research should continue," so people who did got the value 1 for this item. The second box was labeled "Research should stop," so people who checked it got a value of 2. So as it is written and coded, the item measures *opposition* to satellite defense research. Students opposed to it get a higher score than students in favor of it. Conservatives tend to support research on the possibility of satellite defense, so they tend to check the first box; liberals tend to check the second. A high score on the satellite defense item indicates opposition to it, so the negative correlation of −0.41 between conservatism and the satellite defense item is entirely what we would expect.

I have gone over these particular examples to warn you that results such as those in our correlation matrix can be quite confusing if you forget how items were written and coded. Occasionally, even professional researchers make mistakes on this, so it is essential to be alert when interpreting your results. For example, a few years ago an eminent survey researcher reported that religious people were doing slightly less well in their lives than irreligious people. Several people concluded that religion was a bad thing when they saw this result. It was later discovered, however, that the researcher had made a mistake and forgotten how he had coded the religion variable (Hadaway, 1978). In fact, religious people were doing slightly better, on average, than irreligious people. Keep good records of what your variables mean, and avoid mistakes like this!

[3] Rank All Correlations

This option makes the computer do a wholesale search through your correlation matrix, putting the coefficients in order in terms of their size. When you select it, you get a menu with three main choices:

```
[1]    Highest to lowest (+1.00 to -1.00)
[2]    Lowest to highest (-1.00 to +1.00)
[3]    In descending magnitude (ignoring + and -)
[ESC] Return to main menu
```

Try the first choice, using our STUDENTS dataset. The screen goes blank for a moment. Then 1: 0.70 #4 Law - #5 Political science appears. This means the correlation between Law and Political Science is 0.70, and it is the biggest coefficient on the positive side. Soon the screen will fill with other positive coefficients in descending order of magnitude.

The computer is working very hard at the task of hunting through the huge matrix of correlations, so please be patient. When the screen is full, the bottom line will read Highest to lowest correlations. Press [ESC] to escape. Press [ENTER]. If you press [ENTER], the computer will continue finding correlations and putting them in order. If you press [ESC], you will return to the main menu.

Because this procedure involves so much hard work for the computer, I made it possible for you to stop and return to the main menu at almost any time, even before the screen is full. Just press [ESC] and wait. Do wait, please, after pressing [ESC]. The computer may not immediately notice that you pressed [ESC], because it is so busy. But one good press is enough.

Get back to the main menu and press [3] to rank the correlations again. But now do it from lowest to highest (-1.00 to +1.00). This time, the first correlation that appears is -0.41 #34 Satellite defense - #38 Political conservatism. If you were looking for strong negative correlations, you would rank the correlations this way, from lowest to highest.

You can also look for strong correlations, irrespective of whether they are positive or negative. To do so, you would select the third choice on the ranking menu, In descending magnitude (ignoring + and -).

It takes a long while to go through the full list of correlations, which-ever of the three kinds of ranking you choose, but there are no mysteries in the procedure that need to be explained. A warning is in order here, however.

There is a crime in quantitative research known as **data dredging.** This means going through your data in an unintelligent way, looking for big correlations or whatever apparently significant finding you can dredge up. Frankly, most researchers do this occasionally, and in moderation and with full awareness of what you are doing, you have my permission to do it. Indeed, the correlation matrix program is a tool well designed for data dredging. But in excess, data dredging is a bad policy.

For one thing, if you merely dredge up a miscellaneous heap of big correlations, you may not be able to interpret them. It is usually far better to start out with a theory about how particular items go together and then analyze the data to see whether they really do. Done with any care, this procedure accomplishes one of the highest aims of science, theory testing. But data dredging typically gives you a heap of statistical junk that tells no coherent story.

Furthermore, it is too easy to get diverted by big correlations and lose sight of the purposes of your research. Big correlations are not by any means the only interesting findings, and sometimes they can be a per-nicious distraction from the real work of advancing scientific knowledge. A big correlation that can't be fitted into an existing theory has the merit of stimulating thought and perhaps launching whole new research projects to verify it and explain why it exists. But often far more important are the in-stances when theory predicts a big correlation and one fails to show up in your data. So don't let big correlations you dredge up deflect you from your original research purposes. Although such unexpected findings can inspire valuable new theories, more often than not they are just troublemakers.

Data dredging goes furthest astray when researchers accidentally find some modest correlations and then pretend they were the aim of the study in the first place. Typically, this happens when researchers fail to achieve their original aims. The results of testing a particular theory may be quite ambiguous, or the key items in a survey may bomb. For example, if every-body in our survey checked the same box in response to the question about satellite defense, we would not be able to study what factors make people oppose or favor this project.

Once analysis has bombed, the researchers are tempted to salvage their research investment by scanning the data for any correlations that stand out. Suppose we wrote a study, vaguely titled "Student Attitudes To-day," in which we confidently reported 10 correlations that achieved the 0.01 level of statistical significance. The correlations might involve 20 differ-ent items, and we would have no particular theory to explain the results, although we struggled to fit the 10 correlations together somehow into a readable article.

But the fact is, purely by chance you expect to get 10 correlations "sig-nificant at the 0.01 level" out of any set of 1000 correlations. This is what statistical significance means. "Significant at the 0.01 level" means you would expect to get a correlation of the given size once in every 100 coefficients, purely by accident. Thus you expect 10 of them, more or less, in any matrix of 1000. Indeed, out of 1000 correlations, you would expect 50 to achieve the 0.05 level of significance, and 1 to achieve the 0.001 level. Thus data dredging even in completely random data, numbers taken from spins of a roulette wheel, will produce a few apparently significant results.

Of course, if a coefficient is significant far beyond the 0.001 level, it deserves respect even if dredged out of a sea of 1000 coefficients. And, again, I don't want to discourage your theoretical imagination from trying to invent explanations for unexpected findings. But beware of mindless data dredging, and use our matrix program with reasonable care.

[4] Find Blocks of Correlations

The final part of the matrix program is a simple but sophisticated tool for finding groups of items that fit together. When you select Find blocks of correlations from the main menu, you get the standard item selector, with the instruction Select the item that is to be Variable 1. You are to choose the first of as many as 20 items for the analysis. You must choose at least 3 items or the computer won't have enough to work with.

For an example, I suggest you select the first 20 items in the STUDENTS dataset, the first 20 preference questions about college subjects. This will take a minute, but work carefully. Type [1] and [ENTER] to start with Item 1, Botany. Then type [2][ENTER] to get Item 2, Astronomy, and continue until you have selected Item 20, Oceanography.

To select fewer than 20 items, you would press [ENTER] a second time after the last item. Because we want the full limit of 20, the ccmputer will automatically stop when we get that many. A new menu will appear, with the following choices:

```
[1] Positive correlations (+) only
[2] Negative correlations (−) only
[3] Both positive and negative ones (+ and −)
```

We will start with the first choice. It will focus the computer's attention only on correlations on the positive side of zero. Frankly, I don't know what possible use the second option has, but I included it so you would have the complete set of options. The third choice will focus on big correlations, whether positive or negative, but it might be too complicated to begin with. Its main use is with agree–disagree items, or with others where a negative correlation might mean a connection between two variables because they are coded in opposite ways. For example, one item might be supporting a movement to prohibit the sale of alcohol, and another might be liking to drink liquor. These two should correlate negatively, but both represent anti-alcoholism. But our STUDENTS dataset is mostly preference items lacking this complexity. So press [1] to focus on positive correlations.

The computer now asks you What is the weakest correlation you want to work with? The computer is going to sift through all the correlations involving the 20 items we selected, to find the big ones. You have to decide how big is big enough. The computer wants you to give it a correlation, from +0.10 through +0.90, and it will find all the correlations of this size or bigger. The screen already says Correlation: +0. Simply type in a two-digit number from 10 through 90 to complete the instruction. For our example, type 25 to get all correlations of +0.25 or greater among the 20 items we have selected. Thus 0.25 will be the cutoff below which the computer will ignore coefficients.

Finally, the screen fills with the part of the program that will find blocks of correlations. To the right, you will see a list of all 20 selected items, from Botany to Oceanography. Each item's number is just to the left of its label. You also see these numbers over on the left, at the top (running from left to right), and near the bottom. Framed by these 4 sets of numbers (1–20) is a pattern of plus signs (+).

What you are seeing is a rough picture of the correlation matrix for the 20 items we selected. In the upper left corner, to the right of 1 and below another 1, is a plus sign representing the correlation between Item 1 and itself. Remember that each item correlates 1.00 with itself, and that a diagonal line of 1.00 correlations cuts across a correlation matrix. Our plus-sign sketch of the correlation matrix does, indeed, have a diagonal line of +s running from upper left to lower right, representing the correlations between each item and itself.

Near the upper left corner, you see a + to the right of 2 and below 1. This means that there is a positive correlation between Item 1 and Item 2, Botany and Astronomy. Wherever you see a plus sign, there is a correlation between the two items identified by the item numbers—a correlation as big as or bigger than the 0.25 cutoff we chose.

So you are seeing a rough version of the correlation matrix linking the items we chose. It is as if the computer had written all the correlations in their proper places, then went back and erased all the coefficients less than 0.25. Then it marked a plus sign wherever a correlation of 0.25 or greater remained. The correlations are too numerous to fit their actual coefficients on the screen, and the computer is not going to pay attention to their precise sizes when it works, so long as they are 0.25 or greater.

The computer is ready to begin rearranging the 20 items in the matrix, switching their order in the list again and again, until it has grouped together items that share positive correlations. Let's watch it do this, before I try to explain how it does this marvelous and useful job.

Press [ENTER] and the machine will go to work. Watch what happens. Items will begin trading places in the list. Their item numbers will automatically switch, on all four sides of the matrix, and their plus signs will hop around. At each point, the matrix shows the same correlations linking pairs of items. It is just the order of the items in the list that changes.

After a while, this will stop, and a message at the bottom of the screen will say `Press [ENTER] to run 100 tries or [ESC] to escape.` Don't escape. Instead, press [ENTER] to make the computer work some more. Not much may happen, but perhaps a couple of items will switch places again. When the message appears again, press [ENTER]. If you wish, you can continue until the machine doesn't seem to do anything between presses of [ENTER]. This means it has come to a stopping point and can't find a way of rearranging the items in the list that would bring more correlations together.

Now look at the plus signs in the matrix. They should be mostly bunched along the diagonal of pluses from upper left to lower right. I can't tell you exactly how your matrix will look, because there is a random element in how the computer moves the items around. But the upper right and lower left corners of the square should be essentially empty of pluses, and there should be some tight blocks of pluses along the diagonal without blank spaces separating them.

I have just made my computer work on the items' order six times, and I have a very clear picture on my screen. Yours may be similar but not identical. At one point along the diagonal, pluses for History, Political Science, Law, Business, and Economics are bunched together. This block of pluses is not quite a complete square, because there are no pluses linking History with Business and Economics. But except for this lack, these five items are connected by correlations and form a solid bunch.

Elsewhere on my screen (yours might be different), I see a block of correlations linking Mathematics, Physics, Astronomy, Chemistry, and Geology. Each of these five subjects correlates with each of the others. Some of them correlate with Botany, Oceanography, and Biology as well. And these three items form a block of five with Anthropology and Nursing. However your computer has done its job, you should find that the list of items has been rearranged to bring correlated items together, helping you find blocks that are solidly connected.

You don't really need to know how the computer did this, but the principle is simple enough, so I will explain it. We want to bring blocks of pluses together in the matrix, and an easy way to accomplish this is to bring the pluses close to the diagonal. Each time you press [ENTER] the computer will try 100 times to move a few pluses closer to the diagonal.

On each try, the computer selects two items at random and measures the total distance of all their pluses from the diagonal. Then the computer imagines what the situation would be like if it switched these two items in the list. It calculates the total distance all their pluses would be from the diagonal if it switched them. If this distance is less than what actually appears on the screen, the computer will go ahead and make the switch. If making this move will not bring pluses generally closer to the diagonal, nothing will happen. Either way, the computer will select two items at random on every try, again and again, as many times as you want.

You can see the computer's progress through information at the lower left corner of the screen. After `Tries` you will see the number of times the computer has considered making a switch. After Moves you will see how many times it went ahead and switched items in the list. After every 100 tries, the computer stops so you can study the pattern in the matrix, and it waits for you to press [ENTER] to continue, or [ESC] to quit.

No two runs of this block-finding procedure will give exactly the same result, because the computer chooses each pair of items at random. So if you are really serious about seeing how variables fit together, you might want to try it several times and compare results.

It can also be very revealing to work with a given set of items but with different cutoff correlations. Therefore, when you press [ESC] to quit, you do not go immediately back to the main menu. Instead, you return to the point where you selected the cutoff correlation. If you select a lower correlation, you will get more pluses. If you select a higher correlation, you will get fewer pluses. To get all the way back to the main menu, just press [ESC] a couple more times.

Unless you go back to the main menu, the computer will remember the 20 items we are working with, in the order you selected them. This lets you try refining an analysis. For example, you can start with a relatively high cutoff and few pluses, and run the program until you get a stable new ordering of the items. Then lower the cutoff, adding more pluses, and run again, comparing the final results you get.

Of course, if you don't see any pluses at all, except the diagonal, you have chosen too high a cutoff point. It is easy to hit [ESC] once and lower the cutoff. If the matrix is full of pluses, with little blank space to move them into, you have chosen too low a cutoff.

The item selector puts the items in whatever order you type them in. If you wanted, you could have typed our 20 items in reverse order, from 20 down to 1, or in any other arrangement you want. This permits you to experiment in many ways, to get the best final arrangement and find the most solid blocks of correlations possible in your data.

I think this program is an efficient and easily understood way of hunting for blocks of correlations. Social scientists do not at present use this procedure for looking at a correlation matrix, however. There is a branch of sociology that has used something very similar to look at charts of friendships linking individual people, an approach that dates back 40 years (Festinger et al., 1950), and I was inspired to create this program by the recent advances in **block modeling** achieved by sociologist Harrison White and his students (White et al., 1976). Most recently, I found this technique very useful when I had a correlation matrix with 125 items in it, a total of 7750 different coefficients, based on responses from the 894 Harvard students who responded to my fall 1986 survey. These 125 were different justifications for the space program, and I needed to discover the way they fitted together in respondents' minds for a book I am currently writing. The program on the *Survey Research* disk can handle only 20 items, to allow room for all of them on the screen and to make the process go swiftly. With 125 items, my computer had to run about 24 hours to get a final result with each cutoff correlation, and the total computing time invested in block modeling was about a week. But the final picture was well worth waiting for, completely clear and meaningful; the original matrix was far too large for a human being to make sense of unaided.

Unfortunately, the principal techniques used by professional researchers to find groups of correlations, or underlying dimensions hidden in a correlation matrix, are mathematically rather complicated and hard to explain. Perhaps the most widely used general approach is **factor analysis,** and I have employed it several times in my own research (e.g. Bainbridge, 1986a). The term **cluster analysis** is applied to a whole family of other methods of hunting for clusters of related items (Everitt, 1974). I will give you a couple of examples of factor analysis in the next chapter, and there I will also refer back to the blocking procedure explained here.

Thus this simple technique for finding blocks of correlations stands as an example of a whole host of more complex techniques for finding overarching patterns in a correlation matrix or in the dataset itself. If you intend to use such techniques in professional research, you will have to study the ones commonly used in your field, and select the right one for your particular project.

▶ ▶ ▶ ▶ ▶ ▶ ▶ ▶ ▶ ▶ ▶

[H] Scaling—Multi-Item Indexes

Go to the program menu and select [H]. The computer does not need a correlation matrix for this program, because it employs the full dataset instead. As usual, the computer will ask you for the name of the survey you want to work with, and for our examples select STUDENTS. If a recoded version of the data exists, the computer will also ask whether you want the original or recoded data. The main menu of the scaling program has many options:

```
[1]   Create a scale
[2]   Throw a scale away
[3]   See statistics on a scale
[4]   Correlate a scale with items
[5]   Correlate two scales
[6]   Save current scales
[ESC] QUIT or change programs
```

This program will allow us to combine as many as 20 items into a new variable reflecting whatever the items share, known as a scale or index. Indeed, you can create as many as 4 different indexes and save them on your disk. At any time in the future, the computer will remind you how you made each scale, what items are in it, and how these items correlate with the scale of which they are a part.

Unfortunately, survey researchers use the words *index* and *scale* in many different ways, and precise definitions are not widely followed (Babbie, 1973:254). Consequently, I will not try to nail down separate definitions for these two terms here. We have already been using the word *scale* to describe the preference questions in our STUDENTS dataset. Each of the preference questions measures how much the respondent likes a particular college subject, almost as if we were weighing the respondent's enthusiasm on a weight scale. This is a widely understood concept that even gave a popular romantic comedy its title a few years ago: *10*. The movie concerned a middle-aged man's fixation on a young woman he considered a 10 on a beauty scale from 1 to 10.

We hear the word **index** frequently in ordinary language, too. The traditional measure of ups and downs at the New York Stock Exchange is the Dow Jones Index. It is figured by combining the prices of a short list of blue chip stocks, to give a more representative picture of the market than any single stock price could give. Another is the Index of Leading Economic Indicators, calculated by combining several economic statistics that together give a more general picture of the whole economy than any one statistic could.

The phrase Index of Leading Economic Indicators suggests that we should think in terms of indicators as well as indexes. An **indicator** is a statistic that expresses some aspect of reality in a somewhat indirect way. Suppose you were interested in how the construction business was doing. Ideally, you would like to know how much money was going into construction work at the moment, or how many people were employed in construction. But, let's say, you can't get statistics directly about these things. There is a standard statistic known as "housing starts," however, reflecting how many dwellings have recently gone into construction. Builders have to get house construction permits, so such data are readily available, whereas exactly how much money the builders have and how many people are working for them at the moment are not. Housing starts is thus an indicator of the financial and employment health of the construction industry.

In survey research, we could conceive of all our questionnaire items as indicators, because it is hard to ask a question that perfectly gets at the part of reality we want to study. Consider questions about attitudes toward technology. Suppose, for the sake of simplicity, that people vary from very pro-technology to very anti-technology. And suppose what we want to study is people's underlying attitudes toward technology. But maybe we can't get straight answers if we naively ask, "How much do you favor technological development?"

The standard approach is to discover good indicators of the attitude under study, specific ways of measuring the general orientation. For example, Irene Taviss (1972:614) found seven agree–disagree items that combine to make a good pro-technology scale: "Computers make business and government more efficient." "Machines have made life easier." "Television makes people more aware of what is happening." "Supermarkets are a grand advance over the corner store." "In the long run, discoveries made in our space program will have a big payoff for the average person." "Technological advances will eventually solve the overpopulation problem." "Automation creates better working conditions." Each of these touches on a different aspect of technological development, even the one about supermarkets, which refers indirectly to the mechanized system of stocking large numbers of products.

Every good indicator must correlate with the underlying phenomenon we want to study, but usually we have no way of measuring the phenomenon and thus determining the correlation. We can often find several different indicators of the same thing, however. If those seven items are good indicators of pro-technology attitudes, they should correlate highly with each other. And, in fact, Taviss found that they do. The best measure will be a combination of items, a technology index composed of all seven.

Such an index will typically express a more general concept than does any of the items in it. Technology is a more general concept than just television, computers, or the space program. Many indexes will include negative items, and Taviss found several anti-technology items that could be combined profitably with the pro-technology items, including: "Machines have thrown too many people out of work." "Technology has made life too complicated." "Handmade things are better than machine-made things."

If the items are well chosen, the index will be a more precise reflection of the phenomenon than any one item in it is. There is a certain random aspect to a person's response to any question, which reduces the accuracy of that item. But by combining items, much of the randomness cancels out, letting the person's true feeling come through more strongly and clearly.

In the field of radio, and by extension throughout the whole field of communications, the terms *signal* and *noise* help express the concept I am reaching for. Somebody at the other end of the world is sending us a radio message. The message itself is the signal we want to receive. But thunderstorms, spots on the sun, and passing traffic all create random static on the radio frequencies, noise that intrudes on the signal. High-quality radio equipment is especially good at picking up the signal and suppressing the noise.

We want to achieve the same thing with our indexes. We want to hear a message about the phenomenon under study. In our example, we want to learn a person's orientation toward technology. Any one questionnaire item picks up a lot of noise. Liking television for all the nature programs on PBS or the Discovery Channel is not really a pro-technology attitude. And disliking supermarkets simply because the local one carries rotten vegetables is an accidental rather than anti-technology attitude. By combining several technology indicators, perhaps including both pro and anti items, we hope to amplify the signal and suppress the noise.

[1] Create a Scale

As its name suggests, the first option on the scaling program menu lets you create a scale by combining several items. When you press [1] to select this option, the item selector appears on the screen, and the computer instructs `Select the item that is to be Variable 1`. Perhaps you can guess that the computer wants you to select all the items that are going into your new scale.

With the STUDENTS dataset, let's try to create an index measuring preferences for the "hard" sciences. I suggest you take pencil and paper and write down the items we try at each stage, so you will have a record of how the index develops. First, write down the item numbers and names of all the college subjects that look like hard sciences to you. My list is this:

#1 Botany

#2 Astronomy

#9 Physics

#10 Geology

#12 Biology

#13 Chemistry

#20 Oceanography

#29 Zoology

Now type each item number in your list, in turn, and press [ENTER] to register it with the computer. Finally, press [ENTER] again to tell the computer you have finished entering your list. If you type in 20 items, the computer will automatically finish after the 20th.

The computer lists the items you have selected and asks `Decide whether each item should be added or subtracted`. We won't worry about this question now, but will return to it later with a different scale constructed by adding some items and subtracting others. Here we merely want to combine all the values a respondent has for all the items in the scale. Therefore, simply press [ENTER] to get past this decision.

`What name do you want for the new scale?` As with the names you give survey datasets, you should type in from two to eight letters and press [ENTER]. For our example, type SCIENCE and press [ENTER]. Shortly, the computer will return you to the main menu.

[2] Throw a Scale Away

Once you have created a scale, you can always throw it away to make room for a new one. Press [2] to select the second choice in the scaling program main menu, and a list of your existing scales will appear, each one numbered. If you do not want to destroy any at this point, press [ESC] to escape.

[3] See Statistics on a Scale

This option analyzes a scale you have created, giving you information to help you evaluate how well the various items combine to measure the underlying phenomenon. We won't have the background to understand some of the statistics fully until we have considered issues of validity and reliability in Chapter 8, so for now we should be content to describe the statistics in a general way.

Press [3] from the main menu in the scaling program, and the computer will list the scales you have at the moment (even if there is only one), and it will ask which you want to work with. Press [1] to get the SCIENCE scale. The first statistics you will see are all the correlations linking items in the scale with the whole scale itself. These are the r correlations. Because each item is part of the scale, we expect to see a strong positive correlation. In part, the item is being correlated with itself, because it is a component of the scale. But items that lack strong connections to other items in the scale will show much lower correlations.

After the name of each item you will see a plus or minus in parentheses. This is to remind you whether you added $(+)$ or subtracted $(-)$ the score for the item when creating the scale. So far, we have discussed only adding, so the SCIENCE scale will show all pluses.

In the STUDENTS dataset, the Botany item has a correlation of 0.64 with the SCIENCE scale, and the Astronomy item has 0.59. The right side of the screen shows some statistics about the scale as a whole. The mean is 30.81, with a variance of 73.13 and a standard deviation of 8.55. Where did these numbers come from?

When it created the scale, the computer went through the 200 respondents, one by one. For each person, it added together his or her scores on all 8 items we put into our SCIENCE scale. This total became the person's score for the new variable that is the scale. On average, the total was about 31, as expressed through our mean of 30.81. But many respondents would have had totals of much less than this, and many, totals of much more. The distribution of totals around the mean is expressed by the variance and standard deviation.

The computer also displays a statistic called Cronbach's alpha (Cronbach, 1951). We will explain this statistic in the next chapter, but for now suffice it to say that it is a measure of how well the individual items in the scale hold together. It is like a correlation coefficient, and the bigger it is the more tightly the items in the scale are connected with each other. We don't see negative alphas, and only highly positive ones indicate good scales. The 0.71 for the SCIENCE scale is quite solid.

We also see the number of missing cases, which here is 0. If a respondent failed to answer any one of the items in the scale, that respondent is temporarily thrown out, and no scale value is computed for that person. Therefore, whenever you see statistics involving your scales, they will be based only on the cases that have no missing data for any of the items.

[4] Correlate a Scale with Items

As we have just seen, the statistics on a scale give the correlations linking it with each of the items that make it up. But you may also want to see correlations between the scale and other items. In fact, this is generally much more interesting. The reason for creating a scale is to have a good measure of an underlying characteristic of the respondents, and research gets exciting only when we can begin to connect different characteristics with each other.

Press [4] from the main menu of the scaling program to get the option for correlating a scale with items. Next the computer will ask you which scale you want. It does this even if you have only one scale, to remind you what it is. Then you get the item selector and the chance to choose as many as 20 items.

For our example, use the SCIENCE scale we have just created. Then select the following six items to correlate with it, in this order:

#15 Mathematics
#25 Engineering
#19 Nursing
#28 Medicine
#23 Psychology
#26 Sociology

Can you guess why I picked these six? Our SCIENCE scale includes Physics and Astronomy, highly mathematical fields, and one generally associates the hard sciences with math. Physics reminds us of Engineering, and we suspect that the same kind of thinking goes into Engineering as into the hard sciences. So the first two items, Mathematics and Engineering, are included to test these hypotheses.

Our SCIENCE scale also included Botany, Biology, and Zoology, which might be described as life sciences. They would seem to be connected to the medical sciences, and thus we should check the correlations with Nursing and Medicine.

Finally, we can compare the hard sciences that make up our SCIENCE scale with some of the social sciences, sometimes called the "soft" sciences. We have several social sciences to choose from, but Psychology and Sociology seem pretty representative.

To select these items, as usual you type each of their item numbers in, followed by [ENTER], and type another [ENTER] after the last one. In a few moments, a table like Table 7.1 should appear.

The statistics in the table should be quite familiar by now. The left-hand column shows the correlation between each of the items we selected and the SCIENCE scale. The next column shows the statistical significance of that correlation, expressed as the chance we could get such a correlation

▶ ▶ ▶ ▶ ▶ ▶ ▶ ▶ ▶ ▶ ▶

TABLE 7.1   CORRELATIONS WITH THE SCIENCE SCALE

Correlation	Significance	Cases	Variable
0.47	0.001	200	#15 Mathematics
0.44	0.001	200	#25 Engineering
0.31	0.001	200	#19 Nursing
0.56	0.001	200	#28 Medicine
−0.04	n.s.	200	#23 Psychology
−0.04	n.s.	200	#26 Sociology

▶

purely by accident. The third column tells us the number of cases the correlations are based on. If ten people had failed to answer one or more of the items in the scale, or skipped the particular item, then the number of cases would be 200 − 10 = 190. Finally, you see the item itself.

Just as we hypothesized, Mathematics and Engineering correlate highly with the SCIENCE scale, 0.47 and 0.44. These coefficients are significant far beyond the 0.001 shown on the table, and they are extremely solid results. Nursing and Medicine also correlate with SCIENCE, although the correlation with Nursing is pretty low, 0.31. The fact that even this 0.31 achieves the 0.001 level of significance tells you that the much more powerful correlations with Math, Engineering, and Medicine are significant beyond the computer's wildest dreams!

Finally, we see insignificant negative correlations with Psychology (−0.04) and Sociology (−0.04). Apparently, people who like the physical sciences have no tendency to like the social sciences. Because the column about statistical significance says "n.s.," we know that these two coefficients are not significantly different from zero, so we cannot make much of the fact that they are negative.

These correlations with individual items should inspire us to create new scales including them, and then to take the next option on the main menu for correlating two scales.

[5] Correlate Two Scales

First, we must create some new scales. We have just suggested that our SCIENCE scale might have two somewhat separate aspects, physical sciences and life sciences. We have also seen that social sciences are in a very different category. So let's create three new scales, PHYSICAL, LIFE, and SOCIAL. You have to use the scale-creating feature of our scaling program three times, once for each new scale. The items you put in each scale should be these:

Physical:	*Life:*	*Social:*
# 2 Astronomy	# 1 Botany	# 5 Political science
# 9 Physics	#12 Biology	#16 Economics
#10 Geology	#19 Nursing	#18 Anthropology
#15 Mathematics	#28 Medicine	#23 Psychology
#25 Engineering	#29 Zoology	#26 Sociology

Notice that I had to make some decisions in creating these lists of items. Our 30 preference questions include only 5 about life sciences, and I decided it would be interesting to have 3 scales with equal numbers of items in them. Other things being equal, this means they will measure their underlying concepts with equal precision and thus be highly comparable. Taking Botany, Biology, and Zoology from the SCIENCE scale left 7 items, so 2 of them had to go. I dropped Chemistry and Oceanography, thinking they often dealt with biological topics and wanting a PHYSICAL scale very different from the LIFE one.

I must emphasize that you could easily take a different approach. Aside from coming to different personal judgments about the natures of various fields, you could also pick items by looking at the ones most closely correlated with each other.

Next, look at the statistics on each of the three new scales (option 3 on the main menu). The correlations between the PHYSICAL scale and its items range from 0.65 to 0.84, and its Cronbach's alpha is 0.66. For the LIFE scale, correlations range from 0.63 to 0.81, with an alpha of 0.63. The SOCIAL scale has correlations from 0.54 to 0.75, somewhat lower coefficients, and an alpha of only 0.48. This reveals that the SOCIAL scale items are less tightly connected, and thus that it is not so good a scale as the other two. But let's use all three, and our original SCIENCE scale as well, and see how they relate to each other.

From the main menu of the scaling program, press [5] to correlate two scales. The computer will list the scales, numbered 1 through 4, asking Which scale should be Variable X? Press the number of one of the scales you want to correlate, and the computer will ask Which scale should be Variable Y? Select that one, and in an instant it will tell you the r correlation between the two scales and the approximate statistical significance of that coefficient. You will also see the number of cases on which the correlation is based, the number of respondents who gave valid answers to all the items that make up each of the two scales.

Table 7.2 shows the full set of correlations between our four scales. It is not surprising that very strong correlations link PHYSICAL and LIFE with SCIENCE, because the SCIENCE scale contains three items from each of the other two. Generally, researchers set up their scales so that there are no items shared in this way, in order to be sure their correlations are not just reflections of the fact that every item has a perfect positive correlation with itself.

▶ ▶ ▶ ▶ ▶ ▶ ▶ ▶ ▶ ▶ ▶

TABLE 7.2   CORRELATIONS LINKING FOUR SCALES

	Correlation (r) with:		
Scale	SCIENCE	PHYSICAL	LIFE
PHYSICAL	0.74**		
LIFE	0.77**	0.31**	
SOCIAL	0.04	−0.07	0.19*

Significance: *0.01 level, **0.001 level

Far more interesting is the significant correlation of 0.31 between LIFE and PHYSICAL. These two scales do not share any items with each other, and 0.31 is a pretty strong coefficient between really separate variables. Clearly, for all their differences, the physical sciences and the life sciences have enough in common to get similar preference responses from students.

As you can see, SOCIAL has no correlation with either SCIENCE or PHYSICAL, but a slim 0.19, significant at the 0.01 level, with LIFE. Something is shared between SOCIAL and LIFE, but only weakly. It may be that only one of the items in the LIFE scale, such as Nursing, is connected with items in the SOCIAL scale. I mention Nursing because women respondents may like Nursing better and also prefer some of the social sciences more than men do. In any case, a low correlation may reflect correlations linking just a few of the items in the scales, or it may really reflect a broad, weak connection between the entire scales. You can check this out, of course, by switching to the correlation matrix program and looking at correlations linking individual items.

Next, we should explain how to create a scale that combines items through subtraction as well as addition. A good example is an index of sex roles I invented a few years ago while working with criminologist Robert Crutchfield (Bainbridge and Crutchfield, 1983).

The College Sex Roles Index

For a study of delinquent behavior, Crutchfield and I administered to college students a questionnaire containing many items about deviant acts they might have performed when they were teenagers. We were testing a theory inspired by the observation that, traditionally, boys were much more likely than girls to engage in such acts as stealing, fighting, drinking alcohol, and using drugs. It might be that the traditional male role made it more likely for boys to do such things, and the traditional female role prevented girls from doing them. If so, changes in sex roles should produce changes in behavior.

Specifically, as boys move away from their traditional sex role, they should become less and less likely to be delinquent. Conversely, as girls move away from their traditional sex role, they should become more deviant. Actually, Crutchfield and I were skeptical that sex differences in delinquent behavior were reflections of mere social roles, and thus we were quite happy when we found no correlations between sex role attitudes and deviant behavior. But zero correlations could be produced simply by bad questionnaire items, rather than representing real scientific findings, so we had invested much effort on how to measure sex roles while creating our survey.

We included in our questionnaire a 28-item "macho" index invented by Wayne Villemez and John Touhey (1977), because it seemed to measure the aspects of the traditional male role that might encourage delinquency. But we were concerned that this index might not work perfectly, for two reasons. First, we had heard rumors that the scale did not accurately measure variations in women's attitudes, even if it was okay with men. Second, it was composed of items very distant from the daily experience of students, such as a question about whether a woman should be president of the United States, and we were afraid that respondents would give superficial answers that said nothing about their basic personalities.

It seemed to us that preferences for academic fields were very real attitudes for students, and we thought they would reflect very real differences among women as much as among men. I had included our 30 academic preference questions in the survey already, because I was exploring attitudes toward the space program, parallel to my delinquency work with Crutchfield, and was interested in how different fields predicted space-flight attitudes. It seemed reasonable to identify academic fields that men especially liked, and other fields that women especially liked, and combine them into a college sex roles index.

Luckily, there turned out to be 8 fields that showed big sex differences, 4 preferred more by men and 4 by women. Table 7.3 lists these fields and gives statistics revealing the sex differences, for the 498 college women and 364 college men on which Crutchfield and I based our study, all students at the University of Washington in Seattle. If you want, you can compare the correlations in the table with others based on our 200 Harvard students.

As you can see, the UW college men rate Physics, Engineering, Astronomy, and Economics much higher than the women do. And the women rate Art, Foreign Language, Literature, and Social Work much higher. You could create a MALE scale by adding the four male-preferred fields together. Similarly, you could create a FEMALE scale by adding the four female-preferred fields together. We'll do that, but let's also make a combined scale out of all eight items.

First, you have to make room for new scales. So return to the main menu and press [2] to throw a scale away. Probably you should pitch out all the scales we have been working with. First discard SCIENCE by pressing

TABLE 7.3 COLLEGE SEX ROLES INDEX

Academic Subject	Mean Score		Correlation with Being Male
	Women	Men	
Physics	2.59	3.93	0.36
Engineering	3.03	4.23	0.32
Astronomy	3.52	4.33	0.24
Economics	3.65	4.40	0.22
Art	4.73	4.03	−0.20
A foreign language	4.86	4.06	−0.22
Literature	4.88	4.00	−0.25
Social work	4.52	3.41	−0.32

[1]. In a moment you will be back at the main menu. When you choose to throw the second scale away, you will see that SCIENCE has vanished from the list, and PHYSICAL is now number 1, so press [1] again to discard it. Continue until all four are gone and you have room for some new ones.

We are going to create four scales, called MALE, FEMALE, MALFEM, and FEMMAL. The first two are easy. Just add together the four male fields and call the scale MALE. Then add together the four female fields and call the scale FEMALE. Do it like this:

Male:

2 Astronomy

9 Physics

#16 Economics

#25 Engineering

Female:

3 A foreign language

#14 Art

#21 Social work

#27 Literature

Our third scale, MALFEM, will consist of all eight of these items, the four in MALE plus the four in FEMALE. But don't just rush ahead. Stop when the computer says `Decide whether each item should be added or subtracted.`

So far, we have simply been adding. Now we are going to combine adding with subtracting. Our MALFEM scale is going to measure *liking* male fields and *disliking* female fields. That is, a respondent with especially male attitudes will get a high score on the MALFEM scale. It is easy enough to put the four male fields into such a scale; we add them together. But the way to include the female fields in a scale measuring maleness is to *subtract* their scores.

Imagine we were doing this by hand, with a person who had given the four male fields ratings of 4, 5, 6, and 7. We would add these numbers together: $4 + 5 + 6 + 7 = 22$. Suppose the person had rated the four female fields 1, 2, 3, and 4. To get the person's MALFEM score, we subtract these from 22: $22 - 1 = 21; 21 - 2 = 19; 19 - 3 = 16; 16 - 4 = 14$.

Look at the instructions on the screen: A "+" in front of an item means its score will be added in computing the scale. A "-" means the item's score will be subtracted. Type an item's number and press [ENTER] to switch between + and -. Press [ENTER] when you have set all the items correctly.

To start with, all the items listed at the left of the screen have pluses in front of them. This means the computer is ready to add their scores together to make the scale. But we want to subtract the female items. One at a time, type these items' numbers and press [ENTER]. That is, type [3][ENTER] to change the plus in front of 3 A foreign language to a minus. Do the same for 14 Art, 21 Social work, and 27 Literature.

Now the four male fields should have pluses in front of them, and the four female fields should have minuses. If you make a mistake and change the sign in front of the wrong item, you can switch it back by typing its number followed by [ENTER] a second time. When the pluses and minuses are just the way we want them, press [ENTER] again, and the computer will ask you the name for the new scale. Tell it MALFEM.

The fourth scale, FEMMAL, will be the exact opposite of MALFEM. Again, select the same eight items that comprise MALFEM. But this time, add the female items and subtract the male items. That is, when the computer asks you to decide about adding or subtracting items, set plus signs in front of the female fields and minus signs in front of the male fields. Call this fourth and last scale FEMMAL. It measures the extent to which a person prefers the female fields over the male ones.

Now that we have our four new sex role scales, we can examine them, by pressing [3] from the main menu of the scaling program to see the statistics on each. The MALFEM and FEMMAL scales should be exact opposites of each other. Indeed, all the statistics on the MALFEM and FEMMAL scales should be identical, except that the signs in front of the correlations and the mean will be opposite. MALFEM measures liking male fields more than female ones. FEMMAL measures liking female fields more than male ones.

Cronbach's alpha is higher for MALFEM and FEMMAL, 0.58, than for the two shorter scales. Psychologists often use Cronbach's alpha as a measure of how reliable the scale is. Therefore, MALFEM and FEMMAL are better scales than either MALE or FEMALE, although I have to admit to you that psychologists usually like to see higher alphas than this.

In general, other things being equal, the more items we have in a scale, the more reliable it is and the higher Cronbach's alpha will be. Of course, if you just pile in odd items that have little to do with each other, you won't get a good scale. But the larger the number of appropriate items you have the better. The limit to the number of items in a scale is basically practical. If you put in too many items that take much of the respondent's time, you won't have room for questions about other matters you also want to study.

When you have finished inspecting statistics on the four separate scales, you should look at the correlations linking pairs of scales. The correlation between MALE and FEMALE turns out to be -0.28, significant at the 0.001 level. The correlation between MALFEM and FEMMAL, not surprisingly, is -1.00. The two scales are perfectly opposed, so we should get a perfect negative correlation. Can you explain why MALE has a high positive correlation with MALFEM, and FEMALE has a high positive correlation with FEMMAL?

Finally, you can correlate each of these four scales, in turn, with the actual sex of the respondent, Item 39. Remember that the item representing the respondent's sex is coded so that men get the value 2, women get 1. Thus you should expect a positive correlation between sex and MALE, and a negative correlation between sex and FEMALE. Indeed, the correlation between sex and MALE is 0.27; with FEMALE it is -0.45. The correlation between sex and MALFEM is 0.44; with FEMMAL it is -0.44, of course.

But didn't we say MALFEM (or its opposite, FEMMAL) is a better scale because of the number of items in it? And here, the four female fields have a slightly stronger correlation with sex ($r = -0.45$) than does FEMMAL ($r = -0.44$). To be sure, there are random fluctuations in all our calculations, so we can't expect everything to come out exactly as predicted, in all details. But another point is worth considering here.

We must always be careful in deciding what our scales and items measure. In constructing our sex roles scale, we did not say we were going to make a measure of sex itself. Rather, we started with sex to help us identify fields that were relatively masculine or feminine. Then, using those fields, we constructed a matched pair of eight-item indexes that seem pretty good for evaluating respondents' sex role attitudes.

Male fields are not devoid of female students, and vice versa. Rather, students in male fields are playing traditional male academic roles. Students in female fields, whichever their biological sex, are playing traditional female roles. And the whole point of my research with Crutchfield was to study how those roles are changing.

The academic preference questions in our STUDENTS dataset may or may not be ideal for constructing scales that measure a particular phenomenon you might be interested in. But they have afforded us an opportunity for seeing how scales of different kinds might be constructed out of a limited set of items. When you get to the XYZ Management Survey in Chapter 10, you can use this scaling program to test claims certain writers have made about sets of items designed to measure management styles.

[6] Save Current Scales

If you press [6] on the main menu, the scales you have been working with will be saved on your disk, and they will automatically come up again the next time you load the dataset. Only one set of four scales can be saved at a time, although you could always create a second work disk with a second set of four on it. If you have a set of scales already on the disk for the particular dataset and create new scales, you have to decide which of the two you want to keep for the next session of work. If you save your new scales, the old ones will vanish. But you can keep the old ones, and throw the new ones away, by refusing to save the new ones.

The program makes creating scales so easy, I hope you will invent many of your own. And if you discard one, it is simple to re-create it. The projects at the end of this chapter suggest further work you can do with the scales we have already created, and they point out more you can create. Usually, a survey researcher sets out to create scales measuring particular phenomena and writes items with this purpose in mind. But nothing should stop you from exploring the STUDENTS dataset for scales I have not been able to imagine.

▶ ▶ ▶ ▶ ▶ ▶ ▶ ▶ ▶ ▶ ▶

RECODING BEFORE SCALING

Survey researchers usually do some recoding work before creating a scale out of a set of items. Partly, they do this to throw out respondents who failed to follow directions, because otherwise some meaningless data will be injected into the scale. Our scaling program ignores respondents who have missing data (a score of zero) for any of the items in a scale, so you might go through your items recoding bad responses to zero before doing any scaling.

But researchers have a second reason for recoding: to put the items in the best form for use in the particular scale. For example, you might want to combine questions that were originally in very different formats. Consider the political question in the STUDENTS dataset. It has seven possible responses; the range of scores people get on it is 1 through 7. Suppose we have another question: "Which of the following best describes your political orientation: [1] Democrat, [2] Independent, or [3] Republican?" At the moment the Republicans seem more conservative than the Democrats, on average. So this is like a second political conservatism measure, which can be combined with our seven-point scale simply by adding the two together.

But notice that the political party item has only three points, compared with seven in the STUDENTS conservatism item. If we simply added them together, the question with the greater number of points would dominate the one with the lesser number. One solution to this problem might be to use the Democrat–Republican question twice, and the conservatism item once, in making up the scale. This is quite possible with the item selector in our scaling program. Simply select an item twice and you double its influence.

Another solution would be to turn the conservatism item into a three-point scale. In recoding, you would combine "extremely liberal," "liberal," and "slightly liberal," giving them all a value of 1. Then you would recode "moderate" as 2. Then "slightly conservative," "conservative," and "extremely conservative" would be combined as 3. This changes the seven-point conservatism item into a three-point item that is comparable with the three-point Democrat–Republican item.

When items vary in their format and the number of responses, it may be best to recode each of them so that a particular, strong answer is given one code value, and all the other responses get another. The simplest way with most statistical software is for the respondent to be given one point on the scale for every answer of the desired type, and then these points are added up. We use a slightly different method with our programs, but here is a straightforward example of recoding before scaling.

Suppose you were hired by the (fictitious) Asian Ports restaurant chain—which serves a combination of Indian, Chinese, and Japanese cuisine—to determine the market for a new branch in a particular town. Of course, such market research is very serious business, and you would need to attack the problem in several ways. But one approach is to determine how much local people like Asian food, and compare this with the actual restaurants available to them.

Let's imagine you decide to do a survey of town residents, including several questions about restaurants and types of restaurants. You could start with a set of preference questions about existing restaurants, then have a section about different kinds of food in general:

On a scale from 1 (not at all) to 7 (very much), how much do you like each of the following restaurants?

1. Caesar's Pizza Palace 1 2 3 4 5 6 7
2. Lincoln Inn 1 2 3 4 5 6 7
3. Hong Kong 1 2 3 4 5 6 7
4. Viking Smorgasbord 1 2 3 4 5 6 7
5. Just Like Home 1 2 3 4 5 6 7
6. Sally's Steakhouse 1 2 3 4 5 6 7
7. Marseilles Gourmet 1 2 3 4 5 6 7
8. Fisherman's Harbor 1 2 3 4 5 6 7
9. Carolina Moonlight 1 2 3 4 5 6 7
10. Bombay Curry House 1 2 3 4 5 6 7

In general, would you say you agree or disagree with each of the following statements? For each, please check the one box that comes closest to your own, personal opinion.

11. When all is said and done, my favorite meal is traditional American food.
    [1] Strongly agree
    [2] Agree
    [3] Not sure
    [4] Disagree
    [5] Strongly Disagree

12. I love the tremendous variety of food served in the best Asian restaurants.

13. Usually I don't have time for a leisurely meal, so I find fast food very convenient.

14. With all the talk about Japan these days, I would really like to get familiar with Japanese food.

15. When it comes to nutrition, you just can't beat steak, potatoes, and salad.

16. I get enough ordinary food at home, so when I go out to eat I want something different.

Can you see how to construct an Asian food index from some of these items? Two of the ten restaurants, Hong Kong and Bombay Curry House, are Asian, so you might include preferences for them in the index. And agree–disagree questions 12 and 14 deal more generally with attitudes toward Asian food. But these four questions are in two very different formats. How can we combine them?

There are several ways, and you can always try more than one of them to see whether you get the same results. Here's one. Recode the restaurant preferences so that every respondent who likes a given restaurant gets a value of 2 for its item, and every respondent who does not like it gets a 1. That is, recode all responses of 1, 2, 3, or 4 to 1, and recode all responses of 5, 6, or 7 to 2. For the agree–disagree items, we can divide respondents in terms of whether they agree or not. You would recode 1 and 2 (strongly agree and agree) as 2, and 3, 4, and 5 (not sure, disagree, and strongly disagree) as 1.

What we have just suggested is **dichotomizing** the responses. This means collapsing a range of responses into just two. Here, liking a particular Asian restaurant or agreeing with a statement in favor of Asian food are both favorable responses. We have dichotomized responses into favorable (coded 2) and not favorable (coded 1). To make an index out of the four items, simply add their scores. Note that in the process of dichotomizing, we reversed the coding on the agree–disagree items, so that a higher number (2 versus 1) now means agreement, whereas before recoding, a lower number meant agreement.

This simple example illustrates two points about combining miscellaneous items into a simple index. First, the range of responses on all items should be comparable. Unless you have some special reason for giving greater weight to one item or set of items, you should give them equal weight. Second, we have made sure that the items are all coded in the same direction, so that by adding the scores we are building an index in which a high score on various items means the same thing. Of course, if your index includes some items that are opposite in meaning to the others, it is quite appropriate to code them in the opposite direction, as we did in our sex roles index and as we would do if we were combining Taviss's pro-technology and anti-technology items into a single pro/anti technology index.

Depending on the nature of the research, a researcher can take into account the distribution of responses to an item, as well as their substantive meanings, in deciding how to code a question prior to adding it into a scale. Imagine that nobody had given responses lower than 4 in describing the restaurants. I often find topics and groups of respondents that produce mostly high ratings on preference items. Then we may want to distinguish real fans of the restaurant from people who merely like it somewhat. In such a case, you might want to dichotomize differently, perhaps recoding 1, 2, 3, 4, and 5 to 1, and counting only 6 and 7 as really favorable responses by coding them to 2.

Sometimes you may recode individual items in terms of the average score, either the average for each item separately or for all in a group. Let's suppose that the average rating of the Hong Kong restaurant is 4.3. Then you might dichotomize respondents into all those below 4.3 and all those above 4.3. Or you could dichotomize in terms of the overall average rating for all the restaurants. Your decision depends on your research purpose. If the Asian Ports chain which hired you had decided it was definitely going to build a branch in the town and merely wanted to know where to put it, then you can just worry about the Asian restaurants and dichotomize in terms of their means. This can tell you which parts of town like Asian food more, and if you are lucky and Hong Kong and Bombay Curry are elsewhere, then you know where to build Asian Ports. But if the chain is still undecided about building one in town at all, then you'd better take account of the non-Asian restaurants in doing your recoding, dichotomizing either in terms of set numbers, as we did first, or doing so in terms of the average for all restaurants. This way you will wind up with an Asian food index that tells you what proportion of the town's residents like this cuisine and are potential customers for it.

Do you see any other scales you could build out of the items in our restaurant survey? Consider how you would create an index of exotic food, combining the items that refer to foreign restaurants and the ones approving of food other than standard American fare. Or how could you combine items to make an index of traditional American cooking? In a real market survey, we would need several other sets of items allowing us to distinguish potential customers for our product from other people and to describe their purchasing habits. Can they afford what we have to sell? How can we best reach them with advertising? Geographically, where do they live and shop? Where are the other attractions in town they frequent, such as theaters or shopping centers, which we should consider in deciding a location for Asian Ports? We might have to construct indexes on many of these other factors.

I have written enough recoding and analysis capability into the *Survey Research* disk to give you experience with the main kinds of techniques that professional researchers use. When you move on to advanced (expensive!) statistical software packages, you will find all the flexibility and alternatives your imagination could possibly wish for.

▶ ▶ ▶ ▶ ▶ ▶ ▶ ▶ ▶ ▶ ▶

PROJECTS

1. Finding the World of Music. Using the matrix program's Correlations with one variable, find the three college subjects that have the highest positive correlations with preferences for #6 Music. Write down the names of these three items and their correlations with music. Then do the Correlations with one variable procedure for each of them, one at a time, and find the three items with the highest correlations to these three that correlated with music.

This will give you a list of 12 correlations, each linking a pair of college preference items. But how many different items are in the list? In principle, the way we have set up the 12 correlations, they could involve as many as 13 items. But is the number much fewer than 13? That is, do some of the items that correlate with music correlate with each other?

Write a brief essay interpreting the correlations you have found. Why do you think each of the pairs has a strong correlation? Do you see any groups of items that have something in common? If so, how would you describe them?

2. Conflicting College Subjects. With the matrix program, find the seven pairs of college subjects with the strongest negative correlations. To do this efficiently, select Rank all correlations, then choose [2] Lowest to highest (−1.00 to +1.00). When the list of correlations appears, you will have to ignore some involving space items, the political item, and the respondent's sex, and just focus on the seven most negative correlations linking two college subjects.

In principle, there could be 14 different items in these 7 pairs. Are there fewer than 14? Copy the 14 pairs of items and their correlations on a piece of paper. Then make a list of all the items that are in these 7 pairs, and how many pairs each one appears in. Do you think you see any groups of items in the list? Could you suggest a way of dividing the items into 2 groups, so that items in each group seem very similar to each other, and the 2 groups are very different?

Write a brief essay explaining why you think each of the seven pairs of items has a significant negative correlation. Then try to identify underlying aspects of the items that might divide them into two or more groups.

3. The Shape of 20 Subjects. From the main menu of the matrix program, select F i n d b l o c k s o f c o r r e l a t i o n s. Then select the 20 items numbered 11 through 30—Business through Architecture. Tell the computer you want to work only with positive correlations, and select a cutoff point of +0.40.

Run the blocking routine for 500 tries, then write down how many moves there were and list the 20 items in the new order the computer has arranged them in. Then write a paragraph or two describing any blocks of items you see.

Press [ESC] once—just once—to change the cutoff correlation, and tell the computer you want +0.30 this time. Again, run the blocking routine for 500 tries. Write down how many moves the computer makes, and list the 20 items in their new order. Write a description of any new facts you can observe about the blocks in which the computer has arranged the items.

Finally, press [ESC] and change the cutoff correlation to +0.20. Run for 500 more tries, writing down how many moves take place, and the final order the computer puts the items in. Add to your report a description of anything new you discover about the groups of items. Compare the three different attempts at putting the items into blocks with the three different cutoff correlations. Did one of them give clearly superior results, or do you feel that you learned most from two of the attempts, or from all three?

4. A Humanities Scale. Using the scaling program, create a scale composed of several college preference items that are clearly among the humanities rather than among the physical sciences, life sciences, or social sciences. As you go, you should write down every step you take and describe each of four versions of the humanities scale as you create it.

First, select several humanities items, writing them down so this scale can be part of your final report. Combine the items by adding their scores, and give this scale the name HUMAN1.

When the computer has finished making the HUMAN1 scale, look at the statistics on it. Write down the table of correlations and items, and also copy down the summary statistics for the scale, including Cronbach's alpha. Note particularly any items that have especially low correlations with the scale of which they are part, to see whether any should perhaps be dropped. Then check correlations between the scale and other items you did not originally place in it, to see whether any should perhaps be added.

Now create a second scale, HUMAN2, composed of most of the items in HUMAN1. If one or two items in HUMAN1 had especially low correlations with it, don't use them in HUMAN2. If you found some items that correlated with HUMAN1 but were not included in it, include them in HUMAN2. As you add fresh items to the scale, make sure you think they really are humanities, and do not represent some other kind of course that happens for strange reasons to correlate with the humanities.

Examine the statistics about HUMAN2, writing them down as you did with HUMAN1. Which of these two scales looks more solid, on the basis of the correlations linking items with their scale? Does one have a much higher alpha? Keep in mind that scales composed of a larger number of good items might be expected to have higher alphas.

Now create a third scale, HUMAN3, trying to incorporate the best of both HUMAN1 and HUMAN2. Really try to get the best measure of humanities this time. As before, examine its statistics and describe it briefly in the report you are writing.

Finally, consider whether HUMAN3 might be either too short to measure attitudes toward the humanities well, or too long for inclusion in a short questionnaire. Depending on your judgment of this question, create a final scale, HUMAN4, that is either longer or shorter than HUMAN3. Write down its statistics and describe it. Conclude your report with an overview of the four scales you have created, offering your advice to future researchers on which of the four would make the best humanities scale.

5. A Spaceflight Scale. Combine the seven questions about the space program to make a general spaceflight scale, called SPACE. You will not be able to work with the original data, because most of the space items need recoding. So the first step is to use the recoding program to fix the problems with each of the items.

One approach to recoding the space items is to turn each one into a question with two answers, one supporting space exploration and the other not supporting it. For example, with the item about space funding, you could combine people who wanted the amount of money spent on the U.S. space program increased with those who wanted it kept the same, giving them all a value of 2. Also combine those who want it reduced with the person who wants it ended and the people who failed to answer the question, giving them a value of 1.

You don't have to follow this logic, but whatever approach you use, be consistent for all seven space questions. In this approach, a pro-space attitude on a question gives the respondent a value of 2, the lack of a pro-space response gives him or her a 1. Then the scale itself can be created, using the scaling program and the recoded form of the data, combining these seven items and naming the result SPACE.

Write down the statistics on this scale, then correlate it with each of the academic preference questions, and with the sex and politics questions, to see what characteristics of our 200 student respondents might explain support for the space program, or lack of support. Write your report as a brief research study on the sociology of space attitudes.

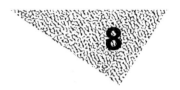

Validity and reliability, though related, are not the same thing. It is quite possible for an item or index to be reliable but not valid, for example. Questionnaire items should be both, and there are several ways of assuring that they are.

A *valid* item or index measures the phenomenon it is supposed to. Today no serious researcher would think it valid to measure people's intelligence by asking them their hat size, although scientists at the beginning of the century held the mistaken belief that bigger heads meant better brains. Thus hat size has no validity as a measure of intelligence.

A *reliable* item or index gives consistent results. If you ask the same question twice, you should get the same answer. The separate items that make up an index should correlate with each other.

Here is a simple hypothetical example of how an item can be reliable but invalid. Suppose we were interested in the power and social status that individuals might enjoy in society, and we included the following item in our questionnaire: "How much influence do you have in your community?" This is phrased as a magnitude item; in the question-processor program, the responses would be "A very great deal," "A great deal," "Quite a bit," "Some," and "Little or none."

Although I haven't tried this item, I imagine it could be very reliable. We could ask the question again, in a second questionnaire a week later, and people might give exactly the same answers. That is, responses to this item could be stable and consistent. A person would be confident in giving a particular answer, and consistently respond a particular way.

But at the same time, this item might not be a valid measure of how

Validity and Reliability

much influence the person actually has in the community. Conceivably, it would not correlate with more direct measures of influence. Community leaders might say Joe has no influence on them. Joe's attempts to get the town to back his favorite projects might always fail. The local newspaper might never even mention Joe. And yet he could consistently check the "A very great deal" box when we asked him how much influence he had.

It may be that our question really measures Joe's arrogance rather than his actual influence on the community. Presumably, every reliable item measures something. Unreliable items might not. Questions that get inconsistent, unstable, uncorrelated answers from people can't be measuring very much at all. Certainly, they are of no use in surveys. On the other hand, there must be a reason that an item gets stable responses, some underlying reality that it reflects. But the reliability of an item does not prove it measures what we want it to.

Thus validity really refers to our *interpretation* of a reliable item. If we have given it the wrong name, if we claim it measures something it really doesn't, then it is invalid. Reliability refers to the consistency of responses achieved by an item or index, and thus it can be evaluated simply through statistical analysis of responses to it. Validity usually requires more, some evidence that we have correctly identified what the item means to respondents.

Perhaps the richest set of examples of the problems around these issues, and the greatest effort from researchers trying to solve methodological problems, can be found in the wide area of human misery. We will consider surveys about illness, emotional trouble, and juvenile delinquency.

213

▶ ▶ ▶ ▶ ▶ ▶ ▶ ▶ ▶ ▶ ▶ ▶

VALIDITY AND INVALIDITY

Many studies have investigated the accuracy of people's reports about their physical health. If we ask you how you are, will you give us medically correct information? This question is important for our society's health care system, because getting accurate information from the patient is a crucial step toward diagnosis and proper treatment. A sensitive professional can coax information out of a patient, probing to clarify misunderstandings, but this can be very time consuming. Accurate health surveys could be valuable tools for preliminary diagnosis and screening of patients for possible problems.

In the 1950s, Edward Suchman, Bernard Phillips, and Gordon Streib (1958) surveyed more than 1000 retired men, asking them several questions about their general health and specific health problems. When they compared the men's responses to doctors' reports about them, they found striking disparities. For example, of the 635 men who the doctors said were in good health, 23% described themselves as in bad health. Of the 361 who the doctors said were in bad health, fully 61% described themselves as in good health. Overall, more than a third of the men disagreed with their doctors over the condition of their health.

You might think the solution to the problem is to ask better-focused questions that zero in on specific health problems. Consider these two apparently clear yes–no questions: "Do you have any trouble with your hearing?" "Did a doctor ever say you had varicose (swollen) veins?" A fifth of the men with normal hearing said they had trouble hearing. Three-quarters of the men with varicose veins denied having them. The researchers dryly observed that "the self-rating of health by a respondent . . . is subject to a great deal of error."

The health self-ratings were not useless, however. They did tend to correlate strongly with doctors' ratings, and thus they could be used in statistical studies if care were taken in interpreting the results. These self-ratings were also better predictors of the person's attitudes about health than were the doctors' diagnoses. For example, self-ratings predicted very well which men would constantly "worry about health."

If validity is a problem with questions about physical health, the difficulties are much worse with questions about mental health. It used to be said that somebody who never wondered whether he or she might be crazy must be crazy. Aren't people with poor mental health by definition bereft of their ordinary faculties, incapable of rendering valid judgments about themselves?

Although this is the common stereotype and may correctly describe some disorders, several studies indicate that the typical mental patient can be counted on to give coherent replies to many questions. During the 1966 and 1968 elections, Morris Klein and Saul Grossman (1971) went into the

Bronx State Hospital and let the psychiatric patients cast straw ballots. As hospitalized mental patients, the respondents had lost the right to vote in the actual elections, and one of the purposes of the study was to determine whether this disenfranchisement was justified. In fact, the inmates voted very much as the people outside the hospital walls did. Percentages voting for the different candidates differed very little between the "insane" and the "sane."

A tremendous amount of skill and effort has gone into the development of psychological surveys that assess a person's mental health and emotional condition. One of the major jobs of clinical psychologists is administering them as part of a professional evaluation of a person's problems. Some, like the Rorschach or the Thematic Apperception Test, employ pictures—inkblots, photographs, or drawings—and are administered in interviews, where the psychologist's training and experience are important parts of the evaluation. But many psychological tests use simple written questions with check-the-box answers.

A common way to validate such a questionnaire is to administer it to a group of normal people and to a group of mentally ill people, then see whether the scores from the survey properly discriminate the two groups. If the survey describes healthy people as ill and gives mentally ill people a clean bill of health, the items are clearly not valid.

Mental health questionnaires have been evaluated in this way many times. For instance, this validity test has been applied to the Leighton instrument, a questionnaire given through interviews (Moses et al., 1971). One hundred outpatients at a psychiatric clinic were compared with a random sample of 100 members of the general public. The average scores were very different, and only a small minority of the general public scored as badly as the typical patient. Of course, some members of the general public undoubtedly are in bad shape, and they have missed getting into treatment for some reason or another. But though we want our research tools to be as good as possible, no survey item or index is perfectly reliable or valid.

The term **criterion group** refers to a group of people, known (on the basis of conclusive, independent evidence) to have the characteristic an item or index is supposed to measure. An item that correctly distinguishes the criterion group from other people is said to have **criterion validity.**

Recall our friend Joe, who claimed to be very influential in his community. We could evaluate the validity of our questionnaire item about community influence by asking it of many respondents, then comparing their answers with more objective evidence of their degree of influence in the community. If we had lots of data about real decisions the community had made, we would know for a fact who was influential and who was not.

We seldom have a perfect standard with which to compare our questionnaire items, however. Usually, we compare our surveys with judgments other people have made, or we compare results from two or more different questionnaire items. In contrasting mental patients with the general public, we are relying on the judgments of doctors that the patients were in need of help, and perhaps on the judgments of the patients them-selves that they wanted help. This evidence of emotional problems may be very convincing, but it is not perfect.

Using Separate Indicators

When Travis Hirschi (1969) administered his huge questionnaire to high school boys, he asked whether they had performed various delinquent acts. His correlations showed that boys who said they were very close to their parents were far less likely to report performing delinquent acts than those who were not close to Mom and Dad. It could be, however, that boys close to their parents had simply learned to lie about the bad things they had done, and thus Hirschi's major research conclusions could have been false.

This is a question about the validity of Hirschi's items on delinquent behavior. Do they validly reflect behavior, or are many of the boys lying? Anticipating this problem, Hirschi had also gone to the police to get infor-mation about which boys had been picked up by the authorities, a very dif-ferent indicator of delinquency. Table 8.1 shows how police records com-pared with the boys' responses to one of the questions in Hirschi's survey.

The survey item asked the boys "Have you ever taken something of medium value ($2–$50) that did not belong to you?" Clearly, boys who said yes were much more likely to have been picked up by the police, 34% of them compared with 15%. Some of the respondents who denied stealing, yet had been involved with the police, had certainly lied on the question-naire. But others undoubtedly had committed different kinds of offense, such as vandalism, being drunk in public, or personal violence, that had gotten them in trouble with the law.

To be sure, trouble with the police is far from a perfect measure of delinquency. Note that 66% of the boys admitting theft on the survey had escaped the notice of the police. Some of them may have done their delin-quent deeds in a different town and gotten into the files of a different police department. And some may have been picked up by the police prior to the two-year period of the records Hirschi examined. So validating question-naire responses by comparing them with official records is not an ideal method, but often it is the best we have.

Hirschi was able to take another step to make sure that his main re-search conclusions were especially well-grounded. When he did his analy-sis, he did not rely on the questionnaire items alone. Instead, he did a par-allel analysis using the police records as his indicator of delinquency. For example, he shows that boys who are close to their parents are much less likely to answer yes to the theft item than boys who are estranged from their parents. Then he also shows, in a separate analysis, that boys who are close to their parents are less likely to have had trouble with the police.

Thus one general solution to the problem of validity in questionnaire measurement is to develop separate indicators that have their own, differ-

▶ ▶ ▶ ▶ ▶ ▶ ▶ ▶ ▶ ▶ ▶

TABLE 8.1   POLICE RECORDS OF BOYS RESPONDING TO A QUESTIONNAIRE

Do the police have a record that the boy was picked up in the past two years?	In responding to a questionnaire item about theft, the boys:	
	Deny Theft	Admit Theft
No	85%	66%
Yes	15%	34%
Total	100%	100%
Number	1054	246

Source: Travis Hirschi, *Causes of Delinquency* (Berkeley: University of California Press: 1969), p. 57.

ent strengths and weaknesses. You can inspect correlations between them to see whether they support each other, and you can run parallel analyses of the relationships between your indicators and the other variables of interest. In fact, Hirschi and his associates have worked constantly on these problems, and they have concluded that different measures of crime and delinquency give very much the same results in research, thus supporting one another's validity (Hindelang, Hirschi, and Weis, 1979).

Validity of an Index

A good example of how to assess the validity of an index is provided by research on self-esteem conducted by Morris Rosenberg (1965). Ten items, in a four-response agree–disagree format, made up the index of self-esteem:

1. On the whole, I am satisfied with myself.
2. At times I think I am no good at all.
3. I feel that I have a number of good qualities.
4. I am able to do things as well as most other people.
5. I feel I do not have much to be proud of.
6. I certainly feel useless at times.
7. I feel that I am a person of worth, at least on an equal plane with others.
8. I wish I could have more respect for myself.
9. All in all, I am inclined to feel that I am a failure.
10. I take a positive attitude toward myself.

If you look through this list, I think you will agree that half these statements express a positive feeling about oneself and half express a negative feeling. Combined in the right way, they make a scale of self-esteem that has considerable **face validity.** This means that each item looks like a reasonable indicator of the concept Rosenberg wanted the scale to measure. Most of us would say, on reflection, that each item primarily expresses high or low self-esteem.

But Rosenberg wanted more than just a strong personal conviction that his scale measured what he wanted it to. He sought independent evidence. If the index were an obesity index, he could easily see if objectively fat people got high scores on it and skinny ones did not. The physical weight of the respondents would be the criterion against which we could evaluate the validity of questionnaire items about obesity. But it is not so easy to identify people having high or low self-esteem. If a definite group of people were objectively known to have high self-esteem and another group known beyond the shadow of a doubt to have low self-esteem, Rosenberg could give his questionnaire to both groups and see whether the scale successfully identified which group each respondent belonged in. This would establish the scale's criterion validity.

With psychological conditions that do not drive a person into psychiatric treatment, it is hard to say what objective evidence we could get to prove that a person was in a particular category. You can weigh people to see whether they are heavy, and check their bank accounts to see whether they are rich. You can't look inside their heads to see whether they have self-esteem. But it certainly is possible to get independent evidence to compare with a self-esteem scale and improve your basis for evaluating it.

Fifty average citizens, healthy volunteers living for a while under hospital observation, answered the ten questions. Hospital nurses then rated each person's apparent mood. None of those scoring high on the self-esteem scale were said by the nurses to be "often gloomy," whereas a third of those scoring low on self-esteem were described in this way. The nurses judged that only 4% of those scoring high had been "frequently disappointed," compared with exactly half of those scoring low.

We often compare the results of one scale with the results of another scale we think should be related to it. Quite logically, Rosenberg argued that people low in self-esteem should be depressed as well, and many clinical observers report depression and low self-esteem go hand in hand. When self-esteem and depression scales were given to 2695 respondents, a powerful connection was found. Only 4% of those high in self-esteem scored as "highly depressed," compared with fully 80% of those scoring low in self-esteem (Rosenberg, 1965:21).

If you think about this for a moment, you might come up with a couple of serious questions. First, if low self-esteem is strongly connected to depression, who is to say they are not really the same thing? The capacity of an item or index to measure something different from what other scales measure is called **discriminant validity.** That is, if an index can be clearly distinguished statistically from other indexes that already exist, it must be measuring something of its own and thus deserves a special name.

On the other hand, if we are assessing the validity of a questionnaire item by examining its correlations with another item in the same survey, aren't we really just measuring the *reliability* of both items, the consistency with which they give a particular result? And at the beginning of this chapter, I said that validity and reliability were two different qualities we sought in an item. These questions suggest that we cannot complete our understanding of validity until we have also considered reliability.

▶ ▶ ▶ ▶ ▶ ▶ ▶ ▶ ▶ ▶ ▶

RELIABILITY AND CONSTRUCT VALIDITY

A reliable item or index gives consistent results. Most simply put, the result we get one time will be the same as the result we get another time. On occasion, we actually put a given item in a questionnaire twice, separated by many other items so the respondent doesn't notice the duplication, and we check to see whether we get the same answer both times. Reliability can become a rather complex topic, however, if we push the concept to its extremes.

Psychologists often speak of **test–retest reliability.** This refers to consistent results when we give the same set of items to a person twice, with some gap of time between the two administrations. Indeed, psychological experiments sometimes begin by giving a questionnaire to the research subjects. Then subjects get whatever experiences the experimenter wants to inflict on them, followed by the questionnaire again. The second administration of the survey is designed to see whether anything has changed as a result of the experiment.

An unreliable survey will give different results a second time even if the experiment had no real effect on the research subjects. A standard experimental approach, of course, is to divide subjects at random into two or more groups that have different experiences. One might be a control group to whom nothing happens, except that the same number of hours go by between the first and second administration of the questionnaire as for the groups that something is done to. Then changes in the experimental group can be compared with changes in the control group, compensating to some extent for any instability in the measuring indexes.

The mere fact that a person has seen the survey before can often produce different responses the second time. With tests of skill or knowledge, this phenomenon is known as the **practice effect.** Taking the test once allows you to do better the second time, either because you actually learn how to handle the problems or simply because you are less anxious the second time.

Thus test–retest reliability is more than just a quality of the items. It also reflects changes in the respondents. Therefore, it may be better to speak of test–retest *stability* rather than reliability. And if you want to assess the pure reliability of your items, giving them twice may not be the best way.

Another approach assesses **parallel-forms reliability.** The survey researcher creates two equivalent forms of an index. For example, you could make one index of ten items that reflect the extent to which the respondent is generally suspicious of other people, and then create another index of ten different items that also measure suspiciousness. Both indexes can be placed in the same survey, even right next to each other. Because each is supposed to measure the same thing, there should be a strong correlation between scores on them. If not, one or both of the indexes is unreliable.

Essentially the same thing is achieved with the **split-halves reliability** approach. You create a 20-item index of suspiciousness. When you have data from a number of respondents, purely to test reliability you create two 10-item indexes out of the 20—two subindexes of suspiciousness. A common method is to create one subindex out of the odd-numbered items and make the other subindex out of the even-numbered items. Because each half of the index is supposed to measure the same thing as the whole index, they should correlate highly with each other.

All these methods can be tried using our statistical analysis programs, and the matrix analysis and scaling programs are designed to do much reliability work for you. I will give practical examples shortly. But one very useful general approach is to look at the set of items that make up your index, either by inspecting the actual correlations linking all the items or by moving items around in the blocking procedure of the matrix program, to see whether the index holds together. Reliable items measuring the same thing should correlate with each other.

If all the items of an index reliably measure the same thing, they will stick pretty well together. But if they easily divide into blocks of correlations, and if a few stray items fail to correlate at all with the others, then the index is not a reliable unit. Perhaps it contains what we call **subscales,** sets of items that measure somewhat different things. Each subscale might be reliable, but if they measure very different phenomena, the combination of subscales might not be a reliable measure of anything.

There is room here for differences of opinion. Should an index always measure just one, narrow phenomenon, or is it appropriate to combine somewhat distinct subscales to measure a wider tendency? For example, several kinds of political conservatism might exist. Religious conservatism is different from economic conservatism. Conservatives who believe in free enterprise are different from conservatives who believe in strong military preparedness. You can create an index to measure each one of these, then combine them into an overall conservatism index. If it gives reasonable results when used in research, it must have some validity. But the attitudes we label "conservatism" may be so different from each other that combining them only causes confusion, and the best course may be to study each separately (Hicks and Wright, 1970).

A standard finding in the sociology of religion is that religiousness has several different dimensions. Glock and Stark (1965) suggested five ways of being religious: believing, observing religious practices, having religious experiences, knowing the facts about one's religious tradition, and behaving as a religious person in one's daily life. These correlate with each other, and it is quite possible to combine them in an index of overall religiousness, but groups of people differ greatly in which of these five are important to them. Studies have shown that the aspects of religion can be measured through reliable, valid indexes (Hilty and Morgan, 1985), and the decision to study religion as one or many dimensions is best made in term of the particular scientific goal a researcher wishes to achieve.

One concept, very popular a few years ago with social scientists but deeply suspected of unreliability and invalidity today, is *modernity*. The assumption behind this concept is that people differ in how modern they are. People in preindustrial and developing societies are believed to have values and personalities different from those of the educated folk who inhabit industrial societies. One interview survey of 1060 people in Guatemala found adequate reliability in a modernity index, but the researcher remained unconvinced that what the index was measuring necessarily had much to do with achieving economic development in the country (Portes, 1973). Another study found that a set of modernity indexes achieved statistical reliability, but they could not easily be distinguished from indexes of other concepts like "alienation" and "anomie" (Armer and Schnaiberg, 1972).

This illustrates the possibility that some indexes may be perfectly reliable without being completely valid. An index that does not allow you to predict anything about the respondents lacks criterion validity. And an index that correlates too well with other indexes adds nothing to what you can learn without it.

The ideal is an index that is both coherent and distinct. It should be coherent in the sense that its items cohere—stick together—as revealed by consistent correlations connecting them. It should be distinct in the sense that its items correlate much more with each other than they do with items from a different index with a different name. An index with both of these good qualities is sometimes said to have **construct validity**.

A **construct** is a concept we use to understand a phenomenon that cannot be observed directly. For example, to speak of some people as having an "authoritarian personality" is to suggest that there is a characteristic or dimension of authoritarianism that can help us understand human behavior. Some people have authoritarianism, and others do not. Or, more subtly perhaps, people vary in how authoritarian they are. But you cannot just look at a person and see authoritarianism. Its existence has to be inferred on the basis of survey results. Authoritarianism is a construct.

If possible, you would like to validate a concept like authoritarianism with respect to some readily observed criterion. But for many concepts in the social sciences, this cannot be done. If surveys find a group of items that cohere as a reliable index, and this index is distinct from other indexes, however, then *it must be measuring something*.

Commonsense interpretation of the items can suggest what we should call the index. And if the items do seem to share meaning, the index has face validity. If an index is reliable and distinct statistically, and if it expresses a meaningful concept, it has construct validity (Cronbach and Meehl, 1955). Although we might like to find appropriate, readily observable data to assess an index's criterion validity, we may have to be satisfied with construct validity. And since the early 1950s, psychologists have been convinced that construct validity is a very strong indication of the value of a survey index.

Construct validity sounds very much like simple reliability, and I said at the beginning of this chapter that reliability was not the same thing as validity. So I must emphasize that distinctness from other indexes is an essential attribute of an index that has construct validity. And many of us would add the requirement that the index reflect some clear theoretical concept before we would be convinced it had construct validity. Therefore, it is vitally important to work out your theoretical assumptions and make explicit the precise concepts you are using, if you want to claim construct validity for an index you have created. But if you do all this, you will find other social scientists very sympathetic toward your index, even if you cannot conclusively establish criterion validity.

Let's explore the reliability of a scale by creating a new one from our STUDENTS dataset. If you look through the list of 30 academic fields, you will see at least 8 of them that are directly related to professional careers. You can use the scaling program to combine these 8 in a CAREER index. We can hope that this index will measure the extent to which a student is oriented toward a professional career or prefers courses far removed from the professionalism implied by the 8. Table 8.2 lists the 8 items and their correlations with the complete index of which they are parts.

Cronbach's alpha for this index is 0.53. Such an alpha would not delight psychologists trying to create highly reliable indexes of personality characteristics, and in a moment we will finally explain what alpha measures. As we noted in Chapter 7, our academic fields were not invented in order to measure personalities. They are the actual subjects students take. Because these fields differ along many dimensions, indexes composed of them are apt to be rather weak and less reliable than indexes composed of items designed precisely for our research purpose.

Next, throw out this CAREER index. That seems a waste, but we already have the summary statistics on this index, and we want room to create four more. I am going to do a split-halves analysis, and to do this, I have to create pairs of indexes composed of the items in CAREER split into halves.

A Split-Halves Analysis

Create an index called FIRST4, with these items: #4 Law, #11 Business, #17 Education, and #19 Nursing. Then create an index called LAST4, with #21 Social work, #24 Communications, #25 Engineering, and #28 Medicine.

TABLE 8.2   ITEMS IN THE CAREER INDEX

Item	Correlation with the Entire Index
# 4 Law	0.51
#11 Business	0.49
#17 Education	0.60
#19 Nursing	0.56
#21 Social work	0.51
#24 Communications	0.54
#25 Engineering	0.38
#28 Medicine	0.54

If the CAREER index is reliable, the two halves of it should measure pretty much the same thing. In other words, like CAREER itself, FIRST4 and LAST4 should each be measures of the students' orientation toward or away from professional careers. Therefore, they should correlate with each other. Check the correlation between FIRST4 and LAST4, and you will find it is 0.50.

The correlation between two halves of an index, such as this 0.50, is often used as a simple measure of the whole test's reliability. A slight modification of this coefficient is more often used, however, which bears the formal name **split-halves reliability coefficient.** To get it, you multiply the correlation by 2 and divide the result by 1 plus the correlation. Here 0.50 × 2 is 1.00. Add 1 to 0.50 and you get 1.50. Divide 1.00 by 1.50 and you get 0.67, which is the split-halves reliability coefficient.

The reason we often do this to a correlation is that, compared to other measures, the correlation between two halves of a test can be an underestimate of the reliability. Remember, other things being equal, an index with few items is less reliable than an index with many items. When we went from an eight-item index to one with four items, our statistics were afflicted by what statisticians call **attenuation.** This technical word simply refers to the concept we just mentioned, a decline in a coefficient caused by a reduction in the number of items in the index. I should mention that there is some room for argument whether a correction for attenuation, such as the split-halves reliability coefficient achieves, is always appropriate. Consult the authorities and traditions in your own field for advice.

Among psychologists, a split-halves reliability coefficient of 0.67 is considered good, and some researchers get excited only when the coefficient reaches 0.70 or higher. But I never said we were going to achieve high reliability with the CAREER index, merely that it would help us explore the issue. And different fields of research are satisfied with different levels of reliability, depending in part on how unified the concepts are and how directly they can be measured through survey items.

With a little work, you can use the *Survey Research* software to calculate the split-halves coefficient for any scale you can create. But why didn't I build the calculation into the program, so that you would automatically get it whenever you created an index? The fact is, this coefficient has a serious problem. Years ago, it was used very frequently, but now you see it far less often in the better journals. The problem is a simple one. You can split an index into halves in many different ways. Here, we separated the first four items from the last four items and got a correlation of 0.50 between the two scales that resulted. Let's try splitting a different way, putting every other item into a half-index. Will that give us the same 0.50 correlation? Probably not.

Create two more indexes. ODD4 will consist of #4 Law, #17 Education, #21 Social work, and #25 Engineering. EVEN4 will consist of #11 Business, #19 Nursing, #24 Communications, and #28 Medicine. Once you have created ODD4 and EVEN4, check the correlation between them. You will find it is 0.57, quite different from the 0.50 we got before.

A correlation of 0.57 becomes a split-halves reliability coefficient of 0.73 when we run it through the formula just described. This is greater than the 0.70 that many researchers feel represents high reliability. Had we looked only at the ODD4–EVEN4 split, we might have concluded that the CAREER index is quite reliable and blithely gone on to base many costly research projects on it. The result might have been a scientific career that was nothing but a house of cards, ready to fall when somebody decided to question the reliability of the CAREER index!

In fact, some other ways of splitting the CAREER items into halves produce terribly low split-halves reliability coefficients, 0.36 for example, far below the 0.67 we got the first time, let alone the 0.73 that seemed satisfactory. Which split is right? What is the correct coefficient?

Of course, selecting any particular split as the one, best split is hard to justify. A different approach is to ask what is the average of all the possible coefficients from all the possible splits. Even with fast, modern computers, it seems a waste of time actually to make all the possible splits, calculate a coefficient each time, then take their average. And the mathematicians have come to our rescue.

Cronbach's alpha, developed by Lee J. Cronbach out of earlier work by G. F. Kuder and M. W. Richardson, is an estimate of the average of all the possible split-halves reliability coefficients (Cronbach, 1951; Green et al., 1977). Our program calculates it swiftly, using Cronbach's elegant formula, and today it is very widely used throughout survey research. The alpha for our CAREER scale is 0.53. CAREER may have some power to measure a professional orientation in respondents, but a highly reliable index it is not.

So what's wrong with it? We can use our matrix analysis program to see. Start up the matrix program and select option 4 to find blocks of items. When the computer asks what items you want, tell it you want the eight in our CAREER index. We will check to see whether the eight items form one solid block or whether in fact they break apart into several pieces.

Do the blocking analysis with positive correlations only, and I suggest you start with a cutoff correlation of +0.30. Sometimes the blocking procedure gets stuck, and you might have to start over, even selecting the items in a different order, to get the very best results. But the first time I tried this, I got a clear result. Law and Business wound up in a little block by themselves. Engineering was all by itself, having no correlations as high as 0.30 with other items in the list.

The rest wound up in a string—I cannot call it a block—each connected to the next one, but with no blocks even as big as three items solidly connected to each other. They were in this order: Communications, Education, Social Work, Nursing, and Medicine. Each correlated with those immediately next to it, but failed to correlate with items further along the string. I think if you consider these items in order, you can see a smooth shift in meaning from Communications to Medicine. Education involves communication with children, Social Work involves helping children and their parents, Nursing involves helping people through medicine.

Thus some significant correlations connect items in our supposed CAREER scale, but it is definitely not a solid block of items. This, in turn, implies that no underlying concept ties these eight items together, at least as respondents see them.

Of course, you might want to try the blocking analysis with a lower cutoff correlation. And other parts of the matrix analysis program can show you the actual correlation coefficients. The reliability and unity of indexes are a matter of degree, and we work with the best we can get, rather than holding impossibly high standards in all the research we do. When professional survey researchers examine an index to see whether its items hold together, they typically use more sophisticated statistical tools, such as factor analysis. But this attempt to create an index of professional career orientation has succeeded in demonstrating the main principles of a reliability analysis, even if it has failed to produce a reliable index.

Now let's look at an important research study that raised issues of reliability.

The Reliability of Consciousness

For decades, many social scientists have assumed that every person has a coherent set of beliefs about the world, and every society is organized around a particular set of ideas. As John Lofland and Rodney Stark (1965:862) expressed this perspective: "All men and all human groups have ultimate values, a world view, or a perspective furnishing them a more or less orderly and comprehensible picture of the world." This assumption is certainly widespread in anthropology, psychology, and sociology, and I think the other social sciences often follow it, too. But some of us dispute this assumption.

An alternative perspective is to believe that human beings learn a large number of wholly disconnected facts about the world and receive from many different people the most varied possible collection of ideas about this or that tiny fragment of reality. Societies, composed of people with highly varied experiences of the world, have few if any overarching principles of unity. Although general values and perspectives are desired, they are very hard to achieve. A few human institutions, notably religion, are able to construct coherent ideological systems, but this task is almost impossible in most areas of life where reality itself is so complex and obscure that it defies systematization.

These two theories about human society could hardly be more different. And theories about matters of such great scope are important. Theory is not merely the idle game of ivory tower scholars, but under a different name theory guides all human action. It is our abstract ideas about reality that distinguish us from other creatures on this planet, and nobody can take action without at least some kind of theory about the situation he or she faces. How coherent and well-organized our ideas are is an open question, however, and this is the issue that these two theories engage.

Unfortunately but perhaps predictably, this great debate has hardly ever been the focus of careful empirical research. The issue is so vast that it is hard to get a grip on it. Most often, researchers in this area simply adopt one or the other assumption and then do projects that apply it without testing it. Thus when Robert Wuthnow published a book that appeared to give unambiguous support for the theory that most people do, in fact, possess coherent systems of beliefs and values, scholars took note.

His book, *The Consciousness Reformation* (1976), was based on a survey of 1000 residents of the San Francisco area. It was an expensive project, because each of the 1000 was interviewed at home, and the respondents were a representative sample of the population. The questionnaire itself was a long one, written by Charles Y. Glock and his seasoned team of survey researchers at the University of California at Berkeley.

Many of the items, written in a wide variety of formats, sought to determine the respondent's view of the world, of the sources of human problems, and of the best ways to live a good life. Many questions were about experimentation in religion and lifestyles, including some about deviant cults, drug use, and participation in the New Age and human-potential movements. Wuthnow set himself the task of explaining why some people experiment with new lifestyles while others hold to traditional patterns of behavior.

His main conclusion was that a set of competing **meaning systems** exists in our society, each possessed by a different set of people and each urging its adherents to make different major decisions about life.

There is no question which side of the debate Wuthnow was on. But his book is not merely an expression of faith. He presents evidence that appears to prove that four groups of respondents possess four different meaning systems that organize their lives. Some people may be caught between two of these, but most people have the benefit of a coherent view of the world.

When I first saw Wuthnow's book, it struck me as good news, despite the fact that it contradicted my own theory. First, there is something very optimistic about Wuthnow's theory. It asserts that society is a meaningful, predictable system, not the disjointed and untrustworthy chaos that my theory holds it to be. Furthermore, Wuthnow appeared to have explained much of the variation between individuals in their lifestyles and experimentation with deviant behavior. This looked like a major scientific advance, one that other researchers could build on.

So when I was getting ready to do a survey on the occult with a big class in the sociology of deviance, I included slightly modified versions of the items Wuthnow had used to measure his four meaning systems. Here are the names of the four and the primary force each asserts governs the events in a person's life:

1. Theism: God is the agent who governs life.
2. Individualism: The individual is in charge of his or her own life.
3. Social science: Life is governed chiefly by social forces.
4. Mysticism: The meaning of life and the forces that govern life cannot be understood by the human intellect.

You could, I suppose, turn each of these into an agree–disagree item. Check the appropriate box to say how much do you agree or disagree with the following: "The individual is in charge of his or her own life." Or you could combine the four into a single menu item:

Check the ONE box that indicates which of the following four factors seems most important in determining what happens in your own life:

[1] God
[2] me, myself
[3] social forces
[4] forces I cannot understand intellectually

But single items, in either of these formats, are not so reliable as indexes composed of several items. The menu item, particularly, would place all the weight of Wuthnow's analysis on a single question and would thus be vulnerable to whatever whim or accident might disturb a respondent while finding a box to check. As I understand it, Wuthnow was not in a position to write long, pretested sets of items and had to content himself with items partly written by others for other purposes. But he was able to base measurement of each of the meaning systems on 3 items, for a total of 12, aiming for greater reliability than single items could achieve.

Four of the 12 were phrased in a 5-response agree–disagree format: "If one works hard enough, he can do anything he wants to." "I believe forgotten childhood experiences have an effect on me." "It is good to live in a fantasy world every now and then." "The poor simply aren't willing to work hard." Another was in a 3-response agree–disagree format: "Man evolved from lower animals." An item about belief in God was very similar to the Glock and Stark item we discussed in Chapter 5.

Two items were among a list of seven in which the respondent was supposed to say how much influence the particular thing had on his or her life: "God or some other supernatural force." "New insights about yourself." Three others were among a list of nine in which the respondent was supposed to say how major a cause each was for the suffering in the world: "Suffering is caused by social arrangements that make people greedy for riches and power." "Suffering comes about because people don't obey God." "People usually bring suffering on themselves." Another item was in a yes–no format with four responses: "Have you ever experienced the beauty of nature in a deeply moving way?"

In adapting these questions for my own survey, I thought it would be advisable to put them all into the same format. Most were already agree–disagree items, or phrased appropriately for this format. So I transformed the others to turn them into declarative statements and decided to use 5 response categories. The items had been strewn throughout Wuthnow's survey, with a few bunched together, but I decided to place all 12 together in my own. But I intentionally rotated them, so that the 4 meaning systems alternated and items representing a meaning system would not tend to correlate merely because they stood next to each other. Here I will list them arranged in their meaning systems, however, so you can see how Wuthnow believed they would go together in people's minds (Stark and Bainbridge, 1985:373):

Theism
1. I definitely believe in God.
2. God or some other supernatural force has a very strong influence on my life.
3. Suffering often comes about because people don't obey God.

Individualism
4. People usually bring suffering on themselves.
5. The poor simply aren't willing to work hard.
6. If one works hard enough, he can do anything he wants to.

Social science

7. I believe forgotten childhood experiences have an effect on me.
8. Suffering is greatly caused by social arrangements which make people greedy for riches and power.
9. Man evolved from lower animals.

Mysticism

10. I have experienced the beauty of nature in a deeply moving way.
11. It is good to live in a fantasy world every now and then.
12. New insights about myself have had a great influence on my life.

You can take a moment to see whether these items have face validity, in your opinion. Consider the principle underlying each meaning system, and see whether the three items for the meaning system all seem to express it. Certainly, it is hard to escape the fact that the first three items all contain the word *God* and express a traditional religious faith that might be called theism. Similarly, the individualism items all hint that the individual is in charge of his or her destiny. Two of the individualism items have the word *work* in them. Thus one might worry a bit that the individualism items focus too narrowly on the world of work and work-related action. And when you get to the third and fourth meaning systems, you may have quite a struggle deciding what the items have in common.

Wuthnow's book does not, to my mind, contain a satisfactory discussion of the face validity of the items, and the reader might find cause to doubt that they mean what he says they do. In the back of the book is a rather impressive factor analysis including these 12 items among many others, but it is not clear whether Wuthnow properly assessed the statistical reliability of his 4 indexes. I did not worry about these things, however, when I adapted his items for my questionnaire. He seemed to have gotten such solid results in explaining human behavior with the meaning systems that I rushed excitedly forward, using his indexes as tools to discover new truths of my own.

So it was with great disappointment that I looked at the results of my survey and discovered that something had gone seriously wrong. Knowing that reliability was a key issue with indexes, the first thing I examined was the correlations linking the 12 items derived from Wuthnow's survey. If an index is reliable, the 3 items that make it up should correlate with each other. This was true for the 3 items about God in the theism index. But the 3 other indexes bombed. The items supposedly composing each failed to correlate significantly with one another. On top of that, some items from different indexes correlated highly.

One possibility was that my dataset was simply lousy. I had only 121 respondents, all students in my sociology of deviance class. This wasn't anything like the random sample of 1000 that Wuthnow had used. In collaboration with my friend and colleague Rodney Stark, I decided to try again with a much larger number of respondents.

We administered a big survey, containing my version of the 12 items, to 1439 undergraduates at the University of Washington. Again the results seemed to contradict Wuthnow's. To be sure, the 3 theism items correlated with each other. The highest correlation in the set (gamma = 0.89) was between "I definitely believe in God" and "God or some other supernatural force has a very strong influence on my life." Coincidentally, each of these items achieved the same correlation (gamma = 0.73) with "Suffering often comes about because people don't believe in God," and thus these 2 correlations were tied for second and third strongest.

The fourth strongest correlation (gamma = −0.60) was a negative one, between belief in God and agreement that "Man evolved from lower animals," supposedly one of the three social science items. Tied for fifth and sixth, at −0.59, were the correlations between this evolution statement and the two other theism items. If the indexes were good, there should not be such strong correlations going from one index to an item in another. To make matters worse, none of the three correlations between pairs of items in the social science index were even as high as 0.20!

Stark and I had to conclude that the social science index was completely unreliable. It made more sense to consider the evolution item to be part of the theism index, coded the opposite way from the other three, measuring a person's disagreement with traditional religious beliefs about the origin of the human species. It was not long before we discovered that the great success Wuthnow's four meaning systems had apparently achieved in explaining respondents' tendencies to experiment with radical lifestyles was mainly a reflection of one meaning system only: theism. Traditionally religious people did not experiment with communes, weird cults, drugs, and the like. Respondents lacking traditional religious faith were far more likely to do so.

Perhaps you had some difficulty making sense of the social science meaning system when I asked you to consider the face validity of the items. The statement about forgotten childhood experiences hints at psychoanalytic theory, developed by Sigmund Freud and his many followers. The statement about suffering being caused by social arrangements hints at Marxist critiques of capitalist society, although it may have a broader meaning to many respondents. The statement about evolution, of course, measures acceptance of Darwinism.

Within professional psychology, great controversy still rages about the psychoanalytic approach, and social scientists of many varieties reject Marxism despite its popularity in sociology and related fields. Many anthropologists and sociologists are vehement in their rejection of evolutionary theories as possible explanations for human behavior. Furthermore, it is very hard to find a social scientist who bases his or her work simultaneously on all three. There are some Freudian Marxists, and both Freudians and Marxists have occasionally written about evolution. But the typical social scientist is remote from at least two of these, and often all three.

There is a sense in which the alleged social science items are similar, because all three suggest a natural, scientific explanation for aspects of life. But apparently this point they may have in common weighs hardly at all in respondents' judgments of them, for strong correlations were quite lacking. Thus the social science scale is not at all reliable, and the face validity of the items, seen as a set, is quite unconvincing.

The mysticism index is a bit hard to understand, and Wuthnow himself used a quite different set of items to measure mysticism in his second book (1978). "Beauty of nature" and "insights about myself" showed a fairly strong correlation (gamma = 0.46), the seventh highest in the set. "Fantasy world" hardly correlated with "insights" (gamma = 0.21), however, and not at all with "beauty." Indeed, these three alleged mysticism items achieved six correlations above 0.20 with items supposed to be in other indexes!

Finally, the individualism items hung together weakly, achieving gammas of 0.31, 0.23, and 0.20. This is far, far below the level achieved by the theism items. Of course, all three of those contain the word *God*, and this alone might connect them in people's minds. But the evolution item gets gammas of −0.60 and −0.59 with the theism items, and it does not contain any reference to God or the supernatural.

On the basis of our 1439 Seattle questionnaires, Stark and I could see no convincing evidence for the existence of the individualism, social science, and mysticism meaning systems. Traditional religiousness alone appeared to function as a meaning system that provided a coherent view of life to its adherents and powerfully guided their action.

Our initial results were not entirely convincing, however. The team that administered the San Francisco survey had invested much money and effort in securing a representative, random sample of the population. We, with no research grant and just a little personal and departmental money to spend, had not tried to get even a random sample of students, let alone of the general public. Perhaps our sample of respondents was so poor that our results were worthless.

Always dedicated to advancing scientific knowledge and improving survey methodology, Charles Glock was kind enough to provide us with a computer tape containing the data from the San Francisco survey. When we ran the correlations, we got almost exactly the same results we had found among our 1439 students. There was nothing wrong with our survey. There was everything wrong with the individualism, social science, and mysticism indexes.

Two lessons can be learned from this scientific adventure. First, checking the statistical reliability of any indexes that play important roles in your research is essential. Second, science is not primarily the story of advances achieved by individual researchers with single, massive research projects. Science is in great measure a collective enterprise. To settle any important question, we need many studies, carried out with somewhat different assumptions using a variety of research methods. Pioneers like Wuthnow deserve great honor in our profession, even if some of their conclusions are invalidated by later research.

▶ ▶ ▶ ▶ ▶ ▶ ▶ ▶ ▶ ▶ ▶

SPURIOUSNESS

Spuriousness might be defined as invalidity with respect to correlations rather than to individual variables. Social scientists often worry about "spurious correlations," and a fair proportion of our more sophisticated statistical techniques are designed to guard against these demons of data analysis. Although the problem of spuriousness can be hard to solve, it is easy enough to understand.

The most famous example of spuriousness is a fictitious study of fires and firefighters. Let's say you were doing the research in Boston, arson capital of the cosmos. For several weeks you lurked at various fire stations around town and surveyed the personnel after each fire alarm. You asked two questions: How many firefighters went to the blaze? How much damage was done by the fire?

To the dismay of the fire chief, you discovered that the more firefighters who went to a blaze, the more damage was done. If only one truck was sent to a fire, the damage averaged $10,000. But if two or more trucks went, the damage averaged $50,000. When your result leaked out, the local tabloid newspaper bannered a front-page story illustrated by a cartoon showing vicious firefighters hacking away with their axes, destroying a perfectly good Boston home.

Of course, this story is unfair to the Boston fire department, because the correlation between firefighters and damage has a simple explanation. The key is the seriousness of the fire in the first place. A big fire causes a lot of damage. A big fire causes the fire department to send several fire trucks to fight it. It is the fire, not the firefighters, that causes the damage.

Let's analyze in terms of variables. In the original story, the number of fire trucks is the X variable. The amount of damage, in dollars, is the Y variable. Your research found a very strong correlation between X and Y. The story leaked to the newspaper assumed that X was the independent variable and Y was the dependent variable—that variations in X caused variations in Y. Indeed, the positive correlation between X and Y is real. If you did the study again, presumably you would get pretty much the same results, demonstrating the reliability of your measurements. The problem is in the interpretation of these reliable results. It is a third variable, size of the fire, that determines both the damage and the number of fire trucks sent. Thus both X and Y are really dependent variables, and a third variable, call it Z, is actually the independent variable.

When two variables correlate with each other but their association is really the result of a third variable, the correlation is spurious. Perhaps it would be more precise to say that our *interpretation* of the correlation is spurious, because the correlation itself is quite real and merely misunderstood. The cure for spuriousness is an alert researcher with the imagination to think of possible third variables and include them in the survey. Had you thought to ask firefighters for an estimate of the size of each fire, you could have controlled for this Variable, Z, and you would have found that the apparent correlation between X and Y would vanish.

A simple way of controlling for a third variable is to divide your data into subgroups in terms of Z. For example, you could divide fires into kitchen fires, house fires, and major conflagrations covering many buildings. Then you would look at the association between fire trucks and damage in each of these categories separately, and you might discover that the correlation vanishes. When you do an analysis like this, the third variable is called the **control variable,** and you are said to be *controlling for* Z.

Here is a real example from a classic survey dataset collected in 1968 (Campbell, 1971) that I came across when I was looking for existing surveys to compare associations between religion and migration in different regions of the country. Several studies have shown that church membership tends to be low among people who have recently moved to a new home. Table 8.3 shows how an apparent relationship between migration and religion turned out to be largely spurious.

One of the questions in the 1968 survey was on frequency of church attendance. The largest group, 42.1%, said they attended "regularly," and a further 13.8% said "often." In the table I have combined these as "attending often." The rest attended "seldom" (32.4%) or "never" (11.7%). A question on migration determined whether the respondent had been born in the city, or how many years ago he or she had moved to it. Here, I have coded those who moved in five years ago or more recently as "recent migrants" and the others as "longtime residents."

If we just look at migration and church attendance, as in the first row of figures of the table, we would think we had solid evidence that migration disrupts church attendance. The percent who attend regularly among longtime residents is 57.9, compared to only 41 among recent migrants. The correlation is −0.33, as measured by gamma, and this achieves a very high level of statistical significance.

But I knew that denominations differ greatly in how much emphasis they place on church attendance. In their survey of California church members, Glock and Stark (1966:16) found that 63% of Protestants attended church every week, compared with 80% of Catholics. Thus I suspected that the association between migration and church attendance might be spurious. This was only a suspicion, and I had no solid reason to believe that it was true, but as a precaution I tried a simple test of spuriousness. As shown in Table 8.3, I calculated migration and church attendance statistics separately for each major denomination.

▶ ▶ ▶ ▶ ▶   ▶ ▶ ▶ ▶ ▶ ▶

TABLE 8.3   MIGRATION AND CHURCHGOING IN 15 AMERICAN CITIES

| Religion | Persons | Percent Recent Migrant | Percent Attending Often | | Correlation: Migration– Churchgoing (gamma) |
			Longtime Residents	Recent Migrants	
All	2568	11.4%	57.9%	41.0%	−0.33*
Catholic	1347	7.1%	74.3%	68.8%	−0.14
Protestant	795	17.1%	42.5%	33.8%	−0.18
Jewish	256	10.9%	27.2%	17.9%	−0.26
Other	73	13.7%	60.3%	20.0%	−0.72
None	90	24.4%	4.4%	4.5%	0.02

▶

*Significant at the 0.0001 level, by chi-square. No other associations achieve even the 0.01 level of statistical significance.

The difference in church attendance narrows considerably, for all groups except the tiny, mixed collection of those with "other" faith. Despite the large numbers in the Catholic and Protestant categories, none of the differences achieves the 0.01 level of statistical significance (as measured by a chi-square test for the full crosstab).

In the 1968 data as in other surveys, Protestants attend church less often than Catholics. The Catholic tradition places great emphasis on going to Mass regularly, so this does not prove Catholics are generally more religious than Protestants, something that would have to be examined through other questions about religious beliefs and practices. Protestants are more mobile geographically than Catholics, in this particular set of respondents. The other denominational groups have their own levels of attendance and migration. Together, these facts produce the spurious impression of a direct association between migration and attendance.

Note that Variable Z has to correlate with both X and Y to produce a spurious correlation between them. If denominations did not differ in their rates of geographical mobility, the differences in their traditional rates of church attendance could not produce a spurious correlation between migration and attendance. Also, the correlation between X and Y might be only partly spurious. They might really be associated, and their correlation might only be inflated by the action of Variable Z. Indeed, the substantial percentage differences in attendance that remain after controlling, in Table 8.3, suggest that this is the case for the data we have just analyzed.

As I have said, statisticians have given us many tools for assessing spuriousness. The simplest one is just dividing the data up by categories of Variable Z, as we have done in Table 8.3. Slightly more subtle is the technique of **partial correlations.** When you calculate the correlation between two variables, X and Y, you work with pairs of numbers—the values of X and Y for all your cases. To calculate partial correlations, you use slightly different mathematical procedures with trios of numbers, X, Y, and Z.

I introduced partial correlations briefly in Chapter 6, and the basic statistics program allows you to calculate them. In Table 8.3, the original correlation between migration and churchgoing is −0.33, as measured by gamma. The partial gamma between migration and churchgoing, controlling for denomination, is only −0.16. This is a substantial reduction, greatly eroding our confidence that X and Y are really related in our data.

One problem in testing for spuriousness is that our control variables, such as denomination, may not be measured accurately enough. Consider the Protestant category. Dozens of different denominations are lumped together under the label of Protestant, and they may differ greatly in norms of church attendance and typical rates of migration. Glock and Stark (1966:16) found that only 45% of Congregationalists attended church each week, compared with 84% of Southern Baptists. If we could divide the Protestants up into their denominations, their correlation of −0.18 between X and Y might vanish. Roman Catholics belong to a single denomination but to many ethnic groups. Perhaps controlling for ethnic group could eradicate the weak −0.14 association among Catholics, as well.

This example does not disprove all the research showing a connection between migration and loss of church membership. In essence, the issue of spuriousness is a warning to think deeply about your variables and your theories, trying to identify possible problems of validity. As Herbert A. Simon (1954) pointed out, you must use theoretical judgment as well as statistical tests in evaluating spuriousness. And you should not be discouraged. Spuriousness is probably not very common in well-designed research studies. But you should be on guard, and you should invest enough care in designing your survey that you could catch the most obvious cases of spuriousness. And if your interpretations survive erosion by control variables, they will be all the more respectable.

Sometimes you will find that a third variable has actually reduced the correlation between X and Y, rather than having inflated it. Here's an example from my experience as director of the undergraduate sociology program at the University of Washington. I don't know about your college, but at many schools sociology is considered a "gut major." We got some very fine, hardworking undergraduates in sociology at UW, but we also got some who wanted to graduate as painlessly as possible but didn't want the abysmal stigma of a degree in General Studies.

So it wasn't a great surprise when I found that the grade-point average (GPA) of sociology majors was lower than that for the university as a whole. I also discovered that about two-thirds of our majors were women. Before you leap to a spurious interpretation, let me report that the average GPA of women at the university was actually higher than the GPA of men.

Thus an association existed between being female and majoring in sociology, and between being female and having a high grade-point average. Just on the basis of these two facts, you might expect a spurious positive correlation between majoring in sociology and having a high grade-point average. But I had found sociology majors tended to have low GPAs—that a *negative* correlation existed between sociology and GPA, not the *positive* one that spuriousness would have produced.

When I re-examined the association between sociology and GPA while controlling for sex, the negative correlation got even more negative. The truth was that sociology had a substantial negative correlation with GPA. The fact that femininity correlated with both variables pulled the apparent correlation in the positive direction, making the situation seem better than it really was. When an association between two variables, X and Y, is spuriously reduced by the action of a third variable, Z, we say that the correlation has been *suppressed* and that Z is a **suppressor variable** (cf. Lazarsfeld, 1955).

▶ ▶ ▶ ▶ ▶ ▶ ▶ ▶ ▶ ▶ ▶

RESPONSE BIAS

It has long been recognized that some respondents may have consistent tendencies to answer questions in a particular way, regardless of what the question is about. Such a tendency would introduce spuriousness into our understanding of correlations that show up in the data. Imagine an agree–disagree questionnaire in which each question has five boxes to choose from, printed from left to right: [1] Strongly agree, [2] Agree, [3] Neutral, [4] Disagree, and [5] Strongly disagree. It is possible that right-handed respondents will have an unconscious tendency to check boxes on the right side, and left-handed respondents will have a similar tendency to check boxes on the left. If these tendencies exist, they are what we often call **response biases**.

Now, I don't have any evidence that this particular kind of bias really exists, but let's think about it as an easy example. I am right-handed. I sit with the questionnaire before me, at a slight angle, more or less lined up with my right forearm. I hold my hand a bit to the right of the questions so I can see them clearly. My pencil is poised and ready to make check marks. The item says, "Response bias is a serious problem for survey researchers." Suppose I disagree with this. My hand is right next to the "strongly disagree" box, and it would take some effort to reach over two inches to the "disagree" box, so I check "strongly disagree."

Under the same circumstances, a left-handed person might have checked the "disagree" box. The laziness of my hand may not be so great as to prevent me from expressing my opinion at all. If I agree with the statement, I am unlikely to check the "disagree" box merely because it is convenient. But I might check "agree" rather than "strongly agree," because doing so requires less movement of my hand. My responses will not be completely meaningless, but perhaps a small bias will exist. Because there are more right-handed people in the general population, the overall statistics will be biased toward disagreement.

Again, this is only a hypothetical example, and survey researchers do not worry much about which hand their respondents write with. But there are two kinds of bias that have generated much concern and a good deal of effort to overcome them: acquiescence and social desirability (Block, 1965). Psychologists sometimes call these **response sets,** because *set* is a technical term referring to the predisposition to be attentive to certain stimuli. A set is like a habit in how people perceive the world around them, and a response set is therefore the habit to respond in a particular, consistent way to stimuli.

Acquiescence is the tendency to agree with whatever the survey says, regardless of the content of the items. This is also called *yea-saying,* the tendency to say yes. The opposite of yea-saying is *nay-saying,* the tendency to say no. When survey researchers talk about acquiescence, they are referring to variations among respondents in the tendency to agree <u>or</u> disagree with the items regardless of their content. Agreeable people and disagreeable people can cause equal problems for the researcher through this kind of response bias. For example, in statistical analysis the researcher might find that all the items in a section of the survey correlate with each other, but this could merely be the result of some people having a tendency to agree with statements and other people having a tendency to disagree with statements.

A standard way of overcoming acquiescence in a set of agree–disagree items is to combine a number of them into an index, composed of equal numbers of positive and negative items. Suppose we wanted to learn whether respondents felt Japanese products were better made than American products. To make our work sound very scientific, we could say we were studying philonipponism, defined as a love of things Japanese. In a set of six items, we would want three where "agree" represented philonipponism, and three where "disagree" did. They might look like the following:

1. By and large, Japanese television sets are better made than American ones.

2. If I were in an auto accident, I would prefer to be riding in an American car, rather than a Japanese car, because they are much stronger in a crash.

3. The next breakthrough developments in electronics are more likely to come from Japan than from the United States.

4. All things considered, American products are better bargains than Japanese products.

5. The low price and high quality of Japanese cars make them more attractive than American cars.

6. The Japanese make decent personal computers, but if you really want the best and most advanced machine, you should buy an American one.

The odd-numbered items say Japanese products are better, and the even-numbered ones say American products are better. Chapter 7, on how to make an index, explains in detail how to combine such items as these into a single measure. But, simply put, you could give a respondent one philonipponism point for agreeing with an odd-numbered item, and one point for disagreeing with an even-numbered item.

Some of the classic questionnaires failed to consider this problem, and they are composed primarily of items phrased positively. An example that has generated a vast literature on possible biases is the MMPI, the Minnesota Multiphasic Personality Inventory (Block, 1965). For decades, this has been the most widely used psychological measurement instrument for evaluating emotional problems; just yesterday one of my students reported the MMPI was given to every patient who entered the mental health clinic she was studying.

Another approach to handling acquiescence is through items specifically designed to measure it. For example, you could have a few pairs of items that were the exact, logical opposites of each other, such as this: "In general, American products are better than Japanese products." "In general, Japanese products are better than American products."

Logically, a person who strongly agrees that American products are better should strongly disagree with the statement that Japanese products are better. But people often give slightly inconsistent answers. A respondent who strongly agrees with the first of this pair might only disagree (without the "strongly") with the opposite item. This suggests a shift in the agree direction—yea-saying.

Or a respondent might agree that American products are better, but strongly disagree with the proposition that Japanese products are better. This suggests a shift in the disagree direction—nay-saying.

Responding to questions involves a good deal of imprecision, so you should not jump to conclusions about acquiescence in a respondent on the basis of one pair of items. You should also be very certain that the pair really are opposites. For example, the following pair would not be interpreted as mutually contradictory by all respondents: "American products are the best in the world." "Japanese products are the best in the world." A respondent who felt that the two nations were tied for best might reasonably agree with both of these, perhaps harboring a slight reservation that the items don't permit him or her to express an opinion on this matter with perfect exactness. Conversely, a person who felt that German products are the best in the world would disagree with both of these items.

There are three problems with using pairs of opposite items to measure acquiescence. First, to do the job well you will need to put several pairs in your survey, thus greatly inflating its size beyond what you or your respondents would prefer. Second, respondents might notice that some items are pairs and consciously try to answer them in a consistent way. Third, and as an extension of the first two problems, respondents may resent the extra effort required by the pairs of opposites and even complain that you are treating them in a condescending way by asking the same questions twice. With all these disadvantages to the pairs of opposites approach, it is not surprising most survey researchers are content to write index items so that the numbers of positive and negative are equal.

Acquiescence may be more than a mere bias; it may represent particular personality styles. In a massive survey employing 681 questionnaire items, Arthur Couch and Kenneth Keniston (1960) found it was possible to describe personalities who were most likely to yea-say or nay-say. The yea-sayers appear to be impulsive people who express themselves quickly with little self-control. They actively seek emotional excitement, novelty, change, movement, and adventure. In contrast, nay-sayers have more of what Couch and Keniston called "psychological inertia," carefully controlling their impulses and resisting influences in their environment. Presumably, yea-sayers are easily carried away by the items in a questionnaire, expressing some enthusiasm for almost anything presented to them, whereas nay-sayers resist the psychological pressures some items may impose.

Couch and Keniston carefully devised a 15-item Overall Agreement Scale (OAS), in which agreement with the items indicates a tendency toward acquiescence. Depending on your tastes, the items seem either charming or silly, but they do have the power to identify people especially prone to yea-saying. Many researchers, however, would want items that are not so saturated with meaning as those in the OAS. Indeed, the scale seems to measure the impulsiveness Couch and Keniston believe is associated with acquiescence, rather than acquiescence itself. The first seven of the OAS items are:

1. Novelty has a great appeal to me.
2. I crave excitement.
3. It's a wonderful feeling to sit surrounded by your possessions.
4. There are few things more satisfying than really to splurge on something—books, clothes, furniture, etc.
5. Only the desire to achieve great things will bring a man's mind into full activity.
6. Nothing is worse than an offensive odor.
7. In most conversations, I tend to bounce from topic to topic.

Whereas acquiescence is a bias that has nothing to do with the content of the items, social desirability bias has everything to do with it. People exhibiting **social desirability bias** tend to answer questions in ways that present themselves in an unusually good light. They agree with statements they think good people agree with, and they disagree with statements that bad people agree with. Thus they would deny they had personal problems and deny they engaged in socially disapproved behavior.

Allen Edwards has defined social desirability bias as "the tendency to give socially desirable responses in self-description" (1967:69), but he is quick to emphasize that this is not the same thing as lying about oneself. Often it is quite ambiguous whether a person has a particular trait or not. Are you a helpful person? How helpful? I like to believe that everybody is a little bit helpful to others. Yet we have no precise scale to determine objectively how helpful a person is, as we do for an individual's height or weight. Thus when confronted with a question about how helpful they are, respondents have considerable latitude in selecting an answer. Because helpfulness is a socially desired trait, a person with social desirability bias will express a high level of helpfulness, without really having to lie.

A considerable amount of effort has gone into assessing social desirability biases in the MMPI. As I noted, this is one of the most commonly used psychological instruments, and its application in diagnosing the kind and severity of psychological problems makes it especially important. Edwards identified a number of items in the MMPI that seemed to tap this bias and constructed a scale out of 39 of them that a panel of judges found to be unambiguous with respect to social desirability.

Block has argued that Edwards's social desirability scale is really a scale measuring the degree of anxiety felt by the respondent. Below are listed six true–false items from it, all of which are supposed to get "false" replies from people with social desirability bias. Block (1965:68) says these six are typical of the whole scale. A person with the yea-saying form of acquiescence bias should answer "true"; nay-sayers and those with social desirability bias would tend to answer "false."

1. My sleep is fitful and disturbed.
2. I cry easily.
3. I dream frequently about things that are best kept to myself.
4. When in a group of people I have trouble thinking of the right things to talk about.
5. I feel anxiety about something or someone almost all the time.
6. It makes me nervous to have to wait.

The fact is that psychological problems are socially undesirable. A well-adjusted person will answer "false" to most of these six items, and yet he or she will be accused of social desirability bias for giving such answers. The problem of how to disentangle pure social desirability of items from their substantive meaning is very difficult. Douglas Crowne and David Marlowe (1960) have created a 33-item social desirability scale they hope avoids this problem. Following are 8 of the items, arranged so that the socially desirable response is "true" for odd-numbered items and "false" for even-numbered items:

1. Before voting I thoroughly investigate the qualifications of all the candidates.
2. On occasion I have had doubts about my ability to succeed in life.
3. I have never intensely disliked anyone.
4. There have been occasions when I took advantage of someone.
5. I'm always willing to admit it when I make a mistake.
6. I like to gossip at times.
7. I have never deliberately said something that hurt someone's feelings.
8. I am sometimes irritated by people who ask favors of me.

If you answered "true" to statements, 1, 3, 5, and 7 and answered "false" to statements 2, 4, 6, and 8, either you are a saint or you exhibit extreme social desirability bias. And saints are rarely found among the respondents to surveys. This kind of bias is a serious problem only when the topic of your investigation is something near an extreme in social desirability.

▶ ▶ ▶ ▶ ▶ ▶ ▶ ▶ ▶ ▶ ▶

COPING WITH VALIDITY AND RELIABILITY PROBLEMS

Valid, reliable results are accomplished in a collaboration between your questionnaire and your respondents. You need good questions and good answerers, as Chapter 2 explained. Much can be done to write valid, reliable questions, and much can be done to get the best responses out of the people to whom you administer the survey.

If you have any doubts about your questionnaire items, you should invest more than you might otherwise in a pilot study. Most simply, this can mean giving the survey to a varied, available set of respondents, as similar to the final group as practical, to check that your items get a good distribution of responses, ensuring some variation to analyze in the final dataset, and that your indexes are reliable. But you may want to start with a somewhat long pilot survey, including extra items. Some of these may include standard scales that probe for response biases. Others may be backups for your own items, written a little differently to see whether they turn out to be more reliable than the ones you originally guessed would be best.

The context in which respondents receive your survey is also important. Refer to Chapter 2, where I outline some general rules for gaining the respondents' trust and commitment. I have said that, other things being equal, reliability increases with the number of items, but this will not be true if you burden the respondent with so many questions that he or she is forced to rush through and ends in a state of exhaustion from which any answer looks as good as any other.

If you suspect that some respondents are not competent or honest enough to give valid answers to your questions, you can include items in your questionnaire designed to trap and identify these poor responders. In the survey I administered to participants in the 1978 World Science Fiction Convention, the respondents were supposed to rate a large number of science-fiction authors on a preference scale, and some of the authors were not widely known. The directions explicitly said, "If you are not familiar with an author, please skip that one and go on to the next." I was concerned that some respondents would ignore the directions and rate authors they were unfamiliar with, thus fouling up my data on those authors. So I laid a trap.

The questionnaire listed 140 authors, but 2 of the names were bogus, intended to identify frivolous or inattentive respondents. The names were those of two of my graduate students, Rick Catalano and Diane Samdahl, who volunteered them for this scientific use. I checked carefully to make sure that no real authors in the science-fiction field had used these names. And if many fans professed to like the fiction of Catalano and Samdahl, we thought they should start writing some to capitalize on this popularity!

Of the 595 respondents, 46 claimed to have read the nonexistent works of Catalano, and 23 professed to be familiar with Samdahl. Fifteen respondents rated both fake authors, and 10 awarded the pair identical scores.

Whenever it seemed important to reflect the opinions of all conventioneers, of which my respondents were a sample, I used the responses from all 595. When I was more concerned that my data come from a panel of expert judges who could help me chart the ideological relationships between the authors, I used the 409 respondents who avoided rating either of the fake writers yet who did rate 50 or more of the real writers.

Note that this procedure of finding and rejecting poor responders may not be appropriate when you are trying to estimate characteristics of the population from which you have drawn your sample. True, data from some wayward or incompetent responders may be so bad that you can't learn much from them. But similar people undoubtedly exist in the population from which you drew your sample, and you have to take account of this fact. At the very least, you can compare the poor responders with the others on the basis of whatever data you feel are most valid from them. For example, are they less educated than the average, or less conventional?

When you are worried about various response biases, you can include scales to measure them in your questionnaire. The Crowne–Marlowe social desirability scale is often used in this way. In your final statistical analysis, you can use partial correlations or some other method to control for the effect of social desirability on the relationships of real interest to you. Conversely, you can do a special pilot study to see whether your key questionnaire items are affected by social desirability bias. Include the items and the scale in a survey given to a convenient but varied set of respondents, and look for correlations between the scale and the items of interest.

Finally, we all have to realize that the power of survey research is limited. We cannot learn everything with any one questionnaire, and some topics are better studied through entirely different methods of research. On the one hand, this means that the absolute validity of our research findings cannot finally be determined until research using different methods has achieved essentially the same results. On the other, it suggests that you should keep the strengths and weaknesses of survey research in mind from the very beginning. Perhaps you should not commit yourself at once to a survey on a particular subject, writing a questionnaire without reflecting first on the best way of approaching your topic. The best results will come if you acknowledge the limitations of each scientific approach and design surveys for which this method is well suited.

▶ ▶ ▶ ▶ ▶ ▶ ▶ ▶ ▶ ▶ ▶

PROJECTS

1. Evaluate Face Validity of a Standard Index. Select an index containing 20 or more items, a standard index in a field of your own interest. This is probably easiest to do in the field of psychology, where so many standard indexes have been created and used repeatedly, but it should be possible to find one of interest to you no matter what your field.

In an essay, evaluate the face validity of each item. Does it really seem to measure what the entire scale is supposed to be about? Or can you suggest some other characteristic it might really reflect? Finally, comment on the face validity of the entire index, as you understand it.

2. Experience Writing Medical Items. Create a short questionnaire in two parts, using whatever closed-ended (fixed-choice) item formats you want, to evaluate the state of a person's physical health (part 1) and mental health (part 2). You may want to consult popular books on health problems of both kinds, or even to interview a medical professional, to identify the most important areas where health problems are common.

As you write the items, think seriously about the problem of getting valid medical information through them. This chapter suggested some of the things that can go wrong in a survey about health problems, and you should keep them in mind as you create your survey. Also, see whether you find the job of writing mental-health items very different from writing physical-health items. And do you sometimes find the two overlapping or getting in each other's way? For example, a question asking whether the person frequently runs out of energy during the day will get a yes answer from people suffering from some physical diseases, but it will also get a yes from people who are emotionally depressed. This illustrates the challenge of writing a medical survey.

In the language of mental-health professionals, there is a phenomenon called *somaticizing*—the tendency of some people to express emotional problems as if they were physical problems. Therefore, it can be a good idea to include some questions about the patient's emotional condition in a survey primarily designed to evaluate physical problems. On the other hand, it can be very dangerous for the patient if a real physical problem is mistaken for an emotional one. Certainly, some people may be so unfortunate as to suffer from both kinds of illness. When your survey is finished, write brief comments on any problems you had designing items for maximum validity.

3. A Medical Attitudes Index. Let me suggest that six of the academic subjects in the STUDENTS dataset can be combined to make an index of the students' appreciation of the medical field: Medicine, Nursing, Biology, Chemistry, Zoology, and Botany. How would you assess the reliability and validity of this scale?

Part of this project is to use the programs you think appropriate to evaluate how well these six items fit together. Another part is to write a brief statement giving your analysis of how each of these six might reflect attitudes toward medicine. And the final part of this project is to write a brief essay describing how you might do some simple research to see whether the index has criterion validity. Make sure you have studied this chapter and really understand what criterion validity is, and this part of the project should not be too difficult.

4. New Examples of Spuriousness. This chapter gave examples of spuriousness, and you should look back at them to make sure you understand what this concept means. Now use your imagination to invent two more possible examples of spuriousness. Write a page or more about each of your two examples. State what the three variables are in each example, and suggest how a correlation between two of them might really be the effect of the third variable.

The examples do not have to be in the social sciences. Perhaps the very best examples for educational purposes are those that concern familiar, everyday matters that everybody understands. Each example illustrates the human capacity to misunderstand, because spuriousness is a type of misunderstanding about the causes of events.

If you get stuck and cannot think of any examples, here are two things you can try to get your mind moving. (1) Return to the examples we gave and try modifying each of them slightly, creating a very similar example. For example, instead of firefighters in the fire damage example, think of a story about police officers or forest rangers. When you've got one, see whether you can modify it further until it no longer is just a variation on the firefighters tale. (2) Let your imagination roam free, perhaps starting with some highly unrealistic fantasy fiction you happen to like, or some weird event you have recently heard about. Then you may be able to think of a totally fantastic example of spuriousness, and a few moments' thought may let you find a more realistic example suggested by it.

5. Replicate Wuthnow's Study. Using the question processor, create a new survey, based on Robert Wuthnow's 12 meaning-system items, phrased in an agree–disagree format. For each of the 4 meaning systems, write 3 additional items that you believe reflect the system's basic concept, bringing the total to 24 items, 6 for each meaning system.

Then invent 20 more items that measure respondents' attitudes and behaviors in areas of life that the different meaning systems might relate to. That is, create 20 items that evaluate the possible consequences of meaning systems. If people understand life in very different ways, how will their attitudes and behavior differ?

This new survey is a *replication,* an attempt to verify the results of an earlier study. Here, you can do two kinds of verification. First, are the four meaning-systems scales reliable? Second, do the meaning systems predict or explain attitudes about controversial lifestyles and significant behavioral differences among respondents? This is sometimes called *predictive validity,* although it can also be considered to be a version of criterion validity.

As a class project, this survey could actually be administered to as many as 200 people, then the relationships between the 44 variables could be studied through the statistics programs.

6. Explore Response Bias in a New Survey. This is an advanced project that a class might do collectively. Take the items from four scales or parts of scales mentioned in this chapter and build a survey around them. The four are: the ten-item Rosenberg self-esteem index, the seven-item Couch and Keniston Overall Agreement Scale, the six-item Edwards social desirability scale, and the eight-item Crowne–Marlowe social desirability scale. All should be placed in an identical agree–disagree format, and you should mix the order of the items up so that the items of each scale are no longer together.

This gives you only 31 items, and there is room for several more. So invent your own response-bias scale of any type you think would be interesting, containing about 10 items. You may then want to add a few factual questions that you guess might identify people more or less prone to response bias. You could ask about the respondents' level of education, for example, or whether they considered themselves to be highly optimistic— anything you think might illuminate the meaning of the scales.

Administer the survey to 50, 100, or 200 respondents, selecting a population that you think will have a range of bias. Then examine each scale's reliability and the correlations between them. Prepare a report communicating your main empirical findings and discussing their implications.

The items we have primarily considered so far, and all the ones available through our question-processor program, are fixed-choice items (or sometimes called *forced-choice* items): The respondent faces a fixed set of choices, in the form of boxes to check, numbers to circle, or single keys to press on the computer. This type of item is sometimes called *closed-ended*. Instead of a set of boxes to check, an **open-ended question** gives the respondent a chance to answer an interviewer spontaneously or a blank area of paper on a printed survey on which to write a response.

I once received a phone call from a polling business that wanted to ask me a single, simple question. Survey researchers have a moral duty to respond to other people's surveys, so I consented. The woman on the phone then asked me to name as many airlines as I could. Hmm. I mentioned United first, because that was then the biggest airline coming into Seattle, where I was living at the time. Then several others I had ridden on back east came to mind: American, Eastern, Piedmont, Delta. On and on it went. So I found myself mentioning minor commuter lines like Cardinal, and going through a mental list of all the foreign national carriers. Eventually, around about number 30, I quit and refused to go on.

But the surveyer wouldn't quit. She asked whether I had named all the ones I had ever heard of. No, it seemed to me there were others I could name, but I was worn out and would not go on. Finally, as if to insult me for not reciting all the airlines in the world, she asked, "How do you feel about Braniff Airlines?" Now, suddenly, I understood what the survey was all about. Braniff was considering adding Seattle to its route and wanted to know whether Seattle residents would consider flying with them. The whole point of the open-ended question about airlines was to see how soon people would mention Braniff in the list. The pollster was simply counting how many airlines I mentioned until I thought of Braniff. Well, Braniff ran

Open-Ended Items

into serious trouble shortly afterward, and I recall a report that too rapid expansion of its routes was one cause. Maybe this particular open-ended question had misled the Braniff executives into unfounded optimism, but it does seem a logical way to assess people's awareness of a brand or product, without giving them clues that might distort their responses as a closed-ended item might.

If this were a text about interviewing, rather than one about questionnaires that can be analyzed with computers, I would devote several chapters to the different approaches to creating open-ended questions and making sense of the replies. But here our emphasis will be on how to write open-ended questions that can be coded into computer-analyzable data and on how to derive closed-ended questions from responses to open-ended questions.

To be sure, open-ended questions can be of great use even when we don't intend to transform the responses into computer-readable numbers. Some of them help a respondent mentally get into a particular topic, perhaps establishing some mild rapport with the researcher. Occasionally, I must admit, we stick a few open-ended questions in merely so the respondent won't get angry at being squashed into the uncomfortable boxes of fixed-choice items. Far more important, open-ended questions are the best way to gain complex, freely expressed ideas, impressions, and personal experiences from respondents. I often quote extensively from such responses when I am writing a book or article derived from survey data, because the open-ended items provide so much more in detail, sensitivity, and expressiveness than do checked boxes. Our focus here must emphasize systematic, quantitative analysis.

When we plan to analyze the data quantitatively, or in some manner wish to integrate responses to open-ended questions with quantitative data, we have to work systematically. We need questions that will elicit simple, intelligible responses, and we need methods of handling the data that will give unambiguous results. These will be the themes of this chapter, and we will begin with the simplest open-ended questions, those just one step removed from the closed-ended variety.

▶ ▶ ▶ ▶ ▶ ▶ ▶ ▶ ▶ ▶ ▶

BASIC INFORMATION ITEMS

Question responses should be clear and intelligible, and this goal usually implies the use of fixed-choice items. Sometimes, however, even very simple check-the-box questions fail on this count. When sociology students in my course on survey methods wrote their own questionnaires as the term paper, they typically included a fixed-choice item about which region the respondent had been born in. Very good; many studies find great differences among the regions in the United States, Canada, and other countries. But do people generally know what region they were born in?

Do you know where Washington, D.C., is? Is it in the East Region? Is it part of the Northeast? According to the Census Bureau, Washington is in the South Region, along with Delaware and Maryland, two rather northerly states. What region is Washington State in? The Northwest? The Mountains? The census people say it is simply in the West Region.

The Census Bureau divides the United States into four regions: the Northeast, the North Central, the South, and the West. These four are divided into nine divisions. A list of the official regions, divisions, and states follows. Nowhere in the list do you see a Midwest, Appalachian, or Great Plains region.

I. Northeast Region
   (1) New England Division
      1. Maine
      2. New Hampshire
      3. Vermont
      4. Massachusetts
      5. Rhode Island
      6. Connecticut
   (2) Middle Atlantic Division
      7. New York
      8. New Jersey
      9. Pennsylvania

II. North Central Region
   (3) East North Central Division
      10. Ohio
      11. Indiana
      12. Illinois
      13. Michigan
      14. Wisconsin
   (4) West North Central Division
      15. Minnesota
      16. Iowa
      17. Missouri
      18. North Dakota
      19. South Dakota
      20. Nebraska
      21. Kansas

III. South Region
    (5) South Atlantic Division
        22. Delaware
        23. Maryland
        24. District of Columbia
        25. Virginia
        26. West Virginia
        27. North Carolina
        28. South Carolina
        29. Georgia
        30. Florida
    (6) East South Central
    Division
        31. Kentucky
        32. Tennessee
        33. Alabama
        34. Mississippi
    (7) West South Central
    Division
        35. Arkansas
        36. Louisiana
        37. Oklahoma
        38. Texas

IV. West Region
    (8) Mountain Division
        39. Montana
        40. Idaho
        41. Wyoming
        42. Colorado
        43. New Mexico
        44. Arizona
        45. Utah
        46. Nevada
    (9) Pacific Division
        47. Washington
        48. Oregon
        49. California
        50. Alaska
        51. Hawaii

Although this list is long, it easily could be turned into a fixed-choice question. You could ask where the respondent was born, then give ten boxes to choose from. The first box would be labeled: "Maine, New Hampshire, Vermont, Massachusetts, Rhode Island, or Connecticut." The tenth box would be labeled: "Somewhere else." The remaining eight boxes would list the states of the other regions. But this is a bit cumbersome. With printed questionnaires, unless there is a compelling reason for a check-the-box format, I think asking the person to write in the full name of the place where he or she was born gives you the best information.

When responses are written in, you have to code them. This means turning the responses into a set of numbers that can be typed into the computer. Perhaps you recall the related process of recoding, explained in Chapter 6. First, you need a **coding scheme**. This is a chart, like the preceding census list, that tells you what number to assign to what state. Although it is technically possible to type full names of places into the computer and make it do its analysis on the basis of these words, using code numbers is easier and more traditional.

When asking the respondent where he or she was born, be explicit; label spaces for answers "city or town," "county," "state or province," and "nation"—whatever main geographical units you decide you need. Then when you have entered all the data in the computer, you can recode the values of the state variable to turn it into a region variable, using whatever geographic scheme you want.

Other nations have their regions, too, and you can't count on their citizens to do much better than Americans in responding to a question about region of birth. When I was doing research on the religious geography of Canada, I found it convenient to describe the country in five pieces: British Columbia, Prairie Provinces, Ontario, Quebec, and Atlantic Provinces. The Prairie Provinces are Alberta, Saskatchewan, and Manitoba. Alberta, which lies next to British Columbia, turned out somewhat similar to British Columbia in my data, and I was tempted to split it away from the Prairie Provinces, to combine it with British Columbia in a West Region. Similarly, some parts of New Brunswick are similar to adjacent Quebec. If you ask the specific place of birth, then you have the freedom to try different regional divisions while analyzing your data in the computer.

A clear question encourages, but does not assure, a clear answer. You may have to prompt your respondent a bit. For example, you can ask people to write out the full name of the town and state (or province, or nation) where they were born. Perhaps everyone agrees that NYC stands for New York City, but LA might be Los Angeles or Louisiana. Just Springfield doesn't tell you much. Illinois, Missouri, Ohio, and Massachusetts all have a sizable Springfield. The Portland in Oregon does not even vaguely resemble the one in Maine. Perhaps it's an imposition to ask people to spell out the name of their state, and some may fail to get it right, but state abbreviations will cause more trouble. Does AL stand for Alaska or Alabama? Officially, AL is the postal service code for Alabama (Alaska is AK), but not all respondents may know this. I have often seen Mississippi (correct code: MS) abbreviated MI, which is actually the official abbreviation for Michigan, and there is the possibility of confusion with Missouri (correct code: MO) as well.

Even for the most basic facts, you must phrase a question carefully, using all the insight and experience at your disposal, to orient the respondent as accurately as possible to the information you want. Consider this simple question: "How old are you? ___ years." You'd think nobody would ever get this one wrong! The fact is that people differ greatly in their consciousness of their age. Young, middle-class people have been used to annual birthday parties, to being in schools that separate them by age, and to filling out numerous data forms that ask for age. But older people may have no contact with all these reminders and may not answer accurately.

Furthermore, young people may wish they were older, and old people may wish they were younger. As you know, young people frequently pretend to be older in order to buy liquor, and they may get in the habit of inflating their ages. Old people may lose track of the turning seasons. Thus if you want to know people's age, you should ask them when they were born, and let the computer subtract that year from the year the survey was administered. "In what year were you born? The year: ___." Obviously, the exact date of birth would add accuracy.

In the 19th century, one of the few bits of information collected every ten years in the U.S. census was the age of the population. At first, the census-takers simply asked how many people in the household were in various age groups. Then in 1850 they began asking the age in years of each person. Soon the census was publishing tables of statistics that noted exceptionally large numbers of people with ages ending in 0 or 5. Obviously, the census-taker was getting only rough estimates of many people's ages. In 1900 the census went so far as to ask not only the age but the year and month of birth. In a sense, this was a huge waste of effort—I estimate at least one and maybe two full work lifetimes. A census-taker wrote down redundant information about 72 million times! The results proved that birth-date was a better question than age, however, a small but valuable lesson for survey writers.

Challenges in Coding

Items on birthplace, age, religious denomination, and the like assume a large but finite list of definite words and phrases from which the respondents can draw their answers. For example, the states and cities of the country have standard names that enable respondents to write answers the researchers can understand. But if I were asked the church I was baptized in as an infant, all I could write would be "an old church at the bottom end of town with a British cannonball from the Revolution still lodged in it." Useless information. Sometimes there will turn out to be a common set of answer categories even when you don't expect one, but often luck and hard work are required to find one in a mass of responses.

I remember less than fondly the hours it took to code the many supposed causes of insanity cited for 2258 inmates of U.S. mental hospitals in the 1860 census forms. Hoping to simplify matters, I went through a pile of the records, writing down the different causes in alphabetical order. Then I copied this list more legibly, assigning a number to each cause. They ranged from "1 A. C. Homicide" (I never did decide exactly what that meant) to "166 yellow fever." Included were "80 illegible," for causes I could not read, and "159 unknown," for when the census-taker had listed no cause or had actually written "unknown" or "not known."

Some of the responses were quite similar to one another, but I gave them different codes if I could possibly imagine analyzing them separately. For example, I kept separate "14 business difficulties" and "15 business perplexities." Also separate were "47 dissipation" and "48 dissolute habits"; "49 domestic affliction" and "50 domestic anxiety"; "151 spirit rappings" and "152 spiritualism." These could always be combined later in the computer.

Then I wrote the number code next to the supposed causes in *all* the census records. In so doing, I found a few variants of causes I had already listed and gave them the same code numbers. For example, I had already assigned 19 to "child birth." When I found a case of insanity attributed to "birth of child," I coded it as 19, too. "Injury on the head" and "injuries to head" were given the coding 87, because they seemed to me identical to "87 injury of head."

But many new causes appeared on records I had not used for my original list, raising the total of code numbers to 283, among them some that convey vivid images: "bite of cat," "ill usage in confinement," "fear of witches," and "vicious habits." Frankly, with so many categories strewn across several pages of list, the work progressed slowly and inefficiently. I wish you a better time with your own coding!

Diaries

The **diary** can be a very important tool for collecting practical data. For example, diaries are used by television rating services. The families picked to represent the nation's TV tastes are given weekly diaries and told to jot down which programs they watch. Recent criticism of this method has alleged that the diary method is not entirely accurate, however, and some TV rating services are experimenting with more mechanized means to collect data on viewing patterns.

The Institute of Community Studies in London recently used a diary questionnaire to study the daily routines of families. The diary pages are divided into 15-minute intervals for the waking hours. For each period, the respondent is first supposed to answer the question "What did you do?" Then he or she is supposed to note where they did this, whom they were with, and whether they were doing something else at the same time. To help the respondent understand what was wanted, the questionnaire lists a full day's activities for a fictional Mr. Cribbins, starting with "6:30 Got up, cup of tea. 6:45 Shaved, washed. 7:00 Prepared breakfast. 7:15 Ate breakfast. 7:45 Took wife cup of tea in bed. 8:00 Fetched paper, read it." Then the questionnaire presented the respondent with two days of diary forms to fill in.

▶ ▶ ▶ ▶ ▶ ▶ ▶ ▶ ▶ ▶ ▶

CHARACTER TRAITS AND OTHER SUBTLE OPINIONS

We often use the open-ended format for collecting data that are far more subtle than birthplace, age, or even doctors' diagnoses. Vast libraries of research have used such items to measure character traits and personal opinions of many kinds. For example, an open-ended questionnaire scale of great simplicity, yet with the potential to provide data for systematic analysis of respondents' self-conceptions, is the Kuhn–McPartland 20-statements test (Kuhn and McPartland, 1954). The respondent is given a sheet of paper with the following instructions at the top:

> There are twenty numbered blanks on the page below. Please write twenty answers to the simple question "Who am I?" in the blanks. Just give twenty different answers to this question. Answer as if you were giving the answers to yourself, not to somebody else.

Write the answers in the order that they occur to you. Don't worry about logic or "importance." Go along fairly fast, for time is limited.

1. _____

2. _____

3. _____

.

.

.

Of course, the key to such an open-ended question is the scheme for coding the results. Several are possible, and you might want to invent a new system of your own. Kuhn and McPartland identified two main categories of responses, which they called *consensual* and *subconsensual*. The consensual responses "refer to groups and classes whose limits and conditions of membership are matters of common knowledge." The examples given were: *student, girl, husband, Baptist, from Chicago, pre-med, daughter, oldest child.* In contrast, the subconsensual responses "require interpretation by the respondent to be precise or to place him relative to other people." Examples were: *happy, bored, pretty good student, too heavy, good wife, interesting.*

More recently, researchers have tended to use a slightly different coding scheme in which the first category of response is *social,* those that identify the person in terms of social roles he or she may play, or membership in social groups. A second category is *psychological,* those that describe a mood or mental attribute of the person. It has been suggested that the balance between social and psychological responses changes from decade to decade, some periods being more other-oriented and some more me-oriented. Other possibilities are physical descriptions and those that refer to past events. Conceivably, neurotics give more responses about their pasts, although the same is probably true for older people as well.

Whichever coding scheme is used, each of the 20 self-descriptive statements is assigned to a category, and the numbers in each category are tallied up. Then groups of respondents are compared in terms of the balance of their responses. Do middle-class people give more psychological responses and working-class people more social ones, for instance?

In the section on menu items in Chapter 5, I discussed at length the issue of whether responses must be mutually exclusive, noting that they usually should be. The same question can be asked with respect to the coding of open-ended questionnaire responses. The main point is to be systematic and consistent in coding. But it is quite possible to use more than one coding scheme at once, some of which might overlap. For example, you can separately count how many responses were social and how many referred to family relationships, the latter being a subcategory of social. Groups of respondents might vary not only in terms of what proportion of the 20 responses were social but in what proportion of those referred to family relationships.

Many open-ended items with standard coding schemes have been created, and the raw material exists for many more in the literature of psychology, education, medicine, and other fields. One interesting source is a study by Norman H. Anderson (1968) that got 100 college students to rate 555 personality-trait words in terms of how likable a person to whom they applied might be. The students were given a fixed-choice questionnaire in which they were to rate the words on a scale from 0 ("least favorable or desirable") to 6 ("most favorable or desirable").

The 10 most favorable or desirable words were *sincere, honest, understanding, loyal, truthful, trustworthy, intelligent, dependable, open-minded,* and *thoughtful.* The 10 least favorable or desirable words were *deceitful, dishonorable, malicious, obnoxious, untruthful, dishonest, cruel, mean, phony,* and *liar.* It appears that honesty is the key dimension defining the ends of this set of 555 trait words. With these 555 words as a resource, let's invent some open-ended questionnaire items.

> Following are a few questions that ask you to think of adjectives describing various people's character traits. For example, adjectives describing Abraham Lincoln might include: *honest, decisive, moral, religious,* and *wise.* We will not be interested in purely physical characteristics, such as *tall* or *bearded.* You should feel free to give negative traits as well as positive ones. Lincoln's opponents considered him *belligerent, insolent,* and *conceited,* for example. Write down whatever adjectives come into your mind as you think about the particular person.
>
> After each of the folllowing, on the lines provided, please write down the first ten adjectives that come into your mind to describe the person. There are no right or wrong answers to these questions, and I am sure that different people will give quite different answers. The goal is to find out how you, yourself, would describe each of the following.
>
> 1. The current President of the United States.
>
> _____   _____
> _____   _____
> _____   _____
> _____   _____
> _____   _____
>
> 2. The current leader of the Soviet Union.
>
> _____   _____
> _____   _____
> _____   _____
> _____   _____
> _____   _____
>
> 3. Yourself as you really are, today.
> 4. Yourself as you would like to be.

5. The typical Protestant.
6. The typical Catholic.
7. The typical Jew.
8. The typical mother.
9. The typical career woman.
10. The typical woman college teacher.

The adjectives mentioned in the instructions came from the list of 555, except for *tall* and *bearded,* and they were put in to suggest the kind of word being sought. I included the first 2 stimuli in the list of 10 above just to get the respondent started, so he or she would be used to the response format before getting to the stimuli of greatest importance, those about self, religious groups, and women's roles. It might be possible, however, to use the first 2 to gauge the person's views on international politics.

To analyze responses, you would start by making an alphabetical list of Anderson's 555 words and their desirability score. Then you would look up each adjective given for the U.S. president, noting first whether it was in the list or not. If it was, you would write down the desirability score. Assuming that a substantial number of the responses were in the list, you would then calculate the average desirability rating of the list of 10 words. Then you would do the same for the Soviet leader and note how the average scores differed. Did you give the Soviet leader much less desirable adjectives, or are the leaders described about as favorably?

The pair of items asking for your self rating can be very powerful. A respondent who rates "myself as I would like to be" vastly higher than "myself as I really am, today" probably has self-esteem problems. We all may rate our ideal self higher than our actual self, but the gap between the two can be an indication of the frustration or satisfaction the respondent feels toward himself or herself.

With the three religion items, you would, of course, want to include a question determining which religious tradition the respondent was from. Then you could calculate average desirability scores from members of each group rating their own religious tradition and each of the others. As we suggested in Chapter 5, eliciting prejudiced responses from people these days can be very difficult, because we all know we are not supposed to be prejudiced. But prejudice persists, and items such as these may help us measure it. Finally, the last three stimuli could be used in a study about attitudes toward women's roles in society.

Projective Techniques

Among the classical methods by which psychologists have studied individual personalities, none has been more important than **projective techniques.** This term refers to a host of interview and questionnaire items that use somewhat indirect means to assess desires and attitudes that cannot easily be discerned more directly. The respondent is presented with an ambiguous stimulus, such as the proverbial inkblot, and is asked to describe it or make up a story about it. In principle, the respondent projects inner feelings onto the stimulus that he or she would ordinarily hide or even be unaware of. The trained interviewer, usually guided by a standard interpretative scheme, can then analyze the response to uncover the hidden meanings.

At present, many standard projective techniques remain highly controversial among researchers, and there is an unfortunate tendency for particular techniques to be so closely associated with particular theories that opponents of the theories reject data collected with them. The most familiar example is the dream analysis used by Freud and his disciples. After the better part of a century of research, the controversy has not quieted down a bit, and all the vast literature on the subject leaves us quite free to believe or not believe in the correctness of psychoanalytic dream interpretation, whichever we wish.

The following example of projective techniques suitable for use in a questionnaire has been subjected to much careful evaluation, with the result that the technique clearly has valid uses, despite the fact that the original research study's findings have generally not been replicated: Matina Horner's research on "women's fear of success." Substantively very interesting, this example lets us see how careful research design can be achieved, and it demonstrates beyond the slightest doubt that careful design is essential with projective techniques.

In 1968, working in a tradition that stressed the importance of attitudes toward achievement as major determinants of career success, Horner did a study that appears to prove American women suffered from "fear of success." The idea is not simply that women are discriminated against in some careers and have learned it is not worth trying to achieve in them. Rather, the theory of female fear of success holds that women, from the earliest years of childhood, have been so emphatically socialized to believe that success and femininity are incompatible that they have made avoidance of success a key part of their personalities.

The research design involved a group of college students, 90 women and 88 men, who were asked to write brief stories, expanding on a sentence given them by the researcher. The women were asked to write stories beginning with "After first-term finals, Anne finds herself at the top of her medical school class." The men got a similar but slightly different sentence: "After first-term finals, John finds himself at the top of his medical school class." They were given a few minutes in which to complete this task.

Clearly, it would be easy to include an open-ended item like this in a printed questionnaire. The real work, for the researchers at least, comes when it is time to analyze this material. Horner had assistants go through all the stories, looking for particular imagery. If you did this, you would prepare scoring sheets for your assistants, a copy to go with each questionnaire. The assistants would read the story carefully and check off various entries on the scoring sheet when they found them in the story. This sheet would then be stapled to the questionnaire.

In her publication reporting the research, Horner (1970:59) listed the following kinds of imagery that she considered to be evidence that the respondent harbored fear of success:

1. negative consequences because of the success
2. anticipation of negative consequences because of the success
3. negative affect because of the success
4. instrumental activity away from present or future success, including leaving the field for more traditional female work such as nursing, schoolteaching, or social work
5. any direct expression of conflict about success
6. denial of effort in attaining the success (also cheating or any other attempt to deny responsibility or reject credit for the success)
7. denial of the situation described by the stimulus
8. bizarre, inappropriate, unrealistic, or nonadaptive responses to the situation described by the stimulus

Horner gives examples in her publication of some of the stories to show how her coders identified cases of each of these eight types. When all the data were tabulated, it appeared that 66% of the women wrote stories high in fear-of-success imagery, compared with only 9% of the men. Apparently, women suffer from fear of success. Or do they?

Many, many studies quickly sought to replicate Horner's findings, and more of them failed than succeeded (Condry and Dyer, 1976). Or, to put the point more precisely, Horner's theory has tended to fail in subsequent research. What were the problems with the original study?

A crucial defect was the fact that all the women wrote stories about Anne, and all the men wrote stories about John. This causes two problems, each of them serious. First, we cannot know whether the women were really expressing feminine fear of success in these stories, or something else. Conceivably, women are more colorful writers than men, and so the protagonists of their stories had to face many negative situations to provide the material for interesting fiction. Had some of the women written stories about John, we could compare to see whether women gave male characters as many difficulties as they did female characters. Further, it might be that the women were merely realistically describing what happens to women achievers in our society, something very different from projecting their own subconscious fear onto Anne. If so, the men might write trouble-filled stories for Anne but not for John, so we would like to see what men do with characters of both sexes, too.

The second problem with having the women write about Anne and the men about John is that we can tell the sex of the story writer merely by looking at the name of the character. This means that Horner's coders, who presumably knew the hypothesis behind the study, might distort their interpretations to find more evidence of fear of success in stories they knew had been written by women than in the stories they knew had been written by men. When researchers are making complex, subtle coding judgments about open-ended answers, it is essential that they do so blind. **Blind coding** means the coders must be unaware of the characteristics of the respondents that are key variables in the research, so they will not bias results, whether consciously or unconsciously.

When Levine and Crumrine (1975) replicated Horner's research, they used a far larger number of respondents, 700 of them, and had respondents of both sexes write about characters of each sex. Their study revealed no difference between men and women. The failure of Horner's analysis should not deter you from using projective, story-writing items when they seem appropriate to you. Just make sure the coding is done blind, and that you have done your best to handle other problems that might undercut the reliability and validity of your analysis.

▶ ▶ ▶ ▶ ▶ ▶ ▶ ▶ ▶ ▶ ▶

IN-DEPTH INTERVIEWS

The art of in-depth interviewing is a topic worthy of an entire book (Gordon, 1969), and it is a bit removed from the printed or computerized questionnaires that have been our main focus here. The survey researcher needs some familiarity with **in-depth interviews,** however, for at least three reasons. (1) A standard method of administering questionnaires is through lengthy at-home interviews, and the insights derived from a discussion of in-depth interviews may be valuable for this more superficial kind of interview as well. (2) As open-ended questionnaire items get more and more ambitious, they enter the territory of in-depth interviews, and the two thus have much in common. (3) Researchers using in-depth interviews often work on the same topics that others investigate with fixed-choice questionnaires, and brief examination of their techniques can help us design better items. The projects at the end of this chapter include three that are to be done through interviews, and I think that the experience of these person-to-person interviews would prepare you to write much better questionnaires on the same topics than you might be able to without it.

Because the territory is so vast, I will mainly discuss the general problem of documenting an individual's past and present life circumstances, hoping that you will be inspired to investigate other approaches by reading on your own.

Within the social sciences, the psychoanalysts are notable for their use of extensive, in-depth interviews to uncover the intimate details of individual personalities and base general theories of human behavior on these findings. Yet criticisms were raised from the very beginning of their enterprise that the subjects of their research were abnormal and that the apparent dogmatism of psychoanalytic theories may have created the material found in these interviews rather than having discovered it already latent in their subjects. Thus it was of crucial importance when psychologists began intensive study, through in-depth interviews and other means, of numbers of normal individuals who had not sought the interviews as a form of treatment. The most notable figure in this great work was Henry A. Murray.

Calling his discipline *personology,* Murray was dedicated to understanding the nature of human lives, in all their diversity and depth. He used many different kinds of questionnaire and formal psychological test, but the in-depth interview was the key method of his research. In a famous study of an individual Harvard student, "American Icarus," Murray (1981) had his subject complete a written autobiography and numerous psychological tests before using all this material as the basis for interviews.

Today Harvard continues this tradition in the Henry A. Murray Research Center, and numerous other influential psychologists followed Murray's lead. A study based on Murray's approach which you might like to read is *Opinions and Personality* by Smith, Bruner, and White (1956). This book examined the possible relationships between personality types and political opinions through in-depth analysis of 10 men, three of whom are the subjects of separate chapters.

Early in his work, Murray developed an open-ended autobiography questionnaire as the prelude to extensive, wide-ranging interviews. He would give it to research subjects, asking them to use it as a guide for writing for at least two hours about themselves and their origins. If you simply mailed such a questionnaire out, I suspect that few people would respond adequately. Murray went to great lengths to motivate volunteers to respond. The first sections of the autobiographical questionnaire suggest the nature of the whole (Murray, 1938:413):

Directions. Please glance over this outline to get a general idea of what is required, and then write your autobiography without consulting it. When you have finished writing, read over the outline carefully and add, as a supplement, whatever information you omitted in your original account.

Family History

(a) *Parents:*

  (1) Race, education, economic and social status, occupations, interests, opinions and general temperament, state of health.

  (2) General home atmosphere (harmony or discord). What was the attitude of each of your parents towards you: (affec-

tionate, oversolicitous, domineering, possessive, nagging, anxious, indifferent, etc.)?

Attachment to family (close or distant); favorite parent; fantasies about parents; disappointments and resentments. Which parent do you most resemble?

Discipline in home, punishments, reactions to punishment. Moral and religious instruction.

Special enjoyments at home.

(b) *Sisters and brothers*

Order of birth; characteristics of each.
Attachments and resentments; conflicts.
Did you feel superior or inferior to sisters and brothers?

(c) *Larger family circle*

Grandparents and relatives.

(d) *Physical surroundings of youth*

City or country; nature of home.

This could hardly be more different from the standard, fixed-choice questionnaire. Indeed, it seems to violate all the rules of questionnaire construction. But Murray's aim was not to study particular aspects of life in a systematic and well-controlled way, but to elicit the widest possible range of responses, from which he would later develop coherent hypotheses that might be the topic of narrower interviews later on. The questionnaire continued with the following other major headings: personal history, school and college history, sex history, major experiences, aims and aspirations, and estimate of self and world. Murray's questions could easily be used to guide a face-to-face interview, if the convenience of written answers were not necessary.

In teaching my field research seminar about interviewing, I have always felt it was important to do two things right at the start. First, I must quickly give the student the experience of completing an interview successfully, to build confidence. Second, I must give the student a simple but flexible interview format to give him or her some experience working with a particular aim in mind, even though the format might not be the appropriate one for particular interview projects the student might do later. The solution I settled on was a simple, chronological life-history interview.

Dozens of times now, my students have located an older person with a rich life story to tell and spent between one and four hours charting the main themes of that person's life, year by year. One challenge was to get the events in order, even though respondents might jump from year to year at random. A method that seemed to work well for many interviewers was to use a notebook with the decades written in as main headings, and hop from page to page as the respondent's mind hopped.

Another challenge was keeping the respondent on track. This particular interview was not designed to record anecdotes in detail, merely to sketch the chronological outlines of a life. Both respondents and interviewers found this hard to do, and this was precisely the experience I wanted my students to have—struggling and succeeding at something that took a little concentration. Of course, a full study of a life would be very drab without anecdotes, and they are often crucial information both about past events and about the ways respondents conceptualize their lives. But as an educational experience, and as a potential first interview in a series that would collect anecdotes later, the chronological life-history interview was an effective assignment.

The third and final challenge was discerning what the main themes in the person's life were, in order to know what to ask about when prompting the person to say more about a particular period of his or her life. For example, one person mentioned involvement in politics at one point in his life. Talking about another period, he did not mention politics at all. The interviewer asked about political involvement and was told that the respondent's employer told him to stay out of politics but relented later, and the man's political career resumed. Consider trying this kind of interview, described further in the projects section at the end of this chapter.

The most extensive series of interviews I have done was for my book on an unusual religious group called The Process (Bainbridge, 1978b). The members lived communally, worshiped four gods (Lucifer, Jehovah, Christ, and Satan), engaged in various deviant psychotherapy techniques, and considered themselves the vanguard of a new civilization. There was never a dull moment studying The Process!

One aim of the interviews was to learn how the members had joined the group, or at least to collect a number of their stories about joining to see whether common factors had brought them in. I am not convinced that in-depth interviews are the right way to test a theory of recruitment to a deviant group; done in the field under chaotic conditions, they can never be systematic enough, and there is real danger the respondents will mainly offer the group's ideology about joining rather than their actual individual histories.

Although I knew I could not fully test a theory, I had one in mind to guide my questions, the model of conversion to a deviant perspective proposed in 1965 by John Lofland and Rodney Stark (1965; Lofland, 1966). I used the seven-step model as a kind of checklist.

For conversion a person must:

1. Experience enduring, acutely felt tensions
2. Within a religious problem-solving perspective
3. Which leads him to define himself as a religious seeker
4. Encountering the group at a turning point in his life
5. Wherein an affective bond is formed (or pre-exists) with one or more members

6. Where attachments to people outside the group are absent or neutralized
7. And he is exposed to intensive interaction with members

In my interviews, I always probed for these points, in a gentle way, while letting the respondents tell their story. Had they experienced unusual personal problems or frustrations prior to joining? Did they have a religious orientation to the solution of human problems, in distinction to political, psychotherapeutic, or other kinds of solutions? Were they consciously looking for a new religious involvement? Were they at some kind of turning point when they encountered The Process? What were their friendships and other attachments like at the time? What changes occurred in their social lives as a result of becoming a committed member?

Occasionally, I asked one or another of these questions explicitly, but more often I kept them in mind as I listened and framed follow-up questions to get the respondent to say more about something relevant to this list. And there was a second purpose to my interviews that fitted in with the first: reconstructing the history of the cult as a whole out of the fragments that were individual stories.

Going into one of these interviews with a set list of questions was impossible. Often I did not know when an individual had joined or which aspects of the group's history he or she had been involved in. So I had to make up my questions as I went. Frankly, I found this very difficult. It is hard to resist sitting back and just letting the informant talk, losing sight of the purpose of the interview because of the difficulty of conducting it. My solution was to put all my mental energies into framing questions and use none of them to write down answers. I had a notepad and frequently jotted down notes—always questions suggested by what the respondent was saying, including questions I ought to ask other members. Too much note-taking can distract a respondent, but too little can suggest the interviewer isn't paying attention. With the respondents' permission, I recorded their answers on a tape recorder. Transcribing taped interviews is tough work. Even with the best, foot-pedal-operated tape players and word processors, accurate transcription is demanding.

Many of the interviews captured recruitment stories; others documented particular periods in the group's history. The Process lived for several months in a ruined coconut plantation on the Yucatán coast of Mexico, and at a different period, members traveled in pairs across Western Europe, living off the benevolence of strangers. Once I knew which members had participated in each of the adventures, I could go back and interview them again about that particular episode. One afternoon, the founder of the cult and I sat down with a series of maps and a tape recorder and traced his extensive travels: Where did he go next? What was he seeking? What did he find? What new aspect of cult doctrine and practices came out of that experience?

In my Process research, there was no need to interview the members about their day-to-day lives, because I was experiencing that life with them as a participant observer. But many interview studies have as their main purpose the documentation of an exotic way of life or the experience some category of people has in our own society. An excellent example is a study of 48 mentally retarded people done by Robert B. Edgerton (1967).

The 48 whom Edgerton and his assistants interviewed had been institutionalized at one time in California. Clearly, this group of respondents had to be interviewed, because they couldn't be surveyed through a printed, mailed questionnaire. Each respondent was seen for at least 5 hours, and some spent as many as 90 hours with the interviewer. Edgerton (1967:16) listed the following general topics that guided interviewers:

1. Where and how the ex-patients lived
2. Making a living
3. Relations with others in the community
4. Sex, marriage, and children
5. Spare-time activities
6. Their perception and presentation of self
7. Their practical problems in maintaining themselves in the community

▶ ▶ ▶ ▶ ▶ ▶ ▶ ▶ ▶ ▶ ▶

DEVELOPING FIXED-CHOICE ITEMS

One of the main uses of open-ended questions is as a source of material for fixed-choice questions. Suppose you wanted to determine the kinds of books people in a certain community were reading and to find out which people were reading which ones. First, you might circulate a simple open-ended survey asking people to list books they had read recently. The next step would be to tabulate all the titles people listed. This is not the end of the project, however, because individuals may list fewer books than they have actually read, with unknown biases in which they mention and which they don't. So you have to make a second questionnaire, in the fixed-choice format, using titles tabulated in the first survey, perhaps leaving out books that only a couple of people had listed.

I call this two-stage method for creating survey items the **ethnographic** approach. This word comes from anthropology and signifies the process of documenting the culture of a social group. An alternative approach, which I call the **scholarly** method, draws questions from the writings of intellectuals and is the subject of the following chapter.

The ethnographic method of item creation is often an essential part of a good survey. If you want to predict which political candidates people are going to vote for, you merely have to look up who has been nominated and build the questionnaire around their names. But if you want to understand the political views of a community, you may have to start with an open-ended survey to determine just which political issues the community cares about and which different viewpoints exist. Using those results, you can design a fixed-choice survey to measure the strengths of the different opinions and their correlations with other variables.

Barney Glaser and Anselm Strauss (1967) have written about what they call **grounded theory,** theoretical analyses derived from the concepts that ordinary people use in the situation under study. If you want to know why medical personnel invest more time in some patients than in others, for example, you should interview them, listen to them, and give them open-ended surveys, paying attention to any comments they make about different categories of patient. They will talk about young patients, helpful patients, appreciative patients, talented patients, and about those who have the opposites of these qualities, as well as about many other categories of patient. In the view of Glaser and Strauss, people will tend to share a set of concepts defining the categories they place people and events into. The job of ethnography is to chart these concepts and categories. After that, you can use systematic, quantitative techniques to study how people actually apply them in making decisions.

How do you know when you have done enough ethnography? The basic test, for Glaser and Strauss, is to stop after you have ceased getting data that help you understand the concepts. This is called *saturation,* the point at which you have enough ethnographic information to understand a concept fully, and after which no new revelations about it come from further research (Glaser and Strauss, 1967:61). A concept has achieved saturation when your ethnography allows you to write clear fixed-choice questionnaire items about it.

Another question is what techniques of sampling are best at this preliminary stage of survey research. Your purpose is not to determine how common certain viewpoints are in the population, to correlate opinions with each other, or to test theories about the causes of various attitudes. Those are jobs properly carried out through a fixed-choice survey or other kind of quantitative study designed on the basis of your qualitative, ethnographic research. Rather, at this early stage, you need the full range of concepts that any substantial number of people within the population hold. This does not require a random sample. Indeed, it may be better consciously to oversample minorities. The ideas held by minorities, even tiny minorities, should be included in the final survey administered to a representative sample, because only with these ideas in your final survey can you document which ideas are really minority viewpoints and which are merely seldom mentioned spontaneously by typical respondents.

Perhaps the best way to make these points clear is by describing one of my own studies on the ideologies of spaceflight. It will illustrate the range of things you could do in developing a fixed-choice questionnaire on the basis of an open-ended survey employing a questionnaire, interviews, and simply overhearing what people say.

In 1972 I attended the World Science Fiction Convention in Los Angeles, armed with a tape recorder and an interest in discovering the reasons some people had for supporting the space program. Wandering the halls of the convention hotel, beset by the usual panic experienced by novice researchers, I summoned up the nerve to interview 58 people about their views on the space program. Now, the purpose was not to get the full range of views people might have, but to concentrate on the positive side of the debate about space, to begin research on the pro-spaceflight ideology.

I asked vague and repetitive questions: "Why do you think we ought to go into space?" "What do you think man's ultimate future in space might be?" "Is there any aspect of spaceflight that interests you especially?" "What do you think the result would be if we stopped going into space altogether?" "Looking toward the far future, what do you think ought to be done in space?" These somewhat dumb questions were meant simply to stimulate open-ended talk about the value of spaceflight.

Then, back home, I went through the resulting 5 hours of recordings and wrote out each distinct objective of spaceflight given by each respondent, as I understood them, on file cards. Then, as a test of my intended method of analysis, I sorted the 242 cards into what I saw as distinct categories. In the methodology of grounded theory, each category should become a coherent, distinct statement as it becomes saturated by the addition of more and more utterances from different respondents. When these cards were sorted, I had 28 categories, each of which did seem to state, or hint at, a different reason that the development of spaceflight was a good thing and should be continued.

At the same time, I had been studying a space-boosting group called the Committee for the Future. The CFF was unusual in that it had established the colonization of the planets as its goal, and it had invested considerable money and effort toward promoting this plan. In the process of my research, I had collected a quantity of the group's early spaceflight propaganda, and I had tape-recorded a number of discussions and speeches made at its 1972 convention. I went through this material, culling more utterances that could be taken as reasons for the continuance of the space program.

To generate more material, I sent out 3 surveys that included the open-ended question "In your opinion, what is the most important reason we should continue the space program?" I got replies from 74 members of the New England Science Fiction Association to add to the interviews done in Los Angeles, and 81 people who attended a convention of the Committee for the Future also answered this question.

Both these groups of respondents are from what might be called the radical wing of the spaceflight movement, people excited and confident about really far-out space projects, and I believed it was important to balance their view with those of more pragmatic professionals in the field. So I included the question in a survey sent to a random sample of members of the American Institute of Aeronautics and Astronautics, which 102 of them completed. The AIAA is the leading technical organization in the aerospace field, and perhaps a third of its members were managers of corporations or government agencies.

The AIAA survey contained a few more open-ended items designed to collect thoughts on the possible value of space: "Suggest another reason for space progress that is a good selling point for convincing the intelligent layman to support the space program." "Some perfectly valid and important justifications for the space program are often ignored and deserve greater mention than they commonly receive. Can you give us such a justification?" "Can you name a bad consequence which would follow if progress in space exploration and development were halted at the present level?" "What is a possible long-range result of a vigorous space program which would eventually be significant for mankind?"

All the responses from these surveys were typed out on file cards, 1 utterance per card, with code numbers identifying the source of each statement. All 1260 cards were sorted several times into categories. Both to provide perspectives other than my own and to introduce some checks on reliability, I employed 2 practiced coders to help me do this work.

You may have to do this work yourself sometime, so I should give you a vivid description. Despite my enthusiasm for computers, I have yet to find an adequate method for doing the sorting with them. Instead, we scattered the cards on a huge table so that dozens of them could be seen at once. Step by step, we assembled the cards into piles, so that all the cards in each pile seemed to speak about the same general justification for the space program. Then we went through each pile, pulling out any cards that didn't fit, moving them to their proper piles. Sometimes a pile would split into two, when we discovered that the cards were about two similar but distinct concepts. Sometimes two piles would merge, when we saw they were really talking about the same thing.

Eventually, we settled on 49 piles, plus a small stack of cards that offered unique fragments of ideas or that spoke about the causes of spaceflight rather than its justifications. The next step was to write a summary statement for each pile.

For example, a pile concerning weather satellites generated the following simple summary: "Meteorology satellites aid in making accurate predictions of the weather." But this could be considerably expanded, using statements on cards in the pile: "The satellite has proved an effective tool in increasing the reliability of short-range weather forecasts." "Meteorological satellites have saved hundreds of lives by hurricane warnings that were formerly not possible." "More than 40 nations benefit from the improved weather forecasting based on cloud-cover photos relayed by a space system equipped with satellites." "If you can predict better the weather on the whole earth . . . you could save something like $2 billion annually." "Studying of seasonal changes can lead to prediction of spring floods through knowledge of the northern snow cover." "More sophisticated satellites may someday help predict and track tidal waves, earthquakes, rainfall, floods," and "perhaps even lead to reduction of human life losses due to tornadoes."

A set of 49 paragraphs like this could serve as the manifesto of the spaceflight social movement. I call such an essay, created by the social scientist through surveys and interviews, a **synthetic ideology**. Despite shelves of enthusiastic space-boosting books, a full ideological statement of the movement's beliefs has never been made. You could use this same method to construct a synthetic ideology for any social movement or group that had not yet fully found its own voice.

But all this was only the first step in the research program. Next, with the help of Richard Wyckoff, I constructed a questionnaire incorporating all 49 distinct statements on the value of the space program. The introduction read:

> On the following pages we have listed 49 reasons that have been given for continuing the space program. You will probably feel that some reasons are better than others. Don't worry about all the aspects of each one, but make an overall judgment of it. After each statement please check the box that indicates your opinion. How good a reason is it for supporting the space program?

Four boxes were provided for each item:

[   ] Not a Good Reason   [   ] Slightly Good Reason
[   ] Moderately Good Reason   [   ] Extremely Good Reason

Consider what the study accomplished to this point. Through a combination of open-ended survey, interviews, reading, and listening, a set of 1260 utterances were gathered and typed on file cards. Each card contained a single thought from a single person. These were then sorted by 3 coders into 49 piles, plus a few leftover cards, each pile representing a specific justification for the space program. From these, 49 summary statements were written and incorporated in a fixed-choice questionnaire.

This lengthy research process results in a questionnaire based on the thinking of a large number of people rather than on just the personal notions of the researcher. All too often, questionnaires designed to survey the public's opinions spring full-grown from the mind of a very unrepresentative person, the social scientist. The method I suggest here, though costly in the beginning, has the potential to produce far richer results. And, of course, you can always include some items in the final questionnaire that did pop into your mind from nowhere. This method is no bar to your personal creativity; rather, it is a way of ensuring that you will not miss the full range of thoughts and opinions held by your respondents.

This questionnaire was sent to a small, random sample of registered voters in Seattle, Washington, and 225 questionnaires were returned properly filled out. Immediately, Wyckoff and I could see which of the 49 justifications were judged positively by our respondents. The one on weather satellites did well, with 51% saying it was an extremely good reason and a further 30% calling it moderately good. But soon we could do a more subtle analysis, looking at correlations linking items with each other. Using the statistical technique known as factor analysis, we were able to identify 5 main groups of items.

The factor analysis was very much like the process of sorting the cards on the big table, except that it was done by the computer based on the correlations between items in the dataset from 225 voters. The computer put together into a group all the items that correlated highly with each other.

For example, one group consisted of four items: "Space has military applications; our nation must develop space weapons for its own defense." "Space is an important arena for international competition, and if we do not keep our lead, the Russians will gain an advantage over us." "The success of the U.S. space program increases our prestige in the world, demonstrates the value of democracy, and renews American national pride." "Military reconnaissance satellites (spy satellites) further the cause of peace by making secret preparations for war and sneak attacks almost impossible."

Do you see what those four statements have in common? A hint can be found in the fact that political conservatives tended to think these were good reasons for supporting the space program, and political liberals did not. Clearly, they conceptualize spaceflight as part of international competition, including military activities. For short, we might call this the *military* factor.

A group that illustrates how spaceflight can come up with valuable, practical results can be described as the *economic–industrial* factor. Wyckoff and I called the three other main groups of items the *information* factor, the *emotional–idealistic* factor, and the *colonization* factor. The first of these included the meteorology item and several others that spoke of the information and scientific knowledge that can be gained through the space program. The emotional and idealistic items spoke of such things as challenge, curiosity, sense of purpose, global renewal, adventure, and spirit. The colonization items described a future age in which human beings would inhabit the planets, exploit the natural resources of distant worlds, and create new forms of society beyond the earth.

The research process can be brought full circle. We can take the final quantitative results and return with them to understand better the ideas that people expressed in the qualitative, open-ended survey. For example, we can ask whether the three space-related groups I initially surveyed gave significantly different kinds of justifications for spaceflight.

The five ultimate groups of items can be divided conceptually into two supergroups. The information, economic–industrial, and military factors represent relatively *conventional* justifications. The emotional–idealistic and colonization factors are more *revolutionary* justifications. In a book I wrote on the social movement that produced modern rocketry, I pointed out that small, radical groups had developed spaceflight for revolutionary reasons, to transport society to the planets and achieve a vastly different kind of existence there (Bainbridge, 1976). But today's spaceflight establishment, represented by the AIAA, is oriented toward conventional aims, using space to influence earthbound society in modest ways. Thus

▶ ▶ ▶ ▶ ▶ ▶ ▶ ▶ ▶ ▶ ▶

TABLE 9.1   JUSTIFICATIONS FOR THE SPACE PROGRAM

Group of Justifications	225 Voters Percent "Extremely or Moderately Good Reason"	Percent of Cards from Group That Contributed to Items in the Factor:		
		AIAA	CFF	Science Fiction
Conventional:				
Information	78.7%	44.0%	32.9%	30.4%
Economic	52.8%	25.0%	8.9%	6.7%
Military	47.3%	10.8%	0.9%	1.4%
Revolutionary:				
Emotional	34.0%	11.1%	30.6%	31.6%
Colonization	31.1%	9.1%	26.7%	29.9%
	Total	100.0%	100.0%	100.0%
	Utterances	539	225	278

▶

we would predict that the AIAA would stress conventional justifications, and the science-fiction and CFF respondents would stress revolutionary justifications.

Table 9.1 shows that the 3 groups of respondents to the open-ended survey differed greatly in which of the 2 main factors their utterances contributed to. The first column of figures shows the average percent of the 225 voters who called items in the factor "extremely good reasons" or "moderately good reasons." The conventional justifications rank higher on this popularity measure than do the revolutionary items. A total of 1042 cards contributed to the 5 factors, the remainder going to 9 items that didn't wind up in factors and to the small pile of unusable utterances.

Note that very few of the utterances (statements on file cards) from the American Institute of Aeronautics and Astronautics contributed to the forced-choice items that wound up in revolutionary factors. In contrast, the members of the Committee for the Future and the science-fiction fans were much more likely to give emotional–idealistic justifications for spaceflight or to justify the space program in terms of the colonization of the planets. The fact that this supports my hypotheses about the different space-boosting groups is gratifying, but far more important is the way this final analysis links the open-ended and fixed-choice phases of the research.

Qualitative research and quantitative research are not mutually exclusive ways of doing social science. Rather, they are compatible and ultimately depend on each other. The items on our fixed-choice surveys should be grounded in the experiences and concepts of our respondents, and open-ended surveys can help us achieve this goal. In the best and most complete studies, quantitative analysis has a qualitative basis, and qualitative data are subjected to quantitative tests.

▶ ▶ ▶ ▶ ▶ ▶ ▶ ▶ ▶ ▶ ▶

PROJECTS

1. A Birthplace Question.   Select three foreign countries and find maps showing the major official and geographic boundaries within each of them. Can you write a single, open-ended birthplace question that will work equally well for all three? If not, how can you write a set of questions that will get you the information you need?

Then design a coding scheme, complete with code numbers for the computer, that would allow you to analyze responses you got from people born in all three countries. A good format is a list of the main divisions of each country with a code number for each. If you are writing a report for class on this project, you should include 20 examples, responses people might give to your birthplaces questions, showing what code number you would assign to each.

2. A 20-Statements Test.   Design a 20-statements test of your own (inspired by the Kuhn–McPartland test), focusing on some topic other than the respondent's self-image, and prepare a coding scheme so that you could assign responses to one of two or more categories. For example, you could have respondents describe their favorite college teacher, and then code responses in terms of whether they referred to professional qualities like command of the subject matter or personal qualities like warmth. In a paragraph or two you should justify the coding scheme you plan to use.

Then administer your 20-statements test to 10 people and code all their responses. Note any difficulties you have assigning responses to categories. While doing this work, do you see any other categories of responses, some that you did not anticipate? Do you think your coding categories are so clear that if you hired coders they could work reliably from simple instructions? Or is a lot of personal judgment required to make the coding decisions?

3. A Story-Writing Item.   With Matina Horner's research in mind, create an open-ended questionnaire item that asks respondents to write a brief story, with a stimulus very different from Horner's, and outline a coding scheme for it. As you think about story topic possibilities, you should develop clear ideas about two things. First, how can you use the item to examine a significant question in your field of interest? Second, how can you reliably code the stories to produce scientific results?

When you have finished the question and outlined a coding scheme, administer the story-writing item to five people. Immediately after each person writes the story, code it in his or her presence. Then explain your coding, and get a reaction about whether he or she thinks your item and coding scheme really produce the data you think they do. *Note:* Survey researchers are not obligated to accept respondents' criticisms of their items and coding schemes; respondents are often self-deceived or ill-informed. But their reactions can help us identify possible problems or even new opportunities for our research.

4. A Subcultural Dictionary. This project and the two that follow involve open-ended interviewing rather than the writing of printed questionnaire items. They can contribute material for questionnaires, however, and each might be part of a pilot study in preparation for a questionnaire.

Construct a short dictionary of terms used in a subculture, through observation and asking questions of knowledgeable members of the subculture. The dictionary should contain 50 words or phrases, and if possible should include verbs and adjectives as well as nouns.

There are many subcultures in our society that augment ordinary English with jargon, argot, slang, and lingo of their own. Every profession has its special terms, as does every deviant subculture. An ordinary word can be used in a special way. For example, *line* refers to a thin row of cocaine crystals in the drug subculture; *barbecue* means slow rotation around the longitudinal axis of a spacecraft in aerospace jargon. But in many cases the words are unfamiliar outside the subculture. Examples include *wippen*, the mechanism that fits between the key and hammer of a piano, and *gafiate*, which means to defect from the science-fiction subculture. Sometimes a key concept is expressed in a phrase, such as being *sent up the river*, which means being incarcerated in a penitentiary.

You may find it useful to write out how a word is pronounced, using the system in an ordinary dictionary. And it might be a good idea to give the etymology (origin) of the word or phrase, to help clarify the concept. *Gafiate* is based on the acronym for "get away from it all." *Sent up the river* derives from the fact that New York City convicts were often sent up the Hudson to Sing Sing penitentiary. Finally, some jargon words need to be defined in terms of others in the dictionary, so occasional cross-references will be necessary.

Use whatever form for the dictionary you find convenient. In the past, most of my students used 3 × 5 file cards, one item to a card, arranged in alphabetical order and held together with a rubber band. More recently, students have been typing the material on a word processor that lets them put everything in alphabetical order.

5. Life-History Interview. In a two-hour interview of an older person, sketch his or her life's course. Arrange the information in extended outline form, giving the major life events in chronological order with dates (the year, anyway) when possible. The purpose is *not* to collect interesting anecdotes *nor* to probe deeply into the person's traumas. Indeed, this should be a completely nonthreatening, straightforward interview, simply to chart the course of the person's life in objective terms.

Your outline should note where the person lived in each year, schools attended, jobs held, major recreational activities participated in, what major family events took place (births, deaths, marriages), what public roles the person played (in political, religious, and social organizations), and whatever other events and statuses seem to mark the course of the individual's life. If you were doing a serious in-depth study of the individual's life, this first interview and outline could serve as the guide for deeper probing of particular issues. But this interview should merely establish an outline.

6. Pair of Culture-Informant Interviews.　Carry out a matched pair of interviews, separately, with two representatives of a culture or subculture, such as: an ethnic group, citizens of a foreign country, a religious group, a profession, a sports team, a hobby club, or a network of artists or musicians. Before the first interview, prepare some open-ended questions to get your interview moving, to bring the informants back to the main theme of your questioning if they stray from it, and to restart the interview if conversation stalls. But during the interview, frame new questions to follow up on answers you receive.

The second interview should be conducted as if the first had never happened, not using any information you gained in the first interview, to get two quite distinct views of the culture. The point of the interviews is to discover the distinctive activities, social institutions, customs, and way of life of the culture. You should refer to Chapter 2 to make sure you know the difference between a respondent and an informant, and use the interviewee as an informant.

7. Open-Ended Survey to Create Closed-Ended Items.　Select a topic of general interest, such as a current political or moral issue, and write a questionnaire consisting of 5 open-ended questions designed to elicit a wide range of thoughts about the issue. I suggest you print it on one side of a legal-size (8½ × 14) piece of paper, clearly marking places for respondents to write their answers. Administer it to 25 people, then make a photocopy of all 25 pages.

Cut apart each of the photocopies so that each different idea a respondent wrote is on a separate slip of paper, often more than one slip per question from each respondent because they may give two or more ideas in response to one of your open-ended items. Then sort these slips of paper on a large table, putting any together that seem to communicate the same idea. The point of this stage in your work is to get a small number of piles of slips, each pile expressing a commonly held idea about the topic of your survey. Then create statements for a fixed-choice questionnaire, expressing each of the ideas you find in the piles.

This project can be especially exciting if several people do it together, both to increase the number of respondents whose open-ended material is combined in the fixed-choice items and to generate debates over what some of the respondents are trying to say about the issue.

The purpose of this chapter is twofold. First, I want to provide you with a fresh dataset that you can analyze yourselves. You are welcome to explore the STUDENTS dataset all you want, but I have already told you much about it, and some of the exercises have further exhausted any interest it may hold for you. As you will see, the XYZ dataset is a serious test of some current theories in business and small-groups research, with 200 successful businessmen as the respondents. (Because few of the original group of 400 executives I surveyed were women, I thought it best to focus on men.) You get to do the testing, and I won't spoil your fun by explaining everything about how to perform your research.

The second purpose is to illustrate how to create a survey to test a theory—a theory of any kind, abstractly scientific or concretely practical. The XYZ Management Survey is a simple questionnaire, in an agree–disagree format, with five responses: Strongly agree, Agree, Neutral, Disagree, Strongly disagree. It illustrates how we can derive questionnaire items from the published thoughts of scholars, theorists, or advocates for particular perspectives. It is an example of what I call **scholarly item creation.** Like scholars in other fields, we go to the library searching for the thoughts of great thinkers who have gone before us. But the scholarly method is not restricted to use in the ivory tower. Indeed, it can have very practical applications, as the XYZ Management Survey will illustrate.

One of the most active fields for survey research is business. Various aspects of this important field have a number of names, including organizational behavior, industrial relations, industrial sociology, and of course market research. In many cases the focus is on the behavior of small groups (Homans, 1950), but the increasing international competition of recent years has focused interest on whole social systems as well, notably that of

The XYZ Management Survey

Japan (Vogel, 1979). A widely read book that popularized social scientific thinking about differences in business management between America and Japan is *Theory Z* by William C. Ouchi (1981).

The title refers to an outlook on management that adapts Japanese practices to American conditions, and the book's huge sales testify to avid interest in the United States today in matching the Japanese successes. Japanese companies supposedly follow a distinctive approach to management that Ouchi calls J, and American companies typically follow another approach, called A. Ouchi notes that he was greatly influenced by a popular business book of a generation earlier, written by Douglas McGregor (1960), that contrasted two styles of American management, called X and Y. Theory Z is an extension of Theory Y from McGregor's book, and it is also a special combination of A and J.

If all these letters seem confusing, they represent some very clear and important debates about business management. In the pages that follow, we are going to create a 40-item questionnaire focused on these theories. To do that, we have to examine each of the theories carefully and write questionnaire items expressing their main ideas. When we give the questionnaire to a number of respondents, they will express their agreement or disagreement with each of the ideas. The first thing we would learn from this is how widely held the different ideas about business management happen to be among our respondents. From a deeper analysis of the results, we can also learn whether the various ideas actually fit together, in coherent ways, as three separate theories, X, Y, and Z.

The key ingredient in this alphabet soup of theories is that managers are guided by different sets of assumptions about human nature. Some business leaders think their subordinates are not to be trusted, so they keep close watch on their workers and avoid sharing responsibility. Other business leaders, in contrast, believe their underlings can generally be trusted with responsibility, so their management style is much more participatory. These two management styles are what McGregor called Theory X and Theory Y.

▶ ▶ ▶ ▶ ▶ ▶ ▶ ▶ ▶ ▶ ▶

McGREGOR'S MANAGEMENT THEORIES

McGregor's work is the best place to begin our questionnaire construction. As Ouchi puts it, in McGregor's scheme:

> A Theory *X* manager assumes that people are fundamentally lazy, irresponsible, and need constantly to be watched. A Theory *Y* manager assumes that people are fundamentally hardworking, responsible, and need only to be supported and encouraged. (Ouchi, 1981:58–59)

Immediately, we see the material for two items, both phrased as statements, one based on Ouchi's sentence about X, and one on his sentence about Y.

1. People are fundamentally lazy, irresponsible, and need constantly to be watched.
2. People are fundamentally hardworking, responsible, and need only to be supported and encouraged.

As they stand, these two statements leave something important out. They fail to say that they apply to work situations. The notion that people "need constantly to be watched" would sound extremely paranoid if we thought it reflected a general policy toward all of life. Are you constantly peering out your bedroom window, fearing an attack from your next-door neighbor?

The context for a questionnaire item can be established in two basic ways. One is by adding an appropriate phrase to the item itself: "People are fundamentally lazy, irresponsible, and need constantly to be watched by their supervisors at work before they will do their jobs properly." If the items in our questionnaire concerned many different contexts, we would have to include orienting phrases in many of them. These phrases complicate the items and thus slow down the respondent.

The other way of setting the context is through a written introduction to the survey or section of items:

Opinions About the Workplace

Following are a few statements about how people behave on the job. Some are about managers, others are about workers, and some are about relations between the two. Please express your own, personal views about how people tend to be when they are at work.

Introductions fail if respondents neglect to read them. This may happen if the introduction is very long or embedded in other material, and we cannot rely on such introductions if too many of them are used throughout the questionnaire.

A short introduction should work well in our XYZ survey, however, because only one is needed, and it will stand out clearly at the head of the items. To be absolutely sure respondents are keeping the workplace in mind, we can add brief reminders of the context to a few items as we go along.

You might wonder whether these two items from Ouchi need to be broken apart into a larger number of shorter items. Certainly, each one is made up of a list of words or phrases, separated by commas. Isn't each one of these really a separate idea? This question has no one, objective answer. You would be perfectly justified in turning Ouchi's statements into a set of brief items, perhaps of the following format:

Opinions About the Workplace

Following are a few short descriptions of the ways people might behave on the job. Please express your own, personal views about how people tend to be when they are at work.

After each of the following, please check ONE box telling us whether you feel that people at work tend to be like this. Do you agree, or do you disagree?

At work people tend to	Strongly Agree	Agree	Neutral	Disagree	Strongly Disagree
1. be lazy	[1]	[2]	[3]	[4]	[5]
2. be irresponsible	[1]	[2]	[3]	[4]	[5]
3. need constantly to be watched	[1]	[2]	[3]	[4]	[5]
4. be hardworking	[1]	[2]	[3]	[4]	[5]
5. be responsible	[1]	[2]	[3]	[4]	[5]
6. need only to be encouraged	[1]	[2]	[3]	[4]	[5]

Whether you break Ouchi's statements down into their tiniest parts or leave them as full sentences depends on the purpose of your research. In particular, you must decide how closely you need to look at the ideas in fine psychological detail. My aim in the XYZ questionnaire is to evaluate the ideas as Ouchi and his associates expressed them, and you will see that they repeatedly express themselves in lists of words that they think in combination get across a unified concept. Furthermore, by drawing on related works by several authors, we will get different perspectives on the same concepts, and thus the final items will have quite enough detail, even without splitting the sentences into separate words and phrases.

So we have a brief introduction and two items from Ouchi, summarizing McGregor's X and Y theories. Now it is time to turn to McGregor himself. He introduced Theory X in terms of three assumptions about human nature and human behavior:

1. The average human being has an inherent dislike of work and will avoid it if he can.

2. Because of this human characteristic of dislike of work, most people must be coerced, controlled, directed, threatened with punishment to get them to put forth adequate effort toward the achievement of organizational objectives.

3. The average human being prefers to be directed, wishes to avoid responsibility, has relatively little ambition, wants security above all. (McGregor, 1960:33–34)

The first of these is in perfect form to be a questionnaire statement. It duplicates the beginning of the first item from Ouchi, about people being "fundamentally lazy," but we are looking for a set of items that will measure X, Y, and Z adequately, so some overlap is bound to occur in the statements we use, at least in the pilot version of our questionnaire.

The second Theory X assumption begins with a connecting phrase we can eliminate: "Because of this human characteristic of dislike of work." It ends with a phrase couched in slightly obscure language: "to put forth adequate effort toward the achievement of organizational objectives." This phrase might be rewritten simply: "to work hard." But McGregor's second assumption also suggests the goal of the work, achieving objectives set by the organization: "to work hard for goals set by their employer."

The third assumption needs only an *and* after the last comma to be a perfectly clear agree–disagree statement item. Thus we have three more statements for our survey:

3. The average human being has an inherent dislike of work and will avoid it if he can.

4. Most people must be coerced, controlled, directed, and threat-

ened with punishment to get them to work hard for goals set by their employer.

5. The average human being prefers to be directed, wishes to avoid responsibility, has relatively little ambition, and wants security above all.

In a 1957 essay, McGregor called X "the conventional conception of management's task" (1966:5), and in his book he called it "the traditional view of direction and control" (1960:33). Rather than stigmatizing Y as "the radical view," he described it as "the integration of individual and organizational goals" (1960:45), thus hinting it achieved better management by fitting together the goals of employer and employee in a way that served both more effectively. The assumptions of Theory Y are:

1. The expenditure of physical and mental effort in work is as natural as play or rest. The average human being does not inherently dislike work. Depending upon controllable conditions, work may be a source of satisfaction (and will be voluntarily performed) or a source of punishment (and will be avoided if possible).

2. External control and the threat of punishment are not the only means for bringing about effort toward organizational objectives. Man will exercise self-direction and self-control in the service of objectives to which he is committed.

3. Commitment to objectives is a function of the rewards associated with their achievement. The most significant of such rewards, e.g., the satisfaction of ego and self-actualization needs, can be direct products of effort directed toward organizational objectives.

4. The average human being learns, under proper conditions, not only to accept but to seek responsibility. Avoidance of responsibility, lack of ambition, and emphasis on security are generally consequences of experience, not inherent human characteristics.

5. The capacity to exercise a relatively high degree of imagination, ingenuity, and creativity in the solution of organizational problems is widely, not narrowly, distributed in the population.

6. Under the conditions of modern industrial life, the intellectual potentialities of the average human being are only partially utilized. (McGregor, 1960:47–48)

These Theory Y assumptions vary in their complexity and in how clearly they are the direct opposites of the Theory X statements. Also, there are twice as many of them as X statements. To get a balanced set of items, it would be nice if we could drop some of them. The first Y statement denies that people are inherently lazy, and thus it is the opposite of the first Theory X statement (Items 1 and 3 in our growing questionnaire). Although the first Y statement has more to say, later statements in the list cover similar ground, so we can simply skip it.

Y assumptions 2 and 3 are closely related, so perhaps we can fashion an item based on both of them. Assumption 2 denies what Theory X says about motivating employees, and assumption 3 suggests the Y alternatives. We've already got what X said about this, so we can stress the ideas in Y assumption 3, translating them into plain English: "People can exercise much self-direction and self-control when their work satisfies their needs for personal achievement and social respect."

Y assumption 4 is about responsibility. Its first sentence is nearly right, but it would gain in clarity if we moved the phrase in the middle to the front end: "Under proper conditions, the average person learns not only to accept but to seek responsibility." Qualifying phrases like "under proper conditions" generally go best at the front of an item. In the middle they break up the main idea of the sentence and thus may add ambiguity. The end of the sentence is not a good place, because you want respondents to have the main idea of the sentence sharply in mind when they go to check a box, and a qualifier at the end would blunt this sharpness.

Y assumptions 5 and 6 say, in effect: "Most people have untapped resources of imagination, ingenuity, creativity, and other intellectual potentialities. The phrase "is widely, not narrowly, distributed in the population" can be translated into plain English as "Most people have." So now we can propose three Y items that do not simply duplicate the X items in negative terms.

6. People can exercise much self-direction and self-control when their work satisfies their needs for personal achievement and social respect.

7. Under proper conditions, the average human being learns not only to accept but to seek responsibility.

8. Most people have untapped resources of imagination, ingenuity, creativity, and other intellectual potentialities.

In his 1957 essay, McGregor distinguished Theories X and Y in terms of the roles they had the manager play in the process of management:

> Theory X . . . With respect to people, this is a process of directing their efforts, motivating them, controlling their actions, modifying their behavior to fit the needs of the organization. (1966:5)

> Theory Y . . . The essential task for management is to arrange organizational conditions and methods of operation so that people can achieve their own goals best by directing their own efforts toward organizational goals. (1966:15)

You can try your hand at turning these statements into plain English and making them effective questionnaire items. Question writing is an art, and no one style is best. Here are my versions:

9. The most important things a good manager does are to direct people's efforts, motivate them, control their actions, and modify their behavior to fit the needs of the organization.

10. The most important thing a good manager does is to create a work environment in which people achieve their own personal goals best by working for the goals of the organization.

A survey writer should be on the alert for the possibility that someone else has already tried to write items of the desired type.

An item on sharing information and objectives from a survey on management style in 14 countries (Haire et al., 1966; Juhn, 1972) based on McGregor's ideas looks like a good extension of the Theory X items we already have, and so I'll simply add it to our growing survey. Another item from that survey, on group goal-setting, also looks like a good addition.

We have a Theory Y item that mentions the intangible rewards of self-esteem and social respect; Theory X stresses basic economic as well as security rewards, McGregor says. So perhaps we need an item about the influence a manager has over subordinates through control of their wages. To this point our survey is balanced, equal numbers of X and Y items, and we have avoided items that are simply the opposite of each other. Thus I think this is a good place to include a pair of items that are exact opposites of each other, one representing Theory X and one representing Theory Y.

For some statistical analyses, a pair like this can be very useful. For example, you can examine acquiescence bias—respondents' tendencies to consistently check the "agree" boxes or to check the "disagree" boxes, no matter what the items say. If someone checks the "strongly agree" box for one item, logically he or she should check the "strongly disagree" box for an item that is its exact opposite. If, in fact, he checks an "agree" box for both, then we can suspect he is a pretty unreliable respondent. But if he checks "strongly agree" for one and just "disagree" for its opposite, then we see a slight tendency for him to answer more on the "agree" side than on the "disagree" side. It is possible to combine both items in the computer to make a response-bias scale that measures any tendency to agree or disagree regardless of what the question is.

With the two items drawn directly from the international survey and a pair of opposites about wage incentives, we have four more to add:

11. A good leader should give detailed and complete instructions to his subordinates, rather than merely giving them general directions and depending upon their initiative to work out details.

12. Group goal-setting offers advantages that cannot be obtained by individual goal-setting.

13. To motivate his subordinates, a good manager will use the economic incentive of wage raises more than the intangible rewards of honor and respect.

14. To motivate his subordinates, a good manager will use the intangible rewards of honor and respect more than the economic incentive of wage raises.

A search of the literature revealed another approach to measuring Theory X and Theory Y. In a study of leadership in education, Armand J. Galfo suggested that McGregor's Theory X was based on what psychologists call Machiavellianism, and Theory Y is opposite to "Mach" (pronounced *mock*). Galfo created a survey based on the Mach scale, and "some quotations taken directly from McGregor's description of theory X and theory Y rationale were added" (Galfo, 1975:312). Following the scholarly approach to creating survey items, we must next look up what Machiavellianism is.

▶ ▶ ▶ ▶ ▶ ▶ ▶ ▶ ▶ ▶ ▶

THE MACH SCALE

The Mach scale was developed by Richard Christie out of the writings of 16th-century Italian political theorist Niccolò Machiavelli (1532). As Christie notes, the name Machiavelli "has come to designate the use of guile, deceit, and opportunism in interpersonal relations" (Christie and Geis, 1970:1).

To create Mach, Christie first read through Machiavelli's principal writings and identified a number of statements that expressed his view of human nature. For example, Machiavelli held that people are basically cowardly; Christie extracted the Machiavellian statement "Most men are cowardly." This scholarly delving produced a list of statements a Machiavellian might agree with, but it is always a good idea to balance a list of questionnaire items so that some call for an "agree" answer and others for a "disagree" answer. Therefore, Christie reworked several of the statements so a Machiavellian would tend to disagree with them. Thus "Most men are cowardly" becomes "Most men are brave."

By this time, Christie had a general, intuitive sense of the kind of personality he was looking for, and he added a few similar statements from other sources. A century ago, circus magnate P. T. Barnum responded to a complaint about all the fakery in his sideshow by saying, "A sucker is born every minute." Believing this attitude to be close to Machiavelli's, Christie added to his list of statements: "Barnum was probably right when he said there's a sucker born every minute." Extreme Machiavellians might believe this greatly underestimates the rate at which suckers are born, but it seemed a reasonable addition to the growing list of potential questionnaire items.

An essential part of the questionnaire construction was discussing the basic concepts with other scholars. Christie got much help developing his early concepts, and you too should discuss your budding ideas about survey items with your friends and colleagues. Every successful survey went through a period of refinement and pretesting, and Christie's was no exception.

He typed each of the statements on a 3 × 5 file card, then asked his associates to take this first version of the Machiavellianism test. The associates went through the statements and said how much they agreed with each one. Then they went through again and explained how they interpreted each statement. This revealed which of the statements were ambiguous and should be thrown out.

The 71 statements that survived this first round of development were put together in an agree–disagree questionnaire that was administered to 1196 college students. The students' questionnaires were scored, then divided into 2 groups, those scoring high on Machiavellianism and those scoring low. Then Christie went through the 71 items to see which ones discriminated between high and low scorers—that is, to see which items showed a strong tendency to get Machiavellian responses from people who gave Machiavellian responses on the entire test. This reduced the list to 50 statements that all seemed to be tapping the same personality characteristic.

Fifty statements is a lot if you want to use the test along with many other questions in a questionnaire, so Christie cut the number down still further to just 20. Half of them were written so that a Machiavellian would tend to agree with them, and the other half so he or she would tend to disagree with them. Indeed, Barnum got switched around, so the item read: "Barnum was very wrong when he said there's a sucker born every minute."

Twenty items is rather a large number to add to the 14 rather similar items we already have in our XYZ scale, but it really would be interesting to see how Mach relates to X and Y. Therefore, I asked a student of mine who happened to be working on Machiavellianism, Maryn Jacobson, to see whether she could create a short form of the Mach scale. A short form is a version of a survey that accomplishes almost as much as the original, but with a smaller number of items.

Jacobson had given a survey including Christie's 20 Mach items to 810 college students. Then she had calculated the correlations linking each item with the others and produced a factor analysis showing how the 20 items broke into four groups. She kept 2 things in mind as she selected items for a short form: (1) choosing items that correlated with the others, thus showing they measured the underlying concept of the whole scale, and (2) choosing items that represented the different groups of items expressing somewhat different aspects of Machiavellianism. This second aim was particularly important, because earlier research had shown that the Mach scale was not really a unit but consisted of as many as four parts (Hunter et al., 1982).

The Barnum item and the one about cowardliness both bombed. Neither of them correlated at all well with the other items, indicating they were tapping something other than Mach. One possibility was that American culture may have changed over the quarter-century since the items were originally chosen. Today "Most men are brave" sounds like a sexist item. "Yeah? What about most women?" Today respondents may not know who Barnum was, not recognize the quote, and perhaps not even know what a "sucker" is.

The Barnum item is also a little complex. This reflects the challenge of rewriting a positive statement to make it into a negative statement. Another item among the 20 also bombed, and I suspect its complexity was partly at fault: "Most men forget more easily the death of their father than the loss of their property." Perhaps this means to assert that people are materialistic beasts, loving money more than family. But in any case, the item did not correlate with the others, so we can drop it, leaving 17.

Jacobson's four groups of items were really two pairs of groups, one group in each pair having a Theory X flavor, and the other a Theory Y flavor. The first pair seemed focused on the tactics that different people followed in their interaction with others. The second pair seemed to be general perspectives on human nature, with no definite advice about how a person should behave. So we can identify the two pairs of item groups as *tactics* and *perspectives.*

Jacobson suggested a short form consisting of six tactics items and four perspectives items. People high in Machiavellianism would agree with half of them. People low in Machiavellianism would agree with the other half. Here they are, listed under headings describing the groups:

HIGH MACH: Theory X tactics
15. Never tell anyone the real reason you did something unless it is useful to do so.
16. It is safest to assume that all people have a vicious streak and it will come out when they are given a chance.
17. It is wise to flatter important people.

LOW MACH: Theory Y tactics
18. Honesty is the best policy in all cases.
19. There is no excuse for lying to someone else.
20. One should take action only when sure it is morally right.

HIGH MACH: Theory X perspective
21. Generally speaking, people won't work hard unless they're forced to do so.
22. The biggest difference between most criminals and other people is that criminals are stupid enough to get caught.

LOW MACH: Theory Y perspective
23. Most people are basically good and kind.
24. Most people who get ahead in the world lead clean, moral lives.

This completes our development of the X and Y scales, so it is time to return to Ouchi's work and begin developing Z. And to do that, we must look at his descriptions of A and J, the typical systems in American and Japanese companies.

▸ ▸ ▸ ▸ ▸ ▸ ▸ ▸ ▸ ▸ ▸

JAPANESE AND AMERICAN CAREERS

Ouchi is less concerned with tactics and perspectives than with social realities. For example, he thinks the Japanese tendency toward lifetime employment in the same company is a crucial determinant of behavior by both managers and workers there, and he draws a sharp contrast with the short-term employment common in the United States.

Table 10.1 illustrates Ouchi's suggestion that Theory Z is an adaptation of Japanese approaches to American conditions, some kind of combination of J and A that happens also to be an extension of McGregor's Y and X (Ouchi, 1981:48; Ouchi and Jaeger, 1978:311).

In Japan, at least at the largest companies, employees typically start when they leave school and stay until they retire. Although the same may be true for workers in *some* American industries, our own pattern has always been much more of moving from company to company throughout life. This, of course, means that the Japanese are far more strongly tied to their company and to their work group. The individual Japanese worker will be expected to play a variety of work roles in his company, whereas the American may have to develop specialized skills in order to be easily employable as he or she moves from job to job, Ouchi says. Thus in Type A organizations, short-term employment implies a specialized career path, and in Type J, lifetime employment implies a nonspecialized career path. Type Z employment is long-term, between short-term and lifetime, so the career must be moderately specialized.

Employees with specialized skills can be evaluated quickly and the best of them promoted. And when employees expect to stay in a given company only for a few years, they will be impatient for promotion. On the other hand, if the employee has a long-term mutual commitment with a company, slow evaluation and promotion may be appropriate.

▶ ▶ ▶ ▶ ▶ ▶ ▶ ▶ ▶ ▶ ▶

TABLE 10.1   CHARACTERISTICS OF THREE ORGANIZATIONAL TYPES: A, J, AND Z

Factor	Type A (American)	Type J (Japanese)	Type Z
Employment	Short-term	Lifetime	Long-term
Career path specialization	Yes	No	Moderate
Evaluation and promotion	Rapid	Slow	Slow
Decision making	Individual	Consensual	Consensual
Responsibility	Individual	Collective	Individual
Concern	Segmented	Holistic	Holistic
Control	Explicit and formal	Implicit and informal	Combination

▶

According to Ouchi, responsibility and decision making lie with the individual in America and with the group in Japan. Certainly, an individual is much more likely to be concerned with blending into the group when membership in it extends over many years, as in lifetime employment. Ouchi defines *concern* as follows:

> Concern refers to the holism with which employees view each other and especially to the concern with which the supervisor views the subordinate. In the A organization, the supervisor regards the subordinate in a purely task-oriented manner and may consider it improper to inquire into his or her personal life. In comparison to this segmented view of people, the J organization manager considers it part of the managerial role to be fully informed of the personal circumstances of each subordinate (Ouchi and Jaeger, 1978:309).

Elsewhere, Ouchi (1979, 1980) has described Type J in terms of clans, and a company with holistic concern as very much like a family. In the jargon of sociology, Type J is called Gemeinschaft (community), and Type A is called Gesellschaft (society). In a community, people share many intimate aspects of life with each other and relate to each other as complete beings, as members of a family would. In a society, individuals share only a few aspects of life with most people they know, relating to only small parts of their identities, as a shopkeeper interacts with customers who are practically strangers.

Finally, we come to the factor of control. This refers to the way managers supervise subordinates, and it should be obvious that Type A is essentially McGregor's Theory X in this respect, and Type J is Theory Y. Type A demands explicit, formalized control of the employee; Type J uses much more implicit, informal control. Ouchi suggests that Type Z would combine these by using implicit, informal control with explicit, formalized measures of the employee's performance.

Having acquired a rough picture of Ouchi's ideas, we now face the challenge of turning them into statements for our questionnaire. As Z is just a combination of A and J, we will be content to devise A and J items without creating distinctive Z items. Ouchi describes existing societies and social organizations, but we will be giving our questionnaire to individuals to determine their attitudes, so we will have to phrase our statements in terms of what the individual believes or likes.

We already have items about some of these themes, but if we want to evaluate Ouchi's analysis in terms of the work of other scholars, it would be best to have fresh measures drawing entirely on his thinking. Here are the items, with the odd-numbered ones expressing the American style and the even-numbered ones the Japanese style:

25. So long as I can find good employment, I would prefer to work for several different organizations throughout my life.
26. Personally, I would prefer to work for the same organization for most of my life.
27. It is best to keep some distance from the other people at work and not get too involved with them personally.
28. I like to feel that the people I work with are almost members of my family.
29. Decisions should generally be made by the individual person who is in the best position to have the right answers.
30. The best way to make most decisions is to have all members of a group discuss the issue until they reach a consensus.
31. Responsibility for success or failure basically rests with the individual.
32. To single out one person for praise or blame is wrong, because the members of a group all contribute to its success.
33. To motivate people properly for work, it is essential to evaluate their performance rapidly and reward quick promotions to those who deserve them.
34. Rapid evaluation and promotion of employees is usually bad policy because it produces unhealthy rivalries and tensions in the group.
35. For sound management, a company needs to set explicit standards for performance and use formal statistics to monitor how well employees are meeting these objectives.
36. Rather than monitoring work by rules and statistics, a company should have a general philosophy expressed through informal understandings among employees.

37. The best way to ensure a successful career is to get specific skills, for example from professional training in a well-defined field.
38. The people who do best generally have a bit of experience in many different kinds of work.

I decided that one item from a survey by Ouchi and Johnson on levels of satisfaction of workers in Type A and Type Z companies should be included, written in opposite ways. I chose it both because it would readily make two exactly opposite items, and because it stressed an important topic that other items did not cover well enough: creativity. The item asked "Do you think that really creative ideas come from people working alone, or do they come from people working together?" (Ouchi and Johnson, 1978:317). It is easy to turn this into two opposite statements, giving us a total of 40 items:

39. Really creative ideas usually come from people working *alone*, rather than from people working together.
40. Really creative ideas usually come from people working *together*, rather than from people working alone.

▶ ▶ ▶ ▶ ▶ ▶ ▶ ▶ ▶ ▶ ▶

THE FINAL XYZ SURVEY

Forty items is a substantial number for a short survey, and we have covered all the aspects of X, Y, and Z that seem important. Therefore, we should stop here and invent no more items. To be sure, several of the items overlap in meaning, and there are two pairs of exact opposites. So we could cut the number down significantly if we really had to. But, as the development of the Mach scale showed, it is best to start with too many items, then pare down the list on the basis of actual data from respondents. Jacobson could not have told us which 10 out of the 20 Mach items made the best short form if she hadn't first given the full 20 to all her respondents. Only then could she look for the highest correlations identifying the items most closely associated with the whole scale or with parts of it.

The only thing that remains is to decide what order the items should be placed in. They cover many specific issues, but our theoretical assumption really is that they express just two or three underlying themes. In many cases the best design for a questionnaire is to separate the main topic areas so that respondents can adjust their mental focus for whole blocks of questions. But here we don't want to wave red flags in front of the themes. Quite the contrary. We want the respondents to take each item on its own merits. Then our statistical analysis can determine whether the items really go into solid groups like Theory X and Theory Y.

One possibility would be to rotate items—for example, to have all odd-numbered items be Theory X, or high Mach, or American, and to have the even-numbered items be Theory Y, or low Mach, or Japanese. But this might be too much of a clue for the respondents as well. Thus I decided to put the 40 items in random order, with the proviso that the items in the two pairs of opposites be separated near the ends of the list, so that their connection would not be too obvious. To do this, I used the first part of the random-numbers program, described in Chapter 3. The first time I tried this, however, Items 39 and 40 wound up very close together, entirely by accident. Because these opposites must be kept apart, I simply ran the random-numbers program a second time and got a satisfactory order.

Here's what the final survey looks like. Statements that a Theory X person is supposed to agree with are marked with an X, and Theory Y statements are marked Y. Items that represent Machiavellianism are marked M, and those that Machiavellians are supposed to disagree with are marked lm, for low Mach. Items describing the Japanese style are marked J; American standards are marked A.

A 1. Decisions should generally be made by the individual person who is in the best position to have the right answers.

X 2. People are fundamentally lazy, irresponsible, and need constantly to be watched.

J 3. Personally, I would prefer to work for the same organization for most of my life.

Y 4. Under proper conditions, the average human being learns not only to accept but to seek responsibility.

M 5. The biggest difference between most criminals and other people is that criminals are stupid enough to get caught.

Y 6. People are fundamentally hardworking, responsible, and need only to be supported and encouraged.

lm 7. Most people are basically good and kind.

J 8. Rather than monitoring work by rules and statistics, a company should have a general philosophy expressed through informal understandings among employees.

lm 9. Honesty is the best policy in all cases.

J 10. To single out one person for praise or blame is wrong, because the members of a group all contribute to its success.

M 11. Generally speaking, people won't work hard unless they're forced to do so.

X 12. Most people must be coerced, controlled, directed, and threatened with punishment to get them to work hard for goals set by their employer.

lm 13. One should take action only when sure it is morally right.

Y 14. People can exercise much self-direction and self-control when their work satisfies their needs for personal achievement and social respect.

X 15. The average human being prefers to be directed, wishes to avoid responsibility, has relatively little ambition, and wants security above all.

J 16. Really creative ideas usually come from people working *together*, rather than from people working alone.

A 17. The best way to ensure a successful career is to get specific skills, for example from professional training in a well-defined field.

X 18. The average human being has an inherent dislike of work and will avoid it if he can.

X 19. To motivate his subordinates, a good manager will use the economic incentive of wage raises more than the intangible rewards of honor and respect.

M 20. Never tell anyone the real reason you did something unless it is useful to do so.

Y 21. Group goal-setting offers advantages that cannot be obtained by individual goal-setting.

J 22. Rapid evaluation and promotion of employees is usually bad policy because it produces unhealthy rivalries and tensions in the group.

M 23. It is wise to flatter important people.

M 24. It is safest to assume that all people have a vicious streak and it will come out when they are given a chance.

J 25. The people who do best generally have a bit of experience in many different kinds of work.

lm 26. There is no excuse for lying to someone else.

lm 27. Most people who get ahead in the world lead clean, moral lives.

A 28. To motivate people properly for work, it is essential to evaluate their performance rapidly and reward quick promotions to those who deserve them.

A 29. Responsibility for success or failure basically rests with the individual.

Y 30. The most important thing a good manager does is to create a work environment in which people achieve their own personal goals best by working for the goals of the organization.

A 31. It is best to keep some distance from the other people at work and not get too involved with them personally.

J 32. The best way to make most decisions is to have all members of a group discuss the issue until they reach a consensus.

A 33. So long as I can find good employment, I would prefer to work for several different organizations throughout my life.

Y 34. To motivate his subordinates, a good manager will use the intangible rewards of honor and respect more than the economic incentive of wage raises.

Y 35. Most people have untapped resources of imagination, ingenuity, creativity, and other intellectual potentialities.

X 36. The most important things a good manager does are to direct people's efforts, motivate them, control their actions, and modify their behavior to fit the needs of the organization.

A 37. For sound management, a company needs to set explicit standards for performance and use formal statistics to monitor how well employees are meeting these objectives.

A 38. Really creative ideas usually come from people working *alone*, rather than from people working together.

J 39. I like to feel that the people I work with are almost members of my family.

X 40. A good leader should give detailed and complete instructions to his subordinates, rather than merely giving them general directions and depending upon their initiative to work out details.

The *Survey Research* disk contains a dataset based on 200 respondents who gave valid answers to all 40 items of this questionnaire. They were selected at random from nearly 400 male presidents, vice presidents, and managers of companies and other organizations nationwide.

You are invited to study the results with our statistical programs. I won't give you any instructions on how to do this, beyond the projects that follow, because you should have the chance to make your own voyage of discovery into the data. In developing the 40 items, this chapter has provided all the theory you will need to make sense of the items and their interrelationships.

▶ ▶ ▶ ▶ ▶ ▶ ▶ ▶ ▶ ▶ ▶

PROJECTS

Note: I have created a set of very simple labels for the XYZ dataset. Instead of hinting at the meaning of each separate item, they identify which set of items each is supposed to belong to: Theory X, Theory Y, Machiavellian, low Mach, American, or Japanese. Before you do some of these projects, you might want to jump ahead to the first project for Chapter 12, which asks you to create a set of distinctive labels to identify the 40 items in the XYZ dataset.

You should do all of the following projects on the XYZ work disk that you made in Project 3, Chapter 1.

1. Is the Mach Scale Reliable?   The psychologists who invented and applied the Machiavellianism scale assumed that its items reflected a single, underlying reality: a Machiavellian style of interaction with other people. True, they thought the items might separate slightly, into some merely reflecting a sour view of human nature and others actively promoting cynical exploitation of other people. But these were supposed to be closely related aspects of Machiavellianism.

Your task is to analyze the ten items in our short-form Mach scale to see how well they fit together and what groups they fall into if they are not a unit. Write a report that not only gives your chief statistical results but attempts to explain whatever you find.

2. Do the X and Y Management Styles Really Represent a Single Dimension?

For this project, you should first examine the X items and the Y items separately. Does each set (X and Y) hold together as a reliable scale? The two are supposed to be exact opposites, so it is reasonable to combine them to make an XY scale, in which an X manager gets a high score and a Y manager gets a low score. Is this combined XY scale reliable? *Note:* In addition to looking at correlations between items, you might want to check how many of the respondents give X or Y responses to key items, because there is always the possibility that one of the two philosophies of management simply does not exist in the group surveyed!

Again, write a report communicating your main statistical findings and your analysis of what they mean. For extra credit, you can also examine whether the X scale is closely related to the Mach scale, as Galfo said it was.

3. Are the A and J Scales Reliable and Opposite?

Analyze the A (American) and J (Japanese) items, in the same way as suggested for the X and Y items in Project 2. Remember, however, that Ouchi was not entirely clear on whether these items should form reliable scales or not. They were mainly lists of typical management practices in the two nations and thus could be purely accidental collections of principles. What do you think? Do any underlying concepts hold the A or J items together? If the items do not form reliable scales, does Ouchi have any justification for grouping the items as he does?

4. Laziness and Honesty Scales.

Let me suggest that all this talk of A, J, Mach, X, Y, and Z is quite unnecessary. Instead of this alphabet soup, I have a simpler theory. The XYZ Management Survey really measures two things: opinions about laziness and attitudes toward honesty as a policy for human relations. Please test my theory.

Create laziness and honesty indexes, including both negative and positive items. Does each of them hang together? Are they more reliable than the Mach, X, Y, A, and J scales? Investigate the leftover items to see whether some other scale might be hiding in the data.

5. An Acquiescence Scale.

Create an acquiescence (yea-saying or nay-saying) scale out of pairs of opposite items. Note that some pairs of items are precisely opposite, whereas others are just approximately opposite in meaning. Select the items you think are good pairs of opposites. You will have to think hard for a few minutes, and perhaps experiment a bit, until you see the proper way to combine two items of a pair to make them measure acquiescence rather than the topic they focus on.

Can you create a reliable scale? Does your final acquiescence scale correlate with other, individual items? Explain what your answer to this question means for survey researchers who might want to use your scale.

11

The typical survey asks questions of separate individuals, in a single period of time allocated for administering it, with all the respondents treated the same. But other, more complex approaches are available, and this chapter will outline them. We shall consider:

1. *Panel surveys*—in which a set of respondents is given questionnaires at two or more different times.

2. *Experiments*—in which respondents are divided into two or more groups that receive somewhat different questionnaires.

3. *Linked-respondent surveys*—in which the unit of analysis is larger than the single individual, typically a pair of respondents.

4. *Sociometric surveys*—in which all or many of the questions concern relationships among the people in the group and where the structure of social relations in the group is the prime focus of research.

PANEL SURVEYS

A **panel** is a set of individuals who serve as respondents at least twice. Such a group is often referred to as a **cohort,** a term demographers use to describe people born at the same time but here applied to people surveyed at

Complex Survey Designs

the same time. The main purpose of using panels is to examine the changes that can happen over time. Research carried out over time using such panels is called **longitudinal.**

This kind of research is frequently used in studies of growing up. Adolescents are given some of the same questions every year or two as they mature into adults. A good example is the vast *Youth in Transition* project that surveyed a panel of more than 2000 young Americans repeatedly and produced a huge set of reports (for example, Bachman, 1970). The first stage of the research, technically known as the first **wave** of the survey, was administered in 1966 to tenth-grade boys. They were resurveyed every two years until five waves had been completed, following them through the college years.

One important purpose of longitudinal studies is to distinguish cause from effect. Suppose we ask college students how involved in traditional religion they are, and whether they engage in premarital sexual activity. Suppose we find that the religious students are less likely to be sexually active than nonreligious students. This negative correlation does not tell us which of the two variables is the cause and which the effect. Perhaps religious involvement deters students from having sex; if so, religion is the cause (or independent variable), and low sexual activity is the effect (or dependent variable). But perhaps sexual activity draws students out of church or even gets them expelled from conservative congregations; then sex would be the cause and lack of religious involvement would be the effect.

The distinction between cause and effect is primarily one of time order. The cause comes before the effect. So a study could survey respondents' religion at a point in time when they had not yet become sexually active, then it could come back and survey them about sexual activity years later when some had become active, to see whether religion discouraged engaging in sex.

This is just what Barbara Schulz and her colleagues did with a sample of 2112 students at the University of Wisconsin. In 1964, just before they were to arrive at the university as freshmen, the students filled out a survey that asked several questions about religion. Four years later, when most were seniors, they responded to another survey that inquired about their sexual behavior. Indeed, traditional religiousness was partly responsible for discouraging students from engaging in sex (Schulz et al., 1977).

An alternative to longitudinal research is **cross-sectional research.** Instead of following one cohort (age group) through several years, the researcher studies people of different ages at the same point in time. For example, you could test the theory that adults become more conservative as they age by comparing young adults with older adults in a single survey. Certainly, this approach seems much more practical than chasing after a group of respondents for several years, administering several expensive surveys to them.

Unfortunately, such cross-sectional research has a real likelihood of giving false results. It confuses the changes a person undergoes during his or her life with the changes the society goes through over the decades. Perhaps people born in 1930 were more conservative even in their youth than people born in 1950, and differences between these two groups are attributable to the era when the individuals grew up.

A difference that reflects the historical period in which a cohort of a particular age grew up is called a **cohort effect.** Differences that reflect the aging process are called **maturational effects.** A survey done at one point in time cannot readily distinguish them from each other.

A study done by Charles Peek and his associates used the *Youth in Transition* dataset to analyze the relationship between religion and delinquency both longitudinally and cross-sectionally. Using data from three points in time, the researchers were able to see whether past religiousness predicted the later level of delinquent behavior (longitudinal analysis) as well as to examine how religion and delinquency correlated in data from a single wave of the survey (cross-sectional analysis). They were even able to detect a tendency for boys who lost a previously strong religiousness to become even more delinquent than the average nonreligious young man later on (Peek et al., 1985). This is a particularly subtle finding, and thus it suggests the nearly endless possibilities for analysis of admittedly expensive longitudinal data.

I can illustrate simple longitudinal analysis using some of my favorite old data from the U.S. censuses of the 19th century. I located the original records for some of the famous religious communes, including the Shakers, Oneida, and Zoar. The Shakers are well known, especially for the now highly prized furniture they made, and several of their former communes have been turned into museums. At their peak they had something like

4000 members practicing an extreme form of Christian religion, living communally but completely abstaining from sex and thus having difficulty maintaining their numbers. Oneida was founded in upstate New York by John Humphrey Noyes, mentioned in Chapter 2 as an early social scientist, and it was famous both for a deviant system of group marriage and for producing a popular brand of silverware that is still being sold. Zoar, in Ohio, was a typical example of several German peasant communes that came to the United States in the 19th century, its members living in conventional families within a very traditional religious community.

According to some sociologists, the intense religious rituals of these groups should bind members to them and to the ways of life taught so thoroughly within the commune's closed worlds. Yet the Shakers seemed to me less able than the other two to offer the rewards people enjoy in conventional lives. For example, Oneida and Zoar went through periods of sexual abstinence when they were first getting established, but both offered members the chance to experience sex and to have children later on. The Shakers, however, were always celibate. Thus we might expect Oneida and Zoar to keep members more successfully than the Shakers, especially in the younger age groups, where sexual urges are at their height.

We can turn the old census manuscripts into a longitudinal study by combining data from two years, 1850 and 1860. When census-takers visited the communes, they wrote down the name, sex, and age of each resident. There were many Shaker communities in 1850, with a total of 3842 members. The census-taker who visited Oneida in 1850 found 182 people, and Zoar's membership was 239. I copied down the names and other data for each of these 4263 19th-century communards and looked them up again in the 1860 records. Table 11.1 summarizes what I found.

The left-hand part of the table reports how many people there were of each sex, in each age group, at each commune in 1850. This information came from the first wave of my panel survey, namely the 1850 census. The right-hand part of the table is the longitudinal analysis. Using the second wave of the study, the 1860 census, it reports what percent of the people in each group are still living members of their commune in 1860, ten years after the first wave.

For example, there were 618 male Shakers aged 0–19 in 1850. I looked up all their names in the original forms of the 1860 census, marking the ones who were still there. The missing ones were either dead or gone; in the case of young men, undoubtedly gone out to the freer world beyond the commune. I was able to find only 24% of these 618 still among the Shakers, a percentage that struck me as representing a very low capacity to hold young men in the communes.

But you need valid comparisons to judge whether rates should be considered low. And the data from Oneida and Zoar provide them. Fully 75% of the young Oneida men and 78% of the young Zoar men remained at their communes over the same decade. The Shakers were better able to hold young women from 1850 to 1860 than young men, keeping 41% of the

▶ ▶ ▶ ▶ ▶ ▶ ▶ ▶ ▶ ▶ ▶

TABLE 11.1   LONGITUDINAL STUDY OF SHAKERS, ONEIDA, AND ZOAR

Age and Sex Group	Number in 1850			Percent Kept 1850–1860		
	Shakers	Oneida	Zoar	Shakers	Oneida	Zoar
Males:						
0–19	618	44	45	24%	75%	78%
20–49	533	43	42	51%	81%	52%
50+	475	8	22	49%	63%	41%
Females:						
0–19	669	39	48	41%	87%	73%
20–49	863	37	37	64%	86%	62%
50+	684	11	45	56%	73%	56%

669 they started with. But Oneida kept 87% of the women in the same age group, and Zoar kept 73%. The Shakers had much greater difficulty hanging on to young members than the two communes that allowed them sexual experiences.

This brief study does not prove that sexuality was the factor that produced the very different dropout rates. I mention sex only as a possible explanation, so that the data will not be completely mysterious. The communes differed in other ways as well. But the analysis illustrates the logic of longitudinal research, combining data from surveys done at two or more points in time to chart changes that occurred over the period.

Perhaps the classic example of panel research is a study of the 1940 presidential election done by Paul F. Lazarsfeld, Bernard Berelson, and Hazel Gaudet (1948). A panel of 600 residents of Erie County, Ohio, were surveyed 7 times, every month from May through November 1940. In each of the first 6 waves they were asked what they intended to do at the time of the election—whether they planned to vote, and if so, for whom. Then in November, just after the election, they were asked what they actually had done. The point of the study was not so much to predict the election as to examine the political changes that took place during the election campaign.

Table 11.2 reports data from the October and November waves, showing how respondents would have voted a month before the election and how they actually did vote. The Republican candidate was Wendell Willkie, and the Democrat, who won the election nationally if not in Erie County, was Franklin Delano Roosevelt. Some respondents said in October they did not plan to vote, and some did not in fact go to the polls in November. Table 11.2 shows the party preferences of those who were prepared to vote.

On the basis of Table 11.2, you would have to conclude that the October poll gave a very precise prediction of the November election results. Indeed, it seems to show that hardly any political changes occurred over

▶ ▶ ▶ ▶ ▶   ▶ ▶ ▶ ▶ ▶ ▶

TABLE 11.2   PARTY PREFERENCES FOR THE 1940 ELECTION
IN ERIE COUNTY, OHIO

Party	Number of Voters		Percent of Voters	
	October	November	October	November
Republican	229	232	58%	59%
Democratic	167	160	42%	41%
Total	396	392	100%	100%

Source: Lazarsfeld et al., 1948: xi

▶ ▶ ▶ ▶ ▶   ▶ ▶ ▶ ▶ ▶ ▶

TABLE 11.3   CHANGES IN VOTER PREFERENCES
FROM OCTOBER TO NOVEMBER 1940

November, Actual Vote	Vote Intention in October			
	Republican	Democratic	Don't Know	Don't Expect to Vote
Republican	<u>215</u>	7	4	6
Democratic	4	<u>144</u>	12	0
Didn't vote	10	16	6	<u>59</u>
Total	229	167	22	65

Source: Lazarsfeld et al., 1948: xi

the last month of the campaign. In October, 58% were going to vote for
Willkie, the Republican, and in November, 59% did so, an insignificant
change. But one of the great advantages of longitudinal research is that you
can examine changes very closely, following each individual respondent
from wave to wave. Perhaps many individuals changed their views from
October to November, but in ways that essentially canceled out, leaving
roughly the same percentages voting for each candidate.

Lazarsfeld and his colleagues were very interested in this possibility,
and they looked closely at the data for individuals who changed their positions during the campaign. Table 11.3 shows a finer analysis of the shifts
from October to November, identifying a significant number of people
who changed positions, despite the relative stability of the overall party
strengths.

Table 11.3 covers a total of 483 people. In October, 229 of them expressed an intention to vote Republican, and in November, 215 of these 229
actually did so. Four others switched to the Democratic candidate, and 10
did not vote after all. Of the 167 who said in October they were going to
vote Democratic, 144 actually did so, 7 switched to the Republican, and 16

did not vote. Of the 22 who told the October wave of the survey they did not know what they were going to do, 4 decided for the Republican, 12 for the Democrat, and 6 did not vote. Sixty-five people did not plan to vote, but 6 of them got sufficiently interested over the month to go ahead and cast ballots.

In the table, I have underlined the numbers for the three large groups that did in November exactly what they said they would do in October: 215 solid Republicans, 144 solid Democrats, and 59 solid nonvoters. Together, these 418 constitute 87% of the respondents surveyed. But this leaves 13% who changed their minds in one way or another. Lazarsfeld and his associates note that this small group is often the part of the electorate that actually decides how an election will come out.

> This 13% represents the *turnover* that took place in the few weeks before the election. The concept of turnover is basic to analysis of opinion formation. A large turnover indicates that the opinion or behavior is unstable, that people feel uncertain and that propaganda may be effective, or that clarification and education are required.
>
> If such dynamic research is conducted more frequently in the future, it may be possible to classify social events according to the following dimensions: What types of events show a small or large turnover as they develop? Does the turnover tend to become smaller as the events run their course? At what point is a minimum turnover reached, and what is likely to increase it again? Under what conditions do we have a balanced turnover, as in this case, where the changes in various directions seem to cancel each other? (Lazarsfeld et al., 1948:xi).

► ► ► ► ► ► ► ► ► ► ►

EXPERIMENTS

Questionnaires are often used in conjunction with laboratory experiments, but they also can be the vehicle for experiments outside the laboratory. Before we can see how, we must make sure we understand what an experiment is. The term is used widely in the sciences to refer to many different things, but philosophers of science have identified a particular approach to testing theories as the *experimental method*.

In an **experiment,** the social scientist systematically examines the effect of a particular action performed on people under study, compared with no action or some other action. To be sure, systematic comparison is the essence of all scientific research. But in experiments, the comparison is between results of different things the experimenter does.

In many cases the comparison is between two different groups of people who have experienced somewhat different versions of the experiment. Richard F. Larson (1968) has provided an example based on questionnaires sent through the mails. Larson wanted to know how clergy in different religious denominations would respond to a person seeking help for emotional problems, and he wanted to compare their judgments with those of professional psychiatrists. His survey, administered to 1868 clergymen, included 6 "case histories," thumbnail sketches of people in trouble, and the respondents were supposed to check a box for each, indicating how severe an emotional disturbance the person suffered from: "none," "mild," "moderate," or "severe."

So far we do not have an experiment, just a survey designed to compare different religious groups among the respondents. But Larson added an experimental manipulation. At random, each of the six imaginary people was presented as either male or female. Thus half the respondents read a story about a withdrawn person named Mr. Thompson, while the other half, selected at random, read a similar story about a withdrawn person named Mrs. Thompson. Here is the story for Mr. Thompson:

> Mr. Thompson has been widowed for five years. He is a respectable person whose wife died when he was just 20. They had no children, and he went home to his parents. He has not had a job in five years and does not seem to want to go out and look for one. He is very quiet: he does not talk much to anyone—including his parents. He acts as if he is afraid of people, especially young women his own age. He won't go out with anyone and whenever someone comes to visit his parents, he stays in his own room until the person leaves. He just stays by himself and daydreams about his wife. (Larson, 1968:252)

Create Mrs. Thompson's story for yourself. Read the preceding paragraph aloud, changing the necessary words so that Mr. Thompson becomes Mrs. Thompson. Say *she* instead of *he*, *husband* instead of *wife*. Given the same facts, would you judge a woman in this situation less disturbed than a man? If so, you may be thinking in terms of traditional sex roles that assumed a man had to be active and have a job, whereas a passive, inactive woman might be judged normal.

In Larson's study, 873 clergymen filled out questionnaires presenting the male case history. Just under half, 45.7%, judged this as a case of severe emotional disturbance. In contrast, only 29.9% of the 989 who responded to the female version of the story felt it was a severe disturbance.

Like longitudinal studies, experimental studies are a good way of distinguishing cause from effect. When Larson mailed out his surveys, it had already been decided whether a given respondent would receive the story about Mr. Thompson or Mrs. Thompson. Because they had been divided at random, the only systematic difference between the groups that got the different stories was the sex of the Thompson they read about. Thus the sex of the character in the story had to be the cause of any differences in their response to it.

In general, surveys can show an association between two variables, but they cannot distinguish cause from effect because most survey designs lack the element of time. Logically, a cause occurs before its effect. Many researchers like to use the terms **independent variable** and **dependent variable** to get away from the cause–effect language. An independent variable is like a cause in that it seems to do the work in the relationship, with another variable said to be dependent. But in experiments and longitudinal research, we can talk more confidently about cause and effect.

▶ ▶ ▶ ▶ ▶ ▶ ▶ ▶ ▶ ▶ ▶

LINKED-RESPONDENT SURVEYS

In longitudinal panel studies, we link together data each individual member of the panel gave in different waves of the survey. In experiments, we compare data from different groups of respondents who experienced somewhat different versions of the survey. And in the kind of research we shall consider here, we link data from different individual respondents. Perhaps the best way to explain this is to go back to the concept of informant surveys in Chapter 2 and examine what can happen when one person is asked to give data about another person.

Many surveys have sought to investigate the interaction between personal relationships and individual attitudes. For example, in 1970 the Harris Poll asked a large sample of college students to describe their own political stance and to report those of their parents as well. Table 11.4 shows a small part of the data, as analyzed by political sociologist Seymour Martin Lipset (1976:85).

These data are essential to Lipset's study of the sources of the political rebellion that swept American universities in the late 1960s. One theory was that members of the political left grew up in families that already were on the liberal side of the political spectrum. But a competing theory of the time was that student rebellion of the period represented a "generation gap"—young people disagreed greatly with their parents.

The data in Table 11.4 indicate that children of politically liberal parents strongly tended to be liberal or even members of the far left. Only tiny minorities of children of liberal parents became conservatives. This suggests, first of all, that children tend to follow in the political footsteps of their parents. We also see some tendency for a shift to the left from one generation to the next, at least among the offspring of liberals. But can we really trust these data?

Unfortunately, the Harris Poll did not ask the parents what their political opinions were. Instead, it asked the *students* to say what their parents felt. It is quite possible that students would exaggerate either similarities or

▶   ▶   ▶   ▶   ▶   ▶   ▶   ▶   ▶   ▶   ▶

TABLE 11.4   POLITICAL VIEWS OF CHILDREN OF LIBERAL PARENTS

Student's Politics	Percent of Students Whose	
	Mother Is Liberal	Father Is Liberal
Far right	1%	0%
Conservative	2%	1%
Middle of the road	9%	7%
Liberal	60%	64%
Far left	24%	24%
Not sure	4%	4%
Total	100%	100%

differences between themselves and their parents. The table might represent a combination of both. Students might tend to place their parents on the same side of the political spectrum as themselves, thereby asserting that theirs was the majority and thus correct side in politics. Or they might want to assert their own, personal progressivism by claiming their parents were not so far in the good direction as they. This might happen on either side of the spectrum, but here Lipset's analysis is concerned with the left.

The ideal study would have interviewed each student, that student's mother, and that student's father. Then each set of three respondents would have been analyzed as a unit, student–mother–father, their data linked in the computer. The best strategy in such research has always been to collect data from each survey subject directly (Duncan et al., 1968). But cost has often required that information on the beliefs and opinions of a respondent's friends or relatives be based merely on the respondent's secondhand report.

Several survey studies have asked young people about their drug use and about their parents' use of prescription drugs. The idea is that if Mom relies on tranquilizers and Dad takes pills to keep his blood pressure down, the kids will learn that drugs produce good moods and good health, and the step from prescription drugs to illegal drugs is a short one once a person has accepted the general idea that drugs are good. The results were fairly consistent. Drug-using young people did seem to come from drug-using families. Then Denise B. Kandel (1974; Kandel et al., 1976) attacked the question more seriously, surveying parents as well as offspring. And the results of her careful studies were very different. There was little if any tendency for young drug users to come from drug-using families. Apparently, the young respondents to the earlier studies had simply exaggerated the similarities between their personal drug behavior and that of their parents.

I explored the linked-respondent approach in a study of 424 pairs of close friends at the University of Washington (Bainbridge and Stark, 1981). Rather than single surveys, all the students got a packet of questionnaires to be completed by themselves, by close friends, and by acquaintances. The students getting the packets were supposed to recruit people they knew to participate in the study and then return everything to me.

The questionnaires in each set carried ID numbers and letters designating original respondent, close friend, and acquaintance. This permitted me to reassemble surveys into sets even if they got scattered. The questionnaires were identical, except that friends and acquaintances were asked "How close a friend is the person who gave you this questionnaire?" A seven-point scale was provided for the answer, from 0 (not at all close) to 6 (very close). In most of my analysis, I focused on 424 "close-friend" pairs defined as those in which the friend rated the relationship a 5 or 6 on the closeness scale.

In entering these data into the computer, I linked the pairs, so that each pair was one case. The way to do this is simple enough. Suppose the survey has 100 items. Staple together the pair's 2 copies of the questionnaire and enter them as one 200-item questionnaire. Items 1–100 are the answers of the first person in the pair, and items 101–200 are the answers of the second person. Imagine we gave a pair of surveys to Jack, whose best friend was Jill, and the first question concerned the sex of the respondent. Jack would answer "male," and Jill would answer "female." So their answer to item 1 would be "male," and to item 101, "female."

The focus of the research was on how friendships and religion relate. Do close-friend pairs tend to agree about their religious beliefs? That is, do religious students have religious friends, and nonreligious students, nonreligious friends? If so, this could be because people who are close friends influence each other to become more similar. Or it might reflect the principle "Birds of a feather flock together." People might choose friends partly on the basis of having similar religious views.

Certainly, religion is a very social phenomenon. And the linking of respondents was not the only way I examined social aspects of religion. I also looked at the effect of the religious movement then washing the campus. Various evangelical groups had sprung up, many of them completely informal. Through the movement, people might acquire religious friends, and certainly the movement intended to influence people socially to become more religious.

Although the questionnaire included many questions about religion, the one that was most potent in charting this movement was taken from the Gallup Poll: "Would you say that you have been 'born again' or have had a 'born-again' experience—that is, a turning point in your life when you committed yourself to Christ?" In Gallup's survey, 34% of respondents said they were "born-again" (Gallup, 1977). Despite the secularizing effect of college and the low church-member rates on the West Coast (Stark and Bainbridge, 1985), 25.6% of my college students checked the yes box.

To analyze the results, we are going to look at what I call **concor-dances,** the correlations between how the members of the pairs answer the same question. For example, let's consider the sex item. Call the first person in each pair Person X and the second person Person Y. In running the correlation, the X variable will be Person X's sex and the Y variable will be Person Y's sex. The number of cases is 424, representing the pairs of close friends, with an X and a Y for each pair. So if respondents tend to have close friends of the same sex as themselves, X and Y will have a positive correlation. If they tend to choose friends of the opposite sex, as Jack and Jill did, X and Y will have a negative correlation.

There is a very strong concordance on the "born-again" question, a correlation (gamma) of 0.59. Born-agains constituted 26% of the original students who received the packets of questionnaires. Those of them who were not born-agains chose friends 24% of whom were born-again, essentially the same proportion. But the born-agains in the original group chose close friends 55% of whom were also born-again, showing a very powerful tendency to select friends who shared their involvement in this intense religious movement.

If we find concordances on a number of other questions in the survey, we might wonder whether the born-again movement is producing them, by leading its members to be of one mind on the particular issue. It is easy enough to test this, by removing all the members of the movement from the analysis. If we take all the born-agains out, we are left with 219 close-friend pairs. In the two tables that follow, I will look at concordances both for the full 424 pairs and for the 219 pairs in which neither party is born-again.

Table 11.5 shows concordances on a number of items that are not essentially religious. We see very strong tendencies for pairs in the 424 to be of the same sex (gamma = 0.79) and same year in college (gamma = 0.59). Undoubtedly, many students gave the close-friend survey to their roommate, who, under university rules, would have to be of the same sex and was likely to be of the same year. Among the items were several asking students how much they liked something on a seven-point scale from do not like to like very much. Tobacco cigarettes got a strong concordance (gamma = 0.50), which is not surprising considering the fact that the university asks students whether they want to room with a smoker or a nonsmoker.

Many of the items show substantial concordances, and you may want to think for a moment whether you share viewpoints on these with your friends. But preferences for "the physical sciences" and "the social sciences" show no concordance. Apparently, college students don't often pick friends or roommates on the basis of academic interests. And the two political items at the bottom, one about nuclear energy and the other a political question taken from the General Social Survey (Davis and Smith, 1986), show no concordance. For friendships, intellectual matters seem much less important than what people smoke and drink.

Notice that the concordances in the two columns of figures are about

▶ ▶ ▶ ▶ ▶ ▶ ▶ ▶ ▶ ▶ ▶

TABLE 11.5 SIMILARITIES IN LINKED RESPONDENTS—CLOSE-FRIEND PAIRS

| | Concordance (Gamma) in | |
| | 424 Close-Friend Pairs | 219 Close-Friend Pairs—Neither Being Born-Again |
Survey Item		
Sex of respondent	0.79	0.82
Year in college	0.59	0.62
Preference for tobacco cigarettes	0.50	0.44
Preference for marijuana	0.45	0.41
Preference for beer	0.32	0.33
Preference for diet soda	0.27	0.28
Preference for rock music	0.25	0.22
Preference for the physical sciences	0.01	0.00
Preference for the social sciences	0.04	−0.02
How often respondent has been high on drugs	0.48	0.40
Respondent agrees: "It is all right for an unmarried couple to have sexual relations"	0.57	0.44
Respondent agrees: "The potential dangers of nuclear energy are outweighed by its potential benefits"	0.06	0.05
Respondent's politics, on a seven-point liberal–conservative scale	0.12	0.02

the same. Taking the born-agains out of the analysis does not much affect the tendency for beer-drinkers to hang out with beer-drinkers, for example. Thus the concordances are not just the result of evangelical religious norms influencing some students. The campus is not simply divided into a clean-living born-again subculture and a hard-drinking, hard-smoking, lascivious subculture of rock music fans. Rather, students are linked in a complex social network where close friends tend to share lifestyles but not noticeably to share views on academic subjects or politics.

What about concordances on religion itself? We have already seen that born agains tend to have born-again friends. Does this mean that religious students tend to have religious friends in general, even outside the born-again movement? Certainly this seems plausible. Many students who did not admit to being born-again said they were religious, especially among Catholics who find other ways to express their religiousness than through the primarily Protestant concept of "born again." Table 11.6 re-

▶ ▶ ▶ ▶ ▶ ▶ ▶ ▶ ▶ ▶ ▶

TABLE 11.6 RELIGIOUS SIMILARITIES IN LINKED RESPONDENTS—
CLOSE-FRIEND PAIRS

Survey Item	Concordance (Gamma) in	
	424 Close-Friend Pairs	219 Close-Friend Pairs—Neither Being Born-Again
Frequency of church attendance	0.34	0.14
Importance of religious beliefs	0.28	0.01
Respondent agrees: "I definitely believe in God"	0.22	0.07
Respondent agrees: "God or some other supernatural force has a very strong influence on my life"	0.29	0.05
Respondent agrees: "Suffering often comes about because people don't obey God"	0.25	0.12
Respondent agrees: "Miracles actually happened just as the Bible says they did"	0.34	0.18
Respondent's preference for "religious books and articles"	0.25	0.03
Respondent's preference for "hymns and spirituals"	0.22	0.07

ports the correlations between close friends on a number of religion questions, both for the 424 pairs and the 219 with no born-again members.

The gammas in the first column are all significant, but most are below the concordance on beer in the previous table, and it is hard to say they prove a very strong religious influence on campus. And all these concordances collapse in the second column, when we look at the 219 pairs of close friends that remain after we take out the born-agains. It seems that religion doesn't influence friendships at the University of Washington, except for the minority of students caught up in the born-again movement.

The item on the importance of religious beliefs is especially interesting. Respondents were asked "How important to you are your religious beliefs?" They had to check one of four boxes: "very important," "fairly important," "not too important," or "not at all important." Removal of the born-agains still leaves 18% who say their religious beliefs are "very important" to them and 34% who say they are "fairly important." Perhaps religious beliefs are privately important for many who are not born-again, but they certainly are not relevant for friendship, as the essentially zero concordance (gamma = 0.01) shows.

Although the complex research designs described in this chapter generally require special methods of analysis, to which our simple, teaching-oriented computer programs are not suited, it is easy to do a linked-respondent survey with the *Survey Research* disk. You must create a questionnaire with no more than 24 items, exactly half the 48 items that are the maximum the programs can handle. In writing the survey into the computer, double the questions so that the set is asked twice. Then bring respondents in as pairs to answer the survey.

I will illustrate this with a hypothetical survey consisting of 20 items. Type the items into the computer, from 1 through 20. Then insert a special free-form question, like this: "STOP! Please bring the second member of the pair to the computer. Is that person ready to begin? Press the 1 key when ready. [1] All ready to go!" This is question number 21. Now type in the 20 items over again, as numbers 22–41.

When administering the survey to Jack and Jill, bring Jack to the computer, and have him respond to items 1–20. Then item 21 will alert him to stop, and bring Jill to the machine. Press [1] to get past question 21, which is meant merely to separate the two respondents in the pair, and have Jill answer items 22–41, which are exactly the same as 1–20. Of course, Jack and Jill should not see each other's answers to the questions.

When you analyze the data, correlating item 1 with item 22 gives you the concordance for the first question. Correlating item 2 with item 23 gives you the concordance for the second question, and so on. Suppose you used 200 pairs like Jack and Jill, with the 2 members always of different sexes. You might want to have one sex always go first. Then if you correlate item 1 with item 2, you get a result for the males, and if you correlate item 22 with item 23 you get a result about the same questions for the females. But these would be ordinary correlations, not concordances, because they are not between answers to the same question from the two members of each pair.

▶ ▶ ▶ ▶ ▶ ▶ ▶ ▶ ▶ ▶ ▶

SOCIOMETRIC SURVEYS

One question in my University of Washington survey is a **sociometric item:** "How close a friend is the person who gave you this questionnaire?" The respondent circled a number from 0 (not at all close) to 6 (very close). Any question that seeks to measure the relationship between people is called sociometric, and a survey whose primary purpose is to map the relationships between people is a **sociometric survey.**

The pioneer of sociometric surveys was J. L. Moreno, who created **sociometry,** the measurement and charting of social relationships, and presented it as a cure for the ills of the world in a marvelously inventive 1934 book titled *Who Shall Survive?* In the 20th century, it is not particularly radical to suggest that the world is falling to pieces, stands in great danger, or tilts toward the abyss of social disintegration. But this book went beyond mere warning and proposed remedies. Moreno was a rival of Freud, creating a novel variety of therapy based on sociological rather than psychological principles. And his patient was not the individual neurotic person but the society as a whole. The first sentences of the book state his aims: "A true therapeutic procedure cannot have less an objective than the whole of mankind. But no adequate therapy can be prescribed as long as mankind is not a unity in some fashion and as long as its organization remains unknown."

Sociometry would reveal the hidden structure of social groups, just as psychoanalysis supposedly revealed the hidden structure of the mind. And once they had been identified, the flaws of social relations and social structure could be corrected. Moreno's book is quite remarkable in its combination of serious methodological pioneering and uninhibited promotion of the author's majestic ambitions. The fact is that Moreno's basic research innovations, shorn of the grandiose hopes he invested in them, have become standard techniques in several of the social sciences, but the world has not been transformed by them.

A good example of the practical use to which Moreno's methods have been put is the classic analysis of the "Bank Wiring Room" by George C. Homans (1950). The original research, reported by Roethlisberger and Dickson (1939), was carried out in 1931 and 1932 at the Hawthorne factory of the Western Electric Company, near Chicago; the contribution Homans made was to provide theoretical explanations of the findings.

The bank wiring room was a special room at the factory set aside for the manufacture of telephone switching equipment—banks of terminals that had to be wired—where every aspect of the work could be observed by scientists. Fourteen men assembled the terminals: nine wiremen who put the wires on, three soldermen who soldered the connections, and two inspectors who checked everything.

The factory management was especially interested in learning what factors determined how much the men produced. They had devised a complex system of payment that rewarded the men both for their individual output and for the output of the group as a whole, thus ensuring that each would work hard on his own tasks but would also be prepared to cooperate with the others. To the managers' surprise, the men did not behave quite as expected. Although their level of production was good, they did not work at the maximum rate they could have achieved.

The social scientists observing the men discovered that they had set their own, collective norms on how much work they should do, somewhat lower than the company would have preferred. Apparently, money was not the only incentive that shaped their action. They also played games in spare minutes at work and shared other social rewards with one another. Thus the group of 14 men was a social unit of its own, influencing the behavior of members even though they were also influenced by the wishes of the factory management.

But among the 14 men, levels of productivity varied significantly. The

▶ ▶ ▶ ▶ ▶ ▶ ▶ ▶ ▶ ▶ ▶

FIGURE 11.1 SOCIOGRAM OF THE BANK WIRING ROOM

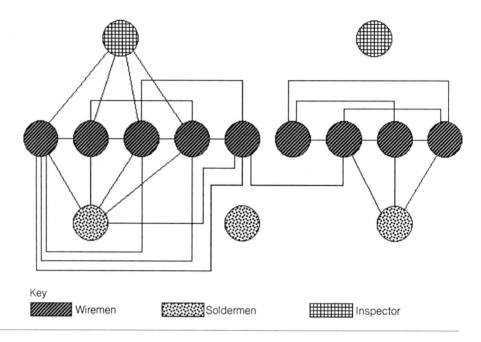

Key

▨ Wiremen   ▨ Soldermen   ▦ Inspector

▶ _____

men were given tests of manual dexterity and intelligence, and neither of these measures explained why some got more work done than others. Part of the answer then came from data on the social relations of the men, data collected in a manner inspired by Moreno's sociometric methods.

One of the scientific observers carefully noted which men played games together and also collected data on many other aspects of their social relations. One of the most convenient and clear methods to represent data on relations in small groups is to draw a **sociogram.** Figure 11.1 shows one of several sociograms of the bank wiring room that Homans (1950:68) published, recording who played games with whom.

Each person is represented by a circle, a square, or some other shape on the page. Relationships connecting them are shown as lines. Here, the two inspectors are at the top, each represented by a circle. The nine wiremen are in a line across the middle, and the three soldermen are at the bottom. Notice that four lines go down from the left-hand inspector to the first four wiremen on the left. These lines mean that this inspector habitually played games with these wiremen.

The inspector on the right is not connected to any of the other men by lines. This means that he did not play games with anyone. A person who is not connected to anyone else in a sociogram is called a **social isolate.** There is one other social isolate in the diagram, the solderman in the center at the bottom.

As you can see, many lines tie together the four wiremen and the solderman on the right. Many more lines tie together the five wiremen on the left, the left-hand inspector, and the left-hand solderman. And one line, representing one game-playing relationship, links these two groups. The whole structure of relationships linking a number of people together is called a **social network**. A subgroup within a network, somewhat cut off from the people around them but closely tied to one another, is called a **clique.**

Clearly, this diagram shows two social cliques. One, on the left, has seven members. The other, on the right, has five members. One social relationship links the cliques, but they are clearly distinct.

This brings us back to the question of what determines the different output levels. One important factor, it turns out, is which clique the man belongs to. Each clique had informally set norms on how much work should be done each day versus the time that should be invested in other things, including sharing social rewards. The two cliques had different standards, and these social norms shaped individual work behavior.

Many social networks, of every imaginable kind, are divided into cliques, and several important social phenomena are shaped by the structure of networks. For example, a religious denomination that is sharply divided into substantial cliques is especially likely to undergo schism, a splitting apart into wholly independent and often rival denominations (Stark and Bainbridge, 1985, 1987). As the analysis by Homans shows, the network structure of work groups has a considerable effect on how well they function. Thus sociograms are important tools for the social scientist concerned with understanding and improving such groups.

Data on the bank wiring room were collected by observation, not through a survey, but writing sociometric survey questions is easy enough. "Please list the men in this room whom you often play games with." "If you were going to relax for a while and play a game, which men in this room would you enjoy being with?" Moreno himself used a variety of sociometric survey questions, specially designed for the particular set of respondents he was studying. For example, when Moreno surveyed schoolchildren, he wrote his key question around the physical situation in the classroom, where the children were sitting.

> You are seated now according to directions your teacher has given you. The neighbor who sits beside you is not chosen by you. You are now given the opportunity to choose the boy or girl whom you would like to have sit on either side of you. Write down whom you would like first best; then, whom you would like second best. Look around you and make up your mind. Remember that next term your friends you choose may sit beside you. (Moreno, 1934:13)

When Moreno surveyed adults, he had them think about whom they would like to have live next door to them. Another approach is to ask members of a group to imagine forming a subgroup, consisting of just the people the respondent chooses to include from the whole group. This was the approach I used the first time I constructed a sociogram.

I was a graduate student, running a sociology tutorial (or seminar) of nine undergraduates. Some students were far more aggressive in the discussions than others, and a couple of the quieter ones became dissatisfied. One of them suggested we split into two separate discussion groups.

Two tutorials, one with four members and the other with five, might have been quite successful. But it would have meant twice as much work for me. Someone suggested taking a vote. I vetoed this idea, saying that voting is for political scientists; we sociologists should use a more distinctively sociological method of deciding: We should do a sociogram.

I had each of the students take a piece of paper and write his or her name at the top. Then I asked them to write the numbers 1 through 4 down the left edge of the page. After the number 1, they were to write the name of the class member they would most like to have in their tutorial, if we split into two. After the number 2, they were to write the name of the person they would like second best, and so on for 3 and 4. Then I went home to analyze.

I wrote the letters A through I, representing the nine members of the class, on a large sheet of paper and began drawing lines connecting people who chose each other to be in their tutorials. For example, student D and student E chose each other, a mutual choice or **mutual pair.** So I drew a line connecting D and E. By the time I had gone through each student's first three choices, there were six such pairs. Students A, B, G, H, and I were connected, forming a clique. C, D, and E were also connected. And F stood alone, none of his choices reciprocated. So at this point it would have been very easy to divide the class. One group would have consisted of A, B, G, H, and I, and the other group would have been C, D, E, and F.

But I sorely wanted to avoid splitting the class and thus doubling my work. So I continued my analysis, adding in each person's fourth choice of a classmate. And success, in my terms, crowned my efforts. There were now ten mutual pairs, and all the students were connected into one big tutorial. It couldn't be divided without separating at least two mutual pairs. The next week I reported the happy result of the sociogram, that we would all stay together.

Perhaps this example suggests to you that sociometry is a slippery technique, one that gives uncertain results and can easily be distorted by the researcher. As a research method, it has some problems, but its very versatility can be a great advantage, allowing you to examine different aspects of social relations in a group and focusing on different levels of intensity in social bonds. An example taken from some serious recent research done by one of my students will make this clear.

I asked the students in my field research seminar to help me create and administer an attitude survey, related to the XYZ survey described in Chapter 10 but including some sociometric questions. Here we will consider just the sociometric items, but the project was really a pilot study on ways to combine sociometric and attitudinal items. The group of nine respondents we will consider here, all of them women, worked at a travel agency. They were the owner, a manager, an accountant, and six agents.

To ensure anonymity, we did not ask respondents to write down the actual names of the other people in their group. Instead, we provided them with a list of ID letters for their coworkers: A, B, C, D, E, F, G, H, and I. We promised we would discard our copies of this list and work only with the anonymous ID letters when we did our analysis. The sociometric section of the questionnaire was like this:

PART ONE: SOCIAL RELATIONS IN YOUR WORK GROUP. First, look at the list of the people in your work group that accompanies this questionnaire and note your own ID letter—that is, see which letter of the alphabet is printed next to your name. Now write your own ID letter below. Please do not write your name, as we want to keep this questionnaire anonymous, but your ID letter is essential for us to analyze social relationships in your work group.

Your ID letter is: _____

A. WORK-RELATED ADVICE. Think for a moment about the people you would go to for advice on the job. Look at the list we have made of your coworkers and decide which one you would be most likely to seek advice from about your work. After the number 1, below, write the ID letter of the person you would be most likely to go to for work-related advice. (Remember, just write the person's ID letter, not the name, so we can ensure anonymity.)

Then, after the number 2, write the ID letter of the person you would be second most likely to ask for work-related advice. Do the same for the numbers 3 and 4, writing the ID letters of the people you would go to for advice third or fourth.

1 _____   2 _____   3 _____   4 _____

B. SOCIAL RELATIONS AWAY FROM WORK. Now look at the list of coworkers and think which person you would most enjoy being with outside of work. Write that person's ID letter after the number 1, below, indicating that you would most prefer to spend social time outside of work with that person.

Then write the ID letter of the person you would second most enjoy being with socially, after the number 2. After the number 3, write the ID letter of the person you would third most like to spend time with socially, and after the number 4, the person you would fourth most like to see socially.

1 _____ 2 _____ 3 _____ 4 _____

C. LEADERSHIP ABILITY. For the last time, look over the list and decide which person, *other than yourself,* has the most leadership ability—is best suited to be a leader at work, whether his or her job formally requires leadership now or not. After the number 1, write the ID letter of the person, other than yourself, with the greatest leadership ability. Then do the same for the other numbers, giving the ID letters of your coworkers with second, third and fourth best leadership ability.

1 _____ 2 _____ 3 _____ 4 _____

The last question, about leadership ability, is more like an opinion question than a sociometric question, because it does not focus on the relationships between the respondent and the other people at work. I include it here so you can see the variety of ways we can use questions of this format. In my analysis of the data, I used this question to learn which people were judged good leaders by their coworkers, and then I compared XYZ attitudes of the leaders with those of the other workers who were not chosen as leaders.

For present purposes, we can concentrate on the questions about work-related advice and social relations away from work. One way to analyze the data is simply to count how many times each of the nine workers was mentioned by her fellows—a kind of popularity poll. Although each person named four coworkers in response to each question, I will analyze just the first three choices.

Table 11.7 shows the number of times each person was chosen, in questions A and B, as well as her job title. You will notice immediately that the people others seek most often for work-related advice are not the same people they would like to socialize with away from work. Person H, the owner, is tied for first choice on advice, but nobody at all wants to spend social time with her away from work. In terms of nonwork social relations, the owner is a social isolate. But of course, she may operate in a social realm away from work very different from that of her employees.

Similarly, the manager, I, and agent D are not popular away from work, but they do get substantial votes as advice-giver. Agents A, E, and G do much better in their social life than in giving advice. This analysis reveals that agent B is a key individual at the travel agency. She is tied with the owner for first place in advice-giving, and she comes in second with respect to socializing.

Figure 11.2 is a pair of sociograms of the travel agency. At the top is one for social relations away from work; work-related advice is shown at

▶ ▶ ▶ ▶ ▶ ▶ ▶ ▶ ▶ ▶ ▶

TABLE 11.7   SOCIOMETRIC VOTES FOR TRAVEL AGENCY WORKERS

ID Letter	Job Title	Votes for Social Relations	Votes for Work Advice
A	agent	7	2
B	agent	6	6
C	agent	3	3
D	agent	1	4
E	agent	4	1
F	accountant	2	1
G	agent	3	0
H	owner	0	6
I	manager	1	4

the bottom. I put social relations at the top because this is the question I used to decide where to arrange the lettered squares representing the nine respondents. Sometimes it is useful to arrange the people as if they were in a graph, putting the most popular ones at the top, for example. But here I have simply tried to fit them so that the lines connecting them will be fairly clear.

You will notice that the social relations between individuals are represented by arrows of two kinds. Thick arrows, with arrowheads at both ends, connect those who chose each other as friends or advice-givers. Thin arrows represent a nonmutual, or nonreciprocated, choice. The person at the tail of the arrow has chosen the person the arrowhead points at, but this person has not returned the favor by mentioning the first person.

The heart of the top sociogram in Figure 11.2 is the triad of agents A, B, and C. Both A and B are very popular, and they like each other. They also like C, who reciprocates. Agents E, F, and G also fit into this social group. These six are all of the same work status, five agents and the accountant, and they form a clique. Nobody chooses H, the owner, for a friend. The only person who chooses I, the manager, is H. Agent D is chosen only by the manager.

The picture changes drastically when we look at work-related advice. B gets many choices as advice-giver, but none of the six reciprocal friendships in the top diagram are translated into reciprocal advice-giving relationships. That is, the six thick, double-headed arrows at the top are in completely different places from the ones at the bottom.

Such comparisons of sociograms on the same group can stimulate many questions about the social functioning of the work group under study. Of course the manager goes to the owner for advice. But why

▶ ▶ ▶ ▶ ▶ ▶ ▶ ▶ ▶ ▶ ▶

FIGURE 11.2   SOCIOGRAMS OF A TRAVEL AGENCY

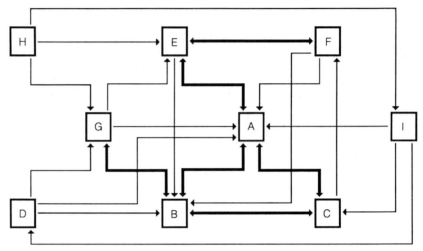

Social Relations Away from Work

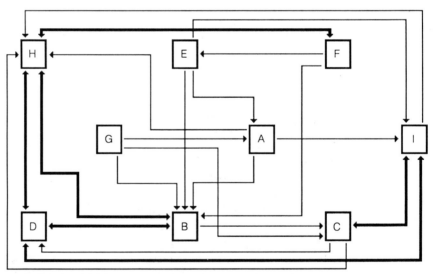

Work-Related Advice

doesn't the owner go to the manager for advice? Because of their jobs, it does make sense for the accountant and the owner to exchange advice. What is there about agent D that makes her so popular for giving advice, including to both manager and owner, but not popular for socializing? One possibility is that D might be older and more experienced than the others. And what does B have that makes her the queen bee among the agents, sought after for both advice and socializing?

Clearly, sociometric questions can be especially effective when combined with other types of information. You can easily bring in the linked-respondent form of analysis described earlier in this chapter. And sociometric analysis of a work group can stimulate the managers themselves to seek improvements in the social relations of the group. For example, agent D seems highly competent, but she is not chosen for socializing by the other agents. Does this mean that D needs some other, nonsocial kinds of rewards to motivate her to keep giving the travel agency her best effort? A valuable social isolate may deserve special positive attention to compensate for the lack of social rewards she receives. B deserves careful consideration as well, perhaps for promotion when a position becomes available, because she is so key in both sociograms. But it is also possible that management might find her influence a threat.

Sociometric questions such as these are really ranking items. Each respondent is supposed to rank the others in terms of advice or socializing. And this means that sociometric questions in this format have all the defects of ranking questions. The owner may not *want* to socialize with any of the employees of the travel agency. But we asked her to list employees she would like to spend time with outside of work, and she dutifully did so. Thus the thin, single-headed arrows that go from her to three others, in the top sociogram, may not represent plaintive, unrequited friendships but simply the best bad answers she could give us.

The fact is, the methodological problems with sociometric questions have not yet been fully solved. Despite great interest in this type of investigation since Moreno proposed it so long ago, there is widespread feeling that the potential value of sociometry has not yet been realized. True, nobody believes today that sociometry will save the world, as Moreno thought it might, but great opportunities clearly exist for extending this technique and for employing sociometric items in a variety of questionnaires.

▶ ▶ ▶ ▶ ▶ ▶ ▶ ▶ ▶ ▶ ▶

PROJECTS

1. Panel Study of an Election.   In an essay of four or five pages, explain step by step how you would do a panel survey of an election in your community. How would you prepare the questionnaires themselves? How would you get your sample of respondents, and how would you arrange to return to the same people for later waves of the survey? Finally, how would you combine several waves of such a survey in a single, final analysis?

Your essay should have a two-page appendix. One page should list the schedule of dates for all steps you would take in the project, including such events as drawing the sample and printing the questionnaires, as well as the dates of the survey waves. The other appendix page should be an inventory of the things you would need. Of course, this will include your printed questionnaires, but you would need many other things for your panel study, and you should think hard about what they might be.

2. Panel Study of Students Going Through College. Many studies have followed college students through their four years, documenting the changes in their attitudes and activities that take place. Design a study of your own, in a brief and imaginative sketch, that would examine changes in two or three student characteristics of interest to you. Of course, your survey might need several questions to evaluate each characteristic. For example, to evaluate the students' political orientation you would need questions about several aspects of politics. In a panel study, we generally avoid flash-in-the-pan issues that are hotly debated for a few weeks and then completely forgotten, unless they are the particular object of our research. Your essay should give some hint of the changes you think might take place over the course of the typical undergraduate career.

Note that students might not all change as a group, from wave to wave of the survey. For example, the course of political changes in college is particularly complex. It used to be thought that students usually got more politically liberal in college, because that was the result of some early, influential studies. But these studies were carried out at liberal colleges, and students at conservative colleges might become more conservative instead. Furthermore, in some ways students may split apart into groups, instead of being made more similar by the college experience. Whereas liberal students might become more liberal, conservative students might become more conservative. Students in each group would choose friends and classes that reinforced their existing political orientations. If you think something similar might happen for the student characteristics targeted by your survey, suggest how these phenomena could be examined with your panel of respondents.

3. Experiment on Stigmatization. Write a brief survey using experimental design to show how a criminal record or mental hospitalization might hurt a person's chances of getting a job. The survey should consist of four thumbnail sketches of people, in the form of recommendation letters written to help four different people get jobs. Each might be just two or three paragraphs long, and the four should describe individuals with somewhat different backgrounds. Imagine that these surveys will be mailed to small businesses that are hiring new employees, supposedly coming from an employment agency but really sent out as part of a scientific experiment. At the end of each of the four simulated recommendation letters should be this question: "Would you like us to send more information about this person, or would you like this person to call for an appointment for a job interview? [1] Have the person call for an appointment, [2] Please send more information, [3] No thank you, we are not interested in this job applicant."

Here is where the plot thickens. Write four sentences that would be inserted at random into the four simulated recommendation letters. One would say that the person had never been in trouble of any kind. The second would say that the person had been accused of a crime but was found innocent by a jury. The third would say that the person had been found guilty of a criminal offense but had paid his or her debt to society and really wanted to be a good citizen now. And the fourth would say that the person had spent several months in a mental hospital but had been well for a while and seemed perfectly normal at the present time.

If you were actually doing this study, you would make several versions of this four-page survey. Everything would be identical from one version to another, except which of the people had which extra sentences inserted. Thus the experiment would be to see how the stigmatizing sentences hurt the job applicant's chances. When psychologists do experiments like this, they often make the survey do double or triple duty. In addition to varying the stigmatizing sentences, they might simultaneously vary the sex of the applicant, the person's social class, and some other characteristic that might bias judgments about him or her.

But if you were actually to do a study like this, rather than merely to write items for one, you could run into serious trouble. Research like this was often done 30 years ago, but today most social scientists believe that to involve unsuspecting people in an experiment for which they did not volunteer is unethical. That is, we are no longer sure it is justified to trick employers into wasting their time on bogus job applications, or to inflict research on people without first getting the design of the study approved by a university committee on the use of human subjects in research. Thus field experiments—experiments done outside the laboratory on people who have not volunteered to do research—are rare today, even though they may offer the most valid scientific data on how people actually behave in the real world.

4. Replication of the Friendship–Religion Survey. From the hints given in this chapter, design a study to redo my linked-respondent survey of students that examined friendships and religion. How would you physically produce the questionnaires and distribute them? How can you most effectively convince pairs of friends to participate? How would you analyze the data when you got them?

Replication studies generally have two purposes. First, the new study can verify whether the results of the original study were correct or not. In some cases the original researcher committed a drastic error, and the research will fail to replicate. On rare occasions, the original researcher might even have been lying, and replication is one of the main ways we have of keeping scientists honest. The second goal of replication is to extend the scope of the research in a new direction. Most simply, you could add questions about other aspects of life that students might share with their friends. Or you could do a quick check of your campus to see what religious movements are currently active and frame questions about students' involvement in them. On a more advanced level, replication research can seek to test theories relevant to the topic that the original research had not included.

5. Linked-Respondent Survey Administered via Computer.

Create and administer a short survey on consumer preferences to pairs of friends. You can adjust this assignment to fit your environment, but let us imagine you are at a large college with a student center where pairs and groups of friends pass through during much of the day. As explained earlier in this chapter, you can use the question-processor program to create a linked-respondent survey with as many as 24 items. Then take a computer to your student center for a day or two, asking pairs of friends who are passing by to be respondents (larger groups can be split into pairs for your study).

If you take the academic preference questions from the STUDENTS dataset, I suspect you won't have interesting results. In my experience, hardly any concordance exists between friends in the academic subjects they like. But you should find significant concordances with simple consumer items, such as tobacco and diet soda. For most students, political attitudes may not show much concordance across friendships, but if you think your campus is especially politicized, they could be the topic of an interesting study.

Indeed, some of the most interesting research findings are the failures to find an expected correlation. You might expect that liberals have liberal friends and conservatives have conservative friends. But maybe this is not so. And if it is not, we shall have to rethink some of our social-scientific ideas about where people get their political orientations and how they act on their political beliefs. A serious study of friendships and politics should include items about a wide range of political issues. For example, there may be high concordances in areas of politics concerning lifestyles, because friends generally share lifestyles. But at the same time there might not be concordances on abstract issues. Why don't you find out?

6. Sociogram of a Group.

Select a group of 7 to 12 people who are all willing to be studied and give them a simple 2-question sociometric questionnaire. Then draw 2 sociograms illustrating results from each of the questions. The sociometric study of the 9 women in the travel agency can be a model for your work, but you do not have to follow it exactly. You might want 2 very different questions. And you probably don't have to use the somewhat confusing ID letter system I used to impress respondents with the fact that the data would be kept anonymous to prevent embarrassment and other potential harm. When I have had students do sociometric studies as part of my field research methods seminar, groups have been quite happy to write the actual names of fellow group members on the page.

The group you choose could be of many kinds—a work group, a friendship group, or even a sports team. One of my students did sociograms of two basketball teams, a winning team and a losing team. The losers turned out to have competing cliques in their sociogram, whereas the winners were more unified. If you are doing this project in a class, it might be good to develop your sociometric questions collectively, so that all your questionnaires are identical, and to survey groups of the same general kind so that comparisons can be most instructive.

12

▶ ▶ ▶ ▶ ▶ This chapter is primarily for advanced students and for faculty who want complete command over the resources of *Survey Research*. We shall mention a few more principles of scientific questionnaire research, but much of this chapter consists of instructions for manipulating information through the utility program, and thus it will not be of interest to all students or appropriate for all courses.

The utility program allows you to do several kinds of advanced work with surveys. Its main sections enable you to enter data conveniently from printed questionnaires. One part lets you make customized labels for variables in the statistical analysis programs. And another part transforms data so that they can be uploaded to a big computer or used in certain micro-computer programs other than those in *Survey Research*. The utility program begins with a main menu of six choices:

```
[1]    Create NEW SURVEY (labels, sounds, ranges)
[2]    Revise EXISTING SURVEY (labels, sounds,
       ranges)
[3]    Input DATA from a survey
[4]    Verify DATA from a survey
[5]    Change DATA from a survey
[6]    Prepare existing DATA for use outside SURVEY
       RESEARCH
[ESC]  QUIT or change programs
```

Except for the capacity to write labels for use in the statistical program, this utility program is intended for advanced students who have already absorbed the important information provided in earlier chapters and

The Utility Program

programs of *Survey Research*. Therefore, I shall begin with simple instructions on how to write labels. After that, I will cover the utilities for working with printed surveys.

▶ ▶ ▶ ▶ ▶ ▶ ▶ ▶ ▶ ▶ ▶

WRITING LABELS

The first two choices on the main menu let you make labels, short phrases, up to 25 letters long (counting spaces), that will appear in the statistical analysis programs and in the parts of this utility that let you input data from printed questionnaires. It is very important to pick the correct one of these choices, 1 or 2.

If you are just beginning to create a new survey, and *absolutely no files exist for this survey yet,* press [1]. This is *not* the case when you merely want to add labels to a dataset that already exists. This option is for the first step in preparing to input data from a printed questionnaire, which will be discussed in a subsequent section. If you select this choice by mistake, when the survey already exists, you may destroy it!

To add labels to an existing survey, press [2]. You will be asked for the name of the survey you want to work with. To write labels for use with the statistical programs, you must type in the name of the dataset you will be analyzing. If you are starting from scratch to input data from a fresh questionnaire, now is the time to decide on a name for this survey. As in earlier programs, the survey's name can be from two through eight letters or numbers long. Type in the name and press [ENTER].

If you had started with option 1, "Create NEW SURVEY (labels, sounds, ranges)," you would now get a stern warning to check what you are doing. If you had named your survey SURVEY, here is what you would see:

```
    BEWARE! You are about to create a NEW SURVEY.
 If one already exists named SURVEY, you will
                 DESTROY it.
        Are you sure you want to create a new SURVEY?
```

If you merely want to add labels to an existing dataset, press [N] for no, or press [ESC] to escape this dangerous situation. If you really do want to create a brand-new survey, however, then you can press [Y] for yes.

If you are creating a new survey, the computer will ask you how many items are in it. This is the exact number of questions (variables) the computer will be prepared to work with, and the number of labels you will be able to write. There can be as few as 1 item in the survey. The maximum number of items possible is 192. If you are adding labels to an existing dataset, the computer will already know the answer to this question, and thus will not ask it.

If you are planning to use the stat programs included in *Survey Research,* you must limit your survey to 48 items. That is the maximum number those programs can hold. But if you plan to transfer the data to a big computer or to some microcomputer program capable of using our raw data files, you can have as many as 192 items. For a new survey, type the number and press [ENTER]. Then you will get a short input format menu giving you the labels, sounds, and ranges options:

```
    [1]    Labels for survey items
    [2]    Sounds to mark pages and sections
    [3]    Set ranges of variables
    [4]    Save work on disk
    [5]    DANGEROUS: Change command file
    [ESC]  Return to MAIN MENU
```

The fifth option is, indeed, very dangerous. Do not use it unless you absolutely understand what it does. This is for very, very special advanced work, as explained at the end of this chapter and in the appendix.

Let's write labels for the XYZ survey. Your disk comes with one set of labels, but they merely identify the group each item is supposed to belong to: Theory X, Theory Y, Machiavellian, low Mach, American, or Japanese. Now I will explain how to create new labels, to identify each separate item clearly. If you want to actually try putting them into the computer, you should make a work disk for XYZ, as explained in the projects section of Chapter 1. To use the statistics programs efficiently, you need labels that will remind you what the items were about. I'm not going to do an ideal job of composing the labels themselves, because one of the projects at the end of this chapter asks you to accomplish that. Instead, we shall use my labels merely to illustrate how to control the program.

Using your XYZ work disk, start up the utility program and type in XYZ when the computer asks for the name of the survey. The computer will take a moment to check information about this survey already on its disk.

Then the menu permitting us to write Labels for survey items appears, and you press [1] to select the labelmaker. The screen clears, and 2 columns of numbers appear, surrounded with vertical bright bands, 1–24 and 25–40. These numbers represent the 40 items in the survey, and you will write the label to the right of the corresponding numbers. At the bottom of the screen are instructions: Type item's label, then press [ENTER]. Press [ESC] to end, [+] or [−] to move.

You should see the existing XYZ labels as well, starting in the upper left-hand corner. Opposite the number 1, at the upper left corner of the screen, is the first label: American. After it is a bright, flashing arrow. If you were creating a new set of labels for a survey of your own, American wouldn't be there; a double-headed arrow would be in its place. The arrow shows us where you can write the label for the first questionnaire item. If your new survey has 48 or fewer items, the arrow will be exactly 25 segments long (23 tiny squares between 2 arrowheads), permitting you to write a label with as many as 25 letters, numbers, or spaces.

To get rid of my American label, backspace a few times. Now you can see the full arrow. Try typing *Very First Item*. This phrase will appear in place of much of the arrow. To change the phrase to *Very First Question*, backspace a few times to get rid of *Item*, and type in *Question*. Backspace again and rewrite the phrase so it reads *Very First Item Goes Here*.

This phrase completely covers the arrow, and the arrow slithers down to flash beside number 2. Now you should backspace enough times to remove my Theory X. Type *Second Item* and press [ENTER]. The arrow hops down to number 3 in the column. Let's say you decide these phrases are not very good labels, and you want to change them. Backspace several times, and what you've written will be eaten away, letter by letter, until you are back where you started, with the complete arrow beside 1.

Now let's type in reasonable labels for the XYZ questions listed in Chapter 10. The first item in the survey says, "Decisions should generally be made by the individual person who is in the best position to have the right answers." This statement is said to be an expression of American management beliefs, in contrast with Japanese beliefs, and thus it is labeled A (for American). A key word in the statement is *individual*. So for your first label, type *A Individual* and press [ENTER]. For the second, type *X Lazy*, because the second statement in the list is a Theory X statement that people are lazy. *Note:* I am not asking you to type the numbers 1 and 2 here to identify items 1 and 2, because the analysis programs will supply them.

Please continue through the whole set of 40 items, eradicating my old

▶ ▶ ▶ ▶ ▶ ▶ ▶ ▶ ▶ ▶ ▶

TABLE 12.1   POSSIBLE VARIABLE LABELS FOR THE XYZ DATASET

[1]A Individual	[25]J Experience
[2]X Lazy	[26]1m Lying
[3]J Same	[27]1m Moral
[4]Y Responsibility	[28]A Promotions
[5]M Criminals	[29]A Success
[6]Y Hardworking	[30]Y Manager
[7]1m Good	[31]A Distance
[8]J Philosophy	[32]J Consensus
[9]1m Honesty	[33]A Organizations
[10]J Praise	[34]Y Honor
[11]M Forced	[35]Y Imagination
[12]X Coerced	[36]X Direct
[13]1m Right	[37]A Statistics
[14]Y Self=direction	[38]A Alone
[15]X Directed	[39]J Family
[16]J Together	[40]X Instructions
[17]A Skills	
[18]X Dislike	
[19]X Economic	
[20]M Useful	
[21]Y Goal setting	
[22]J Evaluation	
[23]M Flatter	
[24]M Vicious	

▶

labels and typing in the labels given in Table 12.1. I have arranged this list so that exactly the right numbers of labels are in the two columns, to fit what is on your labelmaker screen.

Errors are easy to fix. Of course, if you notice an error right away, you can erase it by backspacing. But perhaps you notice something that needs changing several labels back. You can move through the list without erasing anything by pressing [+] or [−] (the plus or minus keys). As in earlier programs, [+] moves you to a higher number, [−] moves you to a lower number. When you reach the label you want to change, you can backspace a few times to erase whatever is wrong and type in the correct label.

Note: It is not possible to use a minus or plus sign or a hyphen in one of these labels. This is because the minus and plus keys are being used to move up and down from item to item. Because the computer can't tell the difference between a minus and a hyphen, hyphens are not possible in these labels, either. You can use an equal sign instead, and the keyboard has several other symbols that work fine. Some of you will be aware that the computer has arrow keys to move you up and down in some software. A major defect of the traditional IBM design, however, is that these arrows get mixed up with the numbers on the keypad, and it is hard for people unfamiliar with IBMs to know when the arrow keys will actually produce arrows instead of numbers, so I avoid them in my educational software.

When all the labels are right, press [ESC] to escape the labelmaker. This returns you to a menu including [4] Save work on disk. Press [4], and your labels will be saved on your disk. When the computer is finished saving, the menu will reappear. Now you can press [ESC] to return to the main menu, where another [ESC] will bring you to the program menu.

If you decide to revise the labels, perhaps weeks after you originally wrote them, the utility program makes it easy. When the program starts up, press [2] to get Revise EXISTING SURVEY and type in the name of your survey. The computer will immediately load information from your disk. When the computer has all the information it needs from the disk, it will give you the menu including [1] Labels for survey items. Press [1] and your labels will leap into place, ready for you to revise them. Of course, after you've done any work like this, you have to save the new version of the labels on the disk. It will automatically replace the old version. This gives you all you need to know to add labels to existing datasets. The rest of this chapter is for the more advanced options.

▶ ▶ ▶ ▶ ▶ ▶ ▶ ▶ ▶ ▶ ▶

CODING A PRINTED QUESTIONNAIRE

Before entering survey data with this program, you must prepare the questionnaires. First, go through your questionnaires, count them, and number them, if they do not already have ID numbers on them. When you are inputting the data, these numbers will keep the questionnaires straight and prevent you from getting lost. After you have entered the data in the computer, you may need to look back and check one questionnaire, so ID numbers are essential.

If the questionnaires already have numbers on them, check whether those numbers are in sequence. For example, you might have numbered the questionnaires before administering them. In the process, many never got returned to you, and those that did may be completely out of order. Consider whether you want to renumber them at this point, or whether the original numbers have some significance.

When you enter data in the computer, each questionnaire is automatically assigned a sequential number, starting from 1 up to the total number of questionnaires you enter. If the questionnaires themselves are numbered in the same way, it is easy to find the one you want. If you want to preserve an old and irregular set of numbers, however, you can easily do so. Let the first variable in your list be ID Number, and type in the numbers on the surveys as if they were answers to questions.

The largest number you can type in for a single variable, in this program, is 999. So if all your ID numbers are 999 or smaller, you can set aside the first variable for ID and simply type the ID as the first datum from each questionnaire. If you have ID numbers going above 999, just set aside the first two variables for ID. Say you have IDs running up to 10,789. For the first variable, type the thousands part of the ID (10 in the case of 10,789), and for the second variable, type the rest of the ID (789).

Next, you have to create a **codebook,** a set of pages that will be your guide for entering and analyzing the data. Many professional surveys go so far as to print up an actual book, listing all the items in the survey and giving information about them. A well-known example is the codebook of the General Social Survey (Davis and Smith, 1986).

The easiest way to make a codebook, usually quite sufficient, is to use a blank copy of your questionnaire, writing information clearly next to the items. Then, if you want, you can make photocopies of it for coworkers and to give you a backup in case the original gets lost. We will go through the steps one at a time, and you can make whatever notes you find useful.

Examine all the items and decide whether they need codings written beside their responses in the codebook. Recoding was discussed in Chapter 6, and Chapter 9 gave advice on coding open-ended items, so the concept is already familiar to you. A coding or a code is the number you would type into the computer to represent each possible answer. Suppose a particular question has only two response choices, a box marked "true" followed by a box marked "false." You would write the number 1 next to the first box and 2 next to the second box. Thus whenever someone answered "true," you would press [1] on the computer. For "false," you would press [2].

You also need to allocate missing-values codes. A missing value is whenever a person fails to answer a question, or answers in a faulty way, such as checking both "true" and "false" boxes. Suppose a particular item has five response choices. Each of them is assigned a number, 1 through 5. The missing values need a number, too. One approach is simply to use the lowest number not already assigned to one of the responses, in this case the number 6. Whenever a person fails to answer this item, you would type in the number 6.

But perhaps the items in your questionnaire have many different numbers of response choices. Some have four valid choices, some five, and some six. In this case, you may want to assign the same number to missing values all the way through. Traditionally, the numbers 9, 99, and 999 are used for missing values, depending on how big the biggest valid response coding is. The statistical analysis programs on the *Survey Research* disk use 0. A standard missing-values code is easier to keep straight while you are doing your analysis. It reduces the error-catching ability of the range specifications we will explain later, however, and you should read the next section of this chapter before deciding.

You may want more than one missing-values code. For example, you could use the number 9 for cases where the person didn't respond at all, and the number 8 for cases where the person responded in an improper way, such as checking two boxes when only one was permitted.

Go through the codebook for your questionnaire, writing in the missing-values codes for each item. For example, a true–false question might look like this before coding:

[   ] True

[   ] False

And like this after coding:

1 [   ] True

2 [   ] False

3   Missing value

Professional survey researchers often use **precoded questionnaires,** which have small code numbers printed on every copy. In the old days, it guided the keypunch operators who banged away at noisy machines, punching holes in the cards that were the primary method of putting data into computers. Now that we can type the data directly into microcomputers or terminals connected to big computers, the cards are completely obsolete. I think precoding should be used much more selectively, now that the cards are gone. Anything on the questionnaire that might confuse the respondent or might bias responses must be avoided.

Today we can write clever programs, like the ones in our utility, to help us keep track of where we are in the input process and to immediately display what we type. If an item has more than five or six response choices, perhaps you should put numbers on the questionnaire. And, of course, some question formats use numbers anyway ("On a scale from 1 to 7, please circle the number . . .").

But for items that have few response choices, such as the typical five-box agree–disagree format, the data entry worker will be able to input numbers accurately, even if they are not printed on the questionnaire. With only five boxes printed across the page, for example, it is no problem at all to find the right key to press: [1] for the left-hand response, [2] for the next one, [3] for the middle one, [4] for the next one, and [5] for the right-hand one. In designing your own questionnaire, you should decide whether precoding is best for your particular project.

Open-ended items require significant coding work. Every response has to be turned into a number and written on the questionnaire itself. For example, if the respondents wrote in their month of birth, you have to turn every January into a 1, every February into a 2, and so on. You should write the appropriate number in a standard spot next to the question, using a bold or colored pencil so that it will stand out. If none of your respondents were born before the year 1900, for year of birth you can simply write the last two digits—for example, 40 for 1940. These items are easy because the set of possible responses is limited. Much more trouble can be caused by open-ended questions about birthplace, occupation, religious affiliation, and the like.

Obviously, there is not room for dozens of little messages next to one item of a questionnaire. For open-ended questions, you will want to write out full codings on separate pages, to be included with the marked-up copy of your questionnaire to comprise the codebook. But you should write the range of numbers assigned to an open-ended question next to it. For example, if you happened to have my cause-of-insanity question, described in Chapter 9, and you found 283 different responses, you would write *1–283* next to this item in your codebook, and staple in the pages listing the 283 different causes.

Finally, you should mark places in the survey where it would be useful for the computer to make a little sound—a beep or a buzz or a siren. These sounds can help the data entry workers keep track of where they are. Of course, my input program is designed to make it very easy to spot where you are, simply by glancing at the screen. But you can enter data much more quickly if you don't have to look at the screen. And I have added a sound-generating feature to save you this trouble.

Almost certainly, you will want the computer to make a distinctive sound at the bottom of each page. But you might want a different sound at the end of each section that is not at the bottom of a page. So you might write *SOUND A* at the bottom of each page, and *SOUND B* at the ends of sections that conclude in mid-page. It is possible to have yet a third sound at some other important place that you could mark, *SOUND C*.

If you want a very pretty codebook—for example, one that you can give to a business client or research sponsor—you can make a special version of the questionnaire with all the codings typed in neatly. This is especially easy to do if the original questionnaire was created on a word processor. You can follow your own imagination, and the practical features of your research, in adding to this basic codebook any other information that might be useful later on. After doing some preliminary analysis of your data, you might want to make a new edition of your codebook, indicating the numbers of respondents who gave each answer. Now you are ready to set up a data entry program, using your codebook as a guide.

▶ ▶ ▶ ▶ ▶ ▶ ▶ ▶ ▶ ▶ ▶

LABELS, SOUNDS, AND RANGES FOR A NEW SURVEY

To prepare the utility program for a new survey, begin from the main menu by pressing [1] for `Create NEW SURVEY (labels, sounds, ranges)`. You will be asked for the name of the survey and, as usual, you should type in a name from two through eight letters long, making sure you don't use the name of an existing dataset, lest you obliterate it. Then the computer will remind you of the consequences of using the name of an existing dataset and ask whether you are sure you want to use the name you just typed. If you are sure you do, press [Y] for yes.

Then the computer will ask `How many items are in the ------ survey?` The maximum number of items that the statistics modules of *Survey Research* can handle is 48, but you can work with as many as 192 if you plan merely to transfer the data to a big computer or to other micro-computer programs.

This brings you to the input format menu. I suggest you prepare the format for data input in the order given in the menu: labels, sounds, and ranges.

Labels

You will want a very different kind of label for data entry than for identifying variables as in our XYZ example. For the statistics programs, you need labels that really express what the variables mean. But for data entry, the labels should quickly tell you where you are in the survey.

Suppose your survey has 60 items, numbered consecutively from 1. And suppose further that the items are divided into 5 equal sections of 12 each, named A, B, C, D, and E. I suggest you give the first item a label that says ⟨1=====A=====. Starting with an arrowhead pointing left is an effective way to visually separate the label from the data you will be typing in. Then comes the item number, exactly as printed on the questionnaire. Because this item starts section A of the questionnaire, you can add =====A=====.

The second item should have a very simple label, to contrast with the section opener, and I suggest ⟨2. When you get to item 13, in this imaginary survey of 60 items, you will have to make a new banner to mark the beginning of the second section: ⟨13=====B=====. Continue like this until the end, and you will have a set of labels like those shown in Table 12.2.

Of course, your questionnaire may have very different sections from this. Imagine another survey of 60 items in which the numbering starts over from 1 at the beginning of each section. Let's say this survey has 7 sections of 10, 12, 5, 15, 4, 6, and 8 items. The labels would look like those in Table 12.3.

▶ ▶ ▶ ▶ ▶   ▶ ▶ ▶ ▶ ▶ ▶

TABLE 12.2   A 60-ITEM SURVEY IN THE LABELMAKER

[1]<1=====A=====	[25]<25=====C=====	[49]<49=====E=====
[2]<2	[26]<26	[50]<50
[3]<3	[27]<27	[51]<51
[4]<4	[28]<28	[52]<52
[5]<5	[29]<29	[53]<53
[6]<6	[30]<30	[54]<54
[7]<7	[31]<31	[55]<55
[8]<8	[32]<32	[56]<56
[9]<9	[33]<33	[57]<57
[10]<10	[34]<34	[58]<58
[11]<11	[35]<35	[59]<59
[12]<12	[36]<36	[60]<60
[13]<13=====B=====	[37]<37=====D=====	
[14]<14	[38]<38	
[15]<15	[39]<39	
[16]<16	[40]<40	
[17]<17	[41]<41	
[18]<18	[42]<42	
[19]<19	[43]<43	
[20]<20	[44]<44	
[21]<21	[45]<45	
[22]<22	[46]<46	
[23]<23	[47]<47	
[24]<24	[48]<48	

▶

If you have a very large number of items, such as the maximum of 192, you will not have room for very long labels. To fit 192 labels on the screen, I had to limit them to 7 letters or symbols in length. But even at this brevity, a prominent banner is possible—for example: ⟨13===B.

When the labels are just the way you want them, press [ESC] to get back to the input format menu. You may want to press [4] at this point, to save your work on labels. In a moment, the menu will return. Then press [2] to get Sounds to mark pages and sections.

Sounds

In a moment, you will see what looks like the labelmaker, except that the flashing double-headed arrow beside the first item has been replaced by a series of musical notes. The instruction at the bottom left corner of the

▶ ▶ ▶ ▶ ▶ ▶ ▶ ▶ ▶ ▶ ▶

TABLE 12.3　　　A 7-SECTION, 60-ITEM SURVEY IN THE LABELMAKER

[1]‹1=====A=====	[25]‹3	[49]‹3
[2]‹2	[26]‹4	[50]‹4
[3]‹3	[27]‹5	[51]‹5
[4]‹4	[28]‹1=====D=====	[52]‹6
[5]‹5	[29]‹2	[53]‹1=====G=====
[6]‹6	[30]‹3	[54]‹2
[7]‹7	[31]‹4	[55]‹3
[8]‹8	[32]‹5	[56]‹4
[9]‹9	[33]‹6	[57]‹5
[10]‹10	[34]‹7	[58]‹6
[11]‹1=====B=====	[35]‹8	[59]‹7
[12]‹2	[36]‹9	[60]‹8
[13]‹3	[37]‹10	
[14]‹4	[38]‹11	
[15]‹5	[39]‹12	
[16]‹6	[40]‹13	
[17]‹7	[41]‹14	
[18]‹8	[42]‹15	
[19]‹9	[43]‹1=====E=====	
[20]‹10	[44]‹2	
[21]‹11	[45]‹3	
[22]‹12	[46]‹4	
[23]‹1=====C=====	[47]‹1=====F=====	
[24]‹2	[48]‹2	

▶

screen says `Press 1-9 for sound & [ENTER].` This, in abbreviated form, is what you do to set a sound to happen right after the particular item is input.

To check this out, try pressing [1]. The computer will emit a beep, and the first two pairs of musical notes will be replaced by ‹‹1››. This means that sound number 1 has been set to happen right after data on the first item have been typed into the computer.

Several other sounds could be set at this point. Try pressing the other number keys, [2] through [9], waiting after each one until the sound it causes has stopped. Notice that the number inside the double arrowheads next to the first item changes to identify the key you just pressed. When you press the zero key, the arrows disappear, and the full set of flashing notes reappears. This means that no sound is set to happen after that item.

Suppose we were working with the hypothetical questionnaire of 60

▶ ▶ ▶ ▶ ▶ ▶ ▶ ▶ ▶ ▶ ▶

TABLE 12.4   A 7-SECTION, 60-ITEM SURVEY IN THE SOUNDMAKER

[1]	[25]	[49]
[2]	[26]	[50]
[3]	[27]<<7>>	[51]
[4]	[28]	[52]<<7>>
[5]	[29]	[53]
[6]	[30]<<9>>	[54]
[7]	[31]	[55]
[8]	[32]	[56]
[9]	[33]	[57]
[10]<<7>>	[34]	[58]
[11]	[35]	[59]
[12]	[36]	[60]<<1>>
[13]	[37]	
[14]	[38]	
[15]<<9>>	[39]	
[16]	[40]	
[17]	[41]	
[18]	[42]<<7>>	
[19]	[43]	
[20]	[44]	
[21]	[45]<<9>>	
[22]<<7>>	[46]<<7>>	
[23]	[47]	
[24]	[48]	

▶

items with 7 sections of unequal length, for which we just created labels. Let's say you were able to get exactly 15 items on each page. Table 12.4 shows how the soundmaker should look to give a siren at the end of each page, a buzz at the end of each section, and a beep at the very end of the survey.

Again, when you are actually typing in data, using other parts of this utility program, these sounds will come after the item they are marked against. For these sounds to be useful, they should be rare. True, you can compose a veritable symphony of them to pour out as you enter data. But such a barrage of electronic music would not help you find your way through the questionnaire.

You may want to avoid sound ⟨⟨1⟩⟩, because it is the same sound most computers make when they respond to a typing error. The other sounds come in pairs, different only in duration. For example, ⟨⟨2⟩⟩ and ⟨⟨3⟩⟩ are the same soft buzz, but ⟨⟨3⟩⟩ is longer than ⟨⟨2⟩⟩. You probably want to use the shorter sound, to avoid excessive noise pollution. On some computers, however, ⟨⟨2⟩⟩ may be lost in the sound made by pressing the key, and you would choose ⟨⟨3⟩⟩ instead. Computers will vary in the sounds they produce, so you should pick the sounds that communicate clearly to you without being irritating.

As with the labelmaker, you can move forward and backward through the soundmaker's items with [+] and [−]. When you have finished setting the sounds, press [ESC] to return to the input format menu, where you can press [4] to save your work and press [3] to set the ranges of variables.

Ranges

The *range* of a variable is the set of values it can take. For example, there are 12 months of the year. If we express them as numbers, 1 through 12, the range of the months variable is 1–12. If the oldest person on Earth is 120 (I am guessing), and babies are 0 years old when born, the range of the age variable is 0–120. If an agree–disagree variable has 5 choices, and you number them 1 through 5, then its range is 1–5. The first number in a range is always the low number, then comes a hyphen and the high number.

You must take account of any missing-values coding you have done back when you created your codebook, however. Consider the months variable. If you decided to write *13* next to the months question when the respondent had failed to answer, thus letting 13 equal missing values, then the range for months would be 1–13. But if you decided to write *99* instead, letting 99 represent missing values, then the range would be 1–99.

When you create your codebook, you probably won't know how old the oldest person is. If you decided the missing-values code for age would be 999, then the range for age is 1–999, even though nobody 500 or even 200 years old ever shows up. Depending on what you decided, the agree–disagree item might have a missing-values code of 6 or 9, and the range would be 1–6 or 1–9.

The important point about setting the range is that the computer absolutely will not accept a number outside the stated range. Suppose you set the range for age at 1–99, intending 99 to represent missing values. Then while you were entering the data, you found somebody who was 120 years old. The computer would refuse to believe it. That is, when you tried to type 120, it would beep and reject the number.

This sounds inconvenient, if not downright stupid. Actually, it is a good system that can help prevent some errors. Suppose the range for agree–disagree questions is 1–6, with 6 being the missing-values code. While you are rapidly typing away, your finger hits the [7] by mistake. Because 7 is outside the stated range, the computer will refuse to take this error, and you will be warned to press the correct key.

A second function the range serves is handling numbers of one, two, or three digits. When you are entering data and the range covers only one-digit numbers, you simply press the correct number key for the data. For example, if the responses for three questions were 2, 4, and 6, you would press [2], [4], and [6]. But with two-digit and three-digit numbers, you have to press [ENTER] after each response. To enter the number 17, you must press [1][7][ENTER]. And to enter three numbers, 17, 19, and 150, you would type [1][7][ENTER][1][9][ENTER][1][5][0][ENTER].

The reason you need to press [ENTER] after entering a two-digit or three-digit datum is that the computer needs to know you have completed typing for that particular item. "How old were you when you first rode in an airplane?" If I were answering the question for myself, I would type [1][6][ENTER], because I was 16 years old. If my eldest son were answering the question, he would type [1][ENTER], because he was only 1 year old when he first flew. His answer is only one digit, but the computer doesn't know that until he presses [ENTER]. The range of the variable has to include both his one-digit age and my two-digit age, and after only one digit has been typed, the computer doesn't know whether the full answer has been given yet. It needs [ENTER] to tell it.

You might want to press [ENTER] after entering each response, especially if the questionnaire has a mixture of one-digit and two-digit responses, to establish a uniform habit in working. You can arrange this easily, by setting the range for one-digit questions to include a two-digit number. If you have an agree–disagree item with an actual range of 1–6, you could set the range as 1–10.

If you plan to use the statistical programs on the *Survey Research* disk, you must limit the range to one-digit numbers. Remember, our statistics programs use 0 for the missing-values code, and it cannot handle values greater than 9. So the maximum range is 0–9 for the analysis programs that come with this book. The range can be as wide as 0–999 if you plan to transfer your data to a big computer system or an appropriate other set of software for the IBM-style microcomputer you are using.

When the rangemaker appears on the screen, it looks very much like the labelmaker and soundmaker, except that each item's number has 0–9 after it. This means that the computer starts with the assumption that all the ranges are 0 through 9. Furthermore, any new ranges you give it will be of the same form: two numbers separated by a hyphen, with the first number lower than the second.

Note: Controlling the rangemaker is a little more complex than controlling the labelmaker or the soundmaker. This is true because the ranges have to make sense. We can't have you specifying crazy ranges like 9–0 or 10–20–30. Consequently, we can't have you type just part of a range before hopping off to a different item. When you are in the midst of typing a range, you cannot use [−], [+] or [ENTER] to move around on the screen. This is good, also, because the computer can't tell a hyphen from a minus sign, and we want you to be able to put hyphens in the ranges, rather than move the cursor when you press [−]. You are permitted to use [ESC] at any time.

Down in the lower left corner of the screen is a brief instruction of how you should type in ranges `low#, hyphen, high#, [ENTER]`. And this is how you do it. First, backspace enough times to remove the 0–9 range for the item. Then type the bottom number specifying the range. This could be 0, 1, or any number up into the hundreds. It is a little hard to imagine variables where the low end of the range is a high number, but I can think of one example. If you have some very old people in your sample and ask year of birth, a few might give years in the 19th century. To cover people born from 1880 through 1999, you could make the range 880–999, and enter the three right-hand digits of the birth year for each respondent.

After the number specifying the bottom of the range, type a hyphen. You can use the minus-sign key, if you want. It won't move you to another item, as explained above. Then type the high end of the range. If you make a mistake, you can backspace, as usual.

Do be careful in typing the ranges, because the instructions are more complicated than with labels and sounds. And don't get angry when the computer refuses to let you leave an item until its range is properly specified. The computer and I are just trying to spare you big problems later on.

To see how a complete set of ranges might look, we can return to our hypothetical survey and imagine what its seven sections are actually like, as suggested by Table 12.5. The first ten items are shown with their original ranges, 0–9. The next section, items 11 through 22, have ranges of 1–6, as five-response agree–disagree questions might if you assigned the number 6 to missing values.

The third section, items 23 through 27, has the largest possible range, 0–999, and you can imagine these are specially coded questions that have many different possible answers, on topics like birthplace or occupation. The next set, items 28 through 42, has about the narrowest possible range, 1–3. Perhaps these are true–false items, with 1 = true, 2 = false, and the number 3 assigned to missing values. The computer will let you set a range as narrow as 1–2, but if you give your respondents two choices, the minimum number, and have to assign a number to missing values, the smallest range will include three numbers.

The fifth section, items 43 through 46, has the widest range again, 0–999. The sixth section has 0–7. These could be preference questions. "On a scale from 0 (do not like) to 6 (like very much), how much do you like fish?" Some people will slip past this fish scale without answering, and the number 7 would be assigned to their missing answers, giving a 0–7 range. Or, as in our programs, the preference scale could run 1–7, with 0 reserved for missing data. Finally, the last section of items shows a variety of ranges.

When the ranges are properly set, you can press [ESC] to get the

▶ ▶ ▶ ▶ ▶ ▶ ▶ ▶ ▶ ▶ ▶

TABLE 12.5   A 7-SECTION, 60-ITEM SURVEY IN THE RANGEMAKER

[1]0-9	[25]0-999	[49]0-7
[2]0-9	[26]0-999	[50]0-7
[3]0-9	[27]0-999	[51]0-7
[4]0-9	[28]1-3	[52]0-7
[5]0-9	[29]1-3	[53]1-4
[6]0-9	[30]1-3	[54]1-5
[7]0-9	[31]1-3	[55]1-3
[8]0-9	[32]1-3	[56]1-6
[9]0-9	[33]1-3	[57]1-4
[10]0-9	[34]1-3	[58]1-3
[11]1-6	[35]1-3	[59]1-7
[12]1-6	[36]1-3	[60]1-12
[13]1-6	[37]1-3	
[14]1-6	[38]1-3	
[15]1-6	[39]1-3	
[16]1-6	[40]1-3	
[17]1-6	[41]1-3	
[18]1-6	[42]1-3	
[19]1-6	[43]0-999	
[20]1-6	[44]0-999	
[21]1-6	[45]0-999	
[22]1-6	[46]0-999	
[23]0-999	[47]0-7	
[24]0-999	[48]0-7	

input format menu, where you should select the fourth choice, "Save work on disk."

▶ ▶ ▶ ▶ ▶ ▶ ▶ ▶ ▶ ▶ ▶

INPUTTING DATA

You can input data from a questionnaire, either for use by the *Survey Research* statistics programs or for uploading to a big computer, using this part of the utility program. Indeed, you may find that some other set of data, having nothing to do with questionnaires, can also be entered conveniently.

Before you can use this utility to input data, you must create a set of labels for the items in your survey, as described earlier in this chapter, and it is useful also to set sounds and specify ranges.

To input data, get the main menu of the utility program and press [3] to select Input DATA from a survey. The computer will ask for the name of the survey, and you should type it in. Next, the computer will call up some information from the disk, including the labels, and the screen will fill with the input setup.

You will see your labels, positioned on the screen exactly as they were in the labelmaker. But instead of the bright columns of item numbers, you will see a string of zeros, one just to the left of each label. As you enter data, each zero will be replaced by numbers you type in.

At the very bottom of the screen, in the center, is Work: followed by the name of the survey you are working on. To the right of this, at the bottom, is Case: 1, signifying that you are going to start with the questionnaire filled out by the first of your respondents.

The very first zero, in the upper left corner of the screen beside the first label, is flashing. This means that the computer is ready for you to type in the response case 1 gave to the first question. You can practice, typing in various numbers to see what happens. Or type in the actual data, pressing [ENTER] if necessary after answers to questions with two-digit or three-digit ranges.

As you enter each datum, it will appear in a bright box to the left of its label, and the zero for the next item will begin flashing. If you have set sounds to happen at certain points in the questionnaire, you should hear them right after you enter the appropriate datum. If you try to enter a number outside the range you set for the particular item, the computer will beep and refuse it.

To return to an item after you have already entered it, press [−] or backspace. The bright column of already entered data will remain, but a single datum will flash to show you where you are. If you want to revise a datum, simply type the correct numbers. There is no need to backspace to erase bad data. To move forward again through the list of items, press [+] or [ENTER]. The last datum in the bright column will show you where you were before you began moving up the list of items.

When your questionnaire contains a mixture of one-digit, two-digit, and three-digit codings, it may take a little while to get used to the pattern of typing you have to follow. But the questionnaire itself—the one you are taking data from, not the codebook—should be a sufficient guide for you. If not, you might consider revising the labels slightly, in whatever way would be useful to you, to make the work go smoothly. For example, if there is a three-digit item that you tend to stumble over because all the others around it are one-digit, you could mark it with III to indicate three digits. Or you could put EN in the label for any items that require you to press [ENTER]. You should keep a copy of the codebook handy, for times when you might need to remind yourself what the ranges are. But my own experience has been that after a few minutes of data entry, you will be comfortable working just from the questionnaire itself.

Sometimes you will get lost. The phone will ring. Or you will sneeze. Or your attention will drift out the window. To find your place, glance at the computer screen. The data you have already entered will be displayed in bright bands, and all you have to do is look to the end of the bands.

If you have set sounds to happen after the last item on each page, I suggest you pause slightly in typing that last datum, to make sure the sound doesn't come too early and to prepare yourself in case it doesn't come at all. Occasionally, when you are rapidly entering data, you will skip a datum by mistake, or some extra mark the respondent put on the page will trick you into pressing an extra number key. Then you will be out of place when you reach the bottom of the page.

You can easily check your work by comparing the data on the screen with the data on the questionnaire. It will take just a few minutes to find where you started entering wrong data. Then you can use [BACKSPACE] or [−] to get back to that point and re-enter the data correctly. You may find, however, that the most efficient way of handling errors is to go back to the beginning of the page and enter the whole page again, regardless of where the error occurred.

After you enter the last datum from a questionnaire, Press [EN-TER] will appear in the lower right corner of the screen. Pressing [ENTER] tells the computer to clean away the data you just entered and prepare for the next case. You can still go back and change data, however, by pressing [−] or [BACKSPACE].

When the data for a case have been entered, and you press [ENTER] to go on to the next case, the screen will again look as it did before you entered any data, except that the number of the new case will be displayed after Case: at the bottom of the screen. Enter data from the questionnaire identified by this case number, and continue until you have typed in the first 25 cases.

After 25 cases, the computer will ask whether you want to save the data you have just been working with. Unless you have been merely practicing data entry, your answer must be [Y] for yes!

You can escape from data entry at any time by pressing [ESC]. If you are in the midst of a case, however, a message will flash in the lower right corner of the screen: ESCAPE? ⟨Y⟩es ⟨N⟩o. This double-checks whether you really want to escape or pressed the key by mistake. To complete your escape, press [Y]. Or press [N] and the escape message will vanish, leaving you right where you were.

▶ ▶ ▶ ▶ ▶ ▶ ▶ ▶ ▶ ▶ ▶

VERIFYING DATA

The data verification option is a standard job in professional data entry. Essentially, it has you enter the data again from the beginning, and it checks to make sure you type exactly the same numbers as you did the first time. This step doubles your data-entry work, but it assures you the data will be correct. It is far more efficient and pleasant than checking the data visually, looking back and forth between the questionnaire and the computer screen, an agonizing task that produces monumental eyestrain.

To verify, go to the main menu and press [4] to get Verify DATA from a survey. The computer will ask you for the name of the survey and will then call up some data about the survey from the disk. If you have not already entered data on any cases, the computer will announce No data yet, so we can't verify.

Suppose you previously entered data on 83 cases. Then the computer will say 83 cases exist. Which should we start with? Type a number from 1 through 83 and press [ENTER]. When you are just starting to verify, you should start with case number 1, thus pressing [1] and [ENTER]. This will let you verify cases 1–25. Repeat the procedure for each bunch of 25 cases, always starting with the lowest-numbered case in the bunch: 1, 26, 51, 76, 101, 126, 151, or 176. You can start with any case that already has been entered, but I think it is wise to verify a whole bunch of 25 at a time.

The verification screen is similar to the one for original data entry. However, the data you already entered will be displayed, instead of zeros. Also, as you type in data, you will find that no sounds you had set will happen. Instead, whenever you enter a datum different from the one in the existing data file, the computer will beep at you and flash a bright rectangle beside the label for the incorrect datum. Then you should very carefully enter the correct datum, and continue on verifying other items.

Suppose the first five variables for case number 1 were originally entered as 11, 12, 99, 14, 15. But in verification mode, you type in 11, 12, 13, 14, 15. The computer will beep after you enter 13. A bright rectangle will flash where 13 had been on the screen, to the left of the third item's label. At this point, you would look carefully at the questionnaire and see what the right answer was. Then enter it carefully. Now the next item is ready to be verified, and you can go quickly through the rest of the questionnaire, stopping to check your work carefully only when the computer beeps.

When you finish a bunch of cases, and save your new data on the disk, the original file that contained an error will be replaced by a corrected file.

► ► ► ► ► ► ► ► ► ► ►

CHANGING DATA

To inspect your data, and to change them in a very flexible format, go to the main menu and press [5] for Change DATA from a survey. As with the verification mode, you will be asked for the name of the survey and for which case you want to begin with. At this point, select whichever case you want to see.

Again, the screen will fill with your item labels, and the data columns will fill with the actual data you had already entered. The first datum will flash, indicating that it is ready to be changed. If you want to change it, just enter the datum you want. As you do down the list of items, data you have passed or re-entered will be displayed in a bright column, just as with original data entry.

Unless you hit some totally wrong keys, either odd letters or numbers outside the given item's range, the computer will remain silent. There will be no verification beeps, and the sounds you originally set for data entry will not happen, either. The "Change DATA" option is for checking data visually and for making very selective changes, and I found that these purposes are best served by a silent computer.

As usual, you should save your work on the disk, and any changes you made to the data will now enter the dataset. Of course, you can always go back and make new changes. And if you have merely looked over the data without changing any of them, there is no need to save your work. Indeed, it's probably a good idea to avoid the one chance in a hundred that the computer will stumble and ruin your data, and not save the file again, if you have done no work on it.

► ► ► ► ► ► ► ► ► ► ►

PREPARING DATA FOR OUTSIDE USE

The sixth option on the utility main menu, Prepare existing DATA for use outside SURVEY RESEARCH, is a really advanced option for people who want to use the data from *Survey Research* with certain other software packages.

Suppose you have been working in *Survey Research* with a set of data and want to try a statistical procedure that doesn't exist in our programs— for example, factor analysis. You can use this option to transform the data so that they can be used in major statistical packages. Here, I will explain how to produce a set of "upload files" on a disk in your microcomputer. You will have to figure out how to transfer those files to a big computer. Some microcomputer programs may be able to use the data in this form, as well, but I will make no promises about which ones—you'll have to experiment.

You should read the appendix to learn the basic facts about the data files on the *Survey Research* disk. If your survey is called SURVEY, they will be named SURVEY.D1, SURVEY.D2, SURVEY.D3, and so on. Each file contains data on a maximum of 25 cases. Therefore, if you have 200 respondents, there will be 8 such files.

The outside-use part of the utility program produces a matched set of files named, for example, SURVEY.U1, SURVEY.U2, SURVEY.U3. Notice that the names are the same as those for your original data, except that the D (for data) after the period in the name is replaced with U (for upload). SURVEY.U1 contains the same data as SURVEY.D1, except that they are in a form much easier for big computers to use.

To get this option, go to the main menu and press [6]. The computer will ask for the name of the survey (let's say you type in SURVEY) and load some basic information about it from the disk. The computer will go to work, displaying messages on the screen telling you which file it is loading or saving at the moment. Assuming there are no problems, it won't stop until it has finished the job and returned you to the main menu. It saves the upload files automatically, and you can ignore the computer for a few minutes as the file preparation is going on.

Information on how to transfer the upload files to another computer will have to come from a local computer consultant or from manuals accompanying your computer equipment and other software. But I need to tell you the form the data will be in.

Again, there is a 25-case file for each bunch of 25 respondents you have. Each file can be conceived of as containing a number of 80-character lines of data, a few lines for each case.

If you want to look at one of these files, using your IBM-type personal computer, quit *Survey Research* and use the DOS command TYPE. I assume, if you are working with an advanced program like this, that you have some familiarity with your computer's disk-operating system. If not, consult your DOS manual. The TYPE command is so simple, however, you can't go far wrong just giving it a try. You will not need your DOS disk if you have already started your machine. When the computer is ready for a DOS command, the screen will show a prompt like this: A⟩__ with the horizontal line flashing. Type TYPE followed by a space and then the full name of the file you want to inspect.

Suppose the file is called SURVEY.U1. In DOS, you can inspect the file by typing TYPE SURVEY.U1 and pressing [ENTER]. The computer will call the file up from the disk and begin displaying it on the screen. If you want to stop the action and look closely, hold down [CTRL] (the control key) and press [BREAK]. Check your computer's manual to find these keys or their equivalent on your machine.

Each 80-character line of data from an upload file contains 20 num-

▶ ▶ ▶ ▶ ▶ ▶ ▶ ▶ ▶ ▶ ▶

TABLE 12.6   EXAMPLE OF CASE 14 FROM AN UPLOAD FILE

14	1	1	2	3	4	5	6	7	8	9	10	11	12	13	14	15	16	17	18
14	2	19	20	21	22	23	24	25	26	27	28	29	30	31	32	33	34	35	36
14	3	37	38	39	40	41	42	43	44	45	46	47	48	49	50	51	52	53	54
14	4	55	56	57	58	59	60	0	0	0	0	0	0	0	0	0	0	0	0

bers, each taking up 4 characters. The number itself is from 1 to 3 digits long, preceded by 1 or more spaces. The first number on each line is always the case number, and the second number is always the number of the line within that case. The remaining 18 numbers on each line are the actual data. The third number in the first line is the datum for item 1. The twentieth number is the datum for item 18. The third number in the second line is the datum for item 19, and so on.

Table 12.6 shows what a case might look like with 60 items. To make the picture especially clear, I have made each datum be simply the item number. We are looking at case number 14.

Notice that the first number in each row is 14, identifying the case we are working on, respondent number 14. The second numbers count the rows, from 1 through 4. The rest are the data, here consecutive numbers from 1 to 60, counting our items. After the last item, the 60 in row 4, the line is filled out with zeros. This information should be sufficient to upload the data and use them in large statistical packages.

In case the upload files are not exactly right for your purposes, I will now tell you how to access the original data files through microcomputer programs you might write yourself. Programmers, who are the only users who can take advantage of this information, will find it quite simple. Although I assume you are writing in BASIC, it is easy enough to create versions in any other popular language. For data files produced by the question-processor program, start with the following array definition: DIM D% (48,24). If you are working with files having more than 48 variables, created with the advanced program described in this chapter, substitute: DIM D% (192,24). At an appropriate point in your program, set the string F$ equal to the full name of the file you want to access, including the period and extension, and let N equal the number of variables in the survey. Then include lines like the following:

```
OPEN F$ FOR INPUT AS #1
FOR V = 1 TO N
FOR C = 0 TO 24
INPUT #1 ,D%(V,C)
NEXT C ,V
CLOSE #1
```

The data will load into the array, with D%(V,C) containing variable V for case C, numbering the 25 cases in the file from 0 to 24. The rest of your program can either be designed to put the data in a form suitable for other software or analyze the data directly.

▶ ▶ ▶ ▶ ▶ ▶ ▶ ▶ ▶ ▶ ▶

CHANGING THE COMMAND FILE

This option is for advanced users only, and you should first become familiar with the various files on the *Survey Research* disk, as explained in the appendix. The command file on a work disk has a name like STUDENTS. KEY or XYZ.KEY. It contains information about all the other files for the given dataset, information that the programs need so that they will know which files to load from the disk. When you change the command file, you alter the information saved in the file with KEY in its name.

This is very dangerous. The programs themselves are constantly changing this file. If you change the file so that it thinks a particular file exists, when it really doesn't, the computer may get into awful trouble when it looks for that file. At the very least, it will complain to you.

Also, the KEY file tells the programs how many items are in the survey and how many people have responded to it. For example, the STUDENTS dataset has 40 items and 200 respondents. Thus STUDENTS.KEY has the numbers 40 and 200 in appropriate places for the programs to find them. If you alter the number of items, the computer may go quite crazy. The program probably will crash, and you will have to start the software over again.

It is possible, however, that advanced users will have a legitimate reason for changing the data in the command file. Two of the projects at the end of this chapter require this, for example, and other reasons are suggested in the appendix. But ordinary student use of *Survey Research* does not require changing anything in the KEY command file; the programs themselves take care of this.

To change the command file, start up the utility program. Select the second option on the main menu, to revise an existing survey. With luck, you need merely type in the name of the survey, and the computer will load the information in the KEY file. If you are struggling to save the disk from some error that has occurred, however, it is possible that the computer will balk at loading the file. For example, the KEY file itself may have been erased from your disk, or the computer could expect to find a labels file that has been removed. If the situation is as bad as this, do not despair. You can select the first option on the main menu, to create a new survey, and make a new KEY file with the appropriate information in it. But be very careful not to go into the labelmaker, the soundmaker, or the rangemaker, because the computer will think you are revising them and will clobber any existing label, sound, or range files when you save your work. Again, it is best to make a backup copy of a disk before trying anything dangerous!

If your situation is not so desperate, an existing KEY file will load easily into the computer when you tell the machine you want to revise a survey. When the revision menu comes on the screen, press [5] to get DANGEROUS Change command file. The information in this file will appear on the screen. Most of the pieces of information concern whether a particular other file exists on the disk or not. The number 1 next to the description of a file means it exists; 0 means it does not. Note that there is a letter in a bright box at the beginning of each line of information. To change information about the existence of a file, press the corresponding letter key. A 1 will change to a 0, or a 0 will change to a 1.

When you press the letter for the number of items or number of cases, the computer will then ask you to type in the number you want. Changing the number of items seems crazy to me, whereas changing the number of cases can be useful, as shown in two of the projects for this chapter. While I was writing my programs, and assembling the two datasets I have given you, it was quite useful to be able to change the KEY command file information. I wanted you to have the freedom to do so, too, although I must warn you that the results could be disastrous if you have not thought your project through carefully.

Especially for advanced work, it is essential to make a backup disk or two you can fall back on if something goes wrong. Also, advanced users can easily transfer files from one disk to another. Just remember that when you move a file, such as STUDENTS.KEY, from one disk to another, a file with the same name already existing on the destination disk will be replaced. The ability to change the KEY command file makes it possible to assemble several files from different sources on one disk and get them to work together—assuming, of course, that they properly harmonize.

Both this advanced option and the one described previously that lets you transfer data to a big computer or to some microcomputer statistics packages were designed to take you beyond the limitations of our instructional programs. And these are appropriate features with which to end our book. I have written these programs and this text to introduce the student to serious survey research. The programs are not exhausted when the semester is over; they can do much work for you in the coming years. But their greatest contribution is to bring you into the exciting field of survey research, where vistas of professional accomplishment and scientific discovery will open for you. With the start this book and software have given you, you are ready to explore other, more advanced tools of survey research.

▶ ▶ ▶ ▶ ▶ ▶ ▶ ▶ ▶ ▶ ▶ ▶

PROJECTS

1. *Labels for XYZ*.   Using the labelmaker part of the utility program, create a set of labels for the 40 items of the XYZ Management Survey in Chapter 10. These labels should be of a sort appropriate for the statistics programs, and thus they should not start with the item number, because the stat program will supply the item number anyway. They should, of course, differ from the labels I wrote for Table 12.1 and from the original set on your disk.

First, go through the 40 items carefully, marking key words in each statement that convey its central concept. Then write a brief phrase for each, one that would fit as a label, based on these key words. It should be no longer than 25 letters, symbols, or spaces long. Note that you cannot use a hyphen in it, because the computer cannot tell the hyphen from a minus sign, which it takes as a command to move, but you could use an equals sign or a slash instead. The point is to create a label that will instantly remind you what the item is about.

If you want, you could start each label with a symbol for the scale the item is supposed to belong to, as I did in Table 12.1. The XYZ Management Survey contains A (American), J (Japanese), lm (low Machiavellian), M (Machiavellian), X (Theory X), and Y (Theory Y) items, as Chapter 10 explains.

Finally, take an XYZ work disk and use the utilities program to create the labels. Now you are ready to do some efficient analyzing with the XYZ dataset.

2. *Create a Codebook*.   Take a classic survey, or a substantial part of one if it is very long, and create a codebook for use in entering and analyzing data. Or you could do this project with a survey of your own if you have already begun serious research.

The codebook should include all the information suggested in the section of this chapter about codebooks, including codings for any complex or open-ended questions, the ranges of all variables, missing-values codes, and any other guidance someone might need to enter or analyze data. It is a good idea to begin the codebook with a brief (one paragraph to one page) description of the sample of respondents who provided the data.

3. *Make an Input System*.   Use the utility program to create a complete system for entering data from a questionnaire into the microcomputer. If you are doing this for a real survey you have administered to real respondents, you should first do the previous project, creating a codebook. Then it will be quite easy to produce the input system. Or you could use all or part of a published questionnaire for this project.

You should create a special, clearly marked work disk. As explained in Project 4 at the end of Chapter 1, you should remove the STUDENTS and XYZ datasets completely from the disk, so you will have a lot of room for your own data. If you are an advanced user, you can consult the appendix to learn which other files can safely be discarded.

Your input system should include carefully chosen short labels, with item numbers as printed on the questionnaire. You should set sounds to mark the ends of pages or sections, and you must also set proper ranges for the variables, following the decisions you made about missing values in writing your codebook.

4. Enter and Verify Data.   This is an advanced project for people who already have some survey data of their own. If a class is doing this project, students can divide up the labor, each doing a dozen questionnaires or so, to give everybody some experience at this vital but tedious work. Of course, if several people are sharing the work, it might be good to make a backup disk after each person, so that nobody can accidentally ruin the whole team's work.

For advanced users only (such as experienced computer instructors), I can suggest an even safer and more convenient way for members of a class to share in data entry. Create a work disk for each person and give each person 25 completed questionnaires, keeping track of who has which ones and marking the disks appropriately. Each person will enter data on his or her own disk, thus creating a file labeled something like SURVEY.D1. Make a copy of the first person's disk, the one with cases 1–25 on it, to be your combined data disk. Take the disk with cases 26–50, and rename its file SURVEY.D2, then copy this file onto the combined disk. Cases 51–75 will be renamed SURVEY.D3, and so on through your whole dataset. When all the files have been renamed and copied onto the combined data disk, use the DANGEROUS Change command file option offered by the utilities program to tell the computer how many cases of data you have altogether. You select the second choice on the main menu, to revise a survey, then the dangerous fifth option from the next menu. You should consult the appendix and make sure you understand something about DOS and disk files before you attempt this. And, as always, keep backup copies of your disks in case anything goes wrong.

5. Separate the Men from the Women.   This is a project using the STUDENTS dataset, but it should be attempted only by advanced users who understand something about DOS and who have studied the appendix.

Make two identical STUDENTS work disks. Label one *Men* and the other *Women*. Take the Women disk and erase the following four data files: STUDENTS.D5, STUDENTS.D6, STUDENTS.D7, and STUDENTS.D8. With this disk in your computer, start the utility program, select the option to revise a survey, and then enter the DANGEROUS Change command file option. Follow instructions to change the number of cases from 200 to 100.

Now take the Men disk and erase the following files: STUDENTS.D1, STUDENTS.D2, STUDENTS.D3, and STUDENTS.D4. Then rename the STUDENTS.D5 file STUDENTS.D1. STUDENTS.D6 should be renamed STUDENTS.D2. STUDENTS.D7 should become STUDENTS.D3, and STUDENTS.D8 should become STUDENTS.D4. Now with this disk in your computer, use the utility program to change the number of cases from 100 to 200.

What you have just done is to split the 200 students into male and female halves, one on each disk. You can now analyze responses to the 40 questions from these two sets of respondents separately.

If you want, you can split the data by year in school, instead. Files STUDENTS.D1 and STUDENTS.D5 are the freshmen and freshwomen. Sophomores are in STUDENTS.D2 and STUDENTS.D6. Can you guess where to find the data from juniors and seniors?

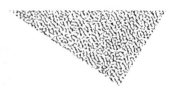

▶ ▶ ▶ ▶ ▶ The typical user of *Survey Research* will not have to know any technical details about the various files of information created by the programs and stored on the work disk. Advanced users might occasionally want to know about these files, however, so I will explain them briefly. For example, if you want to collect data using two or more computers and then combine the data, perhaps for uploading to a big computer, knowledge of the files would be useful. Advanced users may occasionally get into trouble and need some way of repairing a disk. Although the best way to avoid trouble is always to make backup disks, information about the files might help, too. If you want to make work disks with extra room on them, you can use the following information to decide which files you can safely erase from them, including programs.

If you use the DIR command to look at the directory of the *Survey Research* disk, you will see files with several different kinds of names. The nine working programs are called: A.EXE, B.EXE, C.EXE, D.EXE, E.EXE, F.EXE, G.EXE, H.EXE, I.EXE, with the letters A through I identifying the same programs as the choices on the program menu. Another program, S.EXE, is the startup program. Depending on your computer, it may be necessary to go through S.EXE to get to the other programs, because the startup sets a couple of parameters.

The run-time library, used by all the programs, is called BRUN10. COM. Without this important file, none of the programs can work. Two other files, named T and U, provide the city names and data for the simulated national poll program.

All the files for a particular dataset have names in two parts, separated by a period when you type them in as part of a DOS command, but simply separated by space in the disk directory. For example, STUDENTS.

KEY is a file for the STUDENTS dataset, and XYZ.KEY is a file for the XYZ Management Survey. The second part of the name, such as KEY in these two examples, is what we call the *extension*, and it identifies the function of the particular file.

The KEY file contains information on all the other files for the dataset. Many programs on your disk call up the KEY file right at the beginning and learn from it which other files exist on the disk. For example, when you created a recoded version of a dataset, the KEY file is altered so that the computer will know there are two versions of the data, original and recoded, on the disk.

A file with a name like STUDENTS.D1 or XYZ.D8 is a file containing data from as many as 25 respondents. Since both STUDENTS and XYZ have 200 respondents, there will be 8 data files for each on your *Survey Research* disk. STUDENTS.D1 contains data from the first 25 cases. STUDENTS.D2 has the second 25, and so on.

When you save a recoded version of the data on your disk, a second complete set of data files will appear, with names like STUDENTS.R1 and XYZ.R8, the R standing for *recoded*. The advanced utilities program creates still another set of files, with names like STUDENTS.U1 and XYZ.U8, with the U standing for *upload*, containing the data saved in a different form, for uploading to a big computer or porting over to some personal computer statistics packages.

Each correlation matrix is saved as a single file, as many as six for a particular dataset, depending on which ones you have asked the computer to make. STUDENTS.DCR is a correlation matrix based on the original data; XYZ.RCR is a correlation matrix based on recoded data. The first letter of the extension, D for *data* or R for *recoded*, tells you which version of the dataset was used to make the matrix. The two letters that complete the extension identify which coefficient the matrix is composed of. CR means ordinary correlations (Pearson's r), GA means gamma, and TU means tau. There may also exist one file containing as many as four composite scales you created with the scaling program, with the extension SCL for *scale*.

When you create a questionnaire with the question-processor program, the text of the items will be saved as a file with the extension ITM for *items*—for example, STUDENTS.ITM. Another file, with the extension CTL, is the *control* file that helps the question processor by telling it the format and range of each item.

When you prepare a set of labels using the utility program, to help you identify the items in statistics programs or when you use the utility program itself to input data, the labels will be saved in a file with the extension LAB. Finally, when you input data with the utilities program, an INP file is created, containing information about the sounds and ranges you have selected.

A main point to keep in mind is that the KEY file must contain correct information about which files are on the disk. You can change the information in the KEY file through the utilities program. The safest way is to work on an extra disk, so that you can always start over or recover a file that accidentally gets clobbered. Again, whenever you are trying anything fancy that relies on knowledge of the files, you should make a backup disk in case anything goes wrong. The second option on the main utilities menu lets you change a survey, and the DANGEROUS fifth option of the change menu gives you access to the KEY file.

Bibliography

Anderson, Norman H.
   1968 "Likableness Ratings of 555 Personality-Trait Words." *Journal of Personality and Social Psychology* 9:272–79.
Armer, Michael, and Allan Schnaiberg
   1972 "Measuring Individual Modernity." *American Sociological Review* 37:301–16.
Babbie, Earl R.
   1973 *Survey Research Methods.* Belmont, Calif.: Wadsworth.
Bachman, Jerald G.
   1970 *The Impact of Family Background and Intelligence on Tenth-Grade Boys.* Volume 2 of *Youth in Transition.* Ann Arbor, Mich.: Institute for Social Research.
Back, Kurt W., and J. Mayone Stycos
   1973 "The Survey Under Unusual Conditions." In *Comparative Research Methods,* edited by Donald P. Warwick and Samuel Osherson, pp. 248–67. Englewood Cliffs, N.J.: Prentice-Hall.
Bainbridge, William Sims
   1976 *The Spaceflight Revolution.* New York: Wiley-Interscience.
   1978a "Chariots of the Gullible." *Skeptical Inquirer* 3 (Winter):33–48.
   1978b *Satan's Power.* Berkeley: University of California Press.
   1982 "Shaker Demographics: An Example of the Use of U.S. Census Enumeration Schedules." *Journal for the Scientific Study of Religion* 21:352–65.
   1984a "The Decline of the Shakers: Evidence from the United States Census." *Communal Societies* 4:19–34.
   1984b "Religious Insanity in America: The Official Nineteenth-Century Theory." *Sociological Analysis* 45:223–39.
   1984c "Utopian Communities: Theoretical and Methodological Issues." In *The Sacred in a Secular Age,* edited by Phillip E. Hammond, pp. 21–35. Berkeley: University of California Press.
   1986a *Dimensions of Science Fiction.* Cambridge, Mass.: Harvard University Press.
   1986b *Experiments in Psychology.* Belmont, Calif.: Wadsworth.

1987a *Experiments in Sociology.* Belmont, Calif.: Wadsworth (contained in the student's study guide for Stark's sociology textbook).

1987b *Sociology Laboratory.* Belmont, Calif.: Wadsworth.

Bainbridge, William Sims, and Robert D. Crutchfield

1983 "Sex Role Ideology and Delinquency." *Sociological Perspectives* 26:253–74.

Bainbridge, William Sims, and Rodney Stark

1981 "Friendship, Religion, and the Occult: A Network Study." *Review of Religious Research* 22:313–27.

Bauer, Raymond A.

1960 "Executives Probe Space." *Harvard Business Review* (September–October): 6–14, 174–200.

Block, Jack

1965 *The Challenge of Response Sets.* New York: Appleton-Century-Crofts.

Bogardus, E. S.

1925 "Measuring Social Distance." *Journal of Applied Sociology* 9:299–308.

Boyle, Richard P.

1970 "Path Analysis and Ordinal Data," *American Journal of Sociology* 75:461–480.

Campbell, Angus

1971 *White Attitudes Toward Black People.* Ann Arbor, Mich.: Institute for Social Research.

Christensen, Larry B., and Charles M. Stoup

1986 *Introduction to Statistics for the Social and Behavioral Sciences.* Pacific Grove, Calif.: Brooks/Cole.

Christie, Richard, and Florence L. Geis

1970 *Studies in Machiavellianism.* New York: Academic Press.

Condry, John, and Sharon Dyer

1976 "Fear of Success: Attribution of Cause to the Victim." *Journal of Social Issues* 32(3): 63–83.

Couch, Arthur, and Kenneth Keniston

1960 "Yeasayers and Naysayers: Agreeing Response Set as a Personality Variable." *Journal of Abnormal and Social Psychology* 60:151–74.

Cronbach, Lee J.

1951 "Coefficient Alpha and the Internal Structure of Tests." *Psychometrika* 16: 297–334.

Cronbach, Lee J., and Paul E. Meehl

1955 "Construct Validity in Psychological Tests." *Psychological Bulletin* 52: 281–302.

Crowne, Douglas P., and David Marlowe

1960 "A New Scale of Social Desirability Independent of Psychopathology." *Journal of Consulting Psychology* 24:349–54.

Davis, James A., and Tom W. Smith

1986 *General Social Surveys, 1972–1986: Cumulative Codebook.* Chicago: National Opinion Research Center.

Deutscher, Irwin

1973 "Asking Questions Cross-Culturally." In *Comparative Research Methods,* edited by Donald P. Warwick and Samuel Osherson, pp. 163–86. Englewood Cliffs, N.J.: Prentice-Hall.

Dillman, Don A.

1978 *Mail and Telephone Surveys.* New York: Wiley.

Duncan, Otis Dudley, Archibald O. Haller, and Alejandro Portes
1968 "Peer Influences on Aspirations: A Reinterpretation." *American Journal of Sociology* 74:119–37.

Earle, Pliny
1887 *The Curability of Insanity.* Philadelphia: Lippincott.

Edgerton, Robert B.
1966 "Conceptions of Psychosis in Four East African Societies." *American Anthropologist* 68:408–25.
1967 *The Cloak of Competence.* Berkeley: University of California Press.

Edwards, Allen L.
1967 "The Social Desirability Variable: A Review of the Evidence." In *Response Set in Personality Assessment,* edited by Irwin A. Berg, pp. 48–70. Chicago: Aldine.

Everitt, Brian
1974 *Cluster Analysis.* London: Heinemann.

Faris, Robert E. L., and H. Warren Dunham
1939 *Mental Disorders in Urban Areas.* Chicago: University of Chicago Press.

Festinger, Leon, Stanley Schachter, and Kurt Back
1950 *Social Pressures in Informal Groups.* New York: Harper.

Fiedler, Fred E.
1958 *Leader Attitudes and Group Effectiveness.* Urbana: University of Illinois Press.

Flint, Jerry
1987 "Too Much Ain't Enough." *Forbes* 140 (July):92–102.

Furash, Edward E.
1963 "Businessmen Review the Space Effort." *Harvard Business Review* (September–October):14–32, 173–90.

Galfo, Armand J.
1975 "Measurement of Group Versus Educational Leaders' Perception of Leadership Style and Administrative Theory Organization." *Journal of Educational Research* 68:310–14.

Gallup, George
1976 *The Sophisticated Poll Watcher's Guide.* Ephrata, Pa.: Science Press.

Gallup Opinion Index
1973 *Gallup Opinion Index* (December):17–25.
1977 *Religion in America 1977–78.* Princeton, N.J.: American Institute of Public Opinion.

Gardner, Hugh
1978 *The Children of Prosperity.* New York: St. Martin's.

Glaser, Barney G., and Anselm L. Strauss
1967 *The Discovery of Grounded Theory.* Chicago: Aldine.

Glock, Charles Y., and Rodney Stark
1965 *Religion and Society in Tension.* Chicago: Rand McNally.
1966 *Christian Beliefs and Anti-Semitism.* New York: Harper & Row.

Gordon, Raymond L.
1969 *Interviewing: Strategy, Techniques, and Tactics.* Homewood, Ill.: Dorsey.

Green, Samuel B., Robert W. Lissitz, and Stanlen A. Mulaik
1977 "Limitations of Coefficient Alpha as an Index of Test Unidimensionality." *Educational and Psychological Measurement* 37:827–38.

Hadaway, C. K.
1978 "Life Satisfaction and Religion: A Reanalysis." *Social Forces* 57:636–43.

Haire, Mason, Edwin E. Ghiselli, and Lyman W. Porter
   1966 *Managerial Thinking: An International Study.* New York: Wiley.
Hicks, Jack M., and John H. Wright
   1970 "Convergent–Discriminant Validation and Factor Analysis of Five Scales
      of Liberalism–Conservatism." *Journal of Personality and Social Psychology* 14:
      114–20.
Hilty, Dale M., and Rich Morgan
   1985 "Construct Validation for the Religious Involvement Inventory." *Journal for
      the Scientific Study of Religion* 24:75–86.
Hindelang, Michael, Travis Hirschi, and Joseph G. Weis
   1979 "Correlates of Delinquency: The Illusion of Discrepancy Between Self-
      Report and Official Measures." *American Sociological Review* 44:995–1014.
Hirschi, Travis
   1969 *Causes of Delinquency.* Berkeley: University of California Press.
Hollingshead, August B., and Frederick C. Redlich
   1958 *Social Class and Mental Illness.* New York: Wiley.
Homans, George C.
   1950 *The Human Group.* New York: Harcourt, Brace and World.
   1974 *Social Behavior—Its Elementary Forms.* New York: Harcourt Brace Jovanovich.
Horner, Matina S.
   1970 "Femininity and Successful Achievement: A Basic Inconsistency." In *Femi-
      nine Personality and Conflict,* edited by Judith M. Bardwick, Elizabeth Douvan,
      Matina S. Horner, and David Gutmann, pp. 45–74. Pacific Grove, Calif.:
      Brooks/Cole.
Hunter, John E., David W. Gerbing, and Franklin J. Boster
   1982 "Machiavellian Beliefs and Personality: Construct Invalidity of the Ma-
      chiavellianism Dimension." *Journal of Personality and Social Psychology* 43:
      1293–1305.
Ito-Adler, James
   1980 *The Portuguese in Cambridge and Somerville.* Cambridge, Mass.: Cambridge
      Department of Community Development.
Jarvis, Edward
   1855 *Report on Insanity and Idiocy in Massachusetts by the Commission on Lunacy
      Under Resolve of the Legislature of 1854.* Boston: William White.
Juhn, Daniel S.
   1972 *McGregor's Theory X–Y and Maslow's Need Hierarchy Theory: An Empirical
      Study of Managerial Thinking in the New Orleans Area.* New Orleans: Louisiana
      State University.
Kandel, Denise B.
   1974 "Inter- and Intragenerational Influences on Adolescent Marijuana Use."
      Journal of Social Issues 30:107–35.
Kandel, Denise B., Donald Treiman, Richard Faust, and Eric Single
   1976 "Adolescent Involvement in Legal and Illegal Drug Use: A Multiple Classi-
      fication Analysis." *Social Forces* 55:438–58.
Kanter, Rosabeth Moss
   1972 *Commitment and Community.* Cambridge, Mass.: Harvard University Press.
Kennedy, Joseph C. G.
   1860 *Instructions to U.S. Marshals.* Washington, D.C.: Bowman.
Keyser, Daniel J., and Richard C. Sweetland, eds.
   1984 *Test Critiques.* Three volumes. Kansas City, Mo.: Test Corporation of
      America.

Klein, Morris M., and Saul A. Grossman
  1971 "Voting Competence and Mental Illness." *American Journal of Psychiatry* 127:1562–65.
Kuhn, Manford H., and Thomas S. McPartland
  1954 "An Empirical Investigation of Self-Attitudes." *American Sociological Review* 19:68–76.
Larson, Richard F.
  1968 "The Clergyman's Role in the Therapeutic Process: Disagreement Between Clergymen and Psychiatrists." *Psychiatry* 31:250–63.
Lazarsfeld, Paul F.
  1955 "Interpretation of Statistical Relations as a Research Operation." In *The Language of Social Research,* edited by Paul F. Lazarsfeld and Morris Rosenberg, pp. 115–25. New York: Free Press.
Lazarsfeld, Paul F., Bernard Berelson, and Hazel Gaudet
  1948 *The People's Choice.* New York: Columbia University Press.
Levine, Adeline, and Janice Crumrine
  1975 "Women and the Fear of Success: A Problem in Replication." *American Journal of Sociology* 80:964–74.
Lipset, Seymour Martin
  1976 *Rebellion in the University.* Chicago: University of Chicago Press.
Loether, Herman J., and Donald G. McTavish
  1976 *Descriptive and Inferential Statistics: An Introduction.* Boston: Allyn and Bacon.
Lofland, John
  1966 *Doomsday Cult.* Englewood Cliffs, N.J.: Prentice-Hall.
Lofland, John, and Rodney Stark
  1965 "Becoming a World-Saver: A Theory of Conversion to a Deviant Perspective." *American Sociological Review* 39:862–75.
Lusch, Robert F., and Virginia N. Lusch
  1987 *Principles of Marketing.* Boston: Kent.
McGregor, Douglas
  1960 *The Human Side of Enterprise.* New York: McGraw-Hill (1985).
  1966 *Leadership and Motivation.* Cambridge, Mass.: MIT Press.
Machiavelli, Niccolò
  1532 *The Prince.* New York: Mentor (1952).
Mitchell, Arnold
  1983 *The Nine American Lifestyles.* New York: Warner.
Moreno, J. L.
  1934 *Who Shall Survive?* Washington, D.C.: Nervous and Mental Disease Publishing Co.
Morgan, Lewis Henry
  1870 *Systems of Consanguinity and Affinity of the Human Family.* Washington, D.C.: Smithsonian.
Moses, Lincoln E., Allan Goldfarb, Charles Y. Glock, Rodney W. Stark, and Morris L. Eaton
  1971 "A Validity Study Using the Leighton Instrument." *American Journal of Public Health* 61:1785–93.
Murray, Henry A.
  1938 *Explorations in Personality.* New York: Oxford University Press.
  1981 *Endeavors in Psychology.* New York: Harper & Row.
Noyes, John Humphrey
  1870 *History of American Socialisms* Philadelphia: Lippincott.

Osgood, Charles E., George J. Suci, and Percy H. Tannenbaum
1957 *The Measurement of Meaning.* Urbana: University of Illinois Press.
Ouchi, William G.
1979 "A Conceptual Framework for the Design of Organizational Control Mechanisms." *Management Science* 9:833–48.
1980 "Markets, Bureaucracies, and Clans." *Administrative Science Quarterly* 25:129–41.
1981 *Theory Z: How American Business Can Meet the Japanese Challenge.* New York: Avon.
Ouchi, William G., and Alfred M. Jaeger
1978 "Type Z Organization: Stability in the Midst of the Mobility." *Academy of Management Review* 3:305–14.
Ouchi, William G., and Jerry B. Johnson
1978 "Types of Organizational Control and Their Relationship to Emotional Well-Being." *Administrative Science Quarterly* 23:293–317.
Peek, Charles W., Evans W. Curry, and H. Paul Chalfant.
1985 "Religiosity and Delinquency over Time: Deviance Deterrence and Deviance Amplification." *Social Science Quarterly* 66:120–31.
Phillips, Derek L., and Kevin J. Clancy
1972 "Some Effects of 'Social Desirability' in Survey Studies." *American Journal of Sociology* 77:921–40.
Portes, Alejandro
1973 "The Factorial Structure of Modernity." *American Journal of Sociology* 79:15–44.
Przeworski, Adam, and Henry Teune
1973 "Equivalence in Cross-National Research." In *Comparative Research Methods,* edited by Donald P. Warwick and Samuel Osherson, pp. 119–37. Englewood Cliffs, N.J.: Prentice-Hall.
Rabkin, Richard
1967 "Inner and Outer Space." *American Journal of Psychiatry* 124:355–64.
1970 *Inner and Outer Space—Introduction to a Theory of Social Psychiatry.* New York: Norton.
Rand Corporation
1955 *A Million Random Digits with 100,000 Normal Deviates.* Glencoe, Ill.: Free Press.
Robinson, John P., Robert Athansiou, and Kendra B. Head
1969 *Measures of Occupational Attitudes and Occupational Characteristics.* Ann Arbor, Mich.: Institute for Social Research.
Robinson, John P., Jerrold G. Rusk, and Kendra B. Head
1968 *Measures of Political Attitudes.* Ann Arbor, Mich.: Institute for Social Research.
Robinson, John P., and Phillip R. Shaver
1969 *Measures of Social Psychological Attitudes.* Ann Arbor, Mich.. Institute for Social Research,
Roethlisberger, Fritz Jules, and William John Dickson
1939 *Management and the Worker.* Cambridge, Mass.: Harvard University Press.
Rokeach, Milton
1973 *The Nature of Human Values.* New York: Free Press.
Rosenberg, Morris
1965 *Society and the Adolescent Self-Image.* Princeton, N.J.: Princeton University Press.

Rothman, David J.
   1971 *The Discovery of the Asylum.* Boston: Little, Brown.
Schulz, Barbara, George W. Bohrenstedt, Edgar F. Borgatta, and Robert R. Evans
   1977 "Explaining Premarital Sexual Intercourse Among College Students: A Causal Model." *Social Forces* 56:148–65.
Schuman, Howard, and Stanley Presser
   1980 "Public Opinion and Public Ignorance: The Fine Line Between Attitudes and Nonattitudes." *American Journal of Sociology* 85:1214–25.
Simon, Herbert A.
   1954 "Spurious Correlation: A Causal Interpretation." *Journal of the American Statistical Association* 49:467–79.
Skelly, Florence
   1986 "The Stanford/Harvard Survey." *Harvard Magazine* 88 (March–April):21–27.
Smith, M. Brewster, Jerome S. Bruner, and Robert W. White
   1956 *Opinions and Personality.* New York: Wiley.
Srole, Leo, Thomas S. Langner, Stanley T. Michael, Marvin K. Opler, and Thomas A. C. Rennie
   1962 *Mental Health in the Metropolis.* New York: McGraw-Hill.
Stark, Rodney, and William Sims Bainbridge
   1985 *The Future of Religion.* Berkeley: University of California Press.
   1987 *A Theory of Religion.* New York: Toronto Studies in Religion—Peter Lang.
Stark, Rodney, Lori Kent, and Daniel P. Doyle
   1982 "Religion and Delinquency: The Ecology of a 'Lost' Relationship." *Journal of Research in Crime and Delinquency* 19:4–24.
Stouffer, Samuel A.
   1962 *Social Research to Test Ideas.* New York: Free Press.
Suchman, Edward A., Bernard S. Phillips, and Gordon F. Streib
   1958 "An Analysis of the Validity of Health Questionnaires." *Social Forces* 36: 223–32.
Sweetland, Richard C., and William A. O'Connor, eds.
   1983 *Tests.* Kansas City, Mo.: Test Corporation of America.
Taviss, Irene
   1972 "A Survey of Popular Attitudes Toward Technology." *Technology and Culture* 13:606–21.
Taylor, James C., and David G. Bowers
   1972 *Survey of Organizations.* Ann Arbor, Mich.: Institute for Social Research.
Vigderhous, Gideon
   1977 "The Level of Measurement and 'Permissible' Statistical Analysis in Social Research," *Pacific Sociological Review* 20:61–72.
Villemez, Wayne J., and John C. Touhey
   1977 "A Measure of Individual Differences in Sex Stereotyping and Sex Discrimination." *Psychological Reports* 41:411–15.
Vogel, Ezra F.
   1979 *Japan as Number One.* Cambridge, Mass.: Harvard University Press.
Warwick, Donald P., and Samuel Osherson
   1973 *Comparative Research Methods.* Englewood Cliffs, N.J.: Prentice-Hall.
White, Harrison C., Scott A. Boorman, and Ronald L. Breiger
   1976 "Social Structure from Multiple Networks." *American Journal of Sociology* 81:730–80.

Wuthnow, Robert
    1976 *The Consciousness Reformation.* Berkeley: University of California Press.
    1978 *Experimentation in American Religion.* Berkeley: University of California Press.
    1981 "Two Traditions in the Study of Religion." *Journal for the Scientific Study of Religion* 20:16–32.
Young, Michael, and Peter Willmott
    1957 *Family and Kinship in East London.* London: Routledge and Kegan Paul.
    1973 *The Symmetrical Family.* London: Routledge and Kegan Paul.
Zablocki, Benjamin
    1980 *Alienation and Charisma.* New York: Free Press.

Page references follow the definitions.

acquiescence: the tendency of a respondent to agree with whatever a survey item says, regardless of its content, or to disagree; a tendency to agree is called *yea-saying*, the opposite of which is *nay-saying*. (239)

attenuation: a decline in a coefficient because of a reduction of the number of items in an index, reflecting the fact that an index with many items tends to be more reliable than one with few items, other things being equal. (223)

back translation: the translating of a foreign-language version of an English-language questionnaire back into English by a translator who has not seen the original. The two English versions are compared to see what may have been lost or distorted in translation. (37)

binomial distribution: a mathematically defined distribution in which cases are gathered symmetrically around the mean, which is the most common value, while extreme values are rare. As cases increase and measurement categories narrow, it approximates the normal curve. (63)

bipolar concept: a dimension of variation anchored by two equally meaningful opposite concepts, such as *tall–short* or *liberal–conservative*. (106)

blind coding: coding data, such as open-ended item responses, while being unaware of the characteristics of the respondents that are key variables in the research to avoid biasing the results, whether consciously or unconsciously. (258)

block modeling: a statistical procedure for rearranging the order of variables in a list to create clear clusters of coefficients or other data in a matrix based on the variables. (190)

case: an instance of the phenomenon under study—the unit of analysis. Usually each survey respondent is a case. (41)

cell: an element of a table containing a single number. (158)

census: a survey designed to count every person in the nation, city, or group of interest, and in many cases to collect all kinds of factual information about every person and family counted. In a census, the sample is equal to the whole population. (2)

chi-square: a coefficient that measures the difference between the observed values in a table and the values that would be expected purely on the basis of the marginals. (167)

clique: a subgroup within a social network in which members are somewhat cut off from the people around them but closely tied to each other. (311)

cluster: a set of respondents selected together, usually from the same district, in the final stage of a multi-stage sampling design. (81)

cluster analysis: a collection of statistical methods for finding groups of related items in a matrix of correlations or similar coefficients. (191)

codebook: a set of pages that serves as a guide for entering and analyzing data from a questionnaire, usually consisting of an edition of the questionnaire to which code numbers have been added for each response. (328)

coding: assigning a number (value) to each response in a survey item so that the computer can handle the data efficiently. (15, 327)

coding scheme: a system for assigning unique numbers to the different responses to an open-ended item so that the data can be processed by computer. (249)

cohort: in longitudinal research, a set of people who enter the research process at about the same time and are then followed through from stage to stage. (294)

cohort effect: a difference between respondents that reflects the historical period in which a group of a particular age grew up. (296)

concordance: in linked-respondent surveys, the correlation between the response of one person in a linked pair to a given question and the response of the other person to the same question. (305)

construct: a concept we use to understand a phenomenon that cannot be observed directly; its existence has to be inferred on the basis of indirect evidence. (221)

construct validity: the quality of an index that is both coherent and distinct in the responses it receives, measuring a logical construct that cannot be directly observed. To be coherent its items must correlate with each other, and to be distinct they must not correlate highly with other indexes. (221)

contingent questions: items that only a subgroup of respondents are supposed to answer. (140)

control variable: a variable statistically introduced into analysis of the association between two other variables to see whether it affects their correlation. (170, 233)

convenience sample: a collection of respondents selected simply because they are readily available for polling. (68)

correlation coefficient: a number between +1.00 and −1.00, expressing the strength of the association between two variables. (161)

correlation matrix: a table showing all the correlation coefficients between all pairs of variables in a particular list. (175)

cover letter: a letter introducing a questionnaire, usually explaining the purpose of the survey, identifying the researcher and sponsoring agency, and asking the recipient to respond to it. (23)

criterion group: a group of people known to have the characteristic that an item or index is supposed to measure. They can be used to evaluate the validity of the item or index. (215)

criterion validity: the quality of an item or index that successfully distinguishes a criterion group from other people. An item with criterion validity can identify people known to have the characteristic it is supposed to measure. (215)

Cronbach's alpha: a measure of reliability that is an estimate of the average of all possible split-halves reliability coefficients that can be calculated for a given index. (224)

cross-sectional research: an alternative to longitudinal research in which the researcher compares people of different ages at the same point in time. (296)

crosstabulation: a table that tabulates two variables against each other. (158)

data dredging: going through a dataset in an unintelligent way, looking for big correlations without considering any particular theories or other clear scientific purpose. (186)

dependent variable: roughly, the effect in a cause-effect relationship; often the term is used for a variable treated temporarily like an effect with respect to a particular independent variable, variations in the independent variable being said to explain some of the variations in the dependent variable. (302)

diary: a variety of open-ended printed surveys that give informants a schedule of hours and days, asking them to write down what they are doing at each point in time. (252)

dichotomizing responses: collapsing a range of responses into just two by means of recoding. (206)

dichotomous variable: an item or index having just two responses or values. (167)

discriminant validity: the capacity of an item or index to measure something different from what other scales measure. (218)

dispersion: the degree to which respondents' scores are spread out around the mean, usually measured by variance or standard deviation. (156)

ethnographic item creation: collecting open-ended information about people's opinions using interviews or questionnaires as the basis for writing fixed-choice or other kinds of items for a subsequent questionnaire. (263)

experiment: a study in which the social scientist systematically examines the effect of a particular action performed on people under study, compared with no action or some other action. (300)

face validity: the property of an item or index that appears to be an appropriate measure of the concept in question in terms of common sense. (217)

factor analysis: a statistical procedure to find groups of items or underlying dimensions hidden in a correlation matrix. (191, 267)

fixed-choice items: questionnaire items that require the respondent to select from a set of listed choices, for example, by checking one of several boxes printed on the questionnaire. (246)

frequencies: the number of respondents with each particular value for a given item. (153)

gamma: a correlation coefficient designed for use with ordinal data. (167)

grounded theory: theoretical analysis derived from the concepts that ordinary people use in the situation under study. (264)

in-depth interviews: interviews that seek extensive information or private feelings from the interviewee, typically long in duration and using open-ended questions. (258)

independent variable: roughly, the cause in a cause-effect relationship. Often the term is used for a variable treated temporarily like a cause with respect to a particular dependent variable, variations in the independent variable being said to explain some of the variations in the dependent variable. (302)

index: a combination of items designed to measure a quality shared by them. (192)

indicator: a statistic that expresses some aspect of reality in a somewhat indirect way. (192)

informant: a person interviewed or surveyed to obtain objective information. (27)

instrument: a test or set of questionnaire items designed to measure a particular characteristic or set of characteristics of the respondent. (31)

interval variable: an item whose responses are in a logical order and are a constant distance apart. (166)

interview: a session between a researcher and a respondent done face to face or over the telephone in which the researcher asks questions and seeks answers. (22)

linked-respondent survey: a study in which the unit of analysis is larger than the single individual, typically a linked pair of respondents. (302)

longitudinal research: a study carried out over a significant period of time, such as a panel survey. (295)

magnitude item: a question asking the respondent to judge how complete or big something is. (94)

marginals: the numbers along the side of a standard crosstabulation, showing the frequencies for the two variables. (160)

mark-sense forms: specially printed questionnaire forms that can be run through optical scanners to enter their data directly in the computer without typing. (24)

maturational effect: a difference between respondents that reflects the aging process. (296)

mean: the arithmetic average of a set of figures, calculated by adding them together and dividing by the number of figures in the set. (155)

meaning system: general views of the world that people may hold that are their ways of interpreting the events of life. (226)

median: the value on a particular item that exactly divides the group of respondents in half, one part with higher values, and the other with lower values. (156)

menu: a list of choices offered by the computer. (54)

menu item: a survey question that offers several complex choices specially designed for that particular item. (126)

missing cases: respondents who failed to give valid answers to a given question. (157)

missing data: information that is lacking in a dataset, such as a gap where a respondent failed to answer a question. (13)

missing-values code: a number used to indicate missing or faulty data. (15)

mode: the most common value among responses to an item. There can be more than one mode. (155)

multi-response menu item: a menu item that permits the respondent to select two or more of the responses. (132)

multi-stage sampling: drawing cases at two or more levels, for example, first drawing a sample of districts and then drawing samples of individuals in the selected districts. (76)

multiple mailings: in mailed questionnaire research, sending letters and duplicate questionnaires to the respondents, usually to increase the response rate. (26)

mutual pair: two people who choose each other in response to a sociometric question. (312)

nominal variable: an item whose response categories are not in any particular order. The values are equivalent to names and not suitable for most mathematical operations. (165)

normal curve: an ideal, mathematically defined distribution of great importance in social statistics. Cases are gathered symmetrically around the mean, which is the most common value—extreme values are rare. (63)

open-ended items: questionnaire items that give the respondent a blank area of paper on which to write a response in whatever way seems appropriate. (246)

opinion poll: a survey to measure the attitudes held by members of the population toward some set of public issues or the candidates in a political campaign. Typically a random sample is used to estimate the proportions in the population holding each opinion. (2)

ordinal variable: an item whose responses place respondents in categories that are in a meaningful order. (165)

oversampling: drawing more respondents from a group than its proportion in the population would require. (74)

pair comparison: an item asking the respondent to judge how similar or different two things are, or to compare them in terms of some particular quality they might share. (99)

panel: a set of individuals who serve repeatedly as respondents or at least twice at different points in time. (294)

panel survey: a study in which a set of respondents is given questionnaires at two or more different points in time. (294)

parallel-forms reliability: agreement between two different versions of the same measure in a questionnaire, for example, between two different indexes of the same concept. (219)

partial correlation: a method for introducing control variables into the analysis of the association between two variables. (169, 234)

population: the set of people the researcher wishes to learn about, usually studied by drawing a sample of respondents from it. (46)

practice effect: the tendency of respondents to do better on a test, or to give different responses to a survey, merely because they have taken the test or survey previously. (219)

precoded questionnaire: a questionnaire with small code numbers for each response choice printed on every copy to guide the data-entry personnel. (329)

preference scale item: a question asking how much the respondent likes something. (97)

projective techniques: interview and questionnaire items that use an ambiguous stimulus, such as an inkblot, to assess desires and attitudes that cannot easily be discerned more directly. (255)

proportional random sample: a set of respondents designed to include the same proportions of certain groups as are found in the population being polled, created according to procedures that make it impossible to predict which individuals will be included. (72)

proportional sample: a set of respondents designed to include the same proportions of certain groups as are found in the population being polled. (72)

psychological assessment: the professional use of questionnaires and other methods to measure a person's abilities, deep-rooted feelings, and personality type—often with the aim of counseling the individual about his or her problems. (3)

questionnaire: a standardized list of questions and questionlike items designed to obtain information from a number of respondents in a survey, in a printed form given to respondents, or in an outline used to guide an interview. (20)

quota sample: a set of respondents collected in such a way that specified numbers of members from particular groups are included; otherwise, the sample may be random. (73)

r: a correlation coefficient appropriate for use with interval and ratio data. (161)

random: any process the outcome of which cannot be predicted on the basis of any information that ideally could be obtained. (55)

ranking item: a questionnaire item that asks the respondent to put the responses in a particular order, typically by writing numbers in front of them. (133)

ratio variable: an item whose responses are in a logical order, are a constant distance apart, and are measured from a zero point. (167)

raw numbers: data direct from tabulation of responses, before any complicated calculations have been performed on them. (154)

recoding: transforming existing data by reassigning value numbers to various responses and combinations of response. (97, 172, 204)

reference group: the set of people with whom respondents compare themselves, for example, in deciding whether they should be satisfied with their situations. (102)

reliability: the quality of an item or index that gives consistent results; a reliable item tends to get the same response from a respondent if administered twice, so long as the relevant circumstances have not changed. (212)

replication: repeating a previously completed scientific study, often with slightly different methods or kinds of data, to see if the original results will be confirmed. (3)

respondent: a person interviewed or surveyed to discover his or her personal opinions, feelings, and attitudes. (27)

response: a respondent's answer to a question or reaction to a questionnaire item; the box to be checked or key to be pressed in reaction to an item. (90)

response bias: the tendency of a respondent to answer questions in a particular way, regardless of what the question is specifically about. (236)

response rate: the fraction of people given a survey who actually complete it. (22)

response set: the predisposition of a respondent to be attentive to certain stimuli. (237)

sample: a subset of people in the population under study, often selected by random numbers, whose responses to a survey are used to estimate how the entire population would have responded if it had been surveyed. (43)

sampling frame: the plan used by a survey researcher to draw a sample of respondents from the population under study. (49)

scale: an item or combination of items that measures a respondent characteristic along a graduated series of points, usually assumed to be equal distances apart. (97, 192)

schedule: a prepared questionnaire used in interviews that is filled in by the interviewer. (33)

scholarly item creation: writing survey questions on the basis of the writings of academics or other professional experts on a topic, often transforming their statements more or less directly into questionnaire items. (263)

screening questions: items that are used to separate people into subgroups that receive different contingent questions. (140)

semantic differential: a set of items in the paired-opposites format that measures the basic dimensions of meaning a particular concept possesses. (106)

short form: a version of a survey that accomplishes almost as much as the original, but with a smaller number of items. (283)

significance: see *statistical significance.*

simple random sample: a set of respondents taken from the population according to procedures that make it impossible to predict which individuals will be included and that give each individual an equal chance of inclusion. (70)

simulation: a computer program that models an aspect of reality through a precisely defined set of mathematical procedures. (65)

social desirability bias: the tendency of a respondent to give socially acceptable answers to questions, putting himself or herself in a good light. (239)

social distance scale: a set of items written to determine how close the respondent feels to particular categories of people. (124)

social isolate: a person who is not connected to anyone else in a sociogram. (310)

social network: the structure of relationships linking a number of people. (311)

sociogram: a diagram showing relations between individuals. Each person is represented by a circle or some other shape, and relationships connecting them are shown as lines. (310)

sociometric item: any question that seeks to measure the relationship between people. (308)

sociometric survey: a study in which all or many of the questions concern relationships among the people in the group and where the structure of social relations in the group is the prime focus of research. (308)

sociometry: the measurement and charting of social relationships. (308)

split-halves reliability: agreement between two halves of an index, for example, between the odd-numbered and even-numbered index items in the respondents' answers. (220)

split-halves reliability coefficient: a coefficient derived from the correlation between two halves of an index, expressing how well the two halves agree in the responses. (223)

spuriousness: invalidity with respect to correlations rather than to individual variables. The correlation between X and Y is spurious if it is really the result of a third hidden variable, Z. (232)

standard deviation: a measure of dispersion of responses around the mean for the given item. (157)

statistical significance: the probability that a correlation or other statistic is merely the result of chance, rather than representing a real difference. (64, 162)

stimulus: the part of a questionnaire item to which the respondent is supposed to respond—the question to be answered or the statement to be judged. (90)

subscale: a set of items within a scale, measuring a characteristic of the respondent somewhat different from the characteristics measured by other items in the scale. Ideally, the subscales in a scale measure different aspects of the concept behind the entire scale rather than being totally independent of each other. (220)

suppressor variable: the character of a variable, Z, that spuriously reduces the apparent correlation between two other variables, X and Y, which actually do correlate with each other. (236)

survey research: systematic collection and analysis of data from numbers of respondents, in this text synonymous with questionnaire research. (20)

synthetic ideology: a statement of the beliefs and values of a social movement or other social group, created through social scientific research rather than written by adherents. (267)

tau: a correlation coefficient designed for use with ordinal data. (167)

test-retest reliability: the quality of an item or index that yields consistent results when given to a person twice, with some gap in time between the two administrations. Some survey resesarchers prefer to speak of test-retest stability. (219)

unit of analysis: in quantitative research, the thing being counted or the basic element of reality that constitutes a case of the thing being studied. (41)

validity: the quality of an item or index that measures the phenomenon it purports to measure. A valid item accurately reflects the desired aspect of the respondent's thoughts, behavior, or characteristics. (212)

value: the answers people give to a survey question, transformed into a system of numbers so the computer can handle them efficiently. (15, 152)

variable: a quantity that can assume any of a set of values. In analysis of survey data, each item and index composed of several items is a variable. (152)

variance: a measure of dispersion of responses around the mean for the given item. (156)

variation ratio: a measure of dispersion of cases in a distribution, suitable for comparing different variables—the variance divided by the mean. (157)

wave: in panel studies, a stage in the research at which one of a series of questionnaires is administered. (295)

NAME INDEX

Anderson, Norman H., 254–255
Armer, Michael, 221
Asimov, Isaac, 100
Athansiou, Robert, 31

Babbie, Earl R., 192
Bachman, Jerald G., 82, 295
Back, Kurt W., 27
Barnum, Phineas T., 283–284
Bauer, Raymond A., 133
Berelson, Bernard, 298
Block, Jack, 238
Bogardus, E. S., 124
Bowers, David G., 28, 95
Bruner, Jerome S., 259
Buchanan, James, 29
Burroughs, Edgar Rice, 100

Campbell, Angus, 233
Christensen, Larry B., 63, 157
Christie, Richard, 282
Clarke, Arthur C., 46, 100
Condry, John, 257
Couch, Arthur, 239
Cronbach, Lee J., 195, 222, 224
Crossley, Archibald, 44
Crowne, Douglas P., 240
Crumrine, Janice, 258
Crutchfield, Robert D., 199–203

Davis, James A., 16, 154, 305
Deutscher, Irwin, 38
Dickson, William John, 309
Dillman, Don A., 23
Dohan, Daniel, 140
Doyle, Daniel P., 82
Duncan, Otis Dudley, 303
Dunham, H. Warren, 47
Durkheim, Emile, 131
Dyer, Sharon, 257

Earle, Pliny, 42
Edgerton, Robert B., 35–37, 263
Edwards, Allen L., 240

Ellison, Harlan, 100
Everitt, Brian, 191

Faris, Robert E. L., 47
Farley, James A., 43
Festinger, Leon, 190
Fiedler, Fred E., 107–108, 111
Flint, Jerry, 41
Furash, Edward E., 133

Galfo, Armand J., 282
Gallup, George, 44
Gardner, Hugh, 30
Gaudet, Hazel, 298
Geis, Florence L., 282
Glaser, Barney G., 264
Glock, Charles Y., 26, 45, 125–127, 220, 226, 231, 233, 235
Gordon, Raymond L., 39, 258
Green, Samuel B., 224
Grossman, Saul A., 214

Hadaway, C. K., 185
Haire, Mason, 281
Head, Kendra B., 31
Hicks, Jack M., 220
Hilty, Dale M., 221
Hindelang, Michael, 217
Hirschi, Travis, 74, 97, 216–217
Hollingshead, August B., 47
Homans, George C., 102, 274, 309–311
Horner, Matina S., 256–258, 270
Howard, Robert E., 100
Hunter, John E., 284

Ito-Adler, James, 41

Jacobson, Maryn, 283–284
Jaeger, Alfred M., 285–286
Jarvis, Edward, 29
Jarvis, Gregory B., 121
Johnson, Jerry B., 288
Juhn, Daniel S., 281

367

OUTLINE OF PROGRAM MENUS AND COMMANDS, WITH PAGE REFERENCES